# The Hunter Elite

## Manly Sport, Hunting Narratives, and American Conservation, 1880–1925

**Tara Kathleen Kelly**

University Press of Kansas

© 2018 by the
University Press of
Kansas
All rights reserved

Published by the
University Press of
Kansas (Lawrence,
Kansas 66045), which
was organized by
the Kansas Board
of Regents and is
operated and funded
by Emporia State
University, Fort Hays
State University,
Kansas State
University, Pittsburg
State University, the
University of Kansas,
and Wichita State
University.

Library of Congress Cataloging-in-Publication Data

Names: Kelly, Tara Kathleen, author.

Title: The hunter elite : manly sport, hunting narratives, and
   American conservation, 1880–1925 / Tara Kathleen Kelly.

Description: Lawrence, Kansas : University Press of Kansas, [2018]
   | Includes bibliographical references and index.

Identifiers: LCCN 2017054866 | ISBN 9780700625871 (cloth : alk.
   paper) | ISBN 9780700625888 (paperback : alk. paper) |
   ISBN 9780700625895 (ebook)

Subjects: LCSH: Big game hunting—United States—History—
   19th century. | Big game hunting—United States—History—
   20th century.

Classification: LCC SK41 .K45 2018 | DDC 799.2/60973—dc23.

LC record available at https://lccn.loc.gov/2017054866.

British Library Cataloguing-in-Publication Data is available.

Printed in the United States of America

10 9 8 7 6 5 4 3 2 1

The paper used in this publication is recycled and contains
30 percent postconsumer waste. It is acid free and meets the
minimum requirements of the American National Standard for
Permanence of Paper for Printed Library Materials Z39.48-1992.

# The Hunter Elite

# Contents

Introduction, *1*

**Part One. Tales of the Sportsman-Hunter**

1 "What Luxury It Is": Elite Hunting Enters the Gilded Age, *17*
2 Fall of the Workplace, Rise of the Hunt, *33*
3 Making Meaning Out of Moose: Constructing the Hunting Narrative, *50*
4 The Business of Narrative, *83*
5 Whitney Rising, *101*

**Part Two. Fellow Travelers**

6 Diana's Own: Women and the Big-Game Hunt, *137*
7 Sportsmen of the Breed: British and American Hunters, *157*

**Part Three. Discourse and Consequences**

8 Stories of Guides and Gunbearers, *187*
9 Dreaming of Howley: Conservation and the Uses of Discourse, *221*
10 The End of the Hunt: Conservation and the Limits of Discourse, *238*

Afterword, *265*

Acknowledgments, *273*

Notes, *275*

Works Cited, *319*

Index, *337*

# Introduction

In 1898, railway manager and big-game hunter Charles Sheldon visited the Chihuahuan desert in search of antelope. His days were spent riding through the scrub, looking for his elusive quarry but seldom finding them; at night he would sit by the campfire and look forward to the next day's venture. "I can recall many delightful trips," he would write later, "riding for days over wide areas in search of these interesting animals, not all successful in finding and killing game, yet not one of them disappointing to him who had learned to love the desert."[1]

Charles Sheldon was in many ways a typical turn-of-the-century big-game hunter. For him, the hunt was about the chase, rather than the kill, and the test of the true hunter lay in the stalk, the willingness to transform leisured hunting into a kind of work. After all, it would have been far easier to lie in wait by a waterhole and pick off the antelope as they came to drink. Faced with that option, Sheldon, like many big-game hunters, preferred to be unsuccessful. He was also typical in that he was part of a cohort of hunters who shared a remarkably similar profile and background: white, native-born, Protestant, Ivy-educated, and from the East Coast north of Washington, DC. This group yielded almost all the Progressive-Era big-game hunters, the ones who are still remembered now—Theodore Roosevelt, George Bird Grinnell—and those, like Charles Sheldon and his bear-hunting wife, Louisa Gulliver Sheldon, who have been mostly forgotten.

And Sheldon was typical in another way: he wrote about his hunting. The elite big-game hunters were, as a group, avid writers. Roosevelt and Grinnell's exclusive hunting club, the Boone and Crockett Club, did not require its members to publish, but by 1903 roughly half of them had articles or books in print, and over half of those were on hunting. Their writing formed part of an emerging literary genre, the American big-game hunting narrative, that flooded the pages of turn-of-the-century periodicals, appearing not only in recreational magazines but also in such popular generalist venues as

*Harper's*, *Scribner's*, and *Collier's*. Over a century later, the connections that these authors made between hunting and writing are still so much part of our culture that some historians have read these narratives as transparent accounts of experience—as if, after spending days riding through the desert not seeing many antelope, it was the most natural thing in the world for Charles Sheldon to come home, write up the experience, and successfully place it in a published anthology of hunting tales.

Before the 1880s and 1890s, however, very few men were writing tales of big-game hunting, and those that did seldom published in generalist middle-class magazines.

And before 1880, very few middle- and upper-class men of the East Coast were going big-game hunting at all.

To make Sheldon possible, something fundamental in American culture had to shift. This book explores that shift, how and why it happened, and what its consequences were. Combining writing and publishing with their construction of a new meaning for the big-game hunt, Sheldon's cohort brought American readers with them as they pursued game into the American West and then north to Canada and Alaska, south to Mexico, and around the world to British East Africa, South Africa, and India. In their hands the hunting narrative became a place to discuss the meaning of empire for Americans, and what hunters' dependence on guides meant for racial hierarchies, and whether having new reasons to enter the wilderness meant having new reasons to save it. Conservation, imperialism, best-seller lists, and a global market in trophies all became linked to American big-game hunting in this era. So too did the personal identities of men and women struggling to define themselves to each other and to their society.

Examining these hunters, their hunting, and their narratives can thus offer new insight into American society in this period; it also calls into question assumptions that have been with us for too long. One of those assumptions is that hunting has no history, or none that is worth studying, because it has a stable meaning: in any era, it is about violence. The turn-of-the-century hunter-writers explicitly rejected this meaning for the hunt, however. Instead they crafted an interpretation for hunting that centered on willpower, self-denial, and self-discipline. Whether described as the big-game hunt, the still-hunt, the fair-stalk, or, in Roosevelt and Grinnell's memorable phrase, "manly sport with the rifle," refusing the easy kill and turning hunting into a test of a man's character was a new idea that emerged in this period. Also new was the idea that there was an innate link between manliness and wilderness—that a professional man from the East Coast trying to prove himself could do so by going West and hunting there, for instance—and, while that idea remains part of popular culture today, it was also constructed in this period by these writers. Most innovative, however, and least obvious, were the new links these writers forged between hunting and narrative, because every time a new meaning for hunting was offered to readers in print, an underlying connection was being established between going hunting and writing about the experience. But why did so many turn-of-the-century big-game hunters publish? What was writing actually *doing* for hunters? And what did it do for readers?

The answers to these questions provide a new angle of approach to hunting, publication, and American culture at the beginning of the twentieth century—and it was the combination of these elements that gave the narratives both power and influence. It was no coincidence that both a new way of hunting and a new type of hunting narrative emerged in the 1880s. Both were responses to cultural changes at the end of the nineteenth century, and both represented radical breaks from the ways that big-game hunting by middle- and upper-class men had previously been understood and described in print.

In the decades before and immediately after the Civil War, there were very few middle- and upper-class Americans pursuing big game, and those that did seldom wrote narratives of their experiences.[2] The handful who did publish usually described their hunting as a leisurely pursuit, one among many pleasures of travel. Such hunters also didn't consider themselves confined to a single style of hunting but pursued game in a variety of ways, adopting whatever hunting techniques were most popular in the places they visited.

By the 1880s, however, changes in transportation, communications, and the nature of work itself meant that big-game hunting was becoming an ever more popular use of leisure time for a cohort of white, native-born, Protestant, middle- and upper-class men, mostly from urban areas of the East Coast. They went hunting, but in a different form than before. Now, wherever they went, they pursued game through the stalk, also known as the "still-hunt," a time-consuming technique that required both patience and self-discipline from the hunter. They also wrote about their experiences, and in their narratives they argued that the stalk was the only correct way to hunt because it provided a meaningful test of the individual will, one that could reveal the truth about the hunter's inner character.

This was a new way of imagining what hunting could be used for, and it bore little relation to either the experiences or the narratives of their predecessors. Instead, this new interpretation drew on a set of very traditional nineteenth-century ideals that linked manliness, character, and willpower, and that had been generated in a very specific context: the workplace of white, native-born, middle- and upper-class Protestants living in cities in the American Northeast. Those ideals posited a set of virtues—in particular self-control, perseverance, and patience—that were believed necessary for success and were derived from the exercise of the will over the passions and the body. These virtues, often called "the manly virtues," were inseparably connected to rhetorics of both work and manliness. As a result, they were not located in hunting prior to the 1880s, or at least not in hunting done by men on vacation, who were leaving productive work to pursue game for pleasure. Those hunters were instead seen as engaged in a rather dubious form of leisure, and early accounts of their big-game hunting sometimes called not only their judgment but also their manliness into question.

By the 1870s and 1880s, however, the workplace as a site for demonstrating the manly virtues was becoming increasingly compromised. This was partly a result of industrial changes, of the growth of salaried jobs and the loss of workplace autonomy for many middle-class men, but it was also driven by the threats posed to traditional elites by new groups who contested long-standing hierarchies of political and economic power. In response, a cohort of elite men who hunted big game for pleasure began to frame their hunting as a site for the development and display of manly character. This idea was originally promoted by a handful of individuals, including Theodore Strong Van Dyke, Owen Wister, and Theodore Roosevelt, who argued in print that stalking big game was a test of will that revealed the truth about a man's character, and thus "manly sport with the rifle" could complement or even replace work as a site for the display of the manly virtues. Big-game hunting in this reading was about willpower and self-control—and just as definitely *not* about violence or primitivism. By the late 1880s the leisured big-game hunt had been converted, through the process of narrative, into a new site for the display of the traditional manly virtues.

There was no rigid list of those virtues, no single formula that authors had to follow. The big-game hunting narratives that emerged in the 1880s invoked a loosely related group of cultural associations, all centered around manliness and willpower, but displaying considerable variation from one narrative to the next. Some writers connected their hunting to claims of Anglo-Saxon prowess. Others invoked science and exploration as ways to transform leisured hunting into productive work. Many claimed that there was something uniquely American about their hunting, either by comparing it to the hunting of the pioneers or by contrasting it to British hunting. These associations were woven into the narratives over time, affecting both how hunters interpreted their own actions in the wilds and how their reading audiences understood the wider meaning of the hunt.

At the same time, by choosing to write about their hunting, this cohort had made a decision that immediately set them apart from the vast majority of professional and subsistence hunters in North America. It allowed them to corner the market. By 1900 "manly sport with the rifle" had become the dominant way in which big-game hunting by individuals was described in the American middle-class press. This dominance let writers promote certain associations with their hunting while downplaying those that might raise doubts among their audiences. The role of the guide, for instance, was problematic for many sportsmen, who found themselves attempting to display manliness by hunting in places where, as visitors, they needed assistance, often from nonwhite or mixed-race men who were very competent hunters themselves. A variety of ways of negotiating this challenge emerged in the narratives, but they all depended on controlling the public retelling of the hunt, rewriting whatever may have happened in the field in the context of the hierarchies of race and class most familiar to white middle-class reading audiences.

Consumption by those audiences was not just about rhetoric, however. It was also fundamentally about business. The same industrial changes that altered the nature of work in this period were also fueling a publishing explosion, a massive expansion of the book and periodical marketplaces that left them hungry for product and willing to pay for it. Big-game hunting narratives were valuable commodities in these markets, profitable for both hunter-writers and publishers. The end of the nineteenth century also marked a moment when people were beginning to identify themselves through what they consumed as well as what they produced, and the emerging national periodical market was an essential part of that transformation. Subscribing to a middle-class standard like *Harper's* or a recreational magazine like *Outing* connected readers to a national community of like-minded readers, writers, and editors, and that in turn had an impact on how Americans across the country understood the new meanings being given to the sportsmanlike still-hunt. And there were other connections at work as well, behind the scenes. The recreational press in this era was dominated by a handful of men in New York, many of them hunters themselves, who chose for social and economic reasons to publish these narratives both in North America and through transatlantic publishing houses. They dominated the recreational media and controlled access to its presses, creating a nexus through which hunting narratives had to pass on their way to publication. Enthusiastically promoted by this powerful group of publishers, and advertised, marketed, and constantly anthologized and reprinted, by 1900 narratives of manly sport with the rifle were reaching hundreds of thousands of readers every month.

As the new meaning of the hunt achieved wide cultural currency—and as the financial benefits of selling such a story grew—big-game hunting began to attract writers distinct from the original group of elite hunters, including journalists and women, even as British hunters discovered in the American press a second, lucrative market for their tales of hunting and empire. As a result, by 1900 debates were erupting in print over the meaning of the hunt. What role should a hunter's wife play on a safari, especially if she turned out to be a good shot? Was it possible for women to be "sportsmen"? What was the relationship between the American interpretation of the hunt and the very different but equally popular imperial version being promoted by British hunter-writers? As narratives by dozens of authors jostled for space in the pages of *Harper's* and *Outing*, and as hunting narratives by women in particular shot up the best-seller lists, the hunting narratives became fertile sites for public negotiations over ideas about imperialism, national identity, gender roles, and even marital relationships.

This growing popularization came with a price. By 1900 big-game hunting was becoming a profitable and heavily commercialized part of a modernizing global tourist economy, even as both wilderness areas and game animals were rapidly diminishing. In response, the hunter-writers began to assert themselves as a political lobby for conservation using a two-pronged approach: deploying their considerable social and political power to support conservation, while interpreting their actions to the public through the national media. Members of the hunter elite brought political pressure to bear on governors and congressmen, created national parks, and wrote game laws that functioned at state, national, and international levels, restricting the activities of hunters across North America. They accompanied these actions with published pleas for conservation that were grounded in the same values and rhetorics as their hunting tales: appeals to manly self-restraint, to Americanism, and to the value of wilderness as a connection to the pioneer past. They also constantly assured readers that game legislation was *not* class legislation, while framing any opposition to game laws as the work of selfish private interests, motivated by greed rather than by need. This was not always true, especially when it came to those hunting for subsistence, but the hunter elite's monopoly in the media gave them a voice with which no other single group could compete. Those whose hunting they restricted, in particular the thousands of market and subsistence hunters scattered across North America, had no comparable media platform; having never written about their hunting, they had no unified voice with which to argue their case. Nor were these restrictions being imposed only from the top down. Across the country, supporters of conservation reached out to the media, using the international reach of the recreational press to bring pressure to bear on both local hunters and local politicians. Together, the hunter elite and their reading audiences used a potent combination of political power and media access to shape conservation law, to restrict hunting throughout North America, and to preserve American wilderness and game in ways that remain with us to this day.

The following chapters provide the evidence for this argument: the changes to how hunting was interpreted; the cultural meanings given to the stalk and how those were challenged or negotiated by women, British hunter-writers, and guides; the business of publishing that underlay the narratives; and the wide-ranging consequences for American culture and conservation. Since the book focuses on original research, it might be helpful to note here that it contributes to the current historiography in several ways. First, the elephant in the room: the long-standing assumption in the historiography that there is a clear connection between turn-of-the-century big-game hunting and violence, primitivism, masculinity, the frontier, and war. A great deal of attention has been paid to the rise of what has been called "hypermasculinity" in the years after the Civil War: the emergence in American culture of a new vision of manhood that celebrated violence, martial ideals, primitivism, and the male body. Often positioned as part of a wider "crisis of masculinity" that confronted men as part of the rise of modernity—and the rise of the modern woman—the story of this new man found its roots in bloody tales of the frontier and made itself visible in the fiction of Jack London, in middle-class attendance at boxing matches and Wild West shows, and in men withdrawing to "dens" within their houses or setting off into the wilderness.[3] Big-game hunting, especially by elite men, has long been assumed to be part of this movement.[4] Much of the groundbreaking work on both men's history and cultural history in this period has folded hunting into wider arguments about hypermasculinity, with Theodore Roosevelt as the exemplar, and understandably so: if there were an elephant in the room with him, he'd have shot it.[5] He lauded a certain vision of American imperialism, occasionally claimed hunting as a practice ground for war, and consistently posted egregiously large kill counts. He was also the only American elite hunter who did so.

The problem is not just that no other American hunter-writer of the time embraced hypermasculinity, however (and that there are very real limits to how far Roosevelt did); it's also that there were hundreds of such writers, and every one of them explicitly *refused* associations between their hunting and violence or primitivism. Instead, as noted above, elite hunter-writers mobilized traditional nineteenth-century ideals of a manliness based in self-discipline, self-restraint, and the primacy of the will, and imported that into hunting through an unyielding narrative focus, not on the kill, but on the stalk and what the stalk said about the character of the hunter. Offered the chance to mobilize hypermasculinity, many of the most influential and politically powerful men of the era preferred to tell a different story about themselves.

The hunting narratives they wrote show that from the 1880s into the 1920s there were powerful alternate ways to imagine the relationship of gender to hunting that proved useful to both male and female hunters, and immensely popular with readers. Seeing the work that the rhetoric of manliness did for these writers illuminates its nuances, in particular the ways that it allowed men to negotiate divisions within classes as well as between them: while hunting narratives often reveal male anxiety, it is almost always anxiety about other men of their own class with whom they worked and socialized. Recognizing that these hunters were promoting a version of manliness that was not founded in a rejection of the feminine can also help to explain both why so many men went hunting with their wives, and why so many female hunters embraced the narrative of the meaningful stalk. Without primitivism or violence in the rhetorical mix, hunter-writers like Josephine Peary and Grace Gallatin Seton could lay claim to this narrative by insisting that women, too, could display self-discipline and sportsmanship in the field. Over time, the nuances of this gendered rhetoric also had very real consequences for conservation, as hunter-writers insisted in print that wilderness and hunting were vital to American men and boys, in the process defusing or eliding long-standing associations between game legislation and class legislation. The rhetoric of manliness that they invoked remained robustly part of conservation literature well into the 1920s and was eventually adopted by groups ranging from the Boy Scouts to the Women's Clubs of America.

Recognizing the alternate version of manliness being offered in these narratives also raises questions about big-game hunting's relationship with other elements of the hypermasculinity story, especially idealizations of frontier violence and Anglo-American imperial fantasies.[6] Over the past few decades exceptionalist readings of the frontier have slowly been making way for more complicated and global histories, as well as for both transnational and transimperial readings. American big-game hunting is long overdue for such a repositioning, not only within North America but also in terms of Americans hunting abroad in the British Empire.[7] There was never a closed circuit in big-game hunting, at least not where elites were concerned—and, as time passed, many middle-class hunters from the East Coast found that improvements to transportation put hunting in Newfoundland and Canada within their grasp. The American West was also a prime hunting ground for British aristocrats almost as soon as the railways reached the Plains, and this transnational entanglement was only intensified by the development of transatlantic publishing houses, which provided markets for hunting stories throughout the English-speaking world.

Fracturing apart the long-standing connections among masculinity, violence, and the frontier allows us to pluck American hunters from their exceptionalist niche and position them instead as embedded in a set of transnational economies in which hunters, writers, and publishers all participated. Framing big-game hunting this way also moves guides from being "locals" unfairly exploited by visiting hunters into a very different position, that of highly skilled workers in a swiftly modernizing tourist economy that stretched from Alaska to Somaliland, and that was shadowed by the rise of a global market in trophies. It offers a new perspective on the economies surrounding hunting and the laws restricting it, which eventually crossed national and imperial boundaries alike. And it positions hunting narratives both as literary contributions and as desirable commodities in a transatlantic marketplace.

Such an approach also points toward some of the limits of transnational analysis, however. The economies underlying the hunt and its narratives may have been transnational in nature, but in print both American and British writers persistently framed their hunting in nationalist terms. Exploring the insistent focus on the American story of the "wilderness hunter," even when the American in question was hunting in Somaliland or Kumaon, opens the way to ask what nationalist rhetorics were doing for hunters and how they were understood by readers. The combination of cooperation on the ground and competition in print also meant that American hunting narratives had a complex and sometimes uneasy relationship with their British counterparts, one that drew on the rhetoric of Anglo-American solidarity that was part of discussions of imperialism in the era, but that also instructed readers that there was a single, and superior, "American" way to hunt, whether at home or abroad.

That hunting could have radically different national meanings even for men and women sharing the same guides, gear, and hunting grounds highlights the importance of context to understanding hunting, which is as culturally constructed as any other activity. That may seem obvious, but one persistent assumption in the hypermasculinity literature in particular has been that hunting is always primarily about violence.[8] Positioning "manly sport" instead as one among many ways to interpret the hunt places it in a more historical context, one that includes other, contemporaneous groups of hunters who have already drawn the attention of historians. Writers on women's history, for instance, have explored the nuanced meanings of hunting for women throughout the Anglophone world, while historians of hunting in Canada and in the British Empire have thoughtfully examined the relationship of elite hunters with imperialism, conservation, nationalism, and ideas of nature.[9] Environmental historians focused on the United States have also examined hunting in context, especially the experiences of working-class and indigenous peoples, and in the process have created a rich tapestry of the variations, conflicts, and alliances that crisscrossed the nation at the turn of the century.[10]

The hunter elite mattered more than other American hunters, however. They shaped ideas about the meaning of wilderness, hunting, and conservation in the national media, and they used a combination of political power and reader support to write and pass legislation across North America that had an impact on everyone who hunted. The essential contribution of hunters to conservation thought, legislation, and the development of the national parks has long been recognized within environmental history, but even now strikes many readers as paradoxical.[11] This may be partly due to the spurious connections forged in the literature of hypermasculinity between hunting and frontier violence, but the vast majority of hunter-writers preferred to depict their hunting grounds as empty, unpopulated, and uncomplicated, and when they created parks such as Glacier and Denali they gave them histories to match. This aligns them far more closely with what we now think of as histories of wilderness than with histories of the frontier, even as it illuminates the degree to which their vision of an exclusionary Eden continues to inform popular images of wilderness in America, and of the national parks in particular. Their rhetoric of wilderness remains part of our current conversations about the meaning of wild spaces for Americans.

Their most important contribution, however, was the role they played in the reversal in American middle-class attitudes toward conservation. Many historians, ranging from John Reiger to Karl Jacoby, have noted the ways in which middle-class Americans began to support game laws in the late nineteenth century when previously they had (generally) opposed them.[12] There was no single reason for that change, but the hunter-writers had a massive impact on the speed and direction that it took. As they mobilized their narratives and publishing connections on behalf of conservation, hunter-writers substituted a language of gender for that of class, reframing the meaning of game laws even as they linked their cause to already established rhetorics of manliness, sportsmanship, and Americanism. Such rhetorics in turn influenced the writing and implementation of conservation policies across North America.

All this is made even more interesting by the fact that national political influence was not the original goal of the hunter elite when they came to dominate the national media with their hunting tales; the intention to use their published stories as a platform for conservation came later. At heart, this book is about the emergence of a cultural hegemony surrounding hunting and conservation. That hegemony drew a great deal of its power from its mobilization of nineteenth-century ideals of self-controlled manliness that remained part of American cultural life well into the 1920s. It was created inadvertently as part of the process of giving elite big-game hunting a new, gendered meaning, and its consequences ranged from shaping ideas of what wilderness spaces should look like, to restricting hunting across North America, to affecting the ways that men and women imagined themselves, the communities they participated in, and the roles they played in the world. And from the beginning to the end this was about narrative and about social power, about who did and did not have access to the media, and about the roles those elements play in determining the outcome of conflicts over nature.

Finally, this book can also be understood as an argument on method. I would argue that nothing in these popular published hunting narratives can be taken as an unmediated description of events that actually happened, nor it is sufficient to analyze them solely for their literary content. Instead, these narratives must also be placed into context as purposefully constructed commodities.[13] They were deliberately crafted by men and women who were writing in order to publish and who consciously designed them to appeal to an audience made up of potential readers, well-known editors, and popular publishing venues. Approaching the hunting narratives from this perspective demands an extra level of analysis, even as it raises new and intriguing questions. Charles Sheldon's antelope story, for instance, is a charming travelogue, but not much of a hunting tale at all; why, then, did he choose to submit it to an anthology of hunting narratives and why was it accepted? Why did so many hunters include anecdotes in their narratives in which they were outwitted by or even saved by their native guides? Whether such *events* took place or not, why would hunter-writers include them in narratives intended for a white middle-class reading audience? These questions will be answered in the following chapters, but here I want to suggest that positioning these narratives as having both a literary and a very real economic life can help us to better understand these tales and to account for the massive public demand for them. At the very least, it should help to explain why big-game hunting narratives became part of the way that hundreds of thousands of Americans thought about, wrote about, and publicly discussed gender, race, imperialism, wilderness, and conservation at the beginning of the twentieth century.

**A HELPFUL NOTE ON TERMS AND DATES**

*Dates and Eras*: Like many US historians, I use "the Gilded Age" to refer to the period from the end of Reconstruction in 1877 to 1897, with "the Progressive Era" dating from 1897 to the Great War. Of course, nobody at the time divided their experience up neatly into eras, and I also use "turn-of-the-century" to indicate the two decades on either side of 1900 (so 1880–1920).

*Sanity-Saving Shorthand:* While I'll mention this in the text, I use the term "sportsmen-hunters" to indicate a very specific group: white, native-born, Protestant, middle- and upper-class men and women of the urban Northeast who stalked big game. This group exerted a massive influence on hunting, conservation, and American culture at the turn of the century due to their obsessive relationship with writing about the hunt, and they are the focus of the book. (Women hunters in this group were often referred to as sportsmen, so the term "sportsman-hunter" does not exclude them.)

If I refer to "big-game hunters" and don't specify that I'm talking about different hunters than this group, then I mean the sportsmen-hunters. The same applies to big-game hunting itself. There were many other ways to hunt big-game animals and many other groups doing so, but, when it came to first-person narratives, the sportsmen-hunters and their pursuit of the still-hunt dominated the description of big-game hunting in the national press.

# Part One
# Tales of the Sportsman-Hunter

CHAPTER 1

# "What Luxury It Is"
## Elite Hunting Enters the Gilded Age

In his 1913 *Autobiography*, Theodore Roosevelt told his readers that hunting dangerous game required cool judgment and the mastery of nerve. Such mastery, he wrote, could only become the hunter's through

> actual practice. He must, by custom and repeated exercise of self-mastery, get his nerves thoroughly under control. This is largely a matter of habit . . . of repeated effort and repeated exercise of will power. If the man has the right stuff in him, his will grows stronger and stronger with each exercise of it—and if he has not the right stuff in him he had better keep clear of dangerous game hunting.[1]

The connection Roosevelt was making between hunting and willpower would have been familiar to his readers—not only to those who had read other writing by the former president, but also to the hundreds of thousands who had read accounts of big-game hunting written by other men. In those narratives, the hunt was linked to a rhetoric of willpower, self-mastery, and manliness, whether one was reading George Bird Grinnell's claim in *Scribner's* that "hunting the goat is man's work" or skimming *Outing Magazine*, whose editor Caspar Whitney explained that the good sportsman learned to "say No to *[him]self* with a big N" and that "the man who earns and lives up to the honorable title of sportsman, is no more or less than a considerate gentleman—a man."[2] The big-game hunter, the sportsman, the man, was someone with a well-developed will and admirable self-control, and those in turn qualified him to hunt big game, and to hunt it successfully. In 1887, Grinnell and Roosevelt had summarized such hunting in a single phrase: as "manly sport with the rifle."[3]

But just twenty years earlier, there had been no such thing.

In the years immediately following the Civil War, there were very few middle- and upper-class men from the East Coast hunting big game, those who did seldom wrote about it, and those few who did write about it depicted it as play. There were no easy connections between a shooting holiday and nineteenth-century ideals of manliness, and there was no inherent link between manliness and sport, or, for that matter, between manliness and entering the wilderness. Middle- and upper-class American men understood their excursions to the wilds as being about leisure, and the associations they made in print hardly invoked "manly sport." In his popular 1869 account of a shooting trip to the Adirondacks, William Murray assured readers that such a trip was about "luxury . . . easy and delightful. . . . There is nothing in the trip which the most delicate and fragile need fear."[4]

Between Murray's 1869 pronouncement and Roosevelt's 1913 *Autobiography* the entire meaning of the hunting trip had changed. The hunt was reconstructed as "manly sport," given that meaning by a group of elite men who were seeking a way to prove their manhood to an audience of other elite men—and, more and more often, of readers as well. And this conversion of the experience of the hunt into written narrative was as anomalous as was the transformation of leisure-time hunting into manly sport. There was no obvious reason that hunters should write narratives of their trips, and, before the 1870s, very few did. By 1900, however, big-game hunting narratives had become popular offerings, fueling the explosive growth of specialty periodicals such as *Outing Magazine*, as well as appearing regularly in the pages of *Harper's* and *Scribner's*. Suddenly, hundreds of men were going hunting and writing about it; suddenly, readers all over America were consuming such tales. In little more than a generation, American big-game hunting had undergone a sea-change in meaning.

Understanding this change requires stepping back in time to examine the ways that middle- and upper-class men of the East Coast were hunting big game before 1880, and how they were writing about it. Such narratives are rare in comparison with the outpouring at the turn of the century, however, and it is even rarer to find books that were entirely dedicated to the hunt.[5] Instead, descriptions of big-game hunting appear in private letters, in a smattering of articles, and, most often, as minor events in wider travelogues. Taken together, these early sources reveal a world of hunting, and of understanding the hunt, that was unique to white, middle- and upper-class, native-born men of the urban Northeast, and fundamentally different from the ways that most other Americans were hunting in the nineteenth century.

"Hunting" is a word indicating any number of ways of pursuing game, and in mid-nineteenth-century America there were myriad ways to hunt—nor was any single man confined to any single style. A wealthy man of the East Coast might hunt deer in the Adirondacks, but he might also sample fox-hunting on Long Island or visit with friends in Virginia who coursed game with hounds. None of these hunts served the function of making money, however, nor were they necessary for subsistence, and that differentiated such hunting from that of most groups of men in the United States, who were hunting for subsistence or for the market. Also setting these middle- and upper-class hunters apart was the fact that, as urban dwellers, they were among the few Americans who could not reliably find game on their doorstep. As a result, whether doctors in Philadelphia, lawyers in New York City, or political figures in Washington, DC, many of the up-and-coming men of the East Coast found that they had to travel in order to hunt. Together, the absence of any necessity driving the hunt, and the need to travel in order to pursue it, would shape and define hunting for these men.

This traveling hunting took one of three forms. The first was leisurely shooting on the weekend in which men would visit one another's country homes, often indulging in some bird shooting. Such hunting often functioned as an extension of the work world while offering a way for men to demonstrate their grasp of the social niceties. These elements are clear in the foundational text of American sportsmanship, Elisha Lewis's *Hints for Sportsmen*, first published in 1855, reprinted in 1857 and 1871, and then—with its title changed to *The American Sportsman*—again in 1885 and 1906. In *Hints*, Lewis spends a great deal of time describing how the gentleman hunter should comport himself before others, noting, for example, that a gentleman wears gloves at all times while hunting, for "nothing . . . looks more *outré*, if not vulgar, than a coarse, scratched, and scarred hand."[6] The instructional ring of this advice is no coincidence; *Hints for Sportsmen* in fact seems intended to teach men how to appear and behave as gentlemen. Lewis's work shares an affinity with the etiquette manuals that were so popular in the nineteenth century, aimed at the self-improving man eager to climb the social ladder, the man who does not yet know that, by eschewing gloves in hunting, he is saying something about himself that he would rather not say. This hunting is about leisure, although connected to the wider world of social standing and display; it is a social extension of the world that really matters.

Closely linked to this type of pleasure hunting were brief trips to the Adirondacks or another wilderness area close to East Coast urban centers, where deer might be added to the bag—deer probably driven toward the hunter by dogs, in the years immediately after the Civil War, since it was a faster and surer way to kill game than the difficult method of stalking on foot. Murray hunts deer this way during his 1869 trip to the Adirondacks, as well as sampling the pleasures of jacklighting (in which a light is shone into the eyes of animals at night, illuminating them so that the hunter can pick them off while they stand, momentarily blinded). He has guides with him every step of the way, paddling him to his fishing spots and helping him with his camp, and he recommends this mode of hunting, which "takes from recreation every trace of toil. You have all the excitement of sporting, without any attending physical weariness . . . what luxury it is." He estimates the costs for such a venture at about twenty dollars a week, certainly within the reach of many middle-class men, including ministers like Murray himself.[7]

The third major form of hunting available to upper-class (and some middle-class) men was spending a great deal more time and money to travel in search of the most elusive prize, big game. A basic definition might be helpful here. "Big game" as a category was somewhat fluid but was applied to certain animals scattered over four continents.[8] Big-game hunting was thus mainly a rich man's pleasure, and by the mid-nineteenth century what might be described as a Grand Tour of hunting was becoming popular among the wealthy elites of Europe. Such a tour could include hunting tiger and sometimes wild elephant in Asia (most often in British India); lion, rhino, buffalo, leopard, elephant, and various ungulates in Africa; elk in Norway; and bison, moose, caribou, grizzly, mountain goat, mountain sheep, and wapiti (now more commonly known as American elk[9]) in North America. Those adventurous souls tempted further north might add musk-ox, walrus, and polar bear to their lists. This general outline was followed by most big-game hunters, with many variations: members of the deer family were always fair game, for example, whether blacktail deer in Virginia or chamois in the Alps, and some of these animals were defined, not so much by any standard of "bigness," as by the difficulty of hunting them (mountain goat were hardly difficult to kill once reached, but one needed to climb a mountain first). The wild boar of India deserves its own note: while not "big game" by any standard, the sport of pig-sticking that grew up around it attained enormous popularity in British India and was sampled by many visitors; in that case, the danger of the hunt itself qualified the boar as appropriate game.

During the mid-nineteenth century, these animals had become the quarries of a small, wealthy clique with a decidedly English identity.[10] Variety was the goal, and the exotic places that had to be visited in order to fill the hunter's shopping list spoke for themselves of his wealth and leisure. When Englishman Sir Henry Seton-Karr first encountered Lord North Buxton while elk hunting in Norway, he hailed him immediately with "What sport?"—no need for formal introductions; Buxton's presence in the expensive Norwegian elk-grounds told Seton-Karr immediately that he was encountering one of his own set.[11] Long before Theodore Roosevelt popularized hunting in the American West, some of the most famous English hunters were including it in their tours, including Sir Samuel Baker on his well-publicized 1879 round-the-world hunting trip and the Earl of Dunraven, who visited the Rockies in 1872 and remained to build a hunting lodge, cache massive amounts of whiskey, and steal several thousand acres of what is now Estes Park in an impressive piece of land fraud.[12] Some of these men also wrote narratives about their experiences, which enjoyed popularity on both sides of the Atlantic and which framed hunting as one among many pleasures of leisured travel, a distinctive early approach that would change later for both British and American hunter-writers.[13] The British and their relationship to American hunting will be examined closely in a later chapter, but for the moment suffice it to say that the British pioneered leisured big-game hunting, and their adventures in the American West linked such hunting to ideas of play, luxury, and aristocracy for both hunters and readers.

Such associations were often invoked by elite American hunters as well, for whom traveling to the big-game hunting grounds and back again was an adventure as well as a statement about their leisure and wealth. These hunts were constrained both by the time consumed by travel and by the limited access offered by railways and steamships, and before the 1880s that meant that most aspiring big-game hunters from the East Coast headed West. The Plains were the usual destination, and that meant that buffalo were the goal (and not just for dedicated hunters; many travelers seem to have thought that bagging a bison was a quintessential part of any Western trip). Those who wanted to make the full coast-to-coast journey also had the option of hunting bear and a variety of deer in California, but that tended to be as far as traveling hunters seeking the exotic could reasonably venture. Alaska and the Canadian Rockies, as well as the closer hunting grounds of Newfoundland and New Brunswick, would only become easily accessible during or after the 1880s. It was thus to the Great Plains that most American hunters turned when they thought of taking a long trip in the mid-nineteenth century: to the Great Plains, and buffalo.

Before the Civil War, such a journey was an arduous one and was hardly an obvious choice for a there-and-back-again pleasure trip. Henry Ellsworth, leaving home in 1832, summed up his misgivings about his trip west: "I started with a heavy heart . . . the danger from wild Indians, and some of them cannabals too—the exposure to so much inclement weather far from medical treatment & good nursing—the conflagration of the prairies—the reptiles that must every night be my companions & the wild beast[s] on all sides! . . . it was difficult to preserve a cheerful countenance."[14] Like Ellsworth, antebellum travelers, of whom Francis Parkman was the most famous, went primarily for the experience of Western travel, of seeing the great overland trails, and of meeting and interacting with Plains Indians. Parkman also took the time to bag several bison (in some cases simply picking them off from where he was sitting), but these were minor events in his narrative, quickly over and never mentioned again, and this as well seems to have been typical of such early trips.

These early journeys were difficult and enormously time-consuming, but in the years after the Civil War the expansion of the railways made reaching the Plains easier, and two distinct groups of traveling East Coast hunters emerged. One was young men, often on summer vacation from college or just having graduated, who traveled west with friends and classmates to see the country and, inevitably, shoot some buffalo: Elliott Roosevelt did this as a young man, much to the envy of brother Theodore. The other group was grown men who were making a statement about their wealth and ability to take time to play far afield. When George Custer and the Russian Grand Duke Alexis killed three hundred buffalo in a tour of the Great Plains in 1872 or when, the next year, newspaper mogul James Gordon Bennett and the Jerome brothers went hunting on the Plains and cheerfully christened themselves the "Millionaires' Hunting Club," their exploits were understood and reported as leisurely aristocratic outings by the papers of the time. Because Bennett was involved, his expedition was covered by journalists, but it was a participant, Henry Davies, who wrote a book on the adventure—which he then had privately printed and distributed to the other hunters for their personal pleasure. There was no attempt by Davies to interpret the meaning of the hunt for a wider reading audience. Instead, this type of hunting seems to have been perceived, both by the participants and by Americans in general, as having a straightforward enough interpretation: the rich, on vacation, killing things. Such trips also offered an opportunity for a rite of passage for young men, and for a display of status and wealth by adults.[15]

The forms that hunting took for these men were thus dictated by limitations on travel, the need to take time away from work, and their own understanding of why they were in the field. The same factors affected how they hunted once they reached their destinations. Traveling hunters expected to sample a wide variety of hunting techniques, including many that later generations would condemn as deeply unsportsmanlike: jacklighting, for instance, or shooting animals as they swam in the water. The handful of extant hunting tales gives the clear sense that such sampling was not only unremarkable but expected prior to 1880. John Palliser mentions in passing that he has hunted deer at a salt lick, with jacklights, and with dogs, while Joshua Fraser, a minister who went moose hunting in Canada, informs readers that he "had shot abundance of our common red deer in every conceivable orthodox style, by stalking[,] hounds and jacklight" and so was thrilled to experience the novelty of snowcrusting.[16] Snowcrusting consists of a hunter on snowshoes chasing a heavy animal, like a moose or caribou, which breaks through the crust on the snow and flounders; the hunter can then run up beside the animal and shoot it point-blank as it struggles. Fraser enthuses over the ease of this approach and how little it requires from the hunter: "There was no necessity for caution or woodcraft . . . it was simply a matter of running the animal down. . . . The more noise, perhaps, the better. If the moose gets terrified and panic-stricken he comes the more easily blown and exhausted."[17] Henry William Herbert, an Englishman who published under the pseudonym Frank Forester in American sporting magazines, also endorses such variety, telling how he pursued moose in a canoe and shot them as they swam helplessly in the water, and declaring with pride that "great sport . . . fell to the lot of twenty-three officers of the [Coldstream] Guard . . . the flower of the English gentry," who killed ninety-three moose in one day by snowcrusting.[18] Such extreme bags seem to have been more the norm than the exception: Richard Irving Dodge, hunting in the West with four friends, tells readers that his party killed 1,262 animals in twenty days, a count that included "one blue bird, for [a] sweetheart's hat."[19]

There were some who were beginning to question whether these hunting techniques were fair and whether the huge kill counts were necessary, but there is no sense of apology in the writing of these early hunters. Instead they leave an impression of blithe delight in the variety of hunting options. For Fraser, Dodge, and Forester, sampling the wealth of regional variations in hunting was part of the search for novel vacation experiences—and was moreover a sensible way to deal with the time limits facing them.

Snowcrusting, jacklighting, and coursing with hounds all assured hunters of killing game with only a moderate investment of time and effort. This would have mattered to a middle-class minister like Fraser, who spent a great deal of his vacation time simply getting to Canada but was assured of a quick trophy through snowcrusting once there. Dodge advised readers that it was best to chase buffalo down on horseback, noting that those devoted to the technique of stalking could always just dismount for the last part of the hunt, for the "sportsman should never permit his ardour to convert sport into mere labour."[20] Coursing bison from horseback, for him, was the western equivalent of snowcrusting in Canada or jacklighting in the Adirondacks: a new experience, linked to the places he visited and the game he sought, part of the play of the trip.

It's unsurprising that the challenging technique of stalking on foot did not attain much popularity with these hunters. Difficult to learn and to master, the stalk, or still-hunt (so called to differentiate it from "driving" deer with hounds), required the hunter to devote a great deal of time to the hunt and yet made it *less* likely that he would bag the trophy he wanted. (In 1893, for example, Madison Grant would spend weeks stalking moose before finally shooting an animal he considered good enough for his wall; by contrast, snowcrusters could run theirs down in a matter of hours.)[21] Some early hunters even disputed whether stalking was worthwhile at all, including Dodge and Frank Forester: stalking deer "is rather slow work," Forester notes, and is also difficult to learn, so the smart hunter will simply course game with dogs. "He who has ridden once to a good pack, in the open," Forester explains, "[will hold] Deer-stalking as mighty slow sport in all time thereafter."[22] There were men of this set who were stalking animals on foot, and in the 1880s they would emerge into print, but the pre-1880 narratives leave the impression that stalking was not something regularly practiced by traveling hunters.

All these techniques—jacklighting, snowcrusting, hunting with hounds—were also used by subsistence and market hunters seeking to hunt successfully with the least time and effort. This seems not to have troubled well-to-do traveling hunters and in fact eased their passage, since, if they needed assistance, they could just hire local hunters to show them the techniques most common to the region. (This may also help to explain why professional guides didn't appear in many places until much later; there was no need for specialists if all the visiting hunter wanted was a loan of snowshoes or someone to point a light.) As a result, working-class hunters generally appear only as helpers in these narratives, if they appear at all.

Professional market hunters, who were using these same hunting techniques with devastating results, are also invisible in these early narratives. The destruction of the bison on the Great Plains in the late 1860s and early 1870s would have been impossible for travelers to miss: as many as ten thousand professional hunters were at work at the height of the slaughter, with over half a million pelts a year being moved through Dodge City alone.[23] For some travelers it was a shocking illustration of the speed of change in the West, and witnessing it—or seeing the results, how quickly prairies teeming with millions of animals were transformed into desolations—had a formative influence on some well-known hunters who became ardent conservationists, including George Bird Grinnell and William Hornaday.[24] While editorials and articles criticizing the slaughter of the bison were appearing before 1880, however, the writers of these early hunting narratives seem blithely unconcerned with either professional market hunting or the implications of posting large kill counts themselves. Forester reveled in print over "much high and exciting slaughter [of] four or five right Stags . . . whose blood . . . dyed the limpid waters"; Fraser enthused over the ease of snowcrusting; and Dodge boasted of his friends killing over a thousand animals on the Plains *after* the bison had been exterminated from much of the West.[25] These men saw no connection between their actions and those of professional hunters, and why would they? They were gentlemen on vacation, seeking a diverting hunt that guaranteed trophies and that neither involved nor felt like work.

Just as hunting for these men was shaped mainly by practicalities, so too was writing about it. The publishing market, from technology to distribution, was very limited before 1880, at least in comparison to the later developments of the Gilded Age (1877–1897). There was an emerging recreational press in the early 1870s, including the influential *Forest and Stream*, founded in 1873, but such magazines were mostly collations of short reports from readers. Serialized hunting stories that lent themselves to re-publication as books would become common only after 1880 as both the periodical and book markets expanded. Many pre-1880 magazines also seem to have struggled to find their niche: *Field and Stream*, for instance, was founded in 1874 as a journal of field sport but went through two name changes in just seven years, finally settling down as the *American Field* in 1881.[26] All this may help to explain why no particular connections among hunting, writing narratives, and publishing seem to have developed in the pre-1880s period. Part of the alteration both to hunting and to hunting narratives in the Gilded Age would be the result of continuing practical improvements in the technologies of both publishing and distribution.

Those changes would not all be practical, though, because the *cultural* meaning of big-game hunting in the pre-1880 narratives also differed radically from the meanings it would be given by the turn of the century. This is clearest in three areas: the early narratives did not function to create a social network among hunters in print, they framed hunting as part of leisure rather than as work, and they failed to connect their hunting to any concept of manliness. These points are worth underlining because they are counterintuitive in terms of current conceptions of big-game hunting, and because they are the elements that underwent the most massive alteration in the Gilded Age.

First is the issue of social networks, because there is nothing that connects these early hunters clearly to one another in their narratives. This may not appear surprising on the face of it, but, as hunting became ever more popular in the late nineteenth century, the Gilded Age hunter-writers would spin a dense web of connections, describing in print how they hunted together, ran into one another on trains, and met one another unexpectedly in the wilds. They would also use their narratives to exchange information on guides and hunting grounds and to review one another's writing. Eventually, the elite Boone and Crockett hunting club would connect hunting and writing so closely that it would publish entire anthologies based on its members' work. In the process, hunting and the hunting narrative would be woven into the social fabric of upper-class life on the East Coast. None of this is true of the earlier narratives. The social connections certainly existed—men shooting at each other's country homes were building such networks, as were Ivy League classmates traveling west for a summer adventure—but they don't make reference to one another in print. Murray doesn't know Fraser; Fraser never meets the Coldstream Guards; Davies had probably read Parkman, but his narrative isn't grounded in any kind of comparison to *The Oregon Trail*. Overall, the early narratives were too widely separated in time and place to provide such connections.

They were also focused on leisure, and this is perhaps the most counterintuitive cultural element of the early narratives, because both work and manliness have often been assumed to have been part of how American hunting, defined sweepingly, was understood. Historians who have accepted turn-of-the-century hunters' rhetorical connection of their sport to the work of pioneers and cowboys have perhaps overlooked these earlier narratives, where such connections are altogether absent.[27] Fraser doesn't connect his play in the Canadian woods with the hard work of frontier settlement, nor does Dodge or Murray or Forester, and it's difficult to imagine anyone reading these narratives making that connection spontaneously. Valorizing the pioneers was certainly part of American culture, and middle-class readers of narratives like Fraser's and Murray's probably also read the Leatherstocking Tales and stories of Daniel Boone: historian Daniel Herman, in his book *Hunting and the American Imagination*, has done a wonderful job of tracking the trajectory of these various cultural elements.[28] They had not been brought together in the 1860s and 1870s, however; the work of the trailblazing Boone, and Dodge's fear that his sport might become "mere labour," existed in separate cultural and literary worlds. The presentation of hunting in these early narratives *separated* the East Coast man at play from frontier associations, while linking him strongly to leisure, luxury, and, in some cases, the play of aristocrats.

This connection with leisure was so strong that those who did take time away from productive work to go hunting sometimes found themselves under a cloud. This is clear in the conclusion of Fraser's book. It's obvious to him that his hunting has been play, for he is about to return to its opposite: "As I fell asleep . . . it was with a sigh of regret that my moose hunt had come to an end, and now I was to face again the stern realities of work and duty." Those realities turn out to include the opprobrium of his clerical friends, who believe that his hunting has been a scandalous waste of time and "that I might have been much better employed."[29] It might have been easy for someone like James Gordon Bennett, who wanted to be an American aristocrat, to be part of a "Millionaires' Hunting Club"; apparently such associations with frivolous leisure were more difficult to negotiate for a hard-working minister seeking a break from real work.

Connected as it was to play, such hunting also had little to do with ideals of manliness. Far from being the obvious precursors of "manly sport with the rifle," these hunters' connections to leisure opened the way for their sport to be understood as something else entirely. In the nineteenth century, middle- and upper-class native-born men associated manhood with *work*. Leisure was linked to femininity. Visiting a picturesque waterfall or valley scene, sketching and wandering in the woods, and even traveling overseas were seen as women's leisured activities and could be invoked as contrasts to the "real" work of men competing in the marketplace. Hunting was certainly not seen as a woman's activity, but middle- and upper-class men leaving productive work for a hunting vacation were not clearly engaged in manly action either.

There are two indications of this in the early narratives. One is the absence of the rhetoric of manly sport that would permeate later hunting tales. The other is that, on the rare occasions when these hunters do mention gender, the relationship to manliness is often ambiguous. In one letter he sent home, Elliott Roosevelt cheerfully describes being taken out shooting by some locals, noting, "Of course the gentlemen took great care of me as being an effeminate civilian and I had a perfectly glorious time."[30] Henry Ellsworth, describing his first time coursing bison by horseback, explains that "[our guide] said I must yet kill a buffaloe, there was time enough there was a drove ½ mile on our left—I immediately mounted his racer and felt somewhat as a little girl does when she goes to have a tooth pulled, for I was afraid of some accident.... *I never went half so fast before or mean to again.*"[31] Both of these moments occur in letters, not published narratives, but their equivalent is entirely missing from Progressive-Era writing on hunting, public or private.

All this changed in the 1880s. The hunter-writers of the Gilded Age and Progressive Era traveled differently, hunted differently, and gave a different meaning to their hunting than did their predecessors. They also wrote about what they did and used their narratives to shape a social world in print, one linked both to the work of the pioneers and to ideals of manly character. None of these elements can be found in these earlier narratives. The hunter-writers who are the focus of this book remade the American understanding of what it meant to travel to the wilds to hunt. Doing this required first an undoing, for their vacation hunting had to be *disassociated* from luxury, femininity, and aristocracy before it could become manly sport with the rifle. This change happened slowly during the final decades of the nineteenth century, beginning in the early 1880s with the publication of T. S. Van Dyke's seminal book, *The Still-Hunter*.

Theodore Strong Van Dyke was born in New Jersey in 1842, was educated at Princeton, and made his living as a lawyer, but eventually relocated to California because of his health. Throughout his life he hunted deer, and in 1881 he published a serial of thirty articles about the experience in the *American Field*.[32] His timing was exquisite: he hit the beginning of the publishing explosion, the massive expansion of the periodical and book market across North America. Within a year Van Dyke's collected articles were published as a book, entitled *The Still-Hunter*, that went on to be reprinted in 1904, 1912, 1913, 1914, 1923 . . . its most recent reprinting was in 2015. Written in the second person, it is a how-to book that walks the beginning hunter through his experiences, first learning to look for deer, then learning to shoot at them. It would be widely recognized in both the United States and Britain as one of the most important works on hunting ever written; Briton Clive Phillipps-Wolley, in his introduction to the Badminton Library book of *Big Game Shooting*, noted simply that *The Still-Hunter* was the best book ever written by an American. Its status as a classic is in fact well deserved: it was the first American book written on the still-hunt and has lost neither its power nor its charm in more than a century since it was first published.[33]

Among all its outstanding qualities, it was Van Dyke's interpretation of the still-hunt that marks this book as the first of what would become the sportsman-hunter narratives. Still-hunting is another word for stalking, and Van Dyke claimed that stalking deer according to the rules of sportsmanship was better sport than driving, *because it demanded certain qualities from the hunter*. In other words, Van Dyke argued that stalking made the hunt not only more difficult but more meaningful. He recognized that there were easier ways to kill deer than the stalk—indeed, Van Dyke writes, deer are easy prey "to any one of brute strength and brute heart"—but still-hunting, because it is more difficult, ensures that the deer hunt provides "scientific, wide-awake, and manly sport."[34]

If the still-hunt is manly, and easier forms of hunting are not, then hunters like Dodge, Fraser, and Forester were simply expressing their "brute heart" through their hunting. Van Dyke is rewriting the meaning of the hunt here, in part by claiming that the still-hunt can reveal something about the hunter's inner self. This is an entirely new idea of what the hunt can be used for. Hunting like Dodge's and Bennett's certainly said something about their wealth and status, but it was never framed as revealing hidden inner qualities. Van Dyke, however, instructs his readers that the manly qualities of perseverance, determination, patience, and above all self-control are taught by hunting, and are necessary for good hunting. These virtues are linked to their traditional class connotations: Van Dyke's hunter is coming from the city, seeking "the land beyond the pavement," and he is a gentleman. And this construction of the proposed audience is driven home by the use of the second person, as Van Dyke speaks directly to his reader about what kind of man he is, what kind of man he wants to be, and what his hunting experience should be if he is of the "right sort."

A fine bit of work resulting in a good shot. This man was tracking this deer on the hillside where the deer is, but knowing the brush would make him too difficult to see from that side, he left the trail and crossed over to where he could get a good view of the hillside.

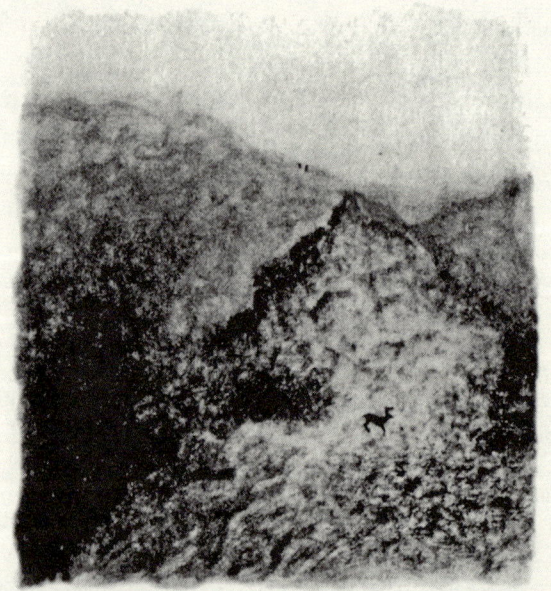

These chaps are on the track of this deer, and both together when they should have separated and gone along the sides of the hill as soon as they found he had gone down the point. But it was better walking on the ridge.

Figure 1.1. Van Dyke illustrated *The Still-Hunter* himself, wanting to show realistic distances between hunters and game, with the deer (*above*) and the hunters (*at left*) barely visible. The captions provide a contrast. The man in the first image, through a "fine bit of work," has positioned himself to make a good (but still difficult) shot; the hunters in the second chose the ridge because "it was better walking," and their laziness means the loss of their trophy. From Van Dyke, *The Still-Hunter*, 1882.

Van Dyke assures his reader that his teachers will be "disappointment and humiliation. If these cure you of still-hunting, it is well; for it proves you were not born for that. . . . But if there is any of the true spirit in you, defeat will only inspire you." This advice is followed by his description of your experience the first time you patiently stalk, yet still lose, your deer. Some men will quit, Van Dyke notes; others will find

> double determination to conquer [the deer] and his tricks. . . . For the first class [of men] this book is not written. The Adirondack guide who holds a deer by the tail in the water for his patrons to shoot from the boat with a shot-gun . . . can give such all the information they are likely to ever need or appreciate. But you, for whom this is written, can learn a good lesson here. . . . You feel rich in a far higher and nobler experience, and feel that to him who has within the true spirit of the chase there is far more pleasure in seeing over a ridge or among the darkening trunks a flaunting flag wave a mocking farewell to hope than in contemplating a gross pile of meat bagged with less skill than is required to wring a chicken's neck on a moonlight night.

Indeed. It is not hard to imagine that, after three hundred pages of this sort of thing, Van Dyke's reader wants to be identified with the true spirit of the chase. This pattern, of telling his audience what happens to them hunting, and then instructing them on what it means, continues throughout the book. Chapter 18 is titled "The Still-Hunter's Cardinal Virtue," which is patience and the constant use of self-control to overcome buck-ague. In this chapter, you fail: as the buck approaches "your desire to shoot is worse than the murderer's secret, and kicks and hammers against your perspiring ribs until you can no longer resist the temptation." But you miss. "Speed of fire is a good servant, but a bad master."[35] You will master it, becoming the Still-Hunter, and your eventual first kill will be patent proof of your mastery, not only of speed of fire, but of yourself. In this formulation, the successful still-hunt offers material proof of the hunter's inner qualities, of his willingness to test himself and of his hard-won self-control. And this formula would lie at the heart of every one of the sportsman-hunter narratives published in the years after *The Still-Hunter* first appeared.

There is nothing obvious about this reading of the hunt, nothing that makes sense at first glance, especially considering the hunting narratives that had preceded it. What relationship does Van Dyke's still-hunter have to Ellsworth, clutching the reins like a nervous little girl, or to Forester glorying in the kill count of the Coldstream Guard, or to Murray's lazy drift through the Adirondacks? In *The Still-Hunter,* a world of associations is being undone. Hunting has suddenly become a manly and meaningful use of leisure, even as the menu of hunting options has been reduced to one. Snowcrusting, jacklighting, and potting deer in the water all remained available, and many hunters would continue to use such techniques. As the nineteenth century drew to a close, however, for middle- and upper-class hunters of the East Coast who wanted to be identified as true sportsmen, there would now be only one kind of hunting that was "wide-awake and manly": the still-hunt.

CHAPTER 2

# Fall of the Workplace, Rise of the Hunt

It's impossible to overstate the importance of *The Still-Hunter* or its influence on the thousands of hunting narratives published in the years after its appearance. The most famous American big-game hunters of the period testified to its impact: Theodore Roosevelt recommended it to Boone and Crockett members as one of the best books on field sport, while Charles Sheldon, in his catalogue of hunting books, described it tersely as the "best book ever written on still hunting."[1] In one stroke, it reinterpreted the stalk as a form of hunting that said something meaningful about the hunter and demonstrated how narrative could be used to make that meaning intelligible to readers. Linking the stalk to a host of manly virtues, and linking hunting to writing a narrative, Van Dyke laid the foundation for all who followed him.

He also left a puzzle for historians, because it is hard to see where this concept of the hunt originated. It certainly didn't evolve from the work of Forester, Fraser, or Dodge, writers who either expressed open contempt for the stalk or, in Fraser's case, listed it as one among many "orthodox" styles of hunting he had sampled, on a par with jacklighting. Van Dyke was certainly not the only man in his era pursuing the stalk, but, while there were other adherents to the method, it's impossible to tell if they saw it as revealing something innate about the hunter. (The absence of any apology among writers like Dodge and Forester who refused the stalk also makes it seem unlikely there was a single agreed-upon meaning for the still-hunt.) Readers who wrote in to the *American Field* about Van Dyke's articles tended to focus on the accuracy of his descriptions: "I can almost imagine . . . that he had followed me through the woods when I first began to hunt deer," one man wrote, while another praised Van Dyke's "scientific exposition."[2] There's no way to know from this how many of these readers had been associating their sport with the *qualities* Van Dyke invests in the still-hunt: manliness, perseverance, and self-control, a very specific set of virtues that seem to bear no more inherent relationship to one another than they do to hunting.

Those virtues hold the clue to solving the puzzle, however, because they were very much part of the culture of the same middle- and upper-class men who had written the earlier narratives, and from which Van Dyke and his followers would be drawn. They were qualities held up as the ultimate goals for native-born, white, Protestant, middle- and upper-class men of the urban Northeast, and were collectively referred to as "the manly virtues." The thing is, they weren't located in leisure. They were located, throughout the nineteenth century, in the workplace.

That workplace had offered a site for the display of the manly virtues for decades, but during the Gilded Age, under the pressures of the Second Industrial Revolution, its role would be irrevocably altered. The Second Industrial Revolution began around 1870 and was characterized by both a flood of technological development and a massive reorganization of American industry, involving corporatization, the growth of trusts, and the ruthless pursuit of monopolies. These changes affected the workplace and in response men began to seek other sites in which to display manliness. The origins of Van Dyke's interpretation of the still-hunt lie here, in the history of middle-class work, its relationship to ideals of manliness, and the massive alterations ushered in by industrial change in the final decades of the nineteenth century.

"Manliness," "manly character," "the primacy of the will": these words and phrases encompassed a set of ideals that were of vital importance to nineteenth-century middle- and upper-class American society. For much of that century, men of those classes defined themselves, and were defined by others, through their occupations, which provided them with both self-definition and social status. Over time a set of ideals emerged, closely linked to workplace performance, that associated worldly success with the possession of certain personal characteristics, the virtues that constituted "character." These virtues, often referred to as the "manly virtues," were those perceived as necessary for economic success: temperance, prudence, self-reliance, and, especially, self-control and willpower. Hard work and self-discipline, an ability to save money and invest it wisely, and the refusal to be tempted by gin, gambling, and loose women, were all believed to be the hallmarks of successful and upstanding men. Character was thus valued because of the results it yielded but was also read from those results, so that any successful man of business could be assumed to possess the manly virtues.[3]

The manly virtues transcended mere economics, however. They had powerful moral significance in a nation devoted to various versions of the Protestant work ethic, where self-discipline, hard work, and a resistance to the temptations of pleasure could all be read as meaningful on the spiritual plane as well as in the business world. They also mattered at the level of family and community obligations for, in an era when women and children were dependent on men for support, a man's success or failure in business determined his family's future as well. The manly virtues were thus part of wider belief systems about what it meant to be not only a good man of business, but also a virtuous man, a family man, a good provider, a man of standing in his community—a man of character.[4]

The wellspring of all these virtues was the will. Nineteenth-century middle- and upper-class Americans believed that the will was the highest faculty that humans had developed, one that granted the possessor control over his mind, body, and emotions. Strengthened through constant deployment, controlled through disciplined effort, the will had to be built up, like a muscle, and then kept strong through ceaseless striving until its use became almost reflexive, a total control over one's body, feelings, passions, thoughts, and actions. A strong will was thus closely identified with personal, economic, and moral success and underlay all the other manly virtues, including temperance, resolution, self-discipline, and self-control.[5]

This well-honed will was not the property of all human beings, however. Instead it was believed to be most developed within those considered to be at the apex of civilization: native-born, Protestant, middle- and upper-class white men. In contrast, women and children, as well as men of other races, classes, religions, and ethnicities, were often represented as slaves of impulse, subject to unconstrained appetites and unreasoning desires. The primacy of the will was not only exercised and displayed by the successful man of business, then, it was also his by right of his gender, race, class, and maturity—and yet he still had to work to possess it. Not every man developed the will to succeed, and, without constant exercise, the will of men of the best families and backgrounds could *devolve*. The concept of the primacy of the will thus allowed native-born American white men to make distinctions between one another, even as it formed a basis for recognition and solidarity in opposition to those excluded from consideration.[6] That solidarity was one whose very language finessed thorny questions of class exclusion, however, because it was almost always framed in gendered terms. "Manliness" and "the manly virtues" were used almost interchangeably with "character," and in the process some of the clear class lines drawn by these ideals were blurred.

Despite this, the ideals of character and the manly virtues remained recognizable as the product and aspiration of one particular set of Americans who shared birth, race, religion, and membership in either the middle or upper classes. The idea that character was fundamentally linked to work seems to have originally been a middle-class creation; historian Mary Ryan has shown how the emerging middle class in Utica, New York, developed both virtues and identity in concert in the antebellum period. One only has to think of Andrew Carnegie and his rags-to-riches personal legend, however, to see that such virtues were often claimed by wealthy men as well. The nineteenth-century "leisure class" in America also tended to be a producing class: politicians, doctors, and gentlemen authors they may have been, but it is difficult to identify a single clear upper class in the nineteenth century through the means of production alone. Rather, on the East Coast, the elite was defined through shared backgrounds, family connections, and, increasingly, a shared education at a handful of Eastern preparatory schools followed by Ivy League colleges. They were far removed in many ways from middle-class men in small cities like Utica, but they also adopted the rhetoric of manly character and were more than willing to view themselves through the lens of the primacy of the will.[7]

It's easy from this description to see why Joshua Fraser's companions looked askance at his decision to take time away from his clerical duties to go moose hunting, and why Elliott Roosevelt had no trouble describing himself as an "effeminate civilian" during his vacation. Such a comment didn't really reflect on Roosevelt's manliness because for him the hunting grounds were a place of play, not of work. These two areas of life existed as complements in the years before and immediately after the Civil War: the workplace culture of manly virtues and willpower embraced by middle- and upper-class men, and a set of leisure activities, including sport hunting, associated with unproductive play. It would take the great changes of the post–Civil War era to transform the identity of both the hunt and the workplace, and to create the context necessary for the emergence of *The Still-Hunter* and the narratives that followed it.

In the wake of the Civil War, throughout the Gilded Age, and into the Progressive Era, the consolidation of the workplace into industrial enclaves, the increasing loss of male autonomy, and the rapidly changing social profile of the United States altered everything. The numbers are still staggering, even at this distance. Between 1870 and 1910, the population of the country more than doubled. Immigrants accounted for almost a third of that increase, and they clustered in cities that were expanding, seemingly without limit. Industry expanded as well: the Gilded Age was an era of railroads and oil trusts, of steel and skyscrapers, and with it came labor unrest and a change in labor itself. The first great mass movements of workingmen emerged, and the violence that accompanied their strikes and demands became linked, in the minds of many, with revolutions in Europe. Such specters were invoked in the railway strikes of 1877, and innocent men with anarchist sympathies were hanged in the wake of the Haymarket bomb throwing of 1886, while men of the upper classes began to mutter about a "volcano under the city," the seething, unpredictable, dispossessed poor. Those poor were the creation of a nation falling at terminal velocity into the Second Industrial Revolution, a country where the laws couldn't keep up with the actions of industry and where opportunity was contracting, until by 1890 some 1 percent of families held 51 percent of the country's wealth. Accompanying these changes was an economy that caromed from one extreme to the other, from one depression to another, culminating in the "savage depression" of 1893–1897: fifteen thousand businesses failed in 1893 alone, and for a while the flood of immigration changed direction. This was new, all of it: the rapid urbanization, the masses of workingmen demanding fair treatment, the McCormicks and Pullmans who opposed them, the brutal chain of depressions.[8]

These changes operated on the levels of the national and international, of the political and economic, and also of the quotidian, the everyday—where people went to work, bought food, dreamed of their futures, and made sense of their worlds. The many poor and the very few rich were affected by these changes, but so was an ever-growing middle class. White, native-born, middle-class men coming of age in the years after the Civil War found themselves entering an economy in which the number of salaried and nonpropertied jobs increased eightfold between 1870 and 1900, and this created opportunity, but a new kind of opportunity: the chance to work for someone else, for life.[9] There was little room in such workplaces for a direct equation between character and performance, while manly virtues such as autonomy and primacy of the will seemingly bore little relation to the qualities needed for corporate success. The workplace as a central site for the performance of manly character was disintegrating. In the new world that was replacing it, men struggled to find their way, to recognize those like themselves, and to understand how traditional ideals of manliness applied to their situations.[10]

Pressure was being applied to these men along at least three axes. The first was that of wealth, of what it had once meant to possess it (proof of character), and of how that meaning had changed, to the point that some self-made men were being jeered at as "robber barons." Walter Lippmann, assessing this era, pointed out that market economics had outrun all the traditional connections between virtue and success: "All I have to do is to choose some well-known stock broker and put myself into his hands. And when I read in books on political economy that any profit I make is a reward for my foresight, my courage in the face of risk, I laugh."[11] Money was also beginning to lose its ability to denote an old-family and identifiable status group. There had been a time when the moneyed elite of the East Coast all knew each other and shared breeding and background, a time when, in the memorable phrase of patrician scion Poultney Bigelow, "all white men spoke English, and there was but one club, and he who was not thereof might better be dead."[12] That club was also failing in the post–Civil War era, as East Coast elites found themselves invaded by robber barons, arrivistes, and nouveaux—people like the Bradley Martins, who threw a ball in 1894 that remade the Waldorf over into a replica of Versailles at an estimated cost of $400,000, and set off a riot among enraged and dispossessed New Yorkers suffering through the worst year of the 1890s depression.[13]

Those rioters represented a second axis of pressure, that of the volcano under the city, the poor who might be provoked, or corrupted, by the unthinking or unethical rich. Many Americans in this period perceived the abuse of wealth, and the dangers posed by the dispossessed, as intimately linked. The connections between the two were drawn in popular periodicals that ran pictures of slum conditions next to muckraking articles on the trusts, in Progressive reform literature that called on factory owners to ameliorate their abuses of their workers, even in presidential speeches that grouped some of the wealthy under the title "the powers that prey." Fear of the wealthy, fear of the poor, fear of the connections between them: for those among the wealthy who felt their elite identity challenged and slipping away, and for those of the middle classes who feared for their autonomy, identity, and prospects, the pressure was coming at once from above *and* below.[14]

At the same time, pressure was being internally generated as well, for the social dislocations accompanying massive immigration, the ever-increasing number of arrivistes, and the expanding geographic and social mobility of the time were intimately connected, and yet different, from the pressures that middle- and upper-class men felt *within* their own groups. The idea of the primacy of the will had always carried this possibility within it: that while some people were clearly excluded, there were also divisions to be made among those who otherwise appeared to belong. Even someone of the "right" race, class, gender, and background might turn out not to be so right after all. Sometimes such men were friends or acquaintances, but they could also be new arrivals: in 1896 writer (and big-game hunter) William Hornaday warned readers against the "stranger of plausible tongue and pleasing appearance [who] is promptly invited to share Mr. Chump's club, his hearth, his table, his box at the theater . . . and sometimes may even marry his daughter" before being exposed as a man of low character—and yet Mr. Chump plays his part in this scenario, he reveals his own foolishness in the act of being fooled.[15] This was the third axis of pressure, one in which questions of identity, character, and manliness came into play as men sought for a way to talk about themselves and those they befriended, worked with, played with, *knew*. That knowledge in turn formed the basis for decisions about business transactions, social contacts, and marriage alliances. It mattered.[16]

It was in this context that the manly virtues took center stage. They served a specific function that was immensely useful in the confusion of the times, because they provided a way to draw distinctions among men. The manly virtues were not, after all, possessed by every man, despite the gendered attribution. This language was instead a way of talking about elements of character that could be used to identify certain men as being of the "right sort." There was a problem, however. Throughout the nineteenth century, for many men, questions about who belonged, who could be trusted, could be answered in part by looking at what kind of work a man did, at what he produced. By the turn of the century, though, the workplace was no longer easily available as a place for men to demonstrate who they were to themselves and to others. Somewhere new had to be sought.

The motivation to find such a site was based not just in the same needs as before, but also in new anxieties. As the workplace became compromised, as the social order began to appear increasingly unstable, as the state of transition became what must have seemed a permanent state of continuous change, it was more urgent than ever for these men to find a way to identify themselves and others, even as the traditional sites for such demonstrations were vanishing. The world of the Second Industrial Revolution was a place where questions of honesty, character, and the reliable fulfillment of obligations were becoming more difficult than ever to answer, but where the need for such answers remained imperative. It was also a world where such answers could provide guideposts, not only for judgments made by others, but also for men to understand themselves.[17]

The dimensions of this challenge were so great that no single response could hope to answer it, nor did only one answer arise. Instead, in the period between the Gilded Age and the Great War, an entire society searched for answers to the questions posed by their nation's transformation. The Progressive movement was one answer, speaking to feelings of dispossession, worries about the marketplace, and anxieties about both the unethical rich and the uncontrollable poor. Cultural responses abounded as well, ranging from the anti-industrial ethic of the Arts and Crafts movement to the embrace of modernity by architects such as Louis Sullivan, "the father of the skyscraper."[18] Many people were seeking the affirmation of traditional values and American writers responded, popularizing a variety of genres in which men proved themselves in almost every setting *but* the workplace. Some of these tales were set in exotic lands, some in the past: Richard Ohmann, looking at fiction in this period, points out that the Western "assure[d] readers whose life chances depend irrevocably on the urban, corporate order that individual action and character still count[ed]," even as stories with modern settings showed young middle-class men leaping into action in response to train crashes and other unexpected emergencies that let them display their manly virtues to admiring onlookers.[19]

Big-game hunting and big-game hunting narratives were part of this change. In the period from roughly 1880 to the beginning of the Great War, more American men went big-game hunting and then produced narratives of their experiences than ever before. Those narratives owed little to the hunting narratives published in America before 1880. Instead, they used the rhetoric of the manly virtues and the primacy of the will to position the still-hunt as a place in which to develop, display, and recognize character. Overwhelmingly produced and consumed by exactly those Protestant native-born white men of the middle and upper classes who had been most devoted to the workplace ideal of manly character, the story of the big-game hunt was a response to the anxieties of its time and drew its moral power from that fact.

"Manly sport with the rifle" thus emerged from cultural anxieties about change, and yet the rise of the stalk as a popular form of hunting was being made possible by many of those same changes, especially those affecting work, travel, and communication. In particular, expanding leisure time and developments in transportation allowed increasing numbers of hunters to choose to stalk game and still be successful. After all, one of the main reasons that the still-hunt had never been widely popular was because of its difficulty: requiring both skill and patience from its disciples, it had been an unreasonable investment of time for middle-class men on a brief vacation from work. By the 1880s, however, expanding leisure time was making the still-hunt a practical option for more and more sportsmen. At the same time, railroads were spanning the continent, steamships moved more rapidly and frequently across the oceans, and as a result hunting grounds formerly difficult to reach suddenly became accessible.

These changes had an impact on every group that hunted,[20] but for the white, native-born, Protestant, middle- and upper-class men of the East Coast who embraced the still-hunt—the group I'm going to be referring to as "the sportsmen-hunters"—the improvements to transportation had four major results. First, they made big-game hunting grounds easier to reach. In 1895, for example, hunter Frederic Irland found to his delight that on September 1 he could receive delivery of his custom-made rifle in Boston, hop an overnight train to New Brunswick, and be moose hunting by noon on September 2. The second major change was that, with hunting grounds more accessible and transport easier, cheaper, and quicker, the number of men hunting afield for pleasure increased dramatically. Now not only the very wealthy, but also middle-class men with an interest in big-game hunting could venture abroad or into the heart of their own continent. The third result was that the stalk, a form of hunting that required a considerable time investment in order to meet with success, became increasingly popular, and began to be invoked as a way to distinguish among hunters—to draw a hard line between gentlemen and market hunters, certainly, but also to make more subtle divisions *among* middle- and upper-class men. Finally, this growth in accessibility made big-game hunting a more attainable goal for an audience that, over time, would include not only hunters but also readers who could reasonably imagine that someday they might find themselves in the places described in the narratives.[21]

All these elements meshed together to inspire and inform sportsmen, beginning a cascade effect that depended not only on new meanings for the hunt but also on growing leisure time, ease of access, and, more and more often, publication. Samuel Davis, in his book *Caribou Shooting in Newfoundland*, describes how he and his friends, relaxing in New York City one afternoon in 1892, read an article on hunting in Newfoundland in *Harper's Weekly*. The article's author, Wakeman Holbertson, lived nearby, so they called upon him, viewed his trophies, received his advice, and set off for Newfoundland. They paid $34 each round trip from New York to St. John's by steamer and had a wonderful time. ("*Wednesday, October 31st.* Thermometer 32; clear. All busy taking care of our trophies. No hunting done, though quite a number of deer were seen crossing the Big Marsh. This was a charming day.") The book urges other sportsmen to "Go and do likewise."[22] It also suggests how to fund such a trip, for Davis presents an imaginary conversation with a friend who says he cannot possibly afford such a vacation. Davis walks the friend through his daily expenses, quickly discovering that the man smokes four ten-cent cigars a day while paying fifty cents for beer and whiskey. $280 a year on beer and smokes? The same money, Davis explains, will pay for

> all the expenses of the grand outing of from six weeks to two months to any point in the United States, Canada or Newfoundland, and with all the advantages and comforts of first-class travel, leaving a balance for extras and some trophies of the chase which money could not purchase, and which are ever a source of pleasure and instruction as specimens of Natural History, and positive evidence of one's prowess and skill with the gun.[23]

There is a moral value being given to the leisure-time hunt here, one implicitly opposed to the drinking and smoking that accompany city life: here, the urban world that surrounds work is something to escape. And the rewards offered by sport are not simply about leisure. Davis's hunt offers health, instruction, scientific knowledge—values that transcend mere materialism—as well as proof of prowess and manly display, all without sacrificing the comforts of first-class travel. Other connections are being made as well. Davis's hunt is intertwined from the beginning with writing and publication, while he and Holbertson are also socially connected, able to call one upon the other (indeed, Davis urges readers to stop by and see his friends' trophies).[24] This is a world that is both nationally available in the pages of *Harper's* and at the same time socially contained, one in which hunting, instruction, social access, and moral issues intertwine, and in which the desire to escape the modern world is being facilitated by the very modern technologies of both transportation and publishing.

Manly display and the Second Industrial Revolution, hunting and writing, the fair-stalk and the railway trip were thus all linked from the beginning. These connections appear in Van Dyke and Davis, and also in Frederic Remington's account of how he hopped a train to Dakota to do some shooting, only to find himself condemned by a railway car full of sportsmen for not being properly outfitted. He wryly informs us that the passengers—an army officer, a phlebotomist from Pittsburgh, and three Harvard men—took up a collection to arm him properly.[25] Anthony Dimock was a stockbroker on Wall Street, educated at Stowe Academy and Harvard, who went on a bear-hunting trip to the Rockies and was pleased to discover that he was camping near "the tent of some Harvard boys, one of whom was Owen Wister."[26] (On his return to New York, he joined the Stock Exchange Rifle Club.) The railways made it possible for these men to travel widely and, everywhere they went, they found other men like themselves. At the same time, however, the hunts they depict are no longer the pleasure trips described by Fraser, Dodge, or Murray. Dimock's hunting is not about time stolen from productive work, but complements it: whether writing a chapter on his "First Corner in Currency" or "Encounter with a Grizzly," Dimock presents himself as a leader, in Wall Street and the wilds. Davis praises his guide, Richard LeBuffe, in terms that cannot be found in Murray's *Adventures in the Wilderness*: "As a still hunter he cannot be excelled."[27] This way of talking about big-game hunting and its role in the lives of hunters was new.

Also new was the fact that these men were *writing* about their experiences—and this is essential to understanding the changing nature of the hunt. Humans had hunted for millennia, but these hunters sat down and converted their experiences into narrative afterward, and those narratives disseminated the new meaning of the hunt to a vast reading audience. Remington reported his adventure in the pages of *Harper's*, where readers would learn that there was a right way to be outfitted, as well as getting an idea of the kinds of men who were going hunting. Dimock wrote a book about his experiences, *Wall Street and the Wilds*, and made sure that an inscribed copy went to the library at Stowe to model his experiences for the next generation of Stowe men.[28] Van Dyke promulgated the new meaning of the still-hunt through the *American Field* and *The Still-Hunter* to thousands of readers he would never meet. If the hunt was now a performance of the will, of the manly virtues, then that display was taking place, not only in the woods, but on the printed page.

The stories these men wrote about the still-hunt quickly came to dominate the presentation of big-game hunting in the middle-class press.[29] Such tales were nonfiction, almost always written in the first person, and told about the hunter's experience stalking his prey. Single articles, featuring titles such as "A Day with the Elk" or "A Remarkable Adventure with Grizzly Bears," normally focused on just one hunt, while serial articles described the drawn-out experiences of hunters like Caspar Whitney as he stalked musk-ox on the Barren Grounds. Such serials were often re-released as books that proved profitable for publishing companies: Whitney's articles were collected and published as *On Snow-shoes to the Barren Grounds: Twenty-Eight Hundred Miles after Musk-Oxen and Wood-Bison*. By 1900 entire series began to appear, so that devotees could collect all the volumes of the American Sportsman's Library from Macmillan or the Outing Adventure Library from the Outing Publishing Company. Whatever the format, all these tales had two things in common: they were aimed at and priced for a middle-class reading audience, and they all focused on the stalk and what it said about the hunter. Their popularity is testified to by their printings and reprintings and by their regular appearances in popular generalist periodicals such as *Harper's*. Delivered into the parlors of nonhunting readers across the country, these stories clearly had an appeal far beyond their subject matter. The idea that the still-hunt said something important about the hunter made such sport meaningful for the men who pursued it; in turn, the creation and distribution of narratives by those men made their interpretation of the still-hunt meaningful for hundreds of thousands of readers.

No one better exemplifies the vital connections between giving meaning to the hunt and writing about it than a man who has been waiting, no doubt impatiently, in the wings: Theodore Roosevelt. If *The Still-Hunter* marked a major transformation in the links among stalking, narrative, and the virtues originally derived from the workplace, then Roosevelt can be credited with linking those elements to the hunting of dangerous game, to a specific language of manliness, and to a certain story about the American West. The legend of Roosevelt in the West has been told too many times to recapitulate in detail here: he bought a ranch in Medora, North Dakota; in 1883, he returned there in grief after the loss of his wife and his mother; and he found solace in ranch life and in hunting. All of which might not have meant much save for one thing: Roosevelt wrote about it. Three of his early books, *Hunting Trips of a Ranchman* (1885), *Ranch Life and the Hunting-Trail* (1888), and *The Wilderness Hunter* (1893), were devoted to hunting in the American West. In these books, and in a host of related articles, Roosevelt rewrote the experience of the wealthy man going hunting into a tale that Richard Irving Dodge would not have recognized. In doing so, he was picking up on trends already underway, for he was one of a group of men who were beginning to write about the West, manliness, the frontier, and Americanism. He was thus never entirely original, but his prolific production and growing personal fame made him tremendously influential. And those things are not easily separable one from the other: Roosevelt's hunts, his written accounts of them, and his love affair with the American public fed into one another in a dizzying spiral of popularity and self-promotion.[30]

While Roosevelt was influential, however, that's a very different thing from being representative. He was, as both a hunter and a writer about hunting, markedly different from most of his native-born, upper-class, Ivy-educated peers. (This is actually true of Roosevelt in general: Christopher Lasch summed the problem up perfectly when, in his article on turn-of-the-century elites, he arrived with a sigh at "the compelling, if slightly bizarre, example of Theodore Roosevelt . . ."[31]) Roosevelt consistently praised sportsmanship, but his massive kill counts were viewed with distaste by his contemporaries, British and American alike, and they overwhelmingly chose not to follow his example. He celebrated elements of the frontier that, as we'll see, almost every other hunter-writer denied or elided, including Indian fighting, violence, and war. He was legendary for his ability to make friends, but not everyone was charmed by him: Poultney Bigelow describes Roosevelt's visit to the Metropolitan Club in 1898, where "we laughed with Teddy and at him as he thumped the table and frothed at the mouth and snapped his teeth and gleamed savagely through his eye-glasses."[32] Despite the private misgivings that some of his peers felt toward him and his hunting, however, his combination of social and political power, ubiquity in the press, and popularity with the public make him central to the story of hunting and conservation in this period. The trick is to note where he diverged completely from other hunters while acknowledging the times when he was influential—and his impact on the development of the big-game hunting narrative was one of those moments. His stories of hunting in the West not only resonated with the American public but had a lasting influence on the associations that surrounded the still-hunt. In 1881 Van Dyke had connected still-hunting to work, primacy of the will, and sportsmanship. In the mid-1880s Roosevelt linked wilderness hunting both to manliness and to an American exceptionalist story.

He began by rehabilitating both the cowboy and the hunter—figures often condemned as vicious in the mid-nineteenth century—describing them instead as admirable Americans and contrasting their putative virtues to those of "civilized" men.[33] In *Ranch Life*, Roosevelt describes the cowboy as having "few of the emasculated, milk-and-water moralities admired by the pseudo-philanthropists; but he does possess, to a very high degree, the stern, manly qualities that are invaluable to a nation."[34] Frederic Remington illustrated the book and caught the flavor of Roosevelt's comparisons in the picture "Which Is the Bad Man?" (see figure 2.1). Is it the cowboy—traditionally considered a wild, lawless sort—or what appears to be the city banker about to fleece him? The anxieties being addressed in this picture, and in Roosevelt's book, are recognizably middle-class anxieties that reach back to the early parts of the nineteenth century. How does one recognize sincerity, manliness, reliability? Remington asks that question visually and Roosevelt answers it in the text, setting up certain cowboys and wilderness hunters as models of manly autonomy. "The hunter is the arch-type of freedom," Roosevelt explains. "His well-being rests in no man's hands save his own."[35]

The manly virtues are on display here, but Roosevelt insists that they are not so much inherent in certain men as derived from the life they lead—a specifically American kind of life, for "there is not in Europe the chance to try the adventurous, wandering life of the wilderness so beloved by the American hunter."[36] That life, "patriarchal in character . . . the life of men . . . who call no man master," develops the qualities of "hardihood, self-reliance, and resolution . . . dogged perseverance and patient persistence": in brief, "vigorous manliness."[37] Certainly self-reliance was a necessary quality for cowboys and frontier hunters, but patience, persistence, and perseverance? Those are markedly middle-class virtues, more appropriate to a Horatio Alger hero than to a woodland hunter trying to procure the most meat with the least effort. Roosevelt is linking nineteenth-century workplace virtues to wilderness hunting here, even as he is disconnecting American hunting from associations with aristocratic play and, especially, from leisured British hunting. Fusing manliness, the wilderness, and Americanism with the still-hunt, Roosevelt literally rewrote the meaning of American big-game hunting.

In the process, he was also reimagining the role of the wealthy man hunting on vacation, in part by shifting his praise of cowboys and frontier hunters into an elegy to their passing. "The great free ranches . . . mark a primitive stage of existence [and] must pass away before the onward march of our people," Roosevelt told readers; the Plains rider "prepares the way for the civilization from before whose face he must himself disappear."[38] That rider's manly qualities, however, could still be derived by a certain set of men, those with the money and leisure to go experience the wilderness for themselves, to hunt, and then to return. On the apex of civilization, a handful of society's elect would find that imitating the wilderness hunter's work and life—however briefly—had become, through Roosevelt's rhetorical alchemy, a way

Figure 2.1. Illustration by Frederic Remington, from Theodore Roosevelt, *Ranch Life and the Hunting-Trail*, 1888.

of experiencing a type of American work, and American manliness, that had previously been unconnected to ideas of leisure-time hunting. Somewhere between North Dakota and Roosevelt's publishers in New York, language, print, and illustration had combined to remake the meaning of the patrician hunt: no longer rich men boasting about their millionaires' hunting clubs, but instead men simulating the experience of the "arch-type of freedom" by pursuing "manly sport with the rifle."

That last phrase comes from the constitution of the hunting club that Roosevelt founded with George Bird Grinnell in 1887: the Boone and Crockett Club. Named for "the tutelary deities of American hunting," it was an exclusive gentleman's club, having one hundred members, usually chosen from among Grinnell and Roosevelt's circle of acquaintances. The requirements for entry shifted over time but always included having killed three big-game animals through still-hunting.[39] Van Dyke was one of the earliest members; so were powerful figures in the publishing world like Caspar Whitney and Grinnell himself, editor and publisher of the recreational periodical *Forest and Stream*. Members embraced the idea of wealthy men's hunting as "manly sport" and wrote about it from that viewpoint, as "man's work" (in Grinnell's words) or "healthy, manly sport" (in Arnold Hague's description of elk hunting).[40] Demonstrating the manly virtues in leisure and then writing about their performances for the national press, Boone and Crockett members disconnected elite hunting from its traditional associations with leisured play and gave it a new meaning. Their rhetoric flooded the pages of popular magazines, including turn-of-the-century publishing powerhouses *Harper's* and *Scribner's*. And all this only makes sense as a whole: the still-hunt's appeal to these men, their access to leisure, railways, and publishing houses, their desire to write, and their need for a new site for the display of the traditional manly virtues.

Over time, the handful of men promoting this narrative would be read by an ever-expanding audience, many of whom would choose to follow Van Dyke's vision of the hunt. Not all of them were patricians. Turn-of-the-century big-game hunters still needed money and leisure, but not enormous amounts of either, and by the 1890s their ranks included struggling lawyers, boys just out of West Point, and professional journalists and editors. These newcomers had a great deal in common with the elite, however: the sportsmen-hunters who followed Van Dyke and Roosevelt were overwhelmingly white, male, native born, Protestant, almost always from urban centers of the Northeast, and born just before, during, or in the decade after the Civil

War.[41] Their values were drawn from that background—their belief in the vital importance of character, the primacy of the will, and the manly virtues—and, in speaking about the meaning of their hunting, they spoke directly to the beliefs and anxieties of those like them. They identified themselves with a group of ideas marked both by their social conservatism and by the radical choice of leisure as a place to seek and demonstrate them. Those choices, in turn, transformed "manly sport with the rifle" into both a phrase and an activity with meaning for thousands of Progressive-Era men.

"Every generation is a secret society," wrote John Jay Chapman in 1915, "and has incommunicable enthusiasms, tastes and interests which are a mystery both to its predecessors and to posterity."[42] Chapman's generation was one in which traditional ideals of what it meant to be a man were caught up in a confluence of forces pushing toward fundamental change, of personal identity and of the nation as a whole. Out of the social and cultural materials at their disposal, some of these men found a new way to talk about and display manliness, using a site that would have mystified their predecessors: the big-game hunt and its interpretation through published narrative. These two things cannot be separated, because the transformation of the hunt into a certain kind of story, and the selling of that story to a national audience, is the reason that these hunters had the influence they did. Van Dyke, Roosevelt, and their ilk created a way to hunt *and* a way to write about it. They were under pressure from some elements of the Second Industrial Revolution and turned to other elements to relieve it, hopping trains for faraway places and displaying their hunting prowess in the pages of *Harper's*. Linking the nineteenth-century manly virtues to leisure-time hunting, they constructed a new meaning for the still-hunt and created an original literary genre in the process. The big-game hunt as it emerged at the turn of the century was neither obvious nor inevitable. It was a product of the Second Industrial Revolution, which made it both necessary and possible. It was new.

CHAPTER 3

# Making Meaning Out of Moose
## Constructing the Hunting Narrative

*One never heard of a bear which travelled all the way from New Mexico to Chicago to kill a man, and yet a man will go 3000 miles to kill a bear—not for love or fear or hate or meat; for what, then?*
—Frederic Remington

In the years after 1880 big-game hunting narratives became tremendously popular, appearing regularly in generalist periodicals such as *Harper's*, in the recreational media, and in best-selling books. The next chapter explores the social and economic networks underlying publication, but it was the new meanings given to the hunt in print that made this genre so popular with readers. Those meanings ranged widely, however, because over the forty years of their greatest popularity—a period stretching roughly from 1880 to 1920—the narratives never conformed to a single predictable formula. A brief glance at three articles that were typical for the era, and yet very different from one another, offers a place to begin exploring the varied ways that meaning was constructed by big-game hunters for their turn-of-the-century reading audiences.

In the mid-1890s, Harry Hale and his friend Hardeman left West Point for St. Mary's, Montana, determined to kill mountain sheep. They had both qualified as sharpshooters and "had broken innumerable bottles"; they figure that sheep hunting can't be that hard. They crawl up and down half the mountains in Montana, looking for sheep. They sit out all night in the freezing cold, waiting for sheep. They become mocked roundly throughout the region as "the sheep-chasers." Finally, the moment comes: they see the sheep, they take their shots—and miss. Hale describes the moment: "As the full extent of the calamity broke upon [Hardeman], he shrieked, 'Great Heavens, man! We have missed them! We have missed them, I tell you.' I was aware of this, and made no reply, but remained sitting where I was, elbows on my knees, and head between my hands. I was trying to puzzle out *how* we had missed them." Discouraged, they go back to camp and begin packing, but then they decide to give it one more try. They find six sheep almost immediately—the shots ring out—they kill four. Hale tells Hardeman, "We have retrieved ourselves, my friend, and may hold up our heads again." This narrative, entitled "At St. Mary's," appeared in the popular middle-class periodical *Scribner's*.[1]

In 1902, explorer and hunter Andrew J. Stone wrote an article about moose: their natural history, their mating battles, his experiences stalking them, and how other hunters might be successful. He describes failing on one stalk because he allowed the moose to scent him after he "became anxious to locate their trail," reminding readers that "eyes and ears should be alert; don't be in a hurry." On the Kenai Peninsula in Alaska he stalks them more successfully and is fascinated to discover "hair of a perfect emerald green" between his trophy's toes.[2] Nor is all his time spent hunting; he describes pleasant days camping by lakes in Maine, trying to confirm a rumor that moose eat pond lilies. His article, "The Moose: Where It Lives and How It Lives," appeared alongside work by Roosevelt and Van Dyke in the anthology *The Deer Family*, published as part of the American Sportsman's Library.[3]

In 1906 the most famous American hunter of big game,[4] Charles Sheldon, went caribou hunting on the Queen Charlotte Islands. C. Hart Merriam, director of the US Biological Survey, had received a report from some missionaries that there were caribou there and "sought for more evidence from somebody personally known to him." Sheldon spends days tracking the elusive caribou but never sees them, nor any living mammal, emerging only with a small sample of caribou dung, which he sends to Merriam. He concludes his account by describing how much he had enjoyed his search, the excitement and eagerness he had felt at the possibility of seeing the mystery caribou appear at any moment—and, in the end, although he had been "continually tramping, slop, slop, slop, through a monotonous level barren waste, most of the time through rain and storm ... even after such a complete failure among dismal surroundings, I felt keen regret at leaving." He devotes a full chapter to the experience in his popular book *The Wilderness of the North Pacific Coast Islands: A Hunter's Experiences While Searching for Wapiti, Bears and Caribou on the Larger Coast Islands of British Columbia and Alaska.*[5]

These three narratives are typical of the big-game hunting stories that appeared in print at the turn of the century and yet they do not share a single pattern of storytelling. They are also strange, counterintuitive even, considering how big-game hunting has been framed in many histories of the Progressive Era. None of these stories is particularly focused on killing animals, for one thing: Hale's sheep simply "drop," Stone skips over the kill to focus on the posthumous toe inspection, and Sheldon doesn't even see any animals. They also are not about dominating nature, or at least not all the time—Stone and Sheldon in particular rather appreciate it, describing pond lilies, bogs, and dung with enthusiasm. And as literary offerings each narrative echoes another genre, a different one in each case: Hale the coming-of-age tale, Stone the natural history article, Sheldon the travelogue.

So what do these narratives have in common? Authors, publishers, and audiences at the time clearly identified these as all being part of a larger genre—nonfiction American hunting narratives—but what links them besides the presence of a hunter intent on locating an animal? The answer is the stalk.

The overwhelming majority of the sportsman-hunter narratives focus on the hunter's experiences reaching the animal—and, while that sometimes takes the form of a wider travelogue or quest narrative, embedded in that, at the heart of the story, is an even closer focus on the stalk. That stalk may take a page, or an article, or a book, but the kill is almost always relegated to a sentence or two. In the mid-nineteenth century, writers such as Frank Forester had dismissed stalking as too time-consuming, even as they regaled middle-class readers with detailed descriptions of animals' death throes, but the sportsman-hunter narratives decisively reversed that formulation, glorifying the stalk and minimizing the kill.[6] Hale's sheep are typical as they "drop"; his story is about the search, and more time in the narrative is given to the boys' reactions after missing the sheep than after killing them. Stone has no comment on what it feels like to shoot a moose, but he has a great deal to say about what it means to stalk them successfully: "the man who has acquired so thorough a knowledge of the habits of the moose as to enable him, unaided, to seek the animal . . . and by fair stalking bring it to bay," he explains, "has reached the maximum standard of the American big-game hunter."[7] And Sheldon's entire chapter can be construed as one long stalk, with scientific evidence (but no kill) to show for it. From Van Dyke on, the stalk, and what it revealed about the hunter, assumed a centrality that in turn helped unite disparate accounts into a single genre recognizable to writers, publishers, and readers.

This meant that the still-hunt was focused on the manly display of character in the stalk and was *not* about killing an animal by any means possible, nor was it ever about violence on the part of the hunter. Van Dyke told a generation of sportsmen that the kill was not the point, and for the most part they appear to have internalized that (or at least to have presented themselves that way to readers).[8] Some writers explicitly disavowed an interest in the animal's death. "I really think that the fun of the hunt is over the minute the rifle comes up to the shoulder and the bead is on the animal," hunter Percy Madeira wrote. "I do not believe any man likes to see animals die. I am sure I do not. The charm lies in the fascination and excitement of the chase, with the killing alone to be regretted."[9] This approach was remarkably consistent. In the hundreds of post-1880 narratives I have read for this work, only three have any drawn-out description of an animal's death (excluding the writing of Roosevelt). The rest move smoothly from the stalk that tests and displays manly character to the trophy that, taken through the still-hunt, offers material evidence of the hunter's mastery both of speed of fire and of himself.

That killing was not the point is also indicated by the existence of accounts in which the hunter chooses not to kill an animal or in which the hunt overall is a failure. Sometimes such narratives detail hunts in which nothing is spotted. Sheldon does this in his account of searching for caribou, nor did he seem to find anything anomalous about including a chapter in a hunting book in which no game is killed or even seen. More often, though, moments in which the hunter does not produce a kill are framed as examples of self-control and self-denial, as when St. George Littledale, having already bagged an auroch on a museum commission, tells readers that he saw a better specimen appear before him, laid down his rifle, and "took off my cap to him out of respect. . . . I had got what I wanted, and mine should not be the hand to hurry further the extermination of a fading race for mere wanton sport."[10] Such moments demonstrate the hunter's character through the *refusal* of the kill; in these cases, the story itself is the trophy that testifies to his manly self-control.[11]

On the other hand, hunters who were not of the right sort were sometimes pilloried in terms of violence. Van Dyke's hunter of "brute heart" is such a man, and his willingness to kill in an unsportsmanlike way reveals his lack of character. Here a love of violence is being recognized as one reason a man might hunt, one that says much about his moral failings. Others made similar comparisons: William Hornaday described sport hunters shooting to the full legal limit as revealing a "savage desire to kill . . . in men in whom we naturally expect to find a very different spirit" while praising "true sportsmen" as those "to whom 'the bag' is a matter of small importance [and who stops] when he has had 'enough.'"[12] The connections among self-restraint, sportsmanship, and a certain kind of hunter are clear here, as is the suggestion that a "savage desire to kill" can indeed be a motivation to hunt for those of the wrong sort. The still-hunt took a central part of its meaning from rejecting that motivation, its adherents instead seeking to display a "very different spirit" through the stalk.

The big-game hunting narratives thus rejected violence; they were also not about connecting with primal male emotions.[13] Hale and Hardeman do not succeed because they become primitives, but because, on failing, they try and try again. Stone presents himself as a dispassionate observer who, on bagging his trophy, thoughtfully inspects its toes in hopes of discovering new information about the animal's natural history. Sheldon finds joy in the careful performance of a challenging task for the improvement of scientific knowledge. This is Van Dyke's vision realized: that each failure only disciplines the right kind of hunter to work harder, that the successful stalk testifies to perseverance and self-control, and that this is why the still-hunt says something meaningful about character. And these meanings lie at the heart of every one of these popular narratives.

The primacy of the will was not all that went into a hunting tale, however, nor was it the only thing that made it meaningful. Over time other associations, some with tremendous cultural power, also became familiar elements in big-game hunting narratives. These elements were never invoked with the unwavering consistency of the stalk, however. Instead they appeared in some narratives but not others, weaving in and out of the stories hunters were telling, and that makes sense, since the narratives were produced by hundreds of different individuals, each with his (or, eventually, her) own interests, beliefs, and social, economic, and political agendas. Instead of a single identifiable formula, then, a web of meanings came to cluster around the still-hunt, and this raises other questions. Why and how did big-game hunting come to be attached to some meanings and not others? How are wider meanings constructed by individual writers, especially when they aren't explicitly coordinating with one another? This diversity also poses a challenge for anyone seeking to understand these narratives now. What is the best way to approach them without reducing or concealing their diversity?

The answer is to approach these works as a discourse.[14] A discourse is a flexible system of meaning made up of links among different elements that have no natural, inherent connection of their own: when Van Dyke described the stalk as the only form of hunting that provided truly "manly sport," he created a new association between two things that had not previously been connected (stalking game and manliness) and that had no essential relationship (there is nothing about being male that necessitates stalking rather than jacklighting). Following Van Dyke, the sportsmen-hunters continued to import new associations into their narratives, ranging from invocations of the pioneer past to rhetorics of work and duty, and in the process they constructed a complex but recognizable discourse around big-game hunting—what I'm going to call "the sportsman-hunter discourse." The entire set of associations never appeared in any single hunting story, but neither was the appearance of any one of these elements ever greeted with surprise; they became, not part of an iron-clad formula, but rather part of a predictable menu of options for hunters attempting to interpret their actions for themselves and for others. Seeing what qualified for inclusion in that web of options, and what did not, can help to illuminate the meaning of the hunt as it was constructed for readers at the turn of the century.

These new meanings can also help to explain the tremendous popularity of these narratives, as well as why they were considered suitable fare for generalist publications such as *Scribner's*. The associations that grew up around the hunt drew in part on wider social anxieties—about the changing meaning of work, for instance, and the importance of manliness—that hunter-writers shared with the middle- and upper-class reading audiences of *Scribner's*, *Harper's*, and *Outing*. By invoking such concerns in their narratives, and offering the stalk as a site where they could be at least temporarily resolved, hunter-writers made both their sport and their stories socially relevant. The discourse they built around their hunting would prove both flexible enough to accommodate individual agendas and powerful enough to persist for decades.

The rest of this chapter examines five of the most important elements of the sportsman-hunter discourse: the redefinition of leisure-time hunting as work; the role played by sportsmanship; the use of invocations of the pioneers and the frontier; the incorporation of exploration and natural history into hunting narratives; and the rhetoric of manliness. Any of these elements could be invoked by any writer of a hunting narrative, and often were. Any of these elements could also be left out. These texts existed in relation to one another in a system that resembled a flowchart far more than it did a checklist. Once taken up into the discourse, however, all five elements proved remarkably stable and, from 1880 through the Great War, appeared in hundreds of published narratives with little variation. (For that reason strict chronology will also be set aside for the moment, opening the way to use a wider range of examples.)

## I. WORK, LEISURE, DUTY, AND CHARACTER

On April 10, 1899, Theodore Roosevelt delivered a speech to the Hamilton Club in Chicago entitled "The Strenuous Life."[15] Roosevelt was speaking mainly about imperialism at the time, but the term quickly came to stand for a life marked by manly performance.[16] To define such performances, Roosevelt fell back on the ideals of the nineteenth-century workplace. He argued that work equaled success, equated luxury and sloth with effeminacy, and urged his listeners to oppose the "doctrine of ignoble ease" and instead embrace the strenuous life that embodies "victorious effort." These ideas were hardly new in 1900; indeed, a more solidly middle-class vision is difficult to imagine.

What was *not* traditional about Roosevelt's vision were the places where the strenuous life could be pursued—not only on the battlefield, but also in the world of leisure. The strenuous life was not a call to toil more assiduously in the industrial workplace. Instead, it was about play, now given the moral valence of work. "If you are rich and are worth your salt," Roosevelt told his audience, "you will teach your sons that though they may have leisure, it is not to be spent in idleness." Leisure could be "wisely used [if] the man still does actual work, though of a different kind . . . in the field of exploration and adventure." Such "different" work would develop and display in wealthy men what Roosevelt called the "virile virtues"—self-control, temperance, resolution, courage, and honesty—in other words, the qualities of manly character, now severed from their traditional site of demonstration in the workplace and transferred into leisure.

Roosevelt was not alone in framing certain kinds of leisured adventure as work that spoke to character; by the 1890s and into the new century, more and more elite hunters described themselves as "working" rather than playing at sport. "Hunting the goat is man's work," wrote Grinnell; "my success with the white sheep had come only with the hardest kind of work," explained James Kidder; "Be a sportsman!" Caspar Whitney urged readers, "after all it is only another name for loyalty to purpose, honesty and charity: the man who does his work modestly and to the very limit of his skill and endurance."[17] Here play and leisure are transformed into "work," albeit of a "different kind." And as leisure vanishes, so too do its long-standing associations with luxury, aristocracy, and femininity, replaced by the "man who does his work" through the hunt.

How much work actually went into big-game hunting? Stalking was certainly more challenging than many other forms of hunting, and I think it says something that the animal that was most difficult to stalk—the moose—was considered the highest test of a hunter's skill. (By contrast, under the "hunting as violence" thesis, one would expect lions or some other predator to be the apex.) That said, the amount of work put into the hunt seems to have varied dramatically from hunter to hunter. Charles Sheldon went into the wilderness around Denali alone, built a cabin by hand, and spent a winter observing mountain sheep and living off the land. When he did bring "guides" with him on his trips, they stayed at camp, dressing his trophies and keeping the fire going; he didn't take them hunting with him, preferring to rely entirely on his own abilities.[18] While not "work" in the nineteenth-century sense, there's no doubt that Sheldon demonstrated an incredible level of self-reliance.

James Kidder, however, who did his "work" with mountain sheep, was a very different kind of hunter, a sportsman from Boston (and a Boone and Crockett member) who visited Alaska in 1900. He has a great deal of help with him: a companion, Blake, as well as local Russian-Aleut guides (whom he describes as "my natives"). Those natives do much of the tracking, at one point bringing "Blake up to within sixty yards, when my friend killed the bear," and also haul canoes through icy water: "the natives were in the glacial stream up to their waists for hours at a time." Dried off, the guides serve as lookouts at camp, watching for bears: at one point Kidder notes that "one of our natives was kept constantly on the lookout, and a dozen times a day both Blake and I would leave our books" to check on him. Of a rainy day, he writes: "Everything was wet, and we passed an uncomfortable day [under the awning]. Our two hunters were camped about fifty yards off under a big rock, and I think must have had a pretty hard time of it, but all the while they kept a sharp lookout."[19] Much more will be said about guides in a later chapter, but many readers will be wondering at this point how Kidder could possibly claim to be the one doing the work. Part of the reason is that he owns his guides' labor, in the sense that he pays for it and directs it, and he asserts that ownership through his choice of rhetoric, in phrases such as "our natives were kept on lookout" that use passive construction and the possessive case to frame the guides as extensions of his will.

Most importantly, however, Kidder is the one stalking the game, and that, to him, is what the work is. "In fact, it was only by the hardest kind of careful and constant work that I was finally successful in bagging my first bear on Kadiak. When the salmon come it is not so difficult to get a shot, but this lying in wait at night by a salmon stream cannot compare with seeking out the game on the hills in the spring, and stalking it in a sportsmanlike manner."[20] When he says that his success killing the sheep came only "with the hardest kind of work," he means the work of the stalk. This is a radical re-envisioning of what matters in the hunt, especially compared to descriptions from earlier narratives—to Murray's trip in the Adirondacks, for example, with its leisure, its appropriateness for the delicate and most fragile. Work, after all, is not a real, recognizable thing. It is an idea: what constitutes work, what do you do in leisure that identifies it as leisure and not work? In Kidder's reading, work is no longer connected to wages, earning a living, or supporting a family, elements that had been essential to the original associations between workplace success and the demonstration of character. Instead, in a sort of reverse shorthand, any performance of character can now be interpreted as being "man's work."

This was not the only way to describe the hunt, however, and there were those who conceded that hunting was about leisure, albeit useful leisure. Anthony Dimock notes in *Wall Street and the Wilds* that his hunting excursions revitalized him after the strains of the financial markets and allowed him to return to Wall Street ready to succeed. For him, hunting and productive labor are separate activities, yet function as clear complements to one another. In a similar vein, Caspar Whitney assures readers of *Collier's Outdoor World* that outdoor recreation gives boys and men "courage to fight, courage to do right, courage to play the game, and courage to play fair, whether in the wilderness or on the playground or in the office. . . . Courage is a national asset."[21] Taking time off to go hunting is being transformed here from an unproductive waste of time into a useful complement to a man's efforts in the workplace. "The solitudes are not a fad to the American man of business," Whitney explains, "they are a duty; a duty he owes his body, his mind and his soul."[22] Such rhetoric reassured middle-class men in particular that visiting the wilds was an appropriate use of their time, where they could strengthen the aspects of character they needed for workplace success.

Other hunter-writers argued that, instead of struggling to reveal character in the corporate workplace, men could perform this vital function in the wilds, then reveal it to their reading audiences on the page. Kermit Roosevelt opens his book of hunting reminiscences by commenting, "There is a universal saying to the effect that it is when men are off in the wilds that they show themselves as they really are," while Robert Steed Dunn explains that the wilds "offer the best field of all to help this knowledge of ourselves . . . in telling the truth about others a man might reveal it about himself which would be best of all."[23] Why would this be best of all? Murray, setting off to the Adirondacks, never presents himself as having the slightest notion of revealing a hidden truth about others or himself, but, by the time Dunn and Roosevelt were writing, the revelation of one's character to others had become a central function of the hunt. This formulation eschews the mention of work entirely and by doing so strips away any connection between manly character and finances, family, or community. Work as a site for manly performance has vanished from the picture. Now it's in leisure that one seeks the truth about a man.

It's not much of a leap from these ideas back to Kidder's assertion that he's the one doing the work on his hunting trip. Repositioning work meant stripping it of some of its most obvious elements, including its relationship to wages. What mattered to the hunter-writers was what work had said about men to other men, not the money they had made from doing it. Resituating the revelation of character from the workplace into leisure transformed the very concept of what "leisure" could mean, while leaving little room to recognize work-for-cash by employees as even being relevant to the discussion. Grinnell's easy dismissal of the Plains buffalo hunters—that "men too lazy to work were not too lazy to hunt"—says it all in just a few words.[24] Professional buffalo hunting in fact appears to have been hard and miserable work and looks a lot more like labor than anything James Kidder was doing, but in the context of the sportsman-hunter discourse all these elements had acquired new meanings. If the elite hunter understood his hunting to be "man's work" because stalking demanded and revealed self-control—and if he condemned hunters of his ilk who depended on jacklights or coursing, who took the easy way out—then how could he understand the professional hunter also using such methods as "working"?

A radical revaluing of the meaning of work and leisure was occurring in the sportsman-hunter narratives. If the manly virtues could be developed and demonstrated in play, if one could do "actual work, though of a different kind" in the world of leisure, then the stage was set for a sea-change in the relationships among work, leisure, and the demonstration of character. The concept of the strenuous life, both in Roosevelt's iteration of it and in the variations that appeared in hundreds of big-game hunting narratives, helped to construct a new cultural meaning for the actions of hunters that transferred the moral power of the workplace into the leisure-time hunt.

## II. SPORTSMANSHIP

Kidder invoked it to turn his hunting into "work"; Van Dyke was near obsessed with it. Sportsmanship was both an ideal and an ever-shifting set of rules governing the hunt, which became codified in constitutions and lists of rules that were widely debated throughout the Gilded Age and Progressive Era. Although they varied tremendously, a brief gloss on typical rules of turn-of-the-century sportsmanship might be helpful here. Most were about what kind of game was fair prey, when it could be hunted, and how it should be hunted. For reasons often framed as chivalrous, but also rather practical in terms of sustainable hunting, sportsmen generally avoided killing young animals and females (killing birds on the nest, for example, was looked on with scorn). Hunting techniques that offered little test of the hunter's character, or that required little effort, were also eschewed by sportsmen. The use of steel traps is an obvious example; others would include jacklighting, snowcrusting, and killing animals swimming in the water.

These methods were more certain for the hunter, and for that reason they were preferred by both subsistence and market hunters who wanted to expend a minimum of time and effort. The rules of sportsmanship thus drew class lines, but it would be a mistake to think that this was primarily about middle- and upper-class men trying to differentiate themselves from working-class hunters. For one thing, it's not clear why they would feel they needed to. The pre-1880 hunting narratives show visiting sportsmen blithely indulging in jacklighting and snowcrusting without any worries over whether using the same techniques as subsistence hunters would reflect poorly on them, or whether readers might confuse them with the locals who assisted them. Also, at least in the sportsman-hunter narratives, the anxiety expressed in debates over sportsmanship was almost always focused on middle- and upper-class men who hunted in unsportsmanlike ways. Van Dyke didn't warn his reader against being mistaken for a working-class hunter, he warned against being the Adirondack tourist who reveals his brute heart by executing a moose swimming in the water. Making things even more interesting, working-class men sometimes chose to still-hunt, and sportsmen-hunters seem to have approved, rather than being concerned about class lines being blurred. Samuel Davis lauds his Newfoundland guide's skill as a still-hunter, while Agnes Herbert, hunting in Alaska, explains that her Aleut guides were "excellent still-hunters" when they chose to hunt for pleasure, noting that it "makes a wonderful difference to a native whether he is hunting because he is hungry, or just for sport. Which is, after all, natural enough."[25] Taken as a whole, this suggests that anxiety about being mistaken for or associated with subsistence or market hunters was not the primary motivation behind the valorization of sportsmanship at the turn of the century. Instead, embracing sportsmanship allowed the sportsmen-hunters to distance themselves further from their leisured predecessors, while drawing lines against those of their own kind who hunted in the "wrong" way.

Sportsmanship was not new to turn-of-the-century hunters, of course. There had been rules governing gentlemanly hunting for at least half a century, if not more, but sportsmanship in antebellum America seems to have mainly functioned as a way in which gentlemen identified their hunting to one another, rather than being a way in which hunting was constructed as work or as a test of will. This is clear in such early writing as Elisha Lewis's *Hints for Sportsmen*, while historian Nicholas Proctor has shown that sportsmanship in the antebellum South was often used as a filter for newcomers, but discarded among hunters who were out with trusted friends and family.[26] Such malleability seems to have been common before 1880. Certainly the early narratives provide evidence of a nuanced attention to local rules: whatever gentlemen's agreements might have applied to shooting ducks at a country home didn't apply in the Adirondacks when deer was the goal, or on the Plains when it was time to course bison.

By the Gilded Age, however, the uses of sportsmanship were changing radically. For one thing, sportsmen-hunters were no longer free to follow local variations on hunting game but were expected to stalk everything by the same rules or risk being identified as "the wrong sort." At the same time, the meaning of sportsmanship itself was under construction, debated by hunters and occasionally quarreled over in print. In 1902, Daniel Elliott made a tentative argument for the despised technique of snowcrusting based on the work involved. "This method of hunting will probably by some be considered as not altogether savoring of true sportsmanship," he writes. "But, my critical friend, have you ever tried to follow a Woodland caribou in winter[?]" The implication that the difficulty of such tracking excuses the act won him no shrift from editor Caspar Whitney, who printed the article but snapped back in a footnote that "it is emphatically unsportsmanlike to follow caribou or any other of the deer family on snow which requires snow-shoes."[27] Exposed here are differing opinions of what constitutes sportsmanship, but also the new grounds on which such claims must rest: Elliott recognizes that making an argument for snowcrusting means reframing it as a challenge, rather than as the easy chase celebrated by earlier writers like Fraser and Forester. Sportsmanship is being reconceived here as a way to impose difficulty on the hunter, transforming his obedience to the rules into a testament to his work and willpower.

This transformation can best be illustrated by comparing two books by William Temple Hornaday. Hornaday was raised in the Midwest and in 1875 was hired by a taxidermist to go on a round-the-world hunting and collecting trip. This was no vacation, but rather a paying job, although Hornaday's instructions allowed him great flexibility ("Plunder Ceylon," his employer told him, "Rake the island over as with a fine-toothed comb; catch everything you can in three months time, and send me the best of it"). Hornaday's account of the trip, *Two Years in the Jungle: The Experiences of a Hunter and Naturalist in India, Ceylon, the Malay Peninsula and Borneo*, was published in 1885 and was a smash hit, going through ten printings by 1900. The five-hundred-page opus lovingly details Hornaday's adventures, the hundreds of animals he shot (ranging from tigers and elephants to flying foxes and orangutans), and the diverse peoples he met, almost all of whom he despised (the Irish, for instance, are described as "howling bog-trotters," while Hornaday was "not ashamed to say that I hate the 'gentle Hindoo'"). The book thoroughly disproves the theory that travel is broadening, but that is not its only point of interest, because it also offers observations on hunting like a sportsman. When Hornaday goes elephant hunting, he explains, "At the very outset I resolved to bag each of my elephants with a single ball through the brain, in a sportsmanlike manner, or else hire a sportsman to do it for me." The idea that there is a right way to hunt is here. What is missing is the idea of sportsmanship as a test. Hornaday does not present his hunting as a challenge to the primacy of the will, although he does use it to make a statement about his skill with a rifle.[28]

Twenty-one years later, in 1906, Hornaday published another hunting book, *Camp-fires in the Canadian Rockies*.[29] This time he was not hunting professionally, but for pleasure, accompanied by vacationing Pennsylvania State Game Commissioner John M. Phillips in a chase after grizzly, moose, and mountain sheep and goat. Those twenty-one years had seen many changes for Hornaday. He had gone from being a relative nobody to being a best-selling author, head of the New York Zoological Park, and one of the founders of the American Bison Society. He had also substantially changed his ideas of what sportsmanship could—and should—mean to hunters.

By 1906, sportsmanship for Hornaday was about self-control, about the refusal to succumb to temptation, and about the strength of character that such refusal demonstrates. Having set (with Phillips) a personal limit on mountain goat well below that allowed by his hunting permit, Hornaday tells us about "temptation goats"—those beautiful ur-goats that appear in camp, frolicking about the fire and nuzzling the hunter's gun, just as soon as he has passed his limit and so cannot take advantage of their presence.[30] Because this limit is personal, Hornaday's refusal to give in to the temptation goats is not simply about obeying the game laws but instead becomes a test of character, for nothing but his will and his promise to himself stand between him and the demonically attractive goats. He resists temptation, however (goat and otherwise), again and again, finally reaching a point where being a sportsman lends itself to high drama: As two sheep appear about to run through the camp,

> Exclamations flew all about.
> "Here they come!" "Sheep!" "Mountain sheep!"
> Mechanically we threw our rifles into position, but [our guide] cried out sharply, "Don't shoot, men! Don't shoot! *They're both ewes!*"[31]

Such moments serve to remind readers that Hornaday and Phillips are more interested in sportsmanship than in a kill count; indeed, at one point, finding the fish coming to his hook too easily, Phillips cries out, "This is nothing but slaughter!" and pauses to consider whether it is morally right to continue fishing.[32] This is taking sportsmanship to an extreme, where good fishing forces the fisherman to place limits on himself that are not provided in any way by nature.

What might be most surprising here is that the refusal to slaughter animals is being identified as a *challenge* to willpower. This is a new reading: before 1880, those who wanted to slaughter large numbers did so, while those who obeyed the various rules of sportsmanship were defined by the fact that they did *not* struggle at it because they were well-bred gentleman. In *Hints for Sportsmen*, Elisha Lewis simply assumes that his reader is a different breed entirely than "the pot-hunter" who carelessly "pots" every animal that crosses his path ("Shun his company and detest his vices," is Lewis's advice).[33]

*Camp-fires*, however, frames containment of appetite as a struggle to be won, with sportsmanship converting hunting into a constant test of will. In the process, Hornaday's performance in the Rockies becomes a display of both sportsmanship and self-control.

This dynamic is especially interesting in comparison to *Two Years in the Jungle*. After all, *Two Years* had been immensely successful, and Hornaday can be seen in *Camp-fires* as departing from a formula that he knew had appealed to readers to embrace sportsmanship-as-struggle instead. At the same time, Hornaday's latter book presents a leisured hunting trip rife with effort, temptation, and self-denial—a trip full of work—that contrasts strangely with *Two Years in the Jungle*, where Hornaday was in fact working for pay, a job he often presented in print as pleasure. In the decades between the books, however, Hornaday had changed. He had been deeply affected by the destruction of the American bison and was moving toward ever stricter definitions of sportsmanship, for himself as well as for other hunters. He had also watched as the hunter elite constructed a discourse in which sportsmanship, the will, work, and manly sport became intertwined, and he mobilized those meanings in his own account of his experiences in the Rockies.

By framing himself this way, Hornaday was also speaking to the anxieties of the time.[34] Containment of appetite and suppression of the passions had always been central characteristics of the Victorian beau ideal, and sportsmanship as it was rewritten by the sportsmen-hunters drew on that image. Historian George Colpitts has suggested that the sportsmanlike hunter offered a utopian figure to turn-of-the-century society—that of the man who voluntarily restrains his appetites for the common good—and that this ideal is on display in *Camp-fires*. No one reading it could doubt that the president of the American Bison Society and his hunting companion, the state game commissioner, were worthy of the public's trust; it would be impossible to confuse them with either bloodstained pot-hunters or greedy robber barons.[35] In an era when both the predatory rich and the unruly poor seemed to threaten the commonwealth, sportsmen-hunters constructed themselves as models of the self-controlled and trustworthy man. Sportsmanship, reimagined as a constant struggle, was far more than just a way of talking about how to hunt. It was also a way for native-born white men with Progressive sympathies to recognize the righteous among them and to signal their desire to belong to that group. A pledge of allegiance to sportsmanship conveyed a wealth of information to other hunters, and to readers, about what kind of man the hunter-writer was. They testified to his character.

## III. PIONEER FOREFATHERS AND THE FRONTIER WEST

The previous chapter touched on the ways that Roosevelt rewrote the history of the pioneer West in order to link it to his own hunting. Rehabilitating the images of the cowboy and frontiersman, even as he altered the connections between wealthy elites and the meaning of the hunt, he established a new set of associations that became central to the ways that the hunter elite described their sport. "Of late years there has been a constantly increasing number of those who have gone back to the old traditions of the American stock on this continent, and have taken delight in the wild sports of the wilderness," he tells readers in one Boone and Crockett book, referring to the club members.[36] This typically Rooseveltian claim does a lot of work in a short space. He makes it sound as if there is a clear cultural connection between the club members and the pioneers (the article mentions Boone, Crockett, and Kit Carson) and locates their hunting as part of a continuous American tradition without specifying exactly what that would be (he certainly doesn't intend his reader to call to mind jacklighting). Roosevelt is creating a lineage that leads from the pioneers directly to the exclusive Boone and Crockett Club and to their performances as presented in the club anthologies.

At first glance this seems somewhat weird and rather fraudulent. Boone and Crockett were many things, but they were certainly not the forerunners of the sportsmen-hunters. Crockett was a slaughterer of game who was also a canny politician (redeemed by his death at the Alamo; there's nothing quite like martyrdom for a political reputation). Boone became a folk hero for the role he played in opening up the continent to white exploration, but he had far less in common with Roosevelt than did Francis Parkman—or, for that matter, the members of the Millionaires' Hunting Club. But consider Roosevelt's phrasing as he explains why he named his elite club after the two pot-hunters: he says that they "have served in a certain sense as the tutelary deities of American hunting lore."[37] Roosevelt understands that the connection is spurious. These frontiersmen have become deities, familiars, free-floating out of history and into the murky sphere of cultural inspiration.

Roosevelt was hardly alone in this. Over time, the invocation of pioneers, explorers, and frontier hunters would become one of the most persistent and powerful elements of the sportsman-hunter discourse, appearing in a variety of forms. Three predominated: passing mentions of the pioneers, actual visits to the frontier, and the use of frontier history to link big-game hunting to a racialized American exceptionalist story.

Most common were passing comments, usually the invocation of Boone, Crockett, Carson, or Lewis and Clark. Some writers simply framed themselves as seeking a general pioneer experience. "Let's go north, to have some of the experiences of the old fellows who explored," Leonidas Hubbard suggests to his friend Dillon Wallace, proposing an exploring and hunting trip to Labrador. Wallace agrees because he yearns to go "even as my forefathers had gone."[38] His actual forefathers seem to have settled in upstate New York, but Wallace isn't talking about his relatives here; he's invoking his *cultural* forefathers.

Mixed in with such casual comments were visits to the actual frontier. This was becoming difficult after 1880, but more than one hunter solved that problem by traveling to the Canadian West, whose frontier was opening on a later timetable than its southern counterpart. There, they were delighted to inform readers, the frontier experience could still be simulated, as if time itself had altered speed.

Caspar Whitney, traveling north to hunt musk-ox, tells readers that Edmonton "raised memories of other frontier days across the line [when] the atmosphere was continuously shattered by cowboy whoops and leaden pellets [and where] duels [took place] between two 'prominent citizens,' with the remaining population standing by to see fair play."[39] This sounds more like a preternatural foreshadowing of a John Ford movie than it does any real place and is made all the more absurd because none of these things appear to have happened in Edmonton during Whitney's visit. The American frontier shadows him here, though; he gives his trip meaning by invoking another frontier, one that now exists only in the past tense. The point is that the frontier is a place where a man can prove himself, and Whitney does so, hunting musk-ox on the Barren Grounds: it is, he explains, "the hardest [journey] a man could make" in these latter days.[40]

Ernest Thompson Seton, who was raised in Canada, offers an even more striking vision as he prepares to travel to the Canadian prairies. "What young man of our race would not gladly give a year of his life to roll backward the scroll of time for five decades and live that year in the romantic by-gone days of the Wild West," he asks. The "miracle [is] possible to-day. For the uncivilised Indian still roams the far reaches of absolutely unchanged, unbroken forest and prairie leagues . . . and still there is hoofed game by the million to be found where the Saxon is as seldom seen as on the Missouri in the times of Lewis and Clark."[41] Seton is explaining, not simply that you can see these forests and prairies, but that you can have a romantic experience in doing so.

Lewis and Clark's experience was meaningful because they were exploring and mapping, but Seton's experience is meaningful because he is thinking about Lewis and Clark. The frontier hovers over his vision, as it does Whitney's—and, as with Whitney, the romantic image elides the fact that these men are traveling much of the way by train, are on vacation, and are armed with survey maps. It's not a historically authentic experience, in other words, but that didn't matter; the point was not to experience the frontier as the pioneers had, but to experience yourself experiencing the frontier. It's about the romance of it all. Seton understands that perfectly.

At the same time, his references to "our race" and "the Saxon" were hardly anomalies. Not every big-game hunter who invoked the pioneers chose to mention race specifically, but bringing up the frontier always offered that possibility and some hunter-writers explored it at length. Remember Roosevelt's comment that recently some hunters have returned to the "traditions of the American stock on this continent"; he's asserting a national lineage for elite hunting, and implicitly denying any link to the British hunt, but he's also envisioning a single American stock from which he, Carson, and Crockett are all drawn. Seton wants to go back to the time when the "Saxon" was new to the prairies; those not of "our race" don't have such an urge, while the Saxon is defined by his yearning for this "miracle." Hubbard and Wallace's trip to Labrador was among the expeditions lauded in the *World Magazine* in an article titled "The Lorelei of the Unknown," who calls to the "Anglo-Saxon . . . place difficulties enough in his way and he will stake his life and do great deeds to get at the answers."[42] Here, having leisure enough to go on a trip to Labrador becomes the mark of both race and greatness. No one put it more bluntly than Owen Wister: "the Anglo-Saxon is . . . forever homesick for the out-of-doors."[43] Van Dyke's "true spirit of the chase" is being racialized here. For men like Wister and his friend and fellow big-game hunter Madison Grant, that spirit is now uniquely Anglo-Saxon.[44]

These rhetorical moves allowed some members of the hunter elite to claim connections to the pioneers while excluding other groups of hunters from consideration, especially mixed-race and nonwhite men. Not every sportsman-hunter chose to push the reading that far, but, for those who did, discussions of the frontier could lend themselves to both exclusion and exclusivity.

Perhaps most strikingly, such exclusions often elided Native Americans completely. While some writers, like Seton, mentioned them in passing, many hunter-writers presented the West as an empty stage waiting for its true inhabitant, the homesick Saxon. This was a new way of imagining both the wilderness and the frontier (which began to blur into one another once they both became uninhabited hunting grounds). It was certainly not part of earlier narratives: for Francis Parkman, seeing the Plains Indians was as essential to his trip West as shooting a Plains buffalo. It also differed from other popular ways of presenting the American frontier at the turn of the century, ranging from Wild West shows to historian Frederick Jackson Turner's claim that violence was essential to the frontier, that settlers needed to "shout the war cry and take the scalp in orthodox Indian fashion" in order to become true Americans.[45] By contrast, sportsmen-hunters discussing the frontier usually shied away from mentioning Indian fighting in their narratives (with the usual exception of Roosevelt); just as they did not invoke violence in relation to their hunting, they also erased it from the histories of the places where they hunted. Instead they framed those places, not as sites of conquest, but rather as stages where true character could be revealed and displayed. Wister explains: "Directly the English nobleman smelt Texas, the slumbering untamed Saxon awoke in him, and . . . galloped howling after wild cattle. . . . It was no new type, no product of the frontier, but just the original kernel of the nut with the shell broken."[46] Here the frontier does not make the man, but simply offers the space where he can reveal the nut he has always been, creating a site for manly performance much like that provided by the still-hunt itself. (There was always some tension between the idea of the frontier as providing the ultimate American experience and as offering an Anglo-Saxon one based on English descent, one resolved in different ways by different writers.)

Interestingly, imagining the frontier this way also changed the meaning of the performances of the *pioneers*. If what mattered most was who the pioneers were—that they were "old American stock"—then both conflicts with Native Americans and the hard work that went into settling the continent became irrelevant. And when the sportsmen-hunters discussed the pioneers in detail, the focus was almost always on character, not on the ways their lives had been entwined with those of America's original inhabitants. There are dozens of references to Kit Carson, but none mention his relationship with the Navajo. In *The Frontier Omnibus*, hunter-writer Emerson Hough describes Boone as a man of "fine social qualities . . . a self-respecting gentleman."[47] In *Outing*, Dillon Wallace airily notes that "most of our first settlers belonged to . . . the middle-class."[48] That meant, of course, that they possessed the manly virtues, the "virile virtues . . . of pioneers and explorers," Roosevelt explains, "the very qualities which are fostered by vigorous, manly out-of-door sports, such as ... big-game hunting."[49]

This was not about history. Instead, it encapsulated what was most significant about the frontier to these writers, and that was its role in shaping character. If the experiences of explorers and pioneers had constituted a performance of manly character, then any activity that offered a way to develop and display manly character could inherit the frontier's function. By demonstrating character in the wilderness, the sportsman-hunter could become the spiritual heir of the pioneer, while the frontier—or a shadow version thereof—became the logical stage for his performance. And two things are happening at once here: the vacation still-hunt is being reimagined as the equivalent of the pioneer experience, while the pioneer experience is being reduced to the equivalent of a six-week hunting vacation. In the process, the conflicts and violence of the frontier, the hard work that went into exploration and settlement, the complexity of figures like Crockett and Carson, and the lack of a clear connection between any of those things and big-game hunting by middle- and upper-class men on vacation are all simplified to the point of caricature, even as the line between work and leisure becomes ever more blurred.

In reimagining the frontier this way, the sportsmen-hunters were once again reflecting and contributing to the tenor of their times. By the late 1880s, talking about the prelapsarian world of the frontier had become a way of talking about the damage being done both to men and to the republic by urbanization, immigration, and the Second Industrial Revolution. This in turn freighted it with layers of cultural significance. Representations of the frontier took many forms in this period, from heroic readings of Custer's last stand, to Turner's frontier drenched in blood, to the sportsmen-hunters' empty wilderness disconnected from war, from violence, and sometimes from ever having been inhabited at all. Their version was one among many, but it would have real consequences, particularly when sportsmen began to lobby for conservation; their desire to preserve a wilderness experience where Anglo-Saxon men and boys could relive the romance of Lewis and Clark would have a marked influence on the ways they sought to preserve wild places at the beginning of the twentieth century.

Their version of the frontier would also leave some confusion for historians, who have sometimes taken these hopefully drawn connections at face value, accepting that there was some inherent connection on which these hunters could draw: that Roosevelt could connect himself to the pioneers simply by hunting in the West, for instance, rather than having to disconnect himself from the Millionaires' Hunting Club first.[50] That disconnection mattered, however; to the degree that the sportsmen-hunters *had* ancestors, they would have been a messy combination of their fathers and grandfathers displaying manliness in the nineteenth-century workplace, and leisured slaughterers of game such as Dodge and Bennett. Concealing that was part of the point.

Invoking the frontier and the pioneer forefathers thus offered ways for hunters to frame themselves—"American stock"—as well as their intended readers—"young men of our race." It let them locate the history of manly character, not in the workplace, but in the pioneer past, creating a lineage for their hunting that concealed their leisured predecessors while avoiding the unrestrained violence associated with other representations of the frontier. Such rhetoric could also lend itself to complex layers of exclusion on the basis of nativism, race, manliness, and class, and sometimes let writers erase entire peoples from the past, from the history of the land itself—but that erasure was a by-product rather than the central point of their writing. By invoking the frontier and their pioneer ancestors, the sportsmen-hunters sought to define their hunting as a specifically American experience. Their claim that the frontier and the wilderness were necessary as stages for the performance of manly character would prove to be one of the most enduring elements of the sportsman-hunter discourse.

### IV. DOING SCIENCE: EXPLORATION AND NATURAL HISTORY

Not every element of the sportsman-hunter discourse represented a complete break with their leisured forebears. There was also continuity, especially when it came to two elements that had been prominent in the writing of both pioneers and well-to-do hunter-writers before the 1880s: exploration and natural history. The sportsmen-hunters embraced both subjects enthusiastically, peppering their narratives with hand-drawn maps and footnotes on debates over bear speciation. Incorporating exploration into their narratives gave their vacations purpose and meaning, while including observations on natural history let them frame both their hunting and their writing as useful and instructive. Over time, such invocations of science would become one of the most commonly deployed elements of the sportsman-hunter discourse.

The link between exploration and big-game hunting was in fact a natural one due to logistics: in an era before freeze-dried food, all explorers needed to live off the land, and there are few exploration books that do not have some hunting, although not all dwell on the details. Logistically, then, hunting in this period was part of exploring, while exploration was a logical outcome of any hunting that ventured beyond the edge of the map in the search for bigger and better trophies. Exploration offered more to the sportsman-hunter than just a logical concomitant to sport, however. It could be recruited as yet another way to transform hunting into work, letting hunters mobilize associations with duty and service to humanity simply by drawing a map or tracing a river to its source. Roosevelt included exploration in his description of the wise uses of leisure and also in the constitution of the Boone and Crockett Club: he and Grinnell hoped the club would promote "exploration in the wild and unknown . . . portions of the country." Roosevelt expanded on this in *Trail and Camp-fire*, praising hunting in its own right but adding that "the man able to be something more, should be that something more—an explorer, a naturalist,"[51] and summed it up in describing his exploring trip to Brazil, where he noted that adding "to our sum of geographical knowledge [is a] hard and valuable type of work."[52]

Presenting exploration as the motive for a hunting trip let hunter-writers assure their readers that they were not traveling just for the fun of it but rather to serve a greater purpose. Arthur Donaldson Smith, setting off to hunt in Africa, gives his trip a gloss by pioneering a new route from Somaliland to Lake Rudolf, explaining to readers that his goal is simply to "add a little drop to the sea of knowledge."[53] On the way he collects plants and butterflies and is struck by lightning while stalking what he hopes is a new variety of gazelle (to the singed Smith's dismay, it turns out to be just another Thompson's). Leonidas Hubbard, headed off to Labrador, has a similar mission: "we'll add something to the world's knowledge of geography at least, and that's worth while. No matter how little a man may add to the fund of human knowledge it's worth the doing, for it's by little bits that we've learned to know so much of our old world. There's some hard work before us. . . ."[54] (Note how this pleasure trip becomes "hard work" through the recruitment of geography.[55]) Such work almost always included the sketching of "traveller's maps," which were published as illustrations and were often characterized by the naming of hills, mountains, lakes, and streams after the hunter and his friends.

There were a few who questioned whether such "exploration" had any real meaning. Frederick Schwatka, an American army officer, surveyor, and big-game hunter, suggested drawing a line between "explorers" who contributed something scientific to the mapping of the world and "discoverers," best at a quick dash and quicker nomenclature.[56] Similar concerns were voiced across the Atlantic, where the Royal Geographical Society issued a plea for its members to resist what it called "promiscuous nomenclature."[57]

Such arguments seem to have made little impact, however, for several reasons. One was that so much "real" exploration was a bit specious in itself: Robert Peary's decades-long effort to reach the North Pole, for no other reason than to get there, does not seem all that different on the face of it from Smith's attempt to reach Lake Rudolf. Another reason was that, for every skeptic, there was an opposing voice encouraging the pursuit of scientific work during pleasure trips. The Harvard Travellers Club's *Handbook of Travel*, for instance, offered instruction on mapmaking, meteorological observation, and natural history collection alongside articles on hunting dangerous game and stalking moose. ("Still-hunting on the track is the high test," readers were reminded. "There is nothing to compare to it."[58]) Zoologist Glover Allen explained earnestly in the preface that he hoped the handbook would be useful "on account of its suggestions for the gathering of objects and facts that shall make the casual pleasure trip of permanent and real value."[59] That the reader would want to do so was taken for granted.

Including exploration in a hunting narrative could thus reinforce connections to work and duty, even as traveling maps and sextant readings created visible traces of the hunter's productive efforts. These connections were only reinforced by the sportsmen-hunters' enthusiasm for natural history. Embracing observations of flora, fauna, geology, and geography, natural history was one of the most popular scientific disciplines at the turn of the century, and one that traditionally had welcomed amateur practitioners. Most of the sportsmen-hunters included natural history observations as part of their hunting narratives for the straightforward reason that successful stalking required detailed knowledge of the habitat, behavior, life history, and anatomy of their quarries. The rules of sportsmanship also required hunters at the very least to be able to distinguish between male and female animals from a distance. Successful still-hunting thus required hunters to display such knowledge, while offering them constant opportunities to observe the natural world.

Many hunters seem to have taken enormous pleasure from this aspect of their trips. Charles Sheldon offers this report of a perfect day: "On the two previous days I had killed one bear and seen another with a cub. Complete was my exultation and bright were my hopes for the days to come. Before sleeping I prepared some shrews and mice that had been taken in the traps."[60] The level of genuine scientific knowledge contributed by big-game hunters varied from writer to writer, and some of it now appears rather arcane (such as Alden Sampson's essay "On Thought Transference among Animals"). Sheldon, however, was a gifted enough amateur that ten species eventually bore his name, while Henry Fairfield Osborn (discoverer of the *T. Rex*) and Daniel Elliott (author of *Synopsis of the Trochilidae* and *Gallinaceous Game Birds of North America*) both contributed articles to the Boone and Crockett anthologies. The presence of such authorities among the sportsmen-hunters strengthened their claims that they were producing valuable knowledge, while positioning them as reliable observers of the natural world.

Further enhancing this sense of scientific legitimacy was the fact that many hunters were collecting for museums. Roosevelt is the most famous American example, procuring Smithsonian support for his trip to Africa and a commission from the American Museum of Natural History for his journey to South America, but it seems that almost everyone at some point mailed off a head or hoof to one museum or another. Contributing to such collections let hunters assure readers that they were taking trophies, not for selfish reasons, but for the purpose of scientific investigation and public education. Nor were such contributions unsolicited: museums depended on hunters to provide them with specimens, and members of the British Museum regularly cruised the workshop of famed taxidermist Rowland Ward to see if any as-yet-undiscovered species had been sent in for mounting.[61] (Considering the social prominence of many of the sportsmen-hunters, some museums may also have seen commissions as a chance to build connections with potential supporters or board members.) Many European countries also had "Head and Horn" collections, and Hornaday started one in the United States, urging Americans to contribute their best trophies for scientific preservation and display.[62] Here trophy taking is being harnessed to patriotic public service through natural history, even as museum endorsements testified to the usefulness of hunters' contributions.

The man who made such contributions was hardly a primitive. Quite the opposite, in fact: he was connected to civilization every step of the way, investigating the world in order to categorize it, map it, report it, and share what he had learned with his peers. This in turn could testify to character, as the sportsman-hunter depicted himself as an observer capable of organizing the scattered, incoherent facts of the landscape and producing knowledge about it that was meaningful, useful, and universal. At the same time, including exploration or natural history in a hunting narrative required the author to know what kind of information about the world mattered—which species of gazelle were already known and which might be new, for example, or why and how he should produce a traveling map. It also required an awareness of current debates in the literature. Arguments raged throughout the era on how many separate bear species existed in North America, for example, and writers describing their bear hunting could weigh in, proffering their opinions while citing other hunters, demonstrating their familiarity with the discussion by participating in it.[63] This required knowledge of natural history, but also of the sportsmen-hunter narratives themselves, even as it made bear hunting sound investigative, about the thrill of discovery rather than any investment in the kill.

It's unsurprising that invocations of science also became a way to draw lines of inclusion and exclusion—and, as usual with the sportsmen-hunters, there were those totally outside the lines and those who otherwise might belong. In a speech given at the Boone and Crockett annual meeting, Henry Fairfield Osborn pointed out that "to the unthinking man a bison, a wapiti, a deer . . . is a matter of hide and meat [but] to the . . . true sportsman, the scientific student . . . they represent an architecture more elaborate than that of Westminster Abbey, and a history beside which human history is as of yesterday."[64] The implication is that subsistence and market hunters pursuing animals do not appreciate them, or at least not in the right way, but Osborn doesn't say that directly; instead, he condemns "the unthinking man"—and that could be any hunter who values animals only for their meat and skin. Lines are being drawn here, not just between subsistence and sport hunters, but also between the Harvard man who makes his casual trip of value and the one who can't be bothered, and between the traveling hunter and the stay-at-home reader: the man who, in John Millais's words, thinks of Newfoundland only as "connected with fogs, dogs, and bogs, just as he imagines Africa to be a 'mass of lions mixed with sand.'"[65] A commitment to science, displayed in print, showed that these hunters knew better: they knew the places they visited well enough to map them; they appreciated the animal for more than just its meat. The pledge of allegiance to science furthered the slicing and splicing among and between groups of men, while reinforcing both the hunter elite's claims to authority and the connections they forged among still-hunting, science, writing a narrative, and the production of valuable knowledge.

## V. MANLINESS

Manliness was the most ubiquitous element of the sportsman-hunter discourse. "Manly" could modify "character" or "sport" or "work" or "virtues." It could underlie the entire meaning of the sportsmanlike still-hunt, so that being an "honorable sportsman" became the simple equivalent of being "a man." It appeared in descriptions of the importance of the frontier and slipped into discussions of the pioneer forefathers. In every case, it functioned to give tremendous cultural weight to the leisured hunting of men in the field. It was also the trickiest, messiest, and most nuanced of all the elements in the sportsman-hunter discourse.

Throughout the nineteenth century, middle-class culture had linked work, character, and the primacy of the will to manliness. The hunter-writers took this already established set of associations and transferred it to a new place of display—the hunt and the hunting narrative. Beginning with Van Dyke, the still-hunt was presented as a site where men could be judged in terms of character, manliness, and self-control, but buried in that assertion was always a deeper argument: that those *were* the terms by which to judge hunters.

Once that assumption was accepted, "character," "self-control," and "manliness" could be used interchangeably in hunting narratives. In particular, the moment when character was revealed was often presented in gendered terms. Such an epiphany occurs in the true tale "A Remarkable Adventure with Grizzly Bears." In this narrative, Elmer Frank and his friend Ed Clark are hunting in Wyoming when they unexpectedly run into a group of five grizzlies and Frank is thrown by his panicked horse. He just manages to grab his rifle when "I was greeted with a terrible growling and the crackling rush of a heavy body. I fired, and was embraced, it seems to me, almost simultaneously . . . calling to Clark as I went down." The bear is covering Frank, preventing any clear shot, so Clark calmly holds his fire. Frank thinks he's been deserted—"the infamy of this act seemed horrible to me"—but then, as the bear ceases mauling his hip and moves to bite through his hand, he hears "the sharp report of a Winchester. . . . It was Clark." The wounded bear leaves

Frank to attack Clark, and after taking fire from both men it "fell dead.... I dragged myself toward Clark.... He asked me if I were much hurt. I told him I thought I was all chewed to a sausage, but that I was indebted to him for my existence; that his was a brave, generous and manly act, and in short, 'You are every inch a man.'"[66]

On the face of it, Frank's statement is nonsensical: biologically, Clark was a man before the grizzly attack. That is not what being "a man" is in this formulation, however; instead, it describes the being who performs a "manly act." That act is one of tremendous self-control, of remaining calm, picking a target with deliberate aim, and choosing to save a friend's life instead of fleeing in terror, but self-control is immediately translated into explicitly gendered terms, the association with manliness constructed in Frank's mind and through his words. This association also draws on preexisting cultural connections for its legitimacy, and that in turn placed certain constraints on hunters: to the degree that they chose to locate either the revelation of character or a certain idea of work in hunting, they also found themselves bound to one particular reading of manliness, the one already associated with the display of character and the manly virtues. This limited the possible uses of gendered rhetoric within hunting narratives, even as it further legitimized the hunt as an alternative to the compromised workplace when it came to the display and recognition of manliness.

This was not the only complex function served by invocations of manliness, however: they also lent themselves to the drawing of lines of exclusion. At first glance, such lines seem obvious. Using a language of gender allowed hunter-writers to conceal class and regional divisions among hunters, for example, so that the time-consuming still-hunt specific to the hunter elite could become the more universal "manly sport with the rifle." It also let them elide hunting by women of their own set and raised complicated questions for female hunters about what their sport might be if it looked like "manly sport" in every particular but the gender of the hunter (this rates a chapter to itself in the next section).

At the same time, this gendered rhetoric concealed less obvious layers of exclusion within itself. "Do not look as a child or woman does—at only one thing at a time—but let your gaze be comprehensive," Van Dyke wrote in *The Still-Hunter*. "This is manly, wide-awake, scientific sport."[67] His still-hunter is a man differentiated from women and children, but he's not Everyman. As noted earlier, Van Dyke went on to separate the still-hunter from other men by his willingness to develop the self-control and willpower to pursue game successfully. He addressed *The Still-Hunter* to that reader, and this is typical. From *The Still-Hunter* to *Outing Magazine*, the rhetoric of manliness appears to have been aimed mainly at a white, native-born, middle- and upper-class reading audience. For those readers, the rhetoric of manliness had traditionally served to draw lines among those who belonged and those who only appeared to, and the sportsmen-hunters continued to use manliness this way. Over time, the dominant function of the rhetoric of gender became complicated parsing *among* white, male, native-born, middle- and upper-class hunters.

These nuances can be illustrated by a passage from Owen Wister. Writing about hunting mountain goat, he makes it clear that the lines he draws among men apply not only to others, but to himself.

> The tenderfoot sportsman . . . frantically pumps his repeating rifle, hypnotized by the glut of destruction . . . for heaven's sake don't let us praise the performance! The best that can possibly be said for it is to call it the seamy side of masculinity; and the seamy side of masculinity fits cowardice like a glove. I am speaking from the sinner's bench; and long back in the years (not so long materially, but miles and miles every other way) I see one or two spots of shame.[68]

Including himself as a past sinner is a fascinating move on Wister's part and may be due partly to overheated prose. (Does he really mean that he once had such a close connection to cowardice? That's not typical of him by any means.) He is both explaining what you are if you do not hunt in a manly manner—"seamy," something close to a coward, something very like Van Dyke's hunter of "brute heart"—and assuring readers that such a condition does not need to be permanent. Instead, men can choose to become manly through their actions (or their refusal to act) in the field.

Would this apply to all men? No, but that makes sense, because manly hunting is linked here, once again, to the exercise of the will. Wister believed that willpower could be strengthened through exercise by those men with the capacity to develop it: Anglo-Saxon Protestant men of the middle and upper classes. He is thus restricting his offer of redemption to those capable of achieving it, a caveat concealed under the essentializing language of gender. At the same time, for the right sort of hunter, he is offering the potential for membership in a very elite group, one that includes men such as himself, Grinnell, and Roosevelt, yet which is being defined through behavior rather than family connections or old money. This is a complex interweaving of exclusion and inclusion, one that draws lines, not only among men of the same social background, but between a single man's past and present, and that holds out the hope of redemption to some unsportsmanlike hunters even as it excludes entire invisible contingents of people.

Such redemption—or the lack thereof—was not only about behavior, however, but also about personal identity. Although it was never entirely separable from ideals of willpower and character, the language of manliness brought its own weight to bear on hunters' performances. It must have cut close to the bone for some writers and readers. After all, if you're a man and your sport isn't manly, then what is it? And what are you? Of all the elements of the sportsman-hunter discourse, gender was the only one that could raise such essential questions. Those who chose to pursue this line of inquiry delved ever deeper into layers of exclusion, even as they presented readers with troubling answers about the nature of the beast lurking within their friends, neighbors, and associates.

George Oliver Shields, editor of the periodical *Recreation*, offered one set of answers to such questions: the man who hunted in an unsportsmanlike way was not a man at all. He was a hog. The so-called game hog was the most commonly invoked antithesis to the manly hunter; he was what a man was when he wasn't a man.[69] Many hunters used the term—Van Dyke, for instance, had strong words for "the trout-swine" and "the great American *porcus*"—but no one promoted it more fervently than did Shields, who published pictures of hunters posed with massive numbers of trophies, labeling them "The Old Hog" or "A Bunch of Seattle Swine" (figure 3.1).[70] Many of *Recreation*'s subscribers seem to have embraced these divisions among hunters. One reader from Colorado Springs sent in a photo of "Herbert Gardner, of this city, who claims to be a hunter, but judging from the picture, I should not class him as such.... [I] should like to have you class him with the rest of your pigs," while C. P. White of Worcester, Massachusetts, wrote to Shields that "I am happy to say RECREATION is having a great influence. It puts gentlemen on their honor and excites the fear of swine."[71]

Again, it is the lack of self-control that divides one hunter from another, but now that failure reveals something innate, something hidden and animalistic that is exposed to view as he revels in the glut of destruction. And again, this is men talking about their own: the hunters Shields read out from the pulpit were white, native born, hunting mainly for pleasure rather than subsistence, and being held to the standards of their peers. There's a disturbing quality to the statements Shields is making, however, one that is lacking

Figure 3.1. "A Bunch of Seattle Swine," *Recreation*, March 1900.

from Wister, as Shields suggests that the man standing next to you might be something altogether alien. Ernest Russell, writing about moose-snarers, sums it up: "There is [an] individual who [is] built like a man, garbed like man, and with many of the superficial masculine attributes, yet whose real nature contrasts so darkly with that of the true sportsman that I hold him up to immediate and merited condemnation."[72] There is no better illustration of the complexity and power of this language. This is about far more than transferring the revelation of character into the hunt or avoiding discussions of class, as complex as those things could be. This is about what it meant, fundamentally, to be a man, and that was not to be sexed male, or dressed as a man, or to present to others as a man. Instead, it had to do with a "real nature" difficult to perceive, one that might be dark, be animal, be swine.

Hunting becomes one of the best and last places to expose such natures, one of the few remaining sites where men can be revealed for what they really are.

We have now come full circle to where we began, back to work and to the social functions that the workplace once served. In 1908, Caspar Whitney took Russell's warning one step further when he told readers in an editorial in *Outing*:

> The conduct of a man in the field is the surest index of that man's character.... Type does not vary in the quality of its expression.... The man who is merciless to his horse and to his dog, is very apt to be inconsiderate to his womankind.... The man who hunts his birds or his animals in an unsportsmanlike manner, is the man of whom you need beware when you come to business or social dealings. *In a word, the man who earns and lives up to the honorable title of sportsman, is no more or less than a considerate gentleman—a man.*[73]

In this passage, work and leisure, the world of business dealings and the world of field sport, are being linked together. The sportsman described here conforms to the nineteenth-century ideal of character—he is considerate of his dependents, fair in his social dealings, honorable, and manly—but he is not necessarily easy to recognize. Instead, he is surrounded by those who pretend to be gentlemen but are not what they seem. It is in the field that such men can be unmasked and that the truth about their behavior in the business world or behind the doors of their homes can be revealed. In the process leisure, not work, has become the site in which to identify a man's true nature. That nature is described in terms of gender as Whitney progresses smoothly from "sportsman" to "gentleman" to "man." If his reader does not have the right to that final title, then what exactly is he? Someone of whom to beware, is Whitney's only answer: someone who needs to be identified, and from whom true gentlemen need to be protected.

The ideas and anxieties being expressed here are hardly new to the Progressive Era. They had been part of middle-class culture for much of the nineteenth century, both in their focus on willpower and the manly virtues, and in worries about the reliable judgment of character. Whitney is at once invoking these anxieties and offering reassurance that palliatives can be found—palliatives grounded in traditional ideas of manly character, but located now in leisure. And he is also telling readers that a man's most fundamental identity can be judged *by* his leisure-time performance.

The language of manliness thus performed a host of nuanced functions within the sportsman-hunter discourse. It could conceal class, reveal character, strengthen other elements of the discourse, and link the narratives both to the cultural past and to contemporary anxieties. It also spoke to what it meant to be a man, and what it meant not to be. The anxieties conjured by the specter of men who proved to be no more than slouching beasts were part of this discussion, but so too was the promise that, by changing the way they hunted, a chosen few could transcend their pasts and join the ranks of true men. Not only character, but manhood itself, could now be revealed, and judged, in the world of the hunt.

**CODA**

The web of associations that surrounded the new meaning of the hunt was irreducible to a simple formula. No single writer was ever bound to use all the elements of the sportsman-hunter discourse, and no one writer ever did. Whitney never stopped invoking work and sportsmanship, but Elliott, gasping on his snowshoes while his caribou floundered away to safety, questioned in print how those terms were being defined. Sheldon was an ardent natural historian who praised his companions, whatever their race, while Wister eschewed science completely and reveled in the rhetoric of Anglo-Saxonism (there's a reason no species are named for Owen Wister). Van Dyke chose not to invoke the pioneers or the frontier; Roosevelt never missed an opportunity to do so. It was a conversation with many voices, an expanding web of options from which hunter-writers could choose, and all the more powerful because of that. It allowed writers to create a range of meanings for the hunt that made room for individual emphases and interests, while uniting the tales they told into a recognizable genre.

Less visible, and more problematic, is the question of what was not included and why it was not. There were always authors who pushed against the limits of this discourse—Elliott and his snowcrusting, for example, or Roosevelt's complete disregard of sportsmanship (although that was never made as explicit in his narratives as it was in his actions)—and, as the new century began, women hunters in particular would find themselves struggling with the rhetoric of manliness as they began writing about their own experiences in the field. Rather than imagining the sportsman-hunter discourse as having some absolute power to include or exclude, however, I would argue that it makes more sense to think of it as a web that could accommodate some ideas, but could not stretch to hold others. And this returns us once again to its origins.

The turn-of-the-century big-game hunt was made meaningful because it was framed as providing a new place in which traditional ideals of manliness, character, and primacy of the will could be displayed. Any addition to the discourse needed to fit with this central meaning. This helps to explain why references to work and to sportsmanship were such consistent themes in the narratives: they slid easily into wider discussions of self-control or the display of character. This also allowed the discourse to accommodate some outlying elements: arch-nativist Madison Grant, for instance, managed to slip antisemitic commentary into his account of moose hunting, while both Whitney and Hornaday took slaps at national immigration policies in their narratives. These did not need to be part of a hunting narrative, and almost always were not, but they *were* part of the culture that gave rise to the nineteenth-century ideals of workplace manliness and could be folded into the wider sportsman-hunter narrative without undue disruption. On the other hand, discussions of primitivism—which were very much part of changing ideas about masculinity in this era—never made inroads into the hunting narratives. This may be because the idea of hunters as men discovering the primitive within would have countered too many of the other elements of the discourse, including primacy of the will, sportsmanship, and the self-control demanded by the stalk, and it was the display of those qualities that made the still-hunt meaningful in the first place. Instead of violence or primitivism, readers were thus given Hornaday and his temptation goats, Seton's romantic pioneer prairie, and Sheldon's thrill at finding caribou dung in a bog. Varied as they were, viewed through the paradigm of a discourse with its own particular history and iterations, what was included and what was left out makes sense as a whole. From these connections, the turn-of-the-century big-game hunt drew its meaning.

**CHAPTER 4**

# The Business of Narrative

> *I made this journey to accomplish a purpose—to get material for a good story for Outing + for a good book. . . . This + the other trip has cost the magazine much money + Outing must have some returns.*
> —Dillon Wallace, Labrador diary, August 30, 1905

> *Hunting should go hand in hand with . . . descriptive and narrative power.*
> —Theodore Roosevelt

Throughout his life, Charles Sheldon was an ardent reader and collector of books on sport, natural history, and conservation, and at his death he bequeathed his collection to his alma mater, Yale. Shortly after the gift was made, conservationist and hunter John C. Phillips and Hugh Morison of the Library of Congress published a catalogue of the collection including annotations, some by Phillips or Morison, most made by Sheldon during his lifetime. That catalogue, *American Game Mammals and Birds: A Catalogue of Books 1582 to 1925: Sport, Natural History, and Conservation*, remains the most complete reference guide to the hunting books of Sheldon's era.[1]

At first glance, however, Sheldon's vast library seems anything but coherent, due to the enormous number of books and the tenuous relevancy they bear to one another in current categories of thinking about hunting and nature. A survey of just two pages of the catalogue, Bass to Beal, reveals the reminiscences of an Oklahoma Scout, a book called *Wild Bird Guests and How to Entertain Them*, a survey bulletin on the eating habits of woodpeckers, a how-to book on camp cooking, and *Oh, Shoot! Confessions of an Agitated Sportsman* (accompanied by the note, "Entertaining writing, the incidents of sport somewhat sacrificed thereto").[2] On other pages one might find books on dog training, or classics of Arctic exploration, or pamphlets on the prevention of mouse plagues. And that's just the general catalogue: there are 155 pages devoted to state and federal conservation publications, and another

64 pages devoted to periodicals ranging from scientific journals to manuals of woodcraft.

Despite Sheldon's omnivorous reading habits, however, not every book rates a comment; Sheldon reserved his personal annotations for those books that he considered outstanding. Among them were Van Dyke's *The Still-Hunter* ("The best book ever written on still hunting"), Caspar Whitney's *On Snow-shoes to the Barren Grounds* ("A real sporting adventure successfully carried out"), and Lewis's *Hints to Sportsmen* ("A standard work of the period, which even survived the more literary 'Field Sports' of Forester"). Almost every hunting book considered here appears in the Sheldon catalogue, and many have an assessment of their quality linked to them. He clearly identified them as belonging together.

At the same time, the boundaries of this group sometimes shifted to allow outliers that reveal some of the other standards Sheldon used. The identity of the author was one: despite almost completely excluding fiction, Sheldon included George Bird Grinnell's children's series on Young Jack, explaining that the books are "based on Dr. Grinnell's own experience or on facts known to him as true. The books are, therefore, accurate representations of the scenes and events described." Despite this excuse, however, to include *Jack in the Rockies*, *Jack among the Indians*, *Jack the Young Hunter*, *Jack the Young Cowboy*, *Jack the Young Explorer*, and *Jack the Young Ranchman* in a catalogue of nonfiction books seems to be more of a nod to Grinnell's status and personal friendship with Sheldon than to any inherently truthful quality of the work in question. (Although this book does not deal with children's literature, it's worth noting the span of Jack's adventures; he was certainly a busy boy, but in a series of activities that connected hunting, exploring, the West, and the pioneer past.)

Another possible exception was for the beauty of the book itself. In his preface to the catalogue, Phillips notes simply that the "subject of American fishing has been, of course, rigidly excluded," and my reader has already noticed that I have followed that lead.[3] Fishing was a pleasure pursued by many big-game hunters but is seldom featured in the narratives, nor was it considered part of the genre. Despite that, however, there is a book on fishing in the Sheldon library, and its description gives an idea why:

> Dean Sage, *The Ristigouche and Its Salmon Fishing*. With a chapter on angling literature [with plates]. Edinburgh, David Douglas, 1888 . . . 71 illus.,

1 map, num. orig. etchings done by Ferraer, on vellum paper, 2 port., helio-gravure reproductions and designs by Burn-Murdoch, eng. by Annan & Swan, with woodcuts by John Adam. Folio. Ed. consists of 105 copies. A sumptuous volume on angling, delightfully written by one of the foremost authorities on the subject. Included in a hunting library because of an appreciative discussion of the feelings and moods of the sportsman enjoying both hunting and fishing, p. 138–141.

This book was not simply a fishing narrative but a "sumptuous volume," beautifully illustrated, printed on rich paper in a limited edition, as much an object for visual consumption as for reading. It reminds us that these narratives had a material reality and that the pleasures of taking these heavy, beautifully bound volumes in hand, and carefully cutting the pages of richly textured paper, are sensual ones bound up in a sense of anticipation and ownership. Possession of such a rare and beautiful book also said something about the owner—about his wealth, his tastes, and his membership in a clique of which Sheldon was a part. Reading a magazine like *Harper's*, or owning a book like *The Ristigouche and Its Salmon Fishing*, were ways of identifying to oneself and to others that one belonged—or aspired to belong—to a particular group, and to indicate allegiance to that group's tastes and interests.[4]

Neither the act of writing nor the production of a book as a material object was an inevitable consequence of the decision to go hunting. The transformation of hunt into bound manuscript was instead the result of a series of choices on the part of individual hunters and editors, facilitated by the massive expansion of the publishing industry in this period. In trying to understand how the big-game hunting narratives fit into American culture, this is the final piece of the puzzle: the relationship between those narratives and the worlds of writing, reading, and publishing at the turn of the century.

Sheldon's catalogue is a good place to start, for through his library he connected a love of hunting with a love of books about the hunt. His collection demonstrates that the line between the hunter-writers and their audiences was hardly inviolable: Sheldon was a hunter as well as a writer, a reader, and a collector. The inclusion of books like Sage's *Ristigouche* also serves as a reminder that these narratives, once in book form, became material possessions that could convey a complex set of messages about their reader. So too could subscribing to recreational magazines and generalist periodicals: in middle-class standards such as *Harper's*, big-game hunting stories were presented side-by-side with fiction, art, and articles on social and cultural issues that together created a certain discourse about the tastes of middle- and upper-class Americans.

Sheldon's catalogue also illuminates the social and economic connections among the hunting and publishing elites. It's there in Sheldon's friendship with Grinnell and his inclusion of *Jack the Young Hunter*, in his careful delineations of the histories of magazines like *Outing* and *Recreation*, and in the knowledge of the publishing world that he reveals in casual asides: where else can one learn that *American Big Game Hunting*, published in 1893 in the United States by the Forest and Stream Publishing Company, was published in the same year in Edinburgh by David Douglas, but with a mild joke about the Marquis of Lorne excised, and that this omission was due to the fact that the Marquis was a friend of Douglas's?[5] Sheldon's notes reveal the connections between sportsmen and publishers, discourses and the books that disseminated them, and Yale-educated hunters and the libraries they left behind.

Finally, the Sheldon catalogue also reveals the boundaries of narrative, because the collection is interesting for what it excludes as much as for what it includes. Some omissions are unsurprising: the general exclusion of books on fishing, for example, and of books by British hunters—Phillips in his preface highlights that fact, drawing the reader's attention to this output as uniquely American, and especially to the game laws as having no European equivalent.[6] Other lines of exclusion seem to have been based on class lines and ideas about the "correct" way to hunt. Sheldon included exploration books, but nothing by the despised Henry Morton Stanley; collections of game laws, but no stories of poaching; and there never was a book called *Jack the Young Game Hog*. These boundaries are not explicitly justified, any more than is the exclusion of fishing. Sheldon and Phillips drew these lines and, in doing so, sketched the outlines of a genre and a rationale.

"Exclusion" is a tricky term, however, one that can make a complex and contingent process sound straightforward. Before assuming that other groups desired to be published and were excluded, it is worth recognizing how truly odd the connections among hunting, writing, and publishing were. There were many ways to construct meaning around hunting at the turn of the century, among groups ranging from Maine poachers to Texan plume hunters to Alaskan subsistence hunters, but none of them connected hunting to producing a written narrative. The role played by writing was one of the things that made the turn-of-the-century still-hunt unique. Only the sportsmen-hunters consistently sought an audience for their actions among a national readership; only for them did their performance in the hunt become most meaningful when it left the presses as a published product.

In the narratives, then, two things are going on at once. One is the decision by hundreds of sportsmen to write and publish narratives of their experiences. This was not an obvious choice by any means, and one that had little precedent in American hunting culture. Why did so many hunters choose to publish? What did writing, specifically, do for them that they could not accomplish otherwise? And did this process go both ways, affecting how writing itself was understood in the period? The other thing that is happening is the massive expansion of the publishing industry, and especially the periodical market, at the turn of the century. This was a matter not just of narrative and discourse but also of economics and technological change, as the Second Industrial Revolution ushered in what Richard Ohmann has described as the "first fully developed, national culture industry."[7] The business of narrative was a lucrative one, and, by choosing to write about their experiences, the sportsmen-hunters became players in a rapidly modernizing publishing marketplace. Connected through narrative, through discourse, and by individual actors, like Sheldon, who straddled the roles of reader, writer, and hunter, both authors and industry need to be placed into their historical context in order to understand how the big-game hunting narratives became an integral part of American culture.

What did writing do for the big-game hunter? The obvious answer is that it allowed him to display his manly character to a wider audience than just his hunting companions and guides, but that's not the only answer. For one thing, hunting and writing interacted to create meanings that linked each with the other. For another, writing had its own history, and its own associations, that made penning a narrative a compromised way of demonstrating manliness. There was nothing inherently manly about *writing*, after all. Instead, throughout the nineteenth century, middle-class writing and middle-class periodicals had overwhelmingly been women's territory, and men seeking a niche for themselves as writers sometimes found themselves mocked for abandoning productive labor.[8]

Sportsmen-hunters most often responded to this challenge by presenting both hunting and writing about hunting as useful activities that served society as a whole. Dillon Wallace claimed that the point of writing *The Lure of the Labrador Wild* was to deliver "Hubbard's Message" of grit and determination, while Ernest Thompson Seton promised that his *Arctic Prairies* would lead his readers back to the "by-gone days of the Wild West," a journey meaningful to any "young man of our race."⁹ Roosevelt hammered at this point, urging big-game hunters to include discussions of natural history or exploration to make their narratives even more worthwhile, and emphasizing adjectives like "valuable" and "useful" in his book recommendations: in one "List of Books" on big-game hunting, he praised *The Still-Hunter* for being an "exceedingly valuable treatise on the science of still-hunting . . . a mine of valuable information."¹⁰ Whether claiming, as Whitney did, that hunting revealed the truth about a man's character, or using their narratives like Wister to make statements about manliness, sportsmen-hunters presented their writing as a service to American society at large—as useful and productive work.

Many hunters also offered a more specific use for their writing: to educate the reader about sportsmanship and to expose abuses. In *Camp-fires in the Canadian Rockies*, William Hornaday presented his own sportsmanship as a model of manly self-control but also criticized a Canadian game protection association that allowed the hunting of female goats.¹¹ The Progressive Era was marked by a move toward persuasion as a mode of social control: from Jane Addams to Theodore Roosevelt, the appeal to reason was seen as an appropriate instrument for addressing malefactors, who were expected to respond with a recognition of the rightness of the argument.¹² This Progressive impulse to instruct and persuade was reified in the big-game hunting narrative and often modeled by the hunter's actions as well as reported in his writing. In 1908, Charles Sheldon, who had built a cabin for himself near Mount McKinley intending to spend a solitary year observing mountain sheep, found his peaceful existence intruded on by market hunters.

> Naturally I was deeply disappointed to hear that my sheep, which I had been so carefully observing, were to be disturbed by vigorous market hunting, but could do nothing to prevent it. In the evening however, when the men had heard me discuss the habits of the sheep . . . they realized that their hunting would put an end to my opportunities. Showing a fine spirit, they at once decided to return and hunt caribou in the lower country.¹³

Sheldon, gentle soul that he was, even liked the market hunters (and they appear to have liked him; they gave him a choice lynx skull for his collection). His impulse here is classically Progressive, and the response (with its "fine spirit") exactly what Sheldon hoped—and, through writing, he offered it as an exemplar of how persuasion could work, a model of the ideal. Such connections to wider reform tendencies—even the hint of muckraking on occasion in the exposure and condemnation of lax game laws—gave hunters another way to identify their writing as instructive and useful contributions to society.

Hunting and writing are being rehabilitated here in tandem, as both visiting the wilderness and writing about it are transformed into blameless activities for men.[14] In 1900, a man who visited the wilderness and then wrote about wildflowers was linking himself to a wider world of literature by genteel women and gentle naturalists. Telling a tale of visiting the wilderness, observing wildflowers, and then shooting a moose, however, could associate the same man with the manly virtues and scientific sport. Sportsmen-hunters devoted long passages to descriptions of scenery, wildflowers, and natural beauty; they talked about the joys of camping, the pleasures of the trail, and how freeing it felt to be away from the city; and as long as, in the end, they shot something—even if it took only a sentence—their activities, both in the wilderness and at the typewriter, became blameless. Constructed as useful, exemplary, and educational, the sportsman-hunter narrative allowed men to express their appreciation of nature in print without risking being considered unmanly, effeminate, or unproductive.

Such writing may have served yet another function as well: reforming the act of *reading*. Reading was a growing leisure activity in the turn of the century and one that came in for its share of concern as a possibly pernicious influence. This may help to explain why big-game hunting narratives and recreational writing in general were often explicitly presented as providing wholesome and healthy reading for men and boys. *The Lure of the Labrador Wild* was framed this way, with author Dillon Wallace's lecture tour making stops at men's clubs, YMCAs, and the wonderfully named "BIG MEN'S MEETINGS" in upstate New York.[15] This in turn fed into the book's success: in 1914, when the Cleveland Public Library included *Lure* on its "carefully selected reading list of eighty books for the Boy Scouts of America" for exemplifying "manliness, discipline, courage, resources and loyalty," the book was already in its eleventh edition.[16] Recreational periodicals were also framed as providing wholesome reading. Reporter Zona Gale described *Outing* to her readers as "healthful," while *Outing* positioned itself as encouraging "clean living ... through the best of virile fiction [and] entertaining stories of adventure."[17] These links among manliness, healthy living, and writing are striking in a literary landscape traditionally dominated by female readership. (It would be going too far to frame these tales as some kind of backlash against women's literature, however; *Outing*, like the generalist periodicals, frequently addressed women and girls as well as men.)

Among all the reasons for writing that were given or implied in the narratives, however, there was one that almost never received mention: all these writers received money for their work. Profit was another reason that a man might publish a hunting tale. The amounts paid for articles and books varied widely, but the most popular writers were very well compensated indeed: Albert Bigelow Paine, for example, received $200 an article for his series *The Tent Dwellers*, published in *Outing*.[18] For some hunter-writers, publication and its accompanying pay-off seems to have been an afterthought, but for others the money mattered. Boone and Crockett member Roger Williams wrote to George Bird Grinnell in 1905, explaining that he had a commission to write a book for Caspar Whitney's American Sportsman's Library, but had grown unhappy with Whitney's editorial demands and also with the pay he had been offered. "I wish to have you read this Mss and advise me what probability there will be of having it published by Forest & Stream in book form," he told Grinnell. "What I may lose in reputation by not having it appear under auspices of the Sportsmen's [sic] Library I am positive will be made up by increased profits as my contract price was only $300."[19]

This aspect of writing appears only in private letters and correspondence with editors; no one reading the printed narratives would ever guess that profit was part of the equation. In the quote that opened this chapter, Dillon Wallace confided to his diary that the purpose of his second Labrador expedition was to get material for a book and that he continued onward after he had run dangerously low on food because his sponsor, *Outing*, "must have some returns." In his published narrative, however, such considerations are invisible. Wallace tells readers that he is exploring in Labrador as part of "a call to duty" and that he pushed onward because "To abandon [the expedition] seemed to me a surrender" and "my duty was plain."[20]

There were a multitude of reasons for not revealing the profit motive in print. Prevailing ideas about writing framed it as an art, rather than a profession, and drew a line between gentlemen amateurs and professional journalists. The original members of the hunter elite also came from a social group that considered public discussions of money the height of vulgarity; Owen Wister privately complained about the social pressure he felt never to "talk shop" or to admit that he wrote as a vocation.[21] Some non-elite men may thus have presented themselves as being on the amateur side of that line in order to maintain associations with the elite, if only in print, but there could be other motivations as well. Dillon Wallace might not have received so many paid speaking invitations to YMCA meetings if he had framed his motivation in going to Labrador as pecuniary rather than as the performance of manly duty, or if he had described his purpose in writing a book as producing a profit rather than as offering wholesome inspiration to boys and men.

Writing for a fee also opened up the possibility that the unmediated demonstration seemingly guaranteed by the hunt might be heavily mediated indeed—might even be just another commodity bought and sold on the market. If this aspect of the hunting narrative surfaced, it could undermine the entire story of selflessness and duty that the sportsmen-hunters were telling. They most often dealt with this threat in the same way that they dealt with other money issues surrounding the hunt: by not mentioning it. Nevertheless, by the first decade of the twentieth century, writing about hunting had become a way for some men who were not members of a financial elite to earn a very good living indeed. For those men, the true trophy of the big-game hunt had become the publisher's contract, even as they assured their readers in print that their manly display, hard work in the stalk, and revelation of character were what made their hunts, and their narratives, meaningful.

That readership was made up of hundreds of thousands of Americans by the turn of the century, but how can we know how they understood these narratives—or rather, how can we know that readers understood these stories the way that hunter-writers wanted them to be understood? That can be answered in part by the narratives themselves, because, as time passed, some members of that reading audience took up big-game hunting and wrote about their experiences. It may be no surprise that Roosevelt's son Kermit, writing in 1920, would echo his father's assessment that character is best revealed in the woods, but he was hardly alone. Sheldon had been at Yale, and then working as a general manager for a railroad in Mexico, when Roosevelt first drew the connections between manliness and the hunt, and he only began writing about his own hunting decades later, but in 1911 he would casually note that "hunting prevents the mere contemplative indulgence in the beautiful from producing effeminateness."[22] By the same token, Percy Madeira didn't leave Philadelphia to go on safari to Africa until 1908, and by then, he explains, he had steeped himself in the writing of those sportsmen who had gone before him, so it seemed the most logical thing in the world to this previously unpublished doctor to write a book, *Hunting in British East Africa*. It is tempting to clump all the hunter-writers together—indeed, with the notable exceptions of the founders of the genre, they were for the most part a generational cohort, the vast majority born during or within ten years of the end of the Civil War—but, in the forty years of the big-game hunting narrative's ascendancy, more and more members of the elite, as well as increasing numbers of middle-class men, chose to pursue the still-hunt and to write about it. That choice, and the unwavering focus on self-controlled, manly sport that remained central to these narratives into the 1920s, provide clear evidence that latecomers to the still-hunt had understood these earlier narratives as their writers had meant them to be read—as displays of character in the woods—and that this had become part of how they conceptualized and described their own hunting.

The writers I have been discussing so far have, for the most part, been members of the same status group from which the first sportsmen-hunters derived. They read each other's work, accepted the new significance given to hunting, and picked up and repeated the associations that gave the still-hunt its meaning. As time passed, however, three other mechanisms came into play among hunters, writers, and readers.

The first was that, as more and more narratives were published, new and self-referential associations began to emerge within the genre itself. When Roosevelt wrote about manly American hunting in the 1880s, he was constructing associations as he went, but the hunter who wrote a narrative of manly sport in the early 1900s was associating himself, among other things, with Roosevelt. As the hunter elite produced volume after volume of big-game hunting narratives, writing such a narrative became a way of identifying with that status group and their values, and even to claim membership in that group, at least in the public eye. Percy Madeira was no Boone and Crockett member, but he name-dropped gleefully throughout *Hunting in British East Africa* and even asked famed British hunter Frederick Selous to write the introduction. (Selous, ever courteous, obliged; it's clear that he had never met Madeira, nor, one suspects, read the book.)[23]

Secondly, as the stories proliferated, the manly still-hunter became a recognizable character, even a stock character. By 1908 a neophyte writer like Madeira knew how to present himself in print—knew to emphasize his coolness under fire, his self-control, the testing he underwent—even as, by becoming a big-game hunter, he laid claim to those elements of character through the hunt itself. Hunting narratives from Van Dyke onward instructed their readers about not only what their hunt was supposed to mean but also how they themselves ought to act, what they should feel as they watched the deer approaching, what their mastery of buck-fever said about them. The big-game hunting narrative constructed a type, and stepping into the world of the hunt, and then writing a narrative about one's experiences, allowed the author not only to identify himself outside the story with others who had published, but also to assume a ready-made persona inside that story, and gather all those associations to himself by doing so.[24] The still-hunt also provided an easy narrative arc; whether pursuing mountain sheep like Hale and Hardeman, or engaging in a longer quest like Whitney's journey to the Barren Grounds, hunting and exploration narratives came with a built-in beginning, middle, and end, another factor that must have made them an attractive genre for first-time writers.

Finally, the success of hunting narratives in the middle-class publishing marketplace must have created its own pressures on hunter-writers hoping to see their work in print, while continually reinforcing the central elements of the sportsman-hunter discourse. By the late 1890s, a hunter hoping to market his narrative to *Scribner's* would have been well aware of which elements were most likely to appeal to its reading audience and to its editors, and would also have known that long descriptions of skinning game, for example, were not going to be a welcome addition to a hunting tale for that market. It is impossible to quantify the looping effect of the market's pressures on would-be hunter-writers, but, once the sportsman-hunter discourse had become established and popular, the recognition of which elements were most welcome in the pages of middle-class periodicals must have served to reinforce that discourse for writers and readers alike.

This also makes it all the more interesting that not every element of the discourse was picked up by later writers: just as Roosevelt focused on the pioneers and Van Dyke on sportsmanship, so later arrivals like Whitney and Sheldon included the elements that most appealed to them while neglecting others. This underlines once again the flexibility of the discourse, the ways in which the meanings circling around the still-hunt offered far more than a simple formula, even as the stability of the most central elements provides evidence of both their cultural importance and their persistence. Sportsmanship, self-discipline, and the stalk were never dispensable.

The sportsmen-hunters had constructed both a way to hunt and a way to write about it. They not only presented a certain discourse of the hunt in print but also made new claims about the uses of both writing and reading. By 1900 going hunting and then writing a hunting narrative had become a way to display one's associations and beliefs, to construct a public persona, and to engage in both leisure and art while retaining manliness and character. Rather than simply being about experience and account-of-experience, the relationship between hunt and narrative was instead a dialogue of immense complexity and intimacy.

That relationship was also both material and economic. Hunters' accounts created new meanings for hunting and writing, but they were also commodities hawked on the pages of *Recreation* and *Rod and Gun* and on the shelves of newsstands and bookshops. The size and reach of that marketplace at the turn of the century was also something new in American culture, for hunting narratives accounted for only one small part of the massive expansion of the publishing industry in this period. Hungry for material, capable of national and international distribution, and almost always edited and published by men of the same social profile as the sportsmen-hunters themselves, the rapidly expanding print market provided the stage on which hunters performed. This is the final part of the context from which the hunting narrative emerged. Without the changes to transportation that placed the wilds of New Brunswick only a day's ride from Boston, there would not have been nearly as many big-game hunters. Without the expansion of the publishing industry, they might not have been published often enough to construct any meaning for the hunt in print at all.

"Communication revolution," "publishing explosion": when historians write about the Second Industrial Revolution, no descriptor seems violent enough to convey the change in communications technology. This was the era in which the telephone, the Kodak camera, the phonograph, and the moving picture were invented, and it was also a time of radical innovations in printing and marketing that culminated in the creation of a national print media. The reduction in paper and printing costs that accompanied the 1890s depression, changes in such technological processes as photogravure (in particular the invention of the halftone technique), major alterations to international copyright law, and congressional intervention in the mailing costs for periodicals all combined to encourage a massive expansion of the publishing industry.[25] In the two decades between 1885 and 1905 the number of new books being published tripled, with the "bestseller" emerging as an official trade term in 1895 and quickly becoming part of the way in which books were advertised.[26] The periodical market also experienced unprecedented growth. In 1865 the United States had seven hundred periodicals (not including newspapers); twenty years later in 1885 there were three thousand, marking the emergence of a national media; but over the next twenty years, between 1885 and 1905, approximately eleven thousand periodicals would be published (although almost half of those eventually failed or were absorbed by other magazines).[27] Monthly circulation figures reflected this expansion, more than tripling between 1890 and 1905, with some magazines reaching hundreds of thousands of subscribers: historian Christopher Wilson notes that in the Progressive Era "topical magazines achieved a centrality in American life never duplicated before or since."[28] This was another part of the changes sweeping through America in this period, and it was about business, economics, and the technology of publishing.

Leading the way among the periodicals were the staples of the American middle class—*Harper's*, *Scribner's*, *McClure's*, and the *Ladies Home Journal*—but there were thousands of generalist and specialty publications on topics ranging from bicycling to theosophy. Among the specialty recreational magazines were Grinnell's *Forest and Stream*, Whitney's *Outing Magazine*, and George Oliver Shields's *Recreation*. These magazines scrabbled for survival in a crowded marketplace, jostling one another for readers and in some cases competing for authors, articles, and advertisers. The magazine industry was one in which survival was the exception rather than the rule, and even relatively stable small periodicals might undergo frequent changes of ownership and even title. In 1912, for example, Shields's *Recreation* was absorbed by the *Illustrated Outdoor World* (which a year before that had been the *Amateur Sportsman*) and became *Outdoor World and Recreation*, then switched around to be *Recreation and Outdoor World*, before settling back down to being just *Recreation* again by 1914, although under different ownership and editorship than in 1912.[29]

Survival depended partly on a magazine finding a niche and partly on its having connections to a press with some money at hand. A comparison of two of the powerhouse recreational periodicals of the era—*Outing* and *Forest and Stream*—suggests radically different approaches to issues of advertising, price, and readership. *Outing* was a twenty-five-cent monthly magazine consisting of 120 pages or so an issue, with twelve or more illustrations, some in color, and it accepted advertising only on its front and back covers. Its writers were either staff members or freelance. *Forest and Stream*, on the other hand, was a weekly publication costing a dime, and a typical issue ran about forty pages. On twenty of those, advertising would take up 50 percent or more of the page. Commissioned articles were few, with most of the content provided by letters sent in by correspondents reporting on local club news and describing their own hunting and fishing trips, and were interspersed with pitches for big-game mailing cards, fishing tackle, and Gold Lion Cocktails (for "A Game Dinner!").[30] Both magazines flourished at the turn of the century, probably more because of than despite their differences. Both were also part, or becoming part, of larger commercial enterprises. *Forest and Stream* was connected to the Forest and Stream Press, which also published many of the Boone and Crockett books. The owners of *Outing Magazine* found business so profitable that in 1905 they purchased a manufacturing plant and created the Outing Press, which went on to publish a series called the Outing Adventure Library.[31] And such connections between book and magazine publishing were hardly confined to the specialty market: *Harper's* was part of the publishing house Harper and Brothers, while *Scribner's* was linked to Charles Scribner's Sons.

These connections made it sensible and profitable for presses to print books from serials originally appearing in their attendant magazines, and this was in fact the standard way that books on hunting were assembled. Whitney's *On Snow-shoes to the Barren Grounds* was originally serialized in *Harper's* then published by Harper and Brothers, while Paine's *The Tent Dwellers* appeared in *Outing*, then was published in book form by Outing Publishing Company. Anthologies often followed a similar path, as with Archibald Rogers's *Hunting*, published by Charles Scribner's Sons and composed entirely of articles originally published in *Scribner's*.[32] This double-dipping meant more profit for publishers, and writers found themselves under pressure to sell serial and book rights as a package. By 1906 *Outing* was formally pursuing this policy, with Whitney explaining to as prestigious an author as Jack London that, without book rights, "the plum [of a series of articles] is not good enough for the magazine no matter how rare and juicy it may be."[33]

The rise of the hunting narrative was thus fueled by the economic demands of an expanding publishing industry. Hunting narratives were perceived as profitable investments, forming part of the standard fare of both specialty and generalist periodicals, even as they were collected and reprinted in numerous books and anthologies from mainstream presses. Some of those collections consisted entirely of hunting stories, while others combined hunting tales with other types of writing: in 1909, Sidney Harris Wright gathered together stories of hunting and adventure from a number of magazines to produce *Adventures among Wild Beasts: Romantic Incidents and Perils of Travel, Sport, and Exploration throughout the World* for Lippincott.[34]

At the same time, publishing houses seeking material that would attract readers also began to reprint stories of hunting and adventure from earlier periods, often edited to play up the adventure and bring the older stories more into line with current offerings. A typical example is Edwin Bryant's 1848 *What I Saw in California*, which reappeared in the late 1880s as *Rocky Mountain Adventures, Bristling with Animated Details of Fearful Fights of American Hunters with Savage Indians, Mexican Rancheros, and Beasts of Prey*.[35] Such reprints fed an audience hungry for tales of adventure while offering publishing houses pure profit, with no reduction for author's fees. They also offer further evidence that both hunting and adventure stories were seen as eminently desirable by the men running the publishing industry.

As that industry expanded, the big-game hunting narrative was thus enabled and encouraged to find a home for itself. This happened partly because of the money to be made by authors, partly because of the hunger for material that led to articles being printed and reprinted, and partly because hunting narratives fed an often-ephemeral specialty press as well as the generalist periodical market.[36] In 1880 few men were writing stories of big-game hunting, but that may have been in part because of a lack of outlets for their product. By 1900 a big-game hunter heading out would have had reason to pause and consider whether it might be economically sensible to produce a narrative on the way.

There was yet one more factor in play, however, for if the big-game hunting community was a small fraternity indeed, the same can easily be said of the publishing industry in this period. The hunter elite was shadowed by a publishing elite, especially in the intimate world of the recreational media. Overwhelmingly white, native-born, Protestant, middle- and upper-class men of the urban Northeast, the era's editors and publishers knew the sportsmen-hunters from colleges, clubs, and social events, and shared friendships and hunting trips with them.[37]

These interconnections are difficult to quantify; they emerge from reading the narratives, from the way that over and over the same group of men meet one another, exchange ideas, and collaborate. Frederic Remington, for instance, got his first break from former Yale classmate Poultney Bigelow, who was then editor at *Outing*; Remington would later illustrate an article on musk-ox hunting by Caspar Whitney for *Harper's* and would complain about Whitney's demands to his friend Owen Wister; Whitney would go on to be editor and part-owner of *Outing*, where he would publish numerous articles by Wister, whom he already knew from the Boone and Crockett Club; there, he had gotten advice on cougar hunting from Wister, which Whitney included in an article that Roosevelt published; Roosevelt at the time was fresh off a stint filling in for Whitney's column at *Harper's* while Whitney was touring England; Whitney's tour was turned into a book called *A Sporting Pilgrimage*, which was serialized in *Harper's*; when Whitney took over *Outing*, Fletcher Harper was one of his co-owners; one of Whitney's first moves at *Outing* was to re-publish Roosevelt's *The Wilderness Hunter* and commission illustrations for it from Frederic Remington.[38] And so it goes. Six degrees of separation are seldom reached when one considers the connections among publishers, hunters, and writers in this period. The overall impression is that, if you traveled back to 1900, you could fit the number of men actually publishing the big-game hunting stories into a single room—and, if you arrived during the Boone and Crockett annual dinner, your work would already have been done for you. This last is an exaggeration, but only a slight one.

Why did all this matter? One reason is that a reader turning to the literature of sport and hunting would find an array of books, articles, and periodicals that seemed to span a wide gamut, but that emerged from a surprisingly small nexus of men in New York who were strategically positioned in the publishing industry and controlled access to its presses. That reader, laying down her issue of Caspar Whitney's *Outing*, might pick up a popular travelogue such as Dillon Wallace's *Beyond the Mexican Sierras* (published from a serial originally appearing in *Outing*), or one of the books of the American Sportsman's Library (published by Macmillan and edited by Whitney), or settle down to read a serial in *Harper's* such as John Neihardt's *The River and I* (from an expedition commissioned by Whitney), and would find remarkable congruence between the stories being told in those sources and the stories she had just been reading in *Outing*. In the same way, Grinnell, editor of *Forest and Stream*, also published in *Scribner's*, *Outing*, and myriad other periodicals, and then reprinted his own articles in the anthologies he edited for the Boone and Crockett Club and published through Forest and Stream Press, even as they were also being reproduced in anthologies like Archibald Rogers's *Hunting*. Readers seeking to avoid this cabal altogether might pick up as transnational-seeming an offering as Edgar Fitz Randolph's *Inter-ocean Hunting Tales* only to find themselves reading *Forest and Stream* reprints.[39] It was not quite a monopoly, but it was close to one.

That monopoly also mattered because periodicals were becoming an essential part of middle-class identity in this period. Throughout most of the nineteenth century, people defined themselves in their communities in large part through what they produced, but by the 1890s Americans were increasingly identifying themselves through consumption, and looking to a media with national reach to do so. This was the great age of the magazine. By 1900 subscribing to and reading periodicals had become one of the most common shared cultural experiences in the United States for middle-class men and women. A subscription could reveal which values readers shared (or did not share) with friends, neighbors, and other members of their community, displaying their tastes and aspirations, even as it brought national conversations into living rooms and workplaces from coast to coast.[40]

Those reading audiences were overwhelmingly white, middle- and upper-class, native born, and Protestant, pushed and pulled by the same anxieties and pleasures as the sportsmen-hunters themselves. This may help to explain why the story of the manly still-hunt, propagated by the nexus of the East Coast publishing elite, appears to have resonated with readers across the country. Over time some of them would take up hunting, replicating the sportsman-hunter discourse in their own tales of the still-hunt. Others would become part of a constituency that supported the ideals of sportsmanship, making those standards part of national conversations about hunting. And for thousands more, for whom reading big-game hunting narratives remained one among many leisure activities, the decision to consume *Harper's* or *Outing* supported the continued perception within the industry that these narratives were valuable commodities. For all these readers, the sportsman-hunter discourse would eventually achieve something close to a cultural hegemony, becoming *the* way to understand big-game hunting, manliness, and the display of character in the field. By 1900, only twenty years after its emergence, the story of manly sport with the rifle had become utterly dominant in the nationally distributed middle-class press.

Seen from here, Sheldon's library still conveys the meanings he hoped it would, revealing his tastes and interests—but it reveals other things as well. Sheldon was an ardent reader of the Boone and Crockett books, for instance, tracking their publishing history and noting whenever a particularly good hunting story appeared in the series, but as time passed he began contributing articles as well, and in 1925 he co-edited the Boone and Crockett anthology

*Hunting and Conservation* with Grinnell. Nor was he unique in finding his way from hunting into the business of narrative: by 1903 more than a quarter of the club members had published hunting stories.[41] Publishing, however, was *not* a requirement for club membership. Instead, it was part of its culture, made manifest in the publishing connections and literary proclivities of individual members. This was about hunting, writing, and reading, and it was also about a club whose co-founder controlled Forest and Stream Press and about books and articles that were profitable commodities. And none of this proceeded inevitably from the fact of going to the woods and shooting an animal. Hunting may be one of humanity's oldest activities, but the emergence and explosive popularity of the sportsman-hunter narrative was the unique result of a modernizing age.

Paradox had always lain at the heart of the sportsmen-hunters' quest to find a new place in which to display the traditional manly virtues. Their search was in many ways a reaction against the changes brought on by the Second Industrial Revolution, and yet, from the moment Van Dyke sold "The Still-Hunter" to the *American Field*, the still-hunt as a display of manly character became caught up in the publishing explosion. That explosion created a market that recruited both new hunters and vast audiences to the sportsmen-hunters' view of the world, and it was made possible by technological developments, legal and economic changes, and the emergence of new forms of consumerism and self-identification. Hunters, readers, writers, and editors were all caught up in these changes—indeed, as Sheldon's example shows, a single person could play all those roles in one lifetime. His seamless transition from one to the next illustrates the evolving connections among hunting, manliness, writing, reading, and publishing. The hunter-writers' celebration of the manly virtues may have been grounded in nineteenth-century tradition, but it was brought to life using very modern venues: the revolutionary new worlds of publishing and consumption.

**CHAPTER 5**

# Whitney Rising

*The conduct of a man in the field is the surest index of that man's character.*
—Caspar Whitney, *Outing*, 1908

There was no conspiracy that met on alternate Tuesdays at seven (or even annually at the Boone and Crockett dinners); the gradual dissemination of the network of ideas underpinning the sportsman-hunter discourse was a matter of individual hunters choosing how to interpret their experiences in print, of editors who selected those narratives for publication, and of audiences who fit what they read into their own visions of the world. There was also nothing predetermined about the hunter-writers' decision to focus on manliness and the will, and one might predict that, as more and more narratives were produced, the sheer amount of individual variation would undermine the stability of the discourse. It did not. Throughout the 1890s and into the turn of the century an ever-increasing number of hunters chose the sportsman-hunter discourse as the way to interpret their actions in print to readers. Fewer than twenty years after *The Still-Hunter* was published, that discourse had become the dominant way that individuals wrote about their big-game hunting for the national middle-class press.

Too often historians are left describing a change without being able to identify the mechanisms at work. This is partly because so much of the past is obscured from a distance and partly because the *how* can sometimes seem less interesting than the *why*—and yet here it is vital. The sportsman-hunter narrative became immensely popular in a short period: how did that happen? How did the small group of hunters who were present at the birth of this narrative—Harvard men, Boone and Crockett members, the eastern elite on the cusp of change—disseminate this story nationally, and how did it come to dominate the presentation of big-game hunting in the middle-class press?

These questions can be answered by examining the life of one man: Caspar Whitney, journalist, editor, publisher, big-game hunter, and explorer.

Whitney is useful because he dissolves the barriers between hunt and narrative, product and producer. He reveals why an individual might embrace the story of manly sport with the rifle: although not a member of the elite by birth, Whitney gained acceptance partly through his adoption of the sportsman-hunter persona. He was also a prominent member of the publishing revolution, one of a group of young editors who were redefining the American periodical in this era—and that meant that, having taken the sportsmen-hunter discourse as his own, he disseminated it over decades to hundreds of thousands of readers in his own books, in the popular periodicals that he edited, and in the books he commissioned and published from his position at the Outing Publishing Company. His individual choices played an essential part in the national popularization and eventual dominance of the sportsman-hunter discourse. He reveals how it all worked in practice.

Whitney is a vexing subject for historical biography, however, partly because his origins are obscured by time, partly because of contradictions in his life that stand as challenges to inference. The Whitneys were a famous family with branches throughout New England, and Caspar Whitney may have had some claim to the blue-blood background of that clan; after all, he was one of the original members of the Boone and Crockett Club, and that would have been close to impossible without both elite antecedents and connections. On the other hand, his family history and education seem to indicate that he was *not* born a member of the elite. Raised in what appears to have been a staunchly middle-class family in Boston, he accompanied his family to the West Coast as an adolescent and remained in California to attend the obscure St. Matthews College, where he was mainly noted for excelling at sport. Whitney thus did not share the private school/Ivy college/Ivy club connections of the East Coast elite. Nor did he follow that elite's tradition of intermarriage among their own: his first wife, Cora Chase, was originally from Illinois, and his second, Florence Canfield, was a Californian, albeit from a wealthy and notable West Coast family.[1]

Nor is it entirely clear when Whitney began his rise to what would eventually be fame and fortune (not least because over his lifetime he claimed a variety of birth dates, ranging from 1861 to 1865).[2] After leaving St. Matthews sometime in the early 1880s, he traveled throughout the Southwest and Mexico, trying his hand at gold mining, then moved to New York, where he became the co-owner and writer of a small magazine called *This Week's Sport*. There he drew national attention when he began selecting and publishing a list of the best college football players in the country, which he dubbed "the All-American football team." In 1891, he was asked to join the staff of the tremendously popular and prestigious *Harper's Weekly* to write his own column, Amateur Sport. *Harper's* was not alone in creating a sports department during the 1890s—*Collier's* and *Life* were among the popular periodicals that did the same—but two things made *Harper's* approach distinctive.[3] One was its unrelenting focus on amateurism: although in the 1880s *Harper's* had covered professional baseball and football, in Amateur Sport readers were exposed only to sport considered "amateur" by the strictest definition. The other was the reason for that focus: its young and ambitious author, not yet thirty, who would become "the voice of *Harper's* in this period."[4]

The beginning of Whitney's rise to prominence was thus as a professional, a member of the salaried middle class. He spent most of his life working as a journalist and editor, jobs that paid well but that left him in a very different financial situation than that of an Owen Wister or George Bird Grinnell. Again, then, he seems to have had little in common with the elite. He was just another white-collar worker, benefiting from the publishing explosion made possible by the Second Industrial Revolution.

That Revolution put Whitney in good position to shape his fortune, however. He was white, male, native born, Protestant, originally from the East Coast, and college educated. He was a talented member of a media that was quickly becoming both nationally influential and explosively popular. He also had the luck to be born in a time when the criteria for inclusion in the elite were moving away from strict standards of birth, when some members of the social elect were taking account of behavior and performance as well as breeding and educational background. And Whitney appears to have had a driving desire to belong. He sought out every chance to hobnob with the wealthy, was an almost compulsive name-dropper, and from his first moments at *Harper's* he enforced the rules of amateurism as if he alone were the guardian of elite beliefs and standards.

None of that meant that Whitney had an immediate connection to hunting, however. In the late nineteenth century, amateur sport and hunting were seen as separate elements on a lifetime continuum: the proper progression was the "lad at his rowing, his football, his baseball or his tennis . . . [for his] father riding, shooting, golfing or yachting."[5] Boys were expected to develop character on the sports field and then to graduate to activities more appropriate to grown men; in particular, hunting big game was sport for adults who had already built manly character.

Despite that, however, there were some clear parallels between amateur sport and sportsmanlike hunting. Like "manly sport with the rifle," the amateur movement in sports was a Gilded Age creation and was partly a way of importing middle- and upper-class standards into recreation and play. By the 1890s amateurism was being defined primarily in the sense familiar today, as sport for which the athlete received no monetary gain. Forbidden by this definition, which was elaborated in rules and regulations throughout the sporting world, was the acceptance of *any* money, including prizes, funds for equipment, or athletic scholarships; even a coach paying for a player's travel to training camp could be counted as professionalism. Such rules segregated athletes along lines of class and culture, and yet they were often promoted through a seemingly unobjectionable language of selfless play. Whitney and other sportswriters assured middle-class readers that the goals of amateurism were to ensure that play was fair, with competitors well matched in terms of training and experience, and also to demonstrate that athletes were playing for the "right" reasons, for the sake of individual betterment rather than material reward. Such play developed "manly boys and gentle men" by offering them "tests of patience and self-control and courage."[6] Concealing class exclusion through a language of manliness, the amateur ideal thus sought to discipline and interpret the meaning of behavior on the playing field, rather as the rules of sportsmanship were doing in the same period for hunters.[7]

Caspar Whitney was one of the premier shapers of this ideal, providing snappy, colorful coverage of amateur sport in his column in *Harper's*. His promotion of amateurism matters here because his writing exposes a host of anxieties that he shared both with his middle-class readers and with the hunter elite. His dominance at *Harper's* also positioned him as the leading arbiter of middle-class standards in sport for a rapidly expanding audience of readers, a reputation he would bring with him when he began writing about hunting. And whatever his subject matter, Whitney's voice was consistent: lively, engaging, sometimes verging on the melodramatic, and with an acid edge that came to be feared by his enemies. His Amateur Sport columns, for example, offered energetic descriptions of baseball and football games while providing acerbic commentary on those who (in his view) violated the standards of amateurism. In one column on Ivy League baseball, he explained that, while "*the Brown nine has continued* its victorious [season]," he could not "comment in detail [on the game]. . . . When Brown places its nine on an ethical equality with the others in its playing class, I shall cheerfully give it full credit, but not until then."[8] Colleges had to earn the right to full coverage in Whitney's column; if not, the college, and sometimes specific coaches and players, might find themselves read out from the altar of Amateur Sport. Whitney assured his readers that such criticism was grounded in the best of intentions, explaining that "this Department desires neither to create sensation nor to do injustice," that it exists "solely for the welfare of honest, manly sport" and "criticises only that it may lay bare and expurgate the unclean."[9] Whether readers swallowed such justifications whole is hard to tell, but Whitney's willingness to name names, and his love of controversy, made his column a much-discussed and anticipated feature of *Harper's*.

He became so popular that in 1893 *Harper's* sent him on a lengthy trip to England to report on the condition of sport there, serialized his dispatches, and then published them as a book, *A Sporting Pilgrimage*. (It may speak to his popularity that *Harper's* held space for Amateur Sport in his absence by commissioning a series of articles from Theodore Roosevelt, while assuring readers that Whitney would be returning shortly.[10]) *A Sporting Pilgrimage* shows Whitney wrestling with one of the most fundamental problems of his time: how does one recognize a true man? This question, of such concern to the big-game hunters, also haunted the paladin of amateurism. He fretted that, in England's Amateur Athletic Association, working-class men saw

> the organization of an institution that would officially and conspicuously label them gentlemen—for it was argued that to be an amateur was to be a gentleman. . . . [Soon] the element of greed replaced what there had been of sport. That class which had in times past popularized such brutish spectacles as cock-fighting [recognized] the rare chance at one and the same time of becoming "gentlemen" and winning prizes that could be turned to a pretty penny.[11]

At first glance this is a clear swipe at the working class, but there are complexities below the surface. Is the danger to amateur sport the influx of money from above or of greedy social climbers from below? Note also the specter of "gentlemen" who are not what they appear to be. If sport becomes linked to monetary inducements, then how can observers accurately identify the meaning of performances within it? By asking such questions, Whitney in sport, like Van Dyke in hunting, was hitting notes that had wider resonance for middle- and upper-class American readers.

Interestingly, Whitney never took a stance against professional sport as long as it was not defined as "amateur"; his focus was always on boys and men of his own class. "There is no disgrace in honest professionalism," he reminded readers, but "there is disgrace and inevitable dissolution in dishonest amateurism."[12] This was because amateur sport for Whitney had only one purpose: developing manly character. "As the boy is in his play, so will he be in his life's work," he wrote. "Therefore let college faculties view athletics as the serious factor in the moulding of undergraduate character that it is."[13] Bringing in "ringers," paying athletes, winning through dishonest means, all were of a piece for Whitney, and he was less likely to attack working-class athletes than he was to call out those who were of the right breeding and background but who did not offer fair play by his definition. "Ward played a strong, errorless game at second," Whitney wrote of a Princeton-Yale game, "but he spoiled the otherwise good impression by blocking Yale's runner on second, and on his attempt, by raising his leg, to shut off the umpire's vision." He informed readers that "next year I am going to start a black list, adding to it as the offenders reveal their vicious inclinations . . . to show the men who have played the mucker rather than the sportsman."[14] Even as Van Dyke finds the man of "brute heart" revealed through his hunting, so Whitney finds exposed on the playing field the Yale man who is vicious by inclination.

By the early 1890s, Whitney had gained tremendous popularity and influence. He enjoyed a sterling reputation among the middle-class press, where he was praised as "the first to show that a man could write of athletics like a gentleman and for gentlemen."[15] Readers across the nation waited eagerly to find out who was being denounced this week or to see who had made the All-American football team; newspapers reprinted his opinions and argued over his controversial denouncements of "professionals" on college teams.[16] In 1896, a Congregational minister, signing himself "Pro Corpore Sano" and identifying himself as a *Harper's* reader, wrote to the *Outlook* asking them to interview Whitney on his "practical suggestions" for helping boys take a higher view of athletics. The *Outlook* obliged, describing Whitney as "conduct[ing] with ability and authority the readable 'Amateur Sport' department of 'Harper's Weekly.' . . . He is now by general consent recognized as the leading expert in amateur athletics in the United States."[17] And Whitney's reputation only increased as he grew older: he was the second American chosen to serve on the International Olympic Committee, and the first head of the American Olympic Committee.[18]

Whitney built this reputation without going hunting: a reputation as a columnist, an expert on amateur sport, and a gentleman's sportswriter. He was not content with that, however; he wanted more. To achieve that, he turned to big-game hunting.

Whitney's choice of the hunt as a means of promoting himself would have been mystifying a generation earlier, when big-game hunting was a wealthy man's pleasure and a leisurely break from real work. By the 1890s, however, Whitney found a different story about hunting available to him. In little more than a decade since the publication of *The Still-Hunter*, the sportsman-hunter narrative had become well established as the way to write about hunting like a gentleman, for gentlemen. The Boone and Crockett Club had published its first anthology of hunting tales and *Harper's* was carrying Roosevelt's hunting stories, some of them in place of Whitney's column while he was away in England. When Whitney selected the sportsman-hunter discourse as a way of identifying himself to others, then, he did so understanding what it might do for him and how he would need to present himself, both in the field and on the page. There were many other ways of entering the wilds in the 1890s, and other ways to hunt game, but, out of all the possible options, Caspar Whitney embraced the still-hunt.

There was good reason for him to do so. For one thing, the sportsman-hunter discourse fit well with the story he was already telling. For almost a decade Whitney had positioned himself as the standard-bearer of fair play and manly sport for young men, but with his own college days behind him there was little chance to practice what he preached. The still-hunt, however, was a grown man's sport, and yet was closely associated with the middle-class values and manly virtues that Whitney had made his reputation promoting (so much so that hunting language sometimes found its way into Whitney's columns: at one point, critiquing professionalism in golf, he noted that "a pot-hunting set seems to be in control").[19] Big-game hunting also offered him the chance to engage in some very effective social climbing. That Whitney aspired upward is clear. He often mentioned his encounters with the elite in his columns and also seems to have been intent on obscuring his educational origins, seldom mentioning St. Matthews and instead repeatedly claiming to have "passed the Harvard entrance exams" (he may have, but he never enrolled; nevertheless, by the late 1890s Roosevelt himself would mistake Whitney in print for "a Harvard man").[20] Entrance into the Boone and Crockett Club got Whitney's foot in the door, and, in choosing to pursue big-game hunting, he was also choosing a mode of personal display that would push that door wider. Writing a hunting narrative would allow him to position himself as a model of the virtues he promoted, even as it put him in company, in print and in person, with the hunter elite. The sportsman-hunter discourse fit both who Whitney was and who he most wanted to be. It provided an identity that was fundamentally *useful* to him.

One of Whitney's earliest ventures into hunting narrative was an article he contributed to the 1895 Boone and Crockett anthology *Hunting in Many Lands*. Cougar in Mexico was Whitney's topic, and he shared the volume with some famous names, including Roosevelt, Winthrop Chanler, and Madison Grant. Cougar were not generally regarded as big game because they were nocturnal and tended to tree themselves when hunted; perhaps because of this, accounts of cougar in hunting books often made it sound as if there were something furtive and unpleasant about the animal itself. Moreover, the cougar was often feminized: Whitney notes at different points that the cougar is as "capricious as a woman" and can "screech like a woman in distress." Hunting them was thus not necessarily considered manly sport, but in "The Cougar" Whitney manages to frame his encounters as performances of courage and nerve. He opens by assuring readers that the landscape itself was dangerous, a place where "cut-throat, horse-stealing Mexicans . . . flourished . . . as thickly as cactus." And Whitney's cougars hunt *him*. Readers are regaled first with an encounter with a charging cougar: "although I aimed for one of those hideous eyes, [I] missed far enough to clip off a piece of skin from the top of his skull and to whet his appetite for my gore . . . he was practically on top of me . . . in another instant I had very nearly blown his entire head off. He was a monster." Later, Whitney is stalked at night when armed only with a mining pick, and "summoning all my ancient baseball skill . . . I hurled that pick at those two shining eyes, with a fervid wish that it might land between them. My aim was true." Whitney notes that he told this story to Owen Wister, who suggested that the cougar might just have been curious, and Whitney admits that this is possible, while making curiosity sound sinister: "the cougar's propensity for following people, out of unadulterated wantonness to frighten them, is well known." Whitney does not appear to have been frightened, however; whether seeking his fear or his gore, the cougars have been disappointed. All told, hunting cougars may not always have been considered manly sport, but being hunted *by* them gave Whitney ample opportunity to demonstrate coolness, courage, athletic ability, and unyielding self-control (as well as a chance to mention his acquaintance with Wister).[21]

At the same time, it is quite a stretch, although one Whitney was just able to make: being stalked by cougar, killing one, and maybe hitting another with a pick is highly unusual fare for a Boone and Crockett book. Whitney didn't have a typical hunting story to tell, however; he had been too busy working for a living. If he truly wanted to make a reputation with big game, he would have to go big-game hunting and write about it.

In 1894, Whitney set off on an expedition to the Barren Grounds of Canada to go musk-ox hunting in winter. The Barren Grounds lie to the north of Great Slave Lake in the western part of Canada, a desolate, treeless area of permanently frozen earth that stretches to the shores of the Arctic Ocean. Sport hunters and, for millennia before them, native inhabitants had entered the area in summer to hunt musk-ox, but few if any ventured there in winter, when they would be facing long hours of darkness, freezing temperatures, and life-threatening conditions.

The attraction for Whitney of such a hunt can be summed up in a phrase: no one else had ever done it. This was important for a journalist out to entertain the public by showing them something they hadn't encountered before, but in his book, *On Snow-shoes to the Barren Grounds: Twenty-Eight Hundred Miles after Musk-Oxen and Wood-Bison* (hereafter *Snow-shoes*), Whitney never presents that reason to his readers. Instead, he claims that his purpose is to demonstrate his mettle. The nonsensicality of the venture is transformed into proof of its virtue, as Whitney explains that its difficulties only make it a better test of himself. "I was going into the country for a purpose, and not for a picnic," Whitney tells readers at the beginning of the book. "I had set out to . . . get into the Barren Grounds for musk-oxen, and get back again to Great Slave Lake on snow-shoes—an undertaking that had been never before attempted and which every one assured me I could not carry out."[22] The difficulty of the quest enhances its appeal: "when one's friends have tried to dissuade and natives to intimidate you, [it] fires your blood, and makes you keen to toe the mark and be off."[23] As Whitney travels north, the Hudson's Bay Company factors to whom he turns for help also warn him off; he reports their warnings lovingly and at length. He never presents an argument as to why he is going in winter, leaving the reader to assume that it is simply because everyone says it can't be done. Whitney's not playing—indeed, he's out to write a series of articles, and then a book, to publish at a profit—but there's no hint of *that* work anywhere in *Snow-shoes*. Instead, the work he will do is the "exploring" work of entering a well-traveled land in the wrong season.

From the beginning of the narrative, Whitney gives the sense that he is traveling back into the past as he invokes the explorations of Franklin, Mackenzie, and Hearne, as well as the American frontier: Edmonton, for example, "raised memories of other frontier days across the line [when] the atmosphere was continuously shattered by cowboy whoops..."[24] Nor is traveling on this frontier easy. Whitney approaches Great Slave Lake in stages, traveling from one HBC post to another, and at each stage he needs to hire a local man to guide him. This arrangement proves challenging almost immediately. Whitney tells us that one guide, John, "evidently thought me ... a 'tenderfoot' ... with whom he could play any game he chose; and when he discovered his mistake he grew sulky."[25] Whitney becomes concerned that the man might sneak away in the night, abandoning him.

> So I engaged John's attention on this our first night together, and in my best pantomime I tried to make him understand that ... if he deserted me ... I should follow his trail and kill him.... I wondered that night ... what that Cree must have thought of this white man who was pushing into his country at a time when he himself usually remained in-doors, had pressed him into a service for which he had no liking, and threatened to take his life if he forsook it.[26]

This is as close to a moment of empathy as Whitney ever comes, in any of his writing, but empathy is not the point. This is about his control over his guide. Whitney is also using the encounter, as he does the warnings from the factors, to make a point about the kind of man he is: not someone who will turn back, not a tenderfoot, not the weakling they think him. In one sense the book is constructed as a series of misrecognitions, with the presence of the text itself—Whitney's story of success—drawing its meaning from the alternate proof it offers as to who Whitney really is. He may appear a tenderfoot at first, but soon he is running five miles an hour on snowshoes, running nine miles in an hour and forty minutes, running his white companion Heming off his snowshoes (Heming turns back by the fifth chapter), running the natives into the ground.

(What really happened between Whitney and his guide? Historians can ask, but there is no real way to know—except for a hint given in a book published almost twenty years later, Ernest Thompson Seton's *The Arctic Prairies*. Seton finds himself being guided by John Schott, "the gigantic half-breed, who went to the Barren Grounds with Caspar Whitney.... He seemed to have great respect for Whitney as a tramper, and talked much of the trip, evidently having forgotten his own shortcomings of the time." One cannot help wondering if this might have been because Whitney exaggerated Schott's shortcomings in print. At the same time, it does support at least some of

Whitney's claims of his own abilities, and it testifies to *Seton's* knowledge of Whitney's feats, as well as his assumption that his reading audience would immediately recognize Whitney's name; indeed, Schott rates a sketch illustration in Seton's book, captioned "Caspar Whitney's guide.")[27]

Arriving at Great Slave Lake, Whitney needs to find a group of native hunters willing to accompany him into the Barren Grounds. With the intercession of the HBC factor, who throws the company's weight behind the arrangements, Whitney manages to hire Beniah, the leader of the Dog-Rib Indians, and some of Beniah's men. Even Whitney yields grudging admiration to Beniah and yet that praise is still, at some level, about Whitney: "I was much pleased with Beniah for the pace he set. . . . Beniah was a plucky Indian, the pluckiest in the country. That was why I made such an effort to get him."[28]

They set off into the Barren Grounds. It's miserable, cold, hungry work. Finally, the musk-oxen are spotted—and, instead of hanging back to allow Whitney to stalk the animals, Beniah and his men heft their rifles and charge. Whitney is amazed but quickly recovers:

> I saw at once that it was every man for himself on this expedition, and if I got a musk-ox I should have to work for him. And then I settled grimly to the business of running. . . . Within about two miles I had caught up with the Indians. . . . In another mile I had worked my way through the stragglers. . . . It was going that would test the bottom of the well-fed, best-conditioned athlete; how it wore on a half-starved man may be imagined.[29]

If Whitney wants his musk-ox, he has to beat Beniah and his men to them, and that challenge both makes him "work" for his trophy and reveals him, even half-starved, as the equal of the college athletes he had covered in *Harper's*.

This race against the Indians occurs every time musk-oxen are sighted, and as the book continues two different stories emerge. One is the tale Whitney is telling, in which he is tested not only by the Barren Grounds and the challenge of stalking musk-ox but also by his guides. He explains their behavior in a series of comments on how it feels to have the "chance for a kill spoiled by the stupidity or viciousness of . . . Indians," but in the end they don't spoil it for him; he succeeds, outrunning them all, bagging his ox.[30] In framing events this way, Whitney creates a series of clear oppositions for the reader: self-control, will, and the white man's hunt, contrasted to stupidity, viciousness, and the Indian hunt.

There is another way of understanding what is happening, of course: that Whitney is in fact sponsoring an Indian hunt in midwinter. Beniah and the others appear to have seen this as a chance to bring home meat and skins—including the skins of fetal musk-ox, tremendously prized for what appears to have been their wicking qualities—with Whitney purchasing the privilege of going with them, underwriting their ammunition and supplies, and paying each man a fee in addition. Throughout the adventure they go to lengths to keep Whitney alive, but when it comes to the killing they don't appear to have understood themselves as employees who should stand back and let Whitney have the first shot. (It is very probable that what Whitney describes actually happened: the inhabitants around Great Slave Lake eventually acquired an international reputation for taking over the shooting on expeditions for which they were hired to serve as guides.[31])

Sponsoring an Indian hunt is not the story that Whitney is telling, however, and he negotiates the problem rhetorically, demoting the Indians' behavior to the level of viciousness while elevating himself to a tenuous command that he retains through force of will. In one telling incident, Whitney fears the group might be thinking of turning back (they have all the meat they need, but Whitney has not yet gotten the trophy head he wants). Whitney explains that he keeps them all going with a show of grit and determination that requires him to master his own feelings first: "Even greater than the pangs of hunger in my stomach was the constant dread in my mind that the Indians would become disheartened . . . and turn back. [So at camp] I sang . . . and tried to whistle, hoping by my actions to shame the Indians from showing failing courage. How little I felt like singing may be imagined."[32] Failing courage probably had little to do with it; generally, sportsmen's obsession with trophy heads seems to have been mystifying to subsistence hunters, and Whitney's desire to continue hunting in dangerous conditions would have made little sense to Beniah and the others. By framing it as an issue of courage, shame, heart, and will, however, Whitney repositions his readers' perception of the meaning of this moment, while offering a public performance of his mastery of himself and, in turn, his employees.

In the end, he bags his trophies and returns safely to Edmonton. "All things come to an end," Whitney writes, "and my Barren Ground trip, the hardest a man could make, had run its course. . . . [I] smoked my pipe in the contentment given by the satisfaction of knowing . . . that I had accomplished what I had been told I could not."[33] He had emerged from the trip with both trophies and a gripping tale. Rhetorically linking courage, self-mastery, hard work, perseverance, and the pioneer past, Whitney created a meaningful hunt out of a nonsensical venture, serialized it in *Harper's*, and then published it as a book with Harper and Brothers Press.

The book won Whitney lifelong renown as an explorer. Charles Sheldon described *Snow-shoes* as a "real sporting adventure successfully carried out," while the *New York Sun* informed readers that "the story is told in Mr. Whitney's manly, unpretentious, and straightforward style. Only a man of indomitable pluck could have gone through the ordeal and only a well-balanced man could have written about it so modestly."[34] The book was promoted at the bottom of Whitney's columns in *Harper's*, free advertising that also connected his exertions on the Barren Grounds to Whitney the sportswriter, to his claims that he had the right to judge manliness and self-control in others. Whitney had created a new identity that complemented his already established reputation as a promoter of amateurism, even as he redeemed his position as an undistinguished (to that point) member of the Boone and Crockett Club.

That was not the end of Whitney's musk-ox adventures, however, because as a writer and editor he would revisit the story. In 1904 he edited a series for Macmillan called the American Sportsman's Library. One of the books, *Musk-Ox, Bison, Sheep and Goat*, offered articles by Whitney on musk-ox, George Bird Grinnell on bison, and Owen Wister on mountain sheep and mountain goat. Here, Whitney bound himself between covers with two of the cream of the elite, and, while his story made an argument about what kind of hunter he was, the company he kept in the book made its own implicit statement about Whitney's authority and status.

That said, the story itself is worth attention, because "The Musk-Ox and Its Hunting" condenses *Snow-shoes* into a much-shortened and markedly different version. It opens with an chapter entitled "My First Kill," and here Whitney tells readers that he became worried that the Indians were going to turn back, disheartened, *before they even see musk-ox*, so "in my fear lest the Indians turn back, I sought to make light of our difficulties by breaking into song [hoping] to shame the Indians out of showing their desire to turn homeward. How little I felt like singing may be imagined."[35] We just saw this episode occurring in *Snow-shoes*, but long after the first kill, and much further north, after the Indians had already taken all the musk-ox they wanted. It is clearly a moment that Whitney thought was meaningful enough to retain, and yet one that is not tied to the actual chronology of the hunt. His courage, the Indians' failure of nerve, and his shaming of them tell readers something about Whitney himself that he thinks is worth repeating, even out of context. It's a stock piece, in other words—and, positioned here, it also helps quash any idea that this is the Indians' hunt, because now they aren't even interested in reaching the musk-ox.

All the more interesting to see how the hunt is now described:

> My preconceived notions of the musk-ox hunting game were in a jiffy jolted to the point of destruction. . . . It was natural to suppose some assistance would be given me in this strange environment, and that the consideration of a party of my own organizing and my own paying should be my killing the musk-ox for which I had come so long a distance. But we were a long way from the Post and interpreters and restraining influences. . . . I speedily realized that it was to be a survival of the fittest on this expedition, and if I got a musk-ox it would be of my own getting.[36]

Whitney sounds rather more bitter, considering it all ten years later. It's still not the Indians' hunt, though—now their actions are the result of a lack of "restraining influences"—while the fact that Whitney eventually gets his musk-ox becomes proof both of the triumph of will over instinct and of his position on the evolutionary scale.

Whitney then offers a different version of the chase than in *Snow-shoes*, where he left readers to imagine his feelings as he raced the Indians for his trophy. In this retelling, all the elements of will, courage, and perseverance that were present in the book are condensed into a passage that is worth rendering verbatim, since it also gives an idea of Whitney's narrative abilities when he hit full stride:

> I have done a deal of hunting in my life, over widely separated and trackless sections, and had my full share of hard trips; but never shall I forget the run along that ridge. It called for more heart and more strength than any situation I ever faced. Already I had run, I suppose, about five miles . . . and when the first enthusiasm had passed, it seemed as though I must give it up. Such fatigue I had never dreamed of. I have no idea how much farther I ran,—three or four more miles, likely,—but I do remember that after a time the fancy possessed me that those . . . musk-oxen and I were alone on earth, that they knew I was after their heads, and were luring me deep into a strange land to lose me; thus in the great silent land we raced grimly, with death trailing the steps of each. The dead-white surface reaching out before me without ending seemed to rise and fall as though I travelled

a rocking ship; and the snow and the rocks danced around my whirling head in a grinning, glistening maze. [Then I spotted the musk-ox.] Instantly the blood coursed through my veins and the mist cleared from my eyes; dropping on one knee I swung my rifle into position, but my hand was so tremulous and my heart thumped so heavily that the front sight wobbled all over the horizon. I realized that this might be the only shot I should get.... The agony of those few seconds I waited so as to steady my hand!.... At last the fore sight held true for an instant; and I pressed the trigger. The exultation of that moment when I saw one of the two musk-oxen stagger, and then fall, I know I shall never again experience.[37]

In this description, the kill is made meaningful by what leads up to it: very little space is given to the actual moment of death, with the passage focused on the test that it took to make the shot and what that says about Whitney. It takes heart, strength, and steadiness, and the exultation he feels is due to his own performance and what it means, not just because he has killed an animal. Nor is he the only hunter in this tale: Death stalks them both, as if Whitney must kill or be killed, as if some kind of equivalence is being drawn in that moment between predator and prey. And the Indians have vanished entirely, as Whitney and the musk-oxen are "alone on earth" in a "great silent land," a wilderness emptied and purified of everything but the hunter and the test that he faces.

This is all the room that Whitney gives to hunting; the rest of the article is devoted to descriptions of supplies and equipment, comments on other Barren Ground adventurers, and the natural history of the musk-ox itself. Into his description of only one hunting moment, then, Whitney boiled his entire adventure down into what he believed mattered most: his own fitness, the difficulty of the chase, and his battle with the land, the Indians, and the musk-oxen. The book was illustrated by the most famous of all big-game artists, Carl Rungius, who followed the spirit rather than the letter of Whitney's descriptions with his picture of an enormous musk-ox facing off against midget wolves on the ice (figure 5.1). Musk-ox are short, albeit bulky, and mild creatures; it's the getting-there that qualifies them as big game, and Rungius is drawing the *spirit* of that challenge, presenting readers with a dangerous landscape and a trophy that is proof of a man's prowess. This image worked well with the story Whitney was telling, even as the elements of "The Musk-Ox and Its Hunting" fit well with Wister and Grinnell's contributions to the book. We have already seen part of Wister's contribution,

Figure 5.1. Illustration by Carl Rungius, from Caspar Whitney, "The Musk-Ox and Its Hunting," in *Musk-Ox, Bison, Sheep and Goat*, 1904.

for his condemnation of the seamy side of masculinity is from this anthology as well; together, his, Grinnell's, and Whitney's tales offered readers all the varied elements of the sportsman-hunter discourse. *Musk-Ox, Bison, Sheep and Goat* also allowed Whitney to receive a new paycheck for rewriting an old story, as well as for editing the book in which it appeared.

In narrating and re-narrating his expedition, Whitney successfully combined the elements of the sportsman-hunter discourse, his position in the publishing industry, and his connections (and would-be connections) to the elite to create a web of meaning that fed back on and reinforced itself. Already possessed of both writing talent and a national limelight, Whitney used big-game hunting to further his social and professional ambitions. Telling this kind of story about himself was a deliberate choice, one that made sense in terms of who he was and who he wanted to be. It worked for him.

Those choices were clearly pragmatic, and that in turn raises the question of how internalized the sportsman-hunter discourse was for him. Whitney presents on paper as a classic opportunist, someone who never passed up a chance to make some money or climb the social ladder, and he certainly deployed the sportsman-hunter discourse deliberately and to his own advantage. Discourse happens in the head as well as on the page, however, and using something does not necessarily negate believing in it as well. Did Whitney believe in what he was writing or was it all just a show?

The answer, I think, is that he believed—and here we edge into a more psychological approach, one that holds many pitfalls for the historian and yet seems well supported in this case by Whitney's writing. I am thinking of a particularly famous example from his work, not on hunting, but on sport: because any historian of amateurism knows Whitney best as the man who once, in print, compared working-class athletes to "vermin."[38] This occurred in *A Sporting Pilgrimage*, in a passage in which Whitney was decrying the infiltration of professionals into amateur sport, and urging gentlemen to desert the Amateur Athletic Association and create a new, more restrictive organization. His actual words are, "Now there is nothing left for us but to abandon the bower planted in pride and nourished with such tender solicitude, and raise up another where experience will guard us against the vermin that have made this one uninhabitable."[39] Despite its having been widely cited, however, no one has ever noted that this is only one of a series of distressing images of corruption that pervade the book. The language of the sacred and the profane is everywhere in *A Sporting Pilgrimage*, ranging from the title itself, to such banal usages as "clean sport" opposed to the image of the "great unwashed," to a series of metaphors in which Whitney variously describes those sports that have been infiltrated by professionals as a gangrened limb that must be amputated to save the body; as a polluted sea in which the amateur is submerged, fighting helplessly against the current; and as the Edenic bower now victim to a verminous Fall.[40] This is a powerful series of images for a man whose will was constantly on display, being tested, being judged, and for whom one slip might mean expulsion from the community of character. The story of Eden's fall, after all, is a story not just of invasion from without but of personal weakness, and it is the succumbing of the amateur athlete to the temptation of "money, money, money" that haunts Whitney—the corruption of the inhabitants of the garden, the disease invading the body of the athlete, drowning him in filth as he struggles to retain, in Whitney's words, his "pristine purity."[41]

Nor was such writing anomalous: Whitney repeatedly linked the display of character to vivid images of corruption, personal loss, and failure. He urged readers to learn, above all else, "To say No to *yourself* with a big N": only through self-control could purity be preserved and boundaries drawn against the forces of corruption, whether those threatened from within or without the man of character.[42] Whitney made a career out of railing against such corruption in print, but it also appears that he feared it, was distressed by it, and was willing to risk his life to demonstrate his own pristine purity.

This last is something that may have been lost here, but should not be. Whitney was willing to die to prove his point. His trip to the Barren Grounds in winter was remarkably dangerous, nor were his later hunting adventures marked by a concern for his own safety. In Sumatra, he risked his life by stalking a man-eating tiger through dense vegetation. "To walk up a tiger is the most dangerous form of sport," he explains to readers, only appropriate for the hunter who can "keep cool under nerve-trying conditions."[43] Here again is evidence of Whitney's internalization of the discourse, a public display of his unyielding personal adherence to the rules. Recognizing that something is being deliberately used does not automatically imply a hidden alternate agenda. There is no reason to doubt that Whitney believed. And that belief would never be shaken, even as he continued to gather acclaim and audiences.

Following the success of *Snow-shoes*, Whitney returned to his column at *Harper's*, but his life was about to change dramatically because of two events following close on one another. The first was the advent of the Spanish-American War. Whitney went to Cuba as *Harper's* war correspondent, and while waiting for departure in Florida he managed to insert himself into the exclusive clique of reporters gathered around Richard Harding Davis. There seems to have been no small amount of social snobbery at work in the reporters' hierarchy, and Whitney may have been welcomed into Davis's clique partly because of his elite connections, but it couldn't have hurt that he sided with Davis during an unpleasant controversy with journalist Poultney Bigelow. Bigelow, a former owner of the magazine *Outing*, had publicly critiqued the army's disorganization and inefficiency, and Davis had attacked him in the *Herald*, calling him "un-American." Whitney quickly rallied *Harper's* to Davis's side, while defending the army as well-organized and efficient (which it certainly was not). The affair culminated in Tampa, where Bigelow had a public exchange of words with Davis, who was supported in turn by Whitney; it stopped short of a fistfight, but (one gets the impression) not by much. After that, there was no doubt of Whitney's place in the reporters' hierarchy, and he sailed to Cuba on Shafter's flagship with Davis rather than in the designated press boat. ("I would have died [of boredom]," Davis wrote to his family of the trip, "as it is the men are interesting on our boat.")[44]

During the war, Whitney distinguished himself at home for his zippy and flagrantly patriotic articles. He quickly became one of Roosevelt's favored reporters, his articles painting glowing pictures of the Rough Riders singing "Fair Harvard" in the trenches.[45] Nor was Whitney lacking in personal distinction. British military attaché Arthur Lee, describing the capture of El Caney, noted that "the first man into the fort was James Creelman, the well-known correspondent, and Caspar Whitney, carrying his entire personal effects, was not far behind."[46] (Creelman was shot, but recovered.) Correspondents charging ahead of soldiers into a fort was not unusual for the journalism of the day, in which reporters were expected to do as well as to observe; still, it cannot have harmed Whitney in the eyes of Roosevelt or other members of the elite. He had backed the claims he had made in *Snowshoes*: Whitney was willing to risk his life to practice what he preached. Davis, praising Whitney in an article in *Harper's*, made specific mention of his Barren Grounds exploits: "Caspar Whitney and John Fox were distinctly among the most earnest, honest, and brilliant [of the correspondents]. If each of them had not been well known before the war, one as a novelist, the other as an explorer, their conduct during it would have made their reputations."[47]

Whitney had emerged from the war with another aspect to his reputation, with his social connections only reinforced, and with a new area of authority that he could claim: patriotism, Americanism. He was still not financially independent, however; he might rub elbows with the Roosevelts of the world, but at the end of the war he had to return to his desk. He thus came back to *Harper's*, but this time it would only be temporary. Within less than a year, Whitney gave notice. He was moving up, to *Outing Magazine*, where he would be co-owner and sole editor. In the first decade of the new century, Whitney would lead the vanguard in speaking to American understandings of manliness, sportsmanship, primacy of the will, and the big-game hunting narrative.

On February 15, 1900, the *New York Times* published an announcement by Whitney informing readers that he, along with ten other men, had purchased the magazine *Outing*. His co-owners included Fletcher Harper (of the publishing house) and Robert Bacon (a renowned yachtsman and soon-to-be American ambassador to France). Whitney was going to be the editor, with the "intention of developing *Outing* to the utmost magazine limits in its especial field."[48] What he did not tell the *Times* was that he would receive $8,000 a year for his editorial work; financially, Whitney was moving up in the world.[49]

When Whitney and his partners took control of *Outing*, it was approaching its twentieth anniversary as a mass-market publication. During that time it had led a chameleonic existence. Launched in January 1882 as *Outing: A Journal of Recreation*, by 1884 it had absorbed a magazine, the *Wheelman*, devoted to bicycling, and briefly became *Outing and the Wheelman*, but in April 1885 it changed names again to *Outing: An Illustrated Monthly Magazine of Recreation*, which it remained until March 1906. In 1906 it widened its horizons to become the *Outing Magazine: The Outdoor Magazine of Human Interest*, and in 1913 morphed into *Outing: Sport, Adventure, Travel, Fiction*, which it remained until its demise in 1923. For sanity's sake, I will refer to it here simply as *Outing*.[50]

*Outing* had been founded in Albany in 1882 by William Bailey Howland, who would go on to be general manager of the *Outlook*. After its marriage to the *Wheelman*, it was purchased by Poultney Bigelow, a scion of the eastern establishment and a conservative of the first stripe. In 1925, Bigelow produced a two-volume memoir of his life, much of which was devoted to describing a Hibernian-Judaic conspiracy to take over America, a plan that only the Klan, Bigelow believed, could successfully oppose. Looking back from that context to his experience with *Outing* almost four decades earlier, Bigelow notes only that "when, for my sins, I foolishly founded [*sic*] a magazine of amateur sport

MR. CASPAR WHITNEY
Editor of *Outing*

Figure 5.2. Caspar Whitney as he appeared in Zona Gale's article "Editors of the Younger Generation," *Critic* 44 (April 1904).

in the city of New York [I discovered that] the day of amateur sport had not arrived—or was it that in me was too much amateur?" He explains that he would not demean himself by borrowing money to keep *Outing* afloat and walked away in 1885.[51] (That Bigelow would later face off in the almost-fistfight against Davis and Whitney once again illustrates what a small world the publishing industry was at this time.)

The magazine survived Bigelow's departure but continued to change hands, never quite financially solvent yet never quite going under, either. By the mid-1890s it had assumed a stable outward form: a monthly periodical, running around ninety pages and selling for a quarter, less than the cost of *Harper's* but still far above the cheaper and more plentiful dime magazine market.[52] (The higher price was probably a reflection of the tremendously restricted advertising; throughout most of its life, *Outing* only advertised on the inside of the front cover and both sides of the back cover.) Its contents, however, were best characterized as scattershot. The October 1894 issue, for example, contained an essay on observing squirrels while strolling in the woods; a letter from Szechuan, where *Outing*'s reporter-at-large, Frank Lenz, was bicycling around the world; an article on the naval militia and their pigeons; and a bittersweet serial love story, "Blank Cartridges" (in this episode, Olive returns Alsop de Camp's letters). This last may seem the most incongruous, but *Outing* carried at least one serialized story of love and sentiment in each issue, often historical (typical is "A Jamestown Romance," in which the virtuous orphan Lina West must choose between the "worthless [but handsome] Percy Lynn" and the responsible Geoffrey Dale). Missing from the magazine is any uniting voice or perspective; it is almost impossible to deduce the audience from the mishmash of articles; and, although having their own bicyclist cycling around the world caught some attention from the national press, once Lenz vanished somewhere in Armenia (probably murdered by bandits) *Outing* had no luck finding a replacement for him.[53]

Caspar Whitney transformed *Outing* completely. Outwardly it remained much the same—a twenty-five-cent monthly periodical, free of advertising on the inside pages—although Whitney lengthened it to almost 130 pages an issue and added copious illustrations (an average of twenty full-page photographs and seven pages of illustration, some in color). The content was what changed most dramatically under Whitney's control, however. From the moment he took over, the magazine had both a new and distinctive voice and a growing share of the market.

The Whitney *Outing* immediately revealed a sharpened interest in sportsmanship. The October 1900 issue contained a spread of sport that would not have been unusual in the pre-Whitney *Outing*: football, hunting woodcock, bicycling in Japan, shark fishing, and canoe racing. Sportsmanship, however, now received a good deal of attention: readers were reminded that "if one does not undertake shark-fishing in a sportsmanlike manner, there is very little sport in it . . . [shark must be] fished for with a recognition of what constitutes fair play," even as they were entertained by a hugely dramatic tale of a fisherman face-to-face with a monstrous man-eater like a "living guillotine."[54] The same issue carried an article decrying the planting of trout in

Michigan by the Fish Commission as endangering grayling, a piece of reporting that crossed the line between playing at sport and commenting on its politics.[55] The fiction also began to change under Whitney: the two fiction stories in this issue were "A Treason of Nature," about moose-calling luring the animal to his doom, and "The Lost Ball." This latter was a love story, but with a different flavor than "A Jamestown Romance": here Webster, a banker's son, is pitted in a golf tournament against Courtney Addison—"simply a mighty fine fellow"—for the love of Maxine; when Courtney slices to avoid hitting a child who has strayed onto the course, and Webster refuses to give him a do-over, Maxine's fine instincts of sportsmanship tell her which of the two is the real man.[56] Unlike its predecessors, "The Lost Ball" is actually about sport, at least tangentially—and also unlike them, it is told from the point of view, not of the woman, but of the golfer. This was the beginning of a trend that would intensify throughout the Whitney years: fiction told more and more often from the point of view of a man.

The other major change that Whitney made was the one that would define *Outing* for the next decade: the inception of his column the Sportsman's View-Point. Every month, in a series of short comments on different subjects, running from eight to fifteen pages, Whitney sat in judgment on the events of the American sporting and hunting worlds. Acerbic, concise, and eminently readable, the View-Point brought the voice that had defined *Harper's* into the pages of the floundering recreational magazine and marked it as Whitney's own. A wide range of subjects was covered in each View-Point: in October of 1900, for instance, its headings included "Shore Birds Need Protection; Uniformity in Close Seasons; The Market-Hunter Checked in Massachusetts; Death-Dealing 'Pump' Gun; Professional Trainers in University Athletics; American v. English Foxhounds; Success of Younger Element in Women's Golf Championship." Here he moved easily from bird protection to game legislation, and from market hunters and their weapons to professional influences in college sport. The final two subjects, foxhounds and women's golfing, may seem like outliers, but by including them Whitney was demonstrating a breadth of knowledge that further confirmed his right to pass judgment on the sporting world.

Those judgments were front and center during the years that Whitney wrote the View-Point. As he had in *Harper's*, in *Outing* he positioned himself as both the advocate and the policeman of amateurism, explaining the "right" way to understand performances on the playing field. He sternly condemned any who violated his standards, drawing on the language of the healthy and the sick so evident in earlier writing such as *A Sporting Pilgrimage*: in a 1903 View-Point, for example, under the heading "**Strange Microbe at Annapolis**," Whitney described how undergraduates were being poisoned "with the detestable microbe that makes for the professional spirit!"[57] And Whitney's attention or condemnation was sought after, at least by his readers. In 1907, when he ranked American colleges in rowing, he left Brown off the list due to what he regarded as the professional entanglements of the team, an explanation he offered only after receiving many letters from readers inquiring about the omission.[58]

Whitney did not confine his remarks to the world of amateur sport, however. His musk-ox adventure had given him authority as a big-game hunter, and *Outing* spoke to a readership whose interests extended far beyond the college playing field. Whitney took advantage of that to position himself as the policeman of sportsmanship in hunting as well, sometimes by calling on individuals to effect enforcement, sometimes by naming the offending clubs and threatening to expel them publicly from the community of sportsmen. In 1902, for instance, he told readers that several members of Quebec's prestigious Triton Fish and Game Club had reportedly engaged in snowcrusting moose. "[If the club members] allow those who engaged in this snow crusting to continue members of the club, we shall have to withdraw our respect," he declared. "The Triton club cannot rest under this stigma, for stigma it is and nothing less. There are too many good sportsmen among Canadians to permit such unsportsmanly conduct to go unpunished." In the same issue, he noted a report from Louisiana that three men had killed thirteen hundred ducks in forty-eight hours and asked, "Are there no sportsmen in Louisiana to bring to book such miserable pot hunters as these three[?]"[59]

In speaking to his readers this way, Whitney was participating in larger trends in both American culture and American publishing. Historian Christopher Wilson has shown that the publishing explosion was marked not just by expansion but also by fundamental changes in the periodicals themselves, driven by a cohort of men who were redefining the role of the editor in this era. These editors presented themselves to readers as experts in their fields, based on their personal experience and access to inside information, and imprinted their personalities on their publications.[60] Whitney was one of them. Like S. S. McClure and other prominent editor-publishers of this period, he both framed the terms through which his readers understood his subject and served as gatekeeper. The Whitney *Outing* was in fact a perfect example of what McClure described as the ideal modern magazine, one that "represents the ideas and principles of one man or a group of like-minded men" and "has a single purpose all through."[61]

This was a new way of conceiving both of periodicals and of the editor's role, and in the years after 1890 these more modern magazines surpassed older, more traditional journals both in circulation and in cultural status.[62] Environmental historians have tended to focus on foundational publications such as Grinnell's *Forest and Stream* as exemplars of the recreational media in this period, but that media was changing dramatically in the 1890s. *Forest and Stream* offers a useful contrast to *Outing* here: Grinnell's magazine, founded in 1873, was typically nineteenth century, its content made up of advertisements, letters and reports from readers, and the same jumble of disorganized one-paragraph news items that characterized many newspapers of the time. This meant that it never had a single consistent voice on any issue, and that includes hunting and conservation. While Grinnell himself consistently called for conservation in his editorial columns, his pleas were always bracketed by page after page of advertisements for weapons and taxidermists, by letters columns featuring debates over the terms of sportsmanship, and by reader contributions from unrepentant game hogs. One correspondent cheerfully explained, "Well, this 22nd day of September was not a bad day for snipe, a bag of 1,400 bay snipe in less than one day and a half's shooting to seven guns."[63]

Whitney's *Outing* presented no such ambiguity. Devoid of interior advertising, stamped by Whitney's voice, its content commissioned by him, and with readers' letters invisible unless mentioned by him in the View-Point, it presented readers with a single interpretation of the right way to play sports and to hunt. When reporter Zona Gale described him in the *Critic* as one of the most influential editors of the "younger generation," she was identifying more than just an age difference between him and editors like Grinnell. Whitney's *Outing*, and his role in shaping it, were recognizably products of the emerging twentieth century. Modeling his magazine far more on *McClure's* than on *Forest and Stream*, Whitney centered *Outing* around a consistent story line about himself, his readers, and the standards that should shape their behavior.

This is part of the reason that Whitney so quickly became the arbiter of standards for an international community of sportsmen and athletes. By following *Outing*'s lead, a hunter in Baton Rouge, Denver, or Montreal could learn about that community and identify himself with it through his own performance, for *Outing* gave him vital clues about how he should behave and what his actions could mean to himself and to others. At the same time, the lack of a letters column only increased Whitney's power by letting him control readers' perception of his authority. After all, what mattered most in terms of Whitney's influence wasn't so much whether sportsmen in the Triton Club really denounced their friends on his say-so, but whether *Outing*'s readers believed that they *might* have.

This self-appointed role as enforcer functioned to position Whitney as much as it did his victims, for, by identifying those who stood outside the lines of sportsmanship and amateurism, he was implying both that he stood within those lines and that he had the right to interpret and condemn the behavior of others. While Whitney unquestionably held the line against the working class, however, he remained as always most interested in policing his own.[64] "There are too many shooters . . . whose sportsmanship is a mere veneer, assumed at the club or where else sportsmen congregate," Whitney warned View-Point readers. "Such a man should be published, and I propose creating a selected and indexed list of this kind of creature."[65] Here he is offering once again to protect his readers from those among them who may appear to be of the right sort but are only mimicking the form. Whitney the policeman was also Whitney the protector, separating the wheat from the chaff among the middle- and upper-class men who were his intended audience, speaking to them about where and how to display and recognize manliness. Having proven his right to belong by hewing to the standards of amateurism and sportsmanship, Whitney turned around and offered those standards to every reader of *Outing Magazine* in the first decade of the twentieth century.

At the same time, *Outing* also proved accommodating to some other forms of storytelling and some other ways of viewing the wilds. The November 1901 issue shows writers experiencing the wilderness in a variety of ways, hunting bull moose in Ontario, deerstalking in Scotland, and even being attacked by grizzly bears, but also camping in peaceful forest groves and photographing the belted kingfisher, "one of the shyest of things which fly."[66] Even during Whitney's tenure there was no single way of going into the wilds, so long as one obeyed certain rules. One did not have to kill anything, but, if one did, it must be in a sportsmanlike manner; one did not have to endanger one's life, but, if one did, it should be seen as a chance to demonstrate grit, determination, and character. The mix of possibilities was thus bounded and yet open enough to draw in a variety of audiences. Hardcore sportsmen would be exposed to articles on nature photography, but by the same token middle-class subscribers interested in camping would find themselves reading stories of manly sport. The kingfisher was certainly charming, but who could resist pausing over "A Remarkable Adventure with Grizzly Bears"?

In the process, readers were being exposed to all the varied elements of the sportsman-hunter discourse. Authors might invoke race—Cameron Forbes, writing on college sport, explained to readers, "Football is the expression of the strength of the Anglo-Saxon. It is the dominant spirit of a dominant race"—or they could call on manliness and the West—Leonidas Hubbard compared "the dashing, sunburned stage-driver of the mountains with his sallow, red-nosed contemporary who stands in front of the Grand Central Depot. . . . As the one is to the other, so is wild Nature to an effete civilization. I look at this hardy fellow. . . . He is a man and he has my most profound respect."[67] Equally manly was Daniel Boone, whom Emerson Hough described to readers as the "apostle of adventure," worth knowing about as the "type of those far-off wonder days with which we are now so rapidly losing touch in our America."[68] *Outing* also sent out explorers: Dillon Wallace to Labrador, and Robert Dunn to climb volcanoes in the Aleutian Seas, where he dutifully recorded the temperatures of steam vents with his ever-present thermometer-on-a-wire.[69] *Outing*'s contributors came overwhelmingly from the same middle-class, native-born, Protestant background as Whitney and shared his need to work for a living. The stories they told reified the elements of the sportsman-hunter discourse and disseminated them to readers in a hundred different variations on a recognizable theme.

Having selected the sportsman-hunter's story as the one that would define him to others, Whitney retold that story for years to the reading public. He also continued to perform it by the strictest Boone and Crockett standards, and it was in his later adventures that his identities as editor and publisher, and as hunter and adventurer, melded most seamlessly. Those narratives hit many of the same notes as did *Snow-shoes* and "The Cougar"; what was new was the way he used his position at *Outing* to direct readers' interpretations of his experiences.

To begin with, *Outing* sponsored but also imposed limits on Whitney's later hunting trips. All his later adventures—a series of trips first to South America, then to Asia—were paid for by his position at *Outing*, serialized in *Outing*, and then published in book form. At the same time, many aspects of his trips were dictated (albeit invisibly) by his magazine work. His tales of hunting in South America are all set in the rainy season, with no explanation offered, but his private correspondence reveals that his publication schedule severely limited his opportunities to travel. Even squeezing out the brief trips he did entailed the sacrifice of one kind of business for another. His letters show him trying to outbid Macmillan for the rights to *White Fang* on the morning he sailed for Brazil; more ominously, while he was gone one of his authors attempted to jump ship to *Forest and Stream*, offering the justification that Whitney was out of the country.[70] No trace of these economic realities appear in published print of any kind, however. Like the gentleman he aspired to be, Whitney eschewed any public mention of actual paid labor, and that included the degree to which his job was both shaping and restricting his hunting adventures.

Those restrictions may also help to explain the choppy feel of his two later hunting travelogues, *Jungle Trails and Jungle People* and *The Flowing Road*, which were clearly assembled from stand-alone articles; *The Flowing Road* in particular ends rather anticlimactically, its penultimate chapter on tracking jaguar being followed by a finale in which Whitney solicited from every famous person he ever met "the one luxury you would bring with you into the jungle" (Charles Sheldon picked tea, Roosevelt dental floss, William Lord Smith a portable bathtub).[71] Despite this, the chapters were linked by Whitney's unyielding focus on sportsmanship and by his persistent inability to get along with his guides, a problem that culminated in an incident on the Orinoco River where "the men, who though engaged to take me up-river, persisted in going down-stream, and finally (when I refused to go farther in the direction opposed to my arrangements and desire) taking my canoe and provisions, abandoned me . . ."[72] Not all his adventures were successes.

Despite that, in 1905 Whitney decided to follow his failure to get upstream with a quest—one reminiscent of his adventure in *Snow-shoes*, but this time interpreted through his controlling position at *Outing*. The quest begins when Whitney decides to travel up the Orinoco, beyond the cataracts that mark the end of its navigable downstream portion, in an attempt to "discover" some Indians as yet unknown to white men. He tells us that his adventure begins "On the Threshold of the Mystic Land" that was "Lope de Aguirres' gateway to El Dorado! . . . fable and mystery still enshroud this head-water country. . . . One hears fearsome tales of this region . . . and no Indian will enter it. . . . To get beyond this barrier and have a look at the savages was the sole object of my trip to the upper waters of the Orinoco."[73] No one wants to go with Whitney, but he finally convinces Cristobal, a deserter from the Venezuelan Army, to accompany him. They portage around the cataracts and soon find themselves traveling through an eerie, unpopulated liminal zone, moving always by night—"for five days we rested and for six nights we paddled, with no indication of man or any of his works. But the works of the Almighty enveloped us."[74] On the sixth day Whitney hears a voice and seeks its source.

> The eager first glance was unrewarded; only a jungle-covered bank . . . greeted my eyes. Deliberate scrutiny, however, uncovered a small bay-like recess where . . . was a nude Indian evidently fishing. . . . I studied the Indian and his environment long and minutely with my glasses. . . . Abundant emotion stirred in me [at] the evidence he provided that my long journey was not to be unrewarded.[75]

Whitney's scrutiny reveals to him that the Indian wears his hair long, unlike Indians below the cataracts: he concludes that he has found a lost tribe, "so far as hair evidence went." Later, he climbs a tree and watches more Indians fishing, exulting in "this island adventure."[76] Having undertaken a long and difficult journey through a forbidden zone (much as he did on the Barren Grounds), Whitney fulfills his quest by mastering his own eagerness, locating the Indians through "deliberate scrutiny," and then recording them on the page, revealing them a second time to the reader. He seamlessly directs the interpretation of this moment in his text, but by 1905 he also had *Outing* to frame his readers' perceptions of his journey.

As Whitney's articles appeared (and as he vanished into the jungle), the View-Point continued to run under the hand of an anonymous junior editor, offering up ready-made interpretations of Whitney's jungle feats. The tale of the journey across the barrier into the mystic land "recalls necessarily Mr. Whitney's remarkable achievement on the Barren Grounds of the North," the View-Point reminds readers who might not have made the connection on their own.[77] The goal might be different, but the explorer's motive is the same, as *Outing* explains in the article "Exploring Unknown America": "This magazine has sent out [this expedition] as it has sent out others in the past, not only because it stands for the adventurous American, the man in whom remains, undying, the old-time pioneer spirit, but because as well it believes it is doing a valuable public service in explor[ation.]"[78] Whitney's journey is now about pioneer spirit, public service, and a certain kind of American man. It's also about a wilderness that can be tropical or Arctic as long as it's not much visited, and a goal that can be almost anything as long as it's difficult to achieve.

Even as Whitney leaves civilization behind and crosses the forbidden threshold, then, his twentieth-century magazine shapes the interpretation of his adventure. Why is Whitney going up the river? The View-Point has an answer: he realized that he could not "call the task [of traveling in South America] finished until he should have explored a region in which dwells an Indian race wholly unknown to white men."[79] Here Whitney, through the magazine that he co-owns and edits, is using his employees to write magazine articles about what it is that Whitney's *own* magazine articles mean. This is a discourse indeed: narratives about narratives about experiences, glosses on stories whose actual events are entirely unconfirmable.

It is an excellent illustration of the ways in which content and form, travel and publishing, the elements of discourse and the economics of the culture industry intersected to create the stories sold to a national audience. And those stories were remarkably successful. Although *Outing*'s circulation was less than twenty thousand when Whitney took the helm, he raised it to a paid circulation of one hundred thousand within five years.[80] Those readers wrote to Whitney, read about him in periodicals and newspapers, and paid attention to his column. They were left in no doubt of what their subscription meant. Circulation "interests me mainly in adding to the swelling numbers of those who believe in clean living and whose heart-beats quicken to the strains of the Star-Spangled Banner," Whitney told readers as he announced *Outing*'s approach to the hundred thousand mark. "Through the best of virile fiction . . . I seek to aid in the uplifting . . . of Americanism; through entertaining stories of adventure . . . and thoroughly practical articles . . . I hope first to win and then to help you to the enjoyment of whatever field you choose."[81] Other journalists appear to have agreed; Gale praised him for promoting the idea that the "real value [of outdoor sports] is not their joy; it is not even that they reveal character; it is that they build character . . . camping-out is [not just] the prime revealer of dispositions; it . . . is a maker of dispositions."[82] Her assessment of Whitney's importance as an editor also does not seem to have been exaggerated: decades later, compiling his *History of American Magazines*, Frank Luther Mott granted *Outing* a chapter of its own, concluding that it was "throughout a gentleman's outdoor magazine."[83] Whitney had shown in *Harper's* that he could write "like a gentleman and for gentlemen" about amateur sport. He used the same techniques to transform *Outing* into one of the premiere publications of its day.

His books also sold well, acclaimed by reviewers as "thrilling . . . stirring hunting adventure[s]" "delineated by a hand of masterly certainty."[84] Nor were they the only books he published. Through the Outing Publishing Company Whitney produced some of the most popular books of his era, ranging from Jack London's *White Fang* to Dillon Wallace's *The Long Labrador Trail* to Albert Bigelow Paine's gentle satire of all things outdoors, *The Tent Dwellers*. He also sent John Neihardt down the Missouri for *Harper's* and edited the prestigious American Sportsman's Library for Macmillan.

This circles back to Whitney's professional life, hidden behind the selfless rhetoric of the View-Point. His correspondence with authors reveals a different side of him, a combination of cajolery and confidence that mixed business with his own ideas about *Outing*'s importance. He talked dollars in his letters in a way he never did in print: luring Jack London to *Outing*, he promised that "we will show you a thing or two in advertising you and giving you extensive sales," while he assured Paine that "we are . . . in a position to talk turkey," offering him $200 an article and a 15 percent royalty on book sales.[85] Mixing constantly with the business talk, however, was Whitney's desire to belong. "Our kind of people" is a phrase that often appears in his letters. "You are our kind of people," he wrote to London at one point; in a different letter he told London that "you are our kind of people, and our readers are your kind of people."[86] He repeated the sentiment to Fernand Lungren: "What I want to do with The Outing Magazine is to have it expressive of our kind of people; your kind and my kind is The Outing Magazine kind, and you eminently are of our kind of people. Therefore I want you to think about it, and plan things for the magazine, and I will give you a definite commission." He added, rather wistfully, "Perhaps you and I might go somewhere on a trip . . ."[87] The combination of businessman and social climber was not always seamless. Members of the elite sometimes found themselves on the bad end of a contract deal with Whitney, while others seem to have found his personality grating: "Whitney makes me tired," Stewart Edward White wrote to Lungren at one point.[88] As *Outing*'s circulation and reputation grew, however, Whitney became impossible to ignore, and some of the most popular writers of the day were attracted to the high pay *Outing* was offering.[89] Whitney's ambition, his unflagging energy, and his ownership of *Outing* meant that by 1905 the musk-ox hunter had become a publishing nexus of his own. Even now, if you read anything about exploration, travel, or hunting from the turn-of-the-century periodical press, sooner rather than later you will find yourself reading something that Whitney influenced.

Nor was it only in circulation numbers that Whitney's work paid off: he also achieved the social standing that he longed for. Through *Outing* he became the public voice of the hunter elite: when William Hornaday launched an appeal for donations to a national Head and Horns Collection, or when Frederick Selous decided to publicize the gratuitous slaughter of caribou in

Newfoundland, Whitney was the man to whom they turned.[90] He also became a prominent member of the Explorers Club and in 1905 was invited to be an honored guest at the annual meeting of the Canadian Club, an elite group that met once a year to dine on peculiar fare from the farthest reaches of the globe (that year Whitney would have been served spiral-eared polar mice specially caught by Commander Robert Peary).[91] The performance of Whitney the explorer, sportsman, and social climber was never separable from the hard work of Whitney the editor and publisher.

Whitney's social ambitions and his early experiences at *Harper's* had led him to embrace the sportsman-hunter narrative, and by doing so he had built a national reputation both as a hunter and explorer and as a friend and confidant of the social elite. His personal decision to identify himself to others through the still-hunt highlights the appeal that the sportsman-hunter discourse could have for a member of the middle class, hopeful of better. His choice had ramifications far beyond the personal, however, as, having adopted that discourse as his own, he then spent decades disseminating it to hundreds of thousands of readers through the periodical press, as well as in the dozens of books he edited for Macmillan or produced through the Outing Publishing Company. His influential position at the center of the publishing explosion is the reason that Whitney's embrace of the still-hunt *mattered*.

By 1908, Whitney was riding high, but his association with *Outing* did not survive the year. At this distance, it is difficult to see exactly what happened, except that it was clearly a time of personal and financial crisis in Whitney's life. His wife, Cora, divorced him that year. 1909 began with Whitney leaving *Outing*, which was foundering in severe financial difficulties. This does not appear to have been a problem of circulation but rather of financial incompetence on the part of the owners. The magazine would eventually survive, but it defaulted on loans that in turn brought down a private bank and the Binghamton Trust Company in the same year. Eventually Whitney, entangled with some of those debts, declared personal bankruptcy as well.[92]

1908 thus shows Whitney falling, but within a year he had landed on his feet. Within some six months of his divorce he married the tremendously wealthy and vivacious Florence Canfield, some fifteen years his junior, and was hired by the popular middle-class periodical *Collier's* to write a column, "Outdoor America."[93] His first column was entitled "What We Stand For." "America, getting into the open, demands recognition and needs interpretation," Whitney told his new audience, and then proceeded to offer both, at length. He enthused about camping, noted that sports for young men built courage "to play the game, and courage to play fair, whether in the wilderness or on the playground or in the office," and concluded that "OUTDOOR AMERICA [calls on you] to play like a gentleman—which means, like a sportsman ... be a man, win or lose."[94] Same song, new showcase; Whitney never missed a note.

In later years he would edit *Recreation*, distinguish himself on the American Olympic Committee, report from the front lines of the Great War, and be decorated by both the French and Belgian governments for his work with the relief effort headed by Herbert Hoover. On his death (in bed, from pneumonia), his obituary in the *New York Times* summed it up: "Caspar Whitney, 64, Explorer, Is Dead; Author and Editor Had Visited Many Far Places and Written of His Quest; An Outdoor Authority; Long Headed Outing Magazine and Recreation—Correspondent in Two Wars."[95] Unmentioned was the size of Whitney's estate: $300,000 left to Florence. Whitney died rich.[96] The *Times* hit every other relevant note, though: the hard-earned reputation as an explorer and traveler, the patriotic service, the claims to expertise in the worlds of hunting and sport, and the wide-flung work in the national media. These elements came together in Whitney's life. Together, they illustrate one way in which the sportsman-hunter discourse could find a place in the life of an individual, and in the life of a nation of middle-class readers seeking to understand the changing world in which they found themselves.

# Part Two
# Fellow Travelers

CHAPTER 6

# Diana's Own
## Women and the Big-Game Hunt

*The story shall be chang'd;*
*Apollo flies, and Daphne holds the chase*
   —A Midsummer Night's Dream

*I shall pass over the guns with the bare mention that I use a*
*30.30 Winchester, smokeless.*
   —Grace Seton, 1900

Women were also sportsmen.

That simple statement has a freighted history. For a long time, the image of men as sportsmen and of women as excluded from the hunt has been part of both American culture and American historiography. Women had always hunted, played at sport, and entered the wilderness, however, and they were doing so in increasing numbers at the end of the nineteenth century.[1] While they seldom engaged in still-hunting, they established substantial presences in sports such as fly-fishing, trapshooting, and exhibition shooting. Nor were they absent from the recreational media: *Forest and Stream* introduced a Ladies Department in 1877, and when *Field and Stream* was launched in 1895 it almost immediately began running a Modern Diana column on women's sport.[2]

This meant that women were part of the experience of recreation and the wilds, both for men in the field and for readers of recreational periodicals. *Outing* carried "virile fiction" but also articles by women such as Agnes Laut (who wrote a series on trapping in 1901) and Annie Peck (official US delegate to the 1900 International Congress of Alpinists). Many of those articles were specifically aimed at female readers. Peck encourages women to try mountaineering or at least mountain trekking—"Many ladies, English, German,

137

even French . . . climb high mountains with their husbands, and many, who have none, without; while many more tramp over easy passes and small mountains"—while warning them, especially if climbing, to avoid wearing a corset.[3] Less robust, but more typical of women's writing in *Outing*, is an article on canoeing by Lesley Peabody: she advises her female reader never to let a man do all the paddling, noting that "to me, being told to sit still and enjoy myself is logically incompatible," and describes a solo experience in which "I was alone in the tangled depths exploring old, old water, heavy with the years. My identity was big and supreme."[4] Women also appeared in fictional stories such as "The Transformation of Arline Baird," in which an insufferable prig of a little girl is turned into a happy child by being allowed to play in the mud and beat the boys at tree climbing.[5] These articles co-existed peaceably with stories in which men proved themselves in the wilderness, and Whitney, throughout his career, encouraged women's participation in sports and gave them coverage in the View-Point. This indicates that there were women readers who were interested in the magazine, or at least that the male readership was unthreatened by women urging other women to climb mountains, take off alone in canoes, and discard their corsets.

This view of women canoeing, trekking, and tree climbing sits oddly with some of the historiography related to gender in the Progressive Era. Some feminist scholars have claimed that there were only a few women adventurers in this era, and that they were overwhelmingly spinsters or widows, women who had in one way or another escaped the shackles of marriage.[6] Some historians of masculinity have also assumed that the wilderness was empty of women, based on two assumptions. One is that, if men were going into the woods to rediscover their manliness, then they must have been, to some extent, fleeing women (this in turn requires the woods to be female-free). The other assumption is that there was in fact something manly about going into the woods at all, something inherently linked to male identity.[7] Together, these assumptions have constructed an image of the wilds as somewhere women were not—a place defined by an absence.

Men hardly found the wilds empty of women, however. They were there, canoeing, camping, and traveling, and writing about their experiences. This was partly for the same reasons that more men were doing those things in this era—changes to transportation, increased access to wild places, and the emergence of tourist economies that assisted those seeking wilderness adventure—but there seems to have been social acceptance and even family expectations at work as well. Mary Sharples Schaffer offers an example of how one woman in this period became involved with wilderness travel. The daughter of a wealthy Philadelphia family, Sharples originally went west at the urging of her friend Mary Vaux, who had traveled extensively with her father and brothers to make annual measurements of glacier movement in British Columbia. The Vaux family took Sharples to Canada and there she met botanist Charles Shaffer; the two married in 1891 and spent over a decade exploring the Canadian Rockies together before he died of a heart attack in 1903. After being widowed, Mary Schaffer continued her travels, now with her friend Molly Adams, and began writing about her experiences (her work proved so popular that in 1910 the Geological Survey of Canada asked Schaffer to visit Maligne Lake, hoping that her fame would help advertise the region).[8] Nor were Adams and Schaffer the only women in the wilderness. At one point on a trip deep in the Canadian Rockies, the two women were pleasantly surprised by a visit from a "charming little English lady who was out on an entomological expedition."[9] Even a remote Canadian lake proves to have at least three women camping on its shores. This view of the wilderness hardly accords with the idea of the woods as a female-free retreat for threatened men, nor with images of women as confined at home by male relatives and only set free to travel upon widowhood: both Vaux and Sharples began traveling in the company of male relatives. These women are not separable from the community and experiences of men but rather are part of an entire class that found itself traveling, exploring, and writing about it during this period.

When women big-game hunters took to the field, then, they were pursuing their sport in wild areas populated, in part, by other women. This offers the beginnings of a context in which to place these Dianas. The term was an immensely popular one for women hunters in this period and ranged from the title of the Modern Diana column, to Agnes Herbert's popular hunting memoirs *Two Dianas in Somaliland* and *Two Dianas in Alaska*, to Prentiss Gray's amused caption on a picture of his wife in camp: "Laura Sherman Gray, center, makes plans to hunt elk. Guides think she is the Goddess Diana."[10] As this last example indicates, there is a final part of the context that needs to be put into place: men. Women who went hunting did so most often with their husbands, fathers, or brothers.[11] When we look for women who hunted, the first place we find them is in the narratives of male sportsmen-hunters.

Women are quite simply everywhere in men's narratives. They appear in the accounts of husbands or fathers whom they accompanied on trips to Africa, the Caucasus, Norway, and the Canadian Rockies; they show up in photographs, such as those of Lord Delamere's African safari; and they even make it into an odd little collection of British songs celebrating the sport of pig-sticking, where Mrs. G sounds as if she rather enjoyed hunting wild boar with a spear: "Brave Mrs. G on trappy ground/Got on him first, and G/Followed in dread, being sure that now/A widower he'd be./She gave a real good spear, and then/That gallant pig he fought . . ."[12] In fact, among the English in particular, and in India especially, wives posted with their army officer husbands pursued shooting, riding, and pig-sticking with notable enthusiasm. Their trophies appeared in the standard book on shooting, *Rowland Ward's Records of Big Game*, and having a wife who did not participate in sport was sometimes considered a strike against her husband in the jockeying for promotion and position among officers.[13]

The British were hardly unique, however, for American male hunters were also often accompanied by their wives. Charles Sheldon, Dall DeWeese, Prentiss Gray, and Carl Akeley were among those men who traveled with a hunting spouse, while explorer Robert Peary's wife, Josephine, accompanied him for a year in the Arctic, and yeast magnate Max Fleischmann's sister Bettie Holmes went with him on a hunting trip to Norway. Perhaps even more remarkable (in terms of our expectations) is that their presence was taken for granted. I have yet to find a sportsman-hunter whose wife accompanied him who felt that he needed to offer a justification for it or who presented her in any other than positive terms. DeWeese, writing to Roosevelt about his 1899 hunting trip to Alaska, noted simply that he had brought his wife with him because he "wanted her to see what had at that time never before been a woman's pleasure . . . myself, wife and party killed four [mountain] sheep, two of which were killed by my wife."[14] Sheldon cited a similar reason for taking his bride, Louisa Gulliver, on honeymoon to the Queen Charlotte Islands: she had never hunted before, and he wanted her to have the experience of stalking and shooting a bear. It rained on them for forty straight days. Sheldon describes how his wife slogged without complaint through swamps and rapids, and at one point was almost swept out to sea as she lost her footing while crossing a river; she managed to keep her rifle above water, though, and displayed it proudly to Charles when he hauled her safely to shore. In addition, he notes, she turned out to be "perfectly cool, even more so than most men," when dealing with bear.[15] While DeWeese and Sheldon are among the few who explain why their wives are with them, such partnerships were common enough that, in 1914, guide Andrew Berg wrote to the governor of

Alaska, wondering whether the rule of one guide for each hunter in the party applied to married couples hoping to bag a trophy together.[16]

These women matched the social profile of their male counterparts: in America, white, middle- or upper-class, native-born Protestants, or, in the British case, white women from the middle and upper tiers of society. They traveled where their husbands did, hunted with them, explored with them, and went on safari with them. This meant that women were part of the sportsman-hunter's experience of the landscape, and that those women who did travel alone were often visiting places where other women of their class and background were or had recently been.

Women were thus present in the wilderness—and, of course, that's only counting the women whose social profile matched that of the sportsmen-hunters. There were also women living in the places sportsmen visited. In North America indigenous or mixed-race women could often be encountered at the Hudson Bay Company posts, while in the early days of the safari African women sometimes joined hunters' entourages, either accompanying their husbands or for safety in traveling from one region to another.[17] Local women must also sometimes have given hunters advice and assistance, although descriptions are rare in the narratives; William Baillie-Grohman offers an account of the intrepid Austrian cleaning woman Moidl, who, after listening to a hunter complaining that he couldn't approach chamois successfully, rose before dawn and made her way upwind of the elusive animals to drive them down toward him.[18] And some local women seem to have had extended contact with big-game hunters. Charles Sheldon was traveling upriver in the Yukon when he struck up an acquaintance with a "young English trapper" named Hosfall and his mixed-race wife. Sheldon's praise of her skills gives the impression that he came to know her well: he notes that she could hunt and shoot "as well as most experienced white men" while being able to "cook even better than most white women" and describes her as both "beloved" and "absolutely respected" by the white men who met her. For her part, Mrs. Hosfall gave him the "fine large skull" of a male otter, which he considered interesting enough to forward to the Biological Survey in Washington.[19]

Looking at the narratives, then, we find women both traveling to hunt and present in some hunting grounds already, and that raises two questions. The first is a question for this book: why segregate women in their own chapter? The second goes to the historiography, for, if women hunted, and often hunted with men, why has the scholarship so often represented women as either absent from the wilderness, or as needing to be single or widowed in order to go there?

These two questions have the same answer, which lies in women's big-game hunting narratives. The second question can be answered first: compared to their numbers, very few women who traveled this way seem to have *published*. Moreover, single women appear to have been more likely than married women to publish in relation to their overall numbers (while far more married than single women hunted, narratives by women tend to be split almost fifty-fifty between the two groups). This disproportionate representation of single women's published narratives may have offered historians a misleading image of who was going hunting, one that seems to link freedom from marriage with the likelihood of entering the wilderness, and that conceals the many wives who accompanied their husbands in the field without feeling the need to write narratives about their experiences.

Why did so few women publish in comparison to the number of male hunter-writers? That question is very difficult to answer from this distance. Since the production of a hunting narrative was itself a cultural artifact rather than an inevitable result of choosing to go hunting, it is possible that not all women hunters bought into the idea of publishing as a form of display. The obverse of that, however—that some women apparently accepted the connections between hunting and publishing—only makes those narratives that were published by women more interesting.

This also explains why women hunters and their narratives have their own chapter here, for, while women and men often shared the experiences of hunting and of wilderness travel, women's hunting *narratives* differed from men's in some important ways. The majority of women's hunting narratives appeared after 1900, roughly two decades after Van Dyke published *The Still-Hunter*, and so women seeking to describe their hunting experiences in print did so in the presence of a well-established discourse that associated the stalk with work, hardship, and manliness. That discourse would at first glance seem to preclude women from adopting the mantle of the still-hunter, and yet it did not—neither in practice in the field, nor on the printed page. At the same time, though, women's narratives do not conform perfectly to the original sportsman-hunter discourse. They tell a different story from that of men.

I want to focus mainly on two women hunters and their most popular narratives—Grace Gallatin Seton's *Nimrod's Wife* and *A Woman Tenderfoot*, and Agnes Herbert's *Two Dianas in Somaliland*—and consider them alongside examples from other women explorers and hunters, in particular Josephine Peary and her popular *My Arctic Journal*. These three women had class and race in common, but not circumstance or nationality. Agnes Herbert, a wealthy Englishwoman from the Isle of Man, began hunting big game after she was widowed, accompanied by her cousin Cecily Baird.[20] Together the two women hunted in the Rockies, undertook an extended safari in Somaliland, and then, with two male companions, went on a shooting trip to Alaska. American Grace Gallatin Seton was the wife of famed naturalist and author Ernest Thompson Seton; her books describe her adventures camping and horsepacking with him in the American West. Peary's *Journal* describes the year she spent in Greenland with her husband Robert and his team, which included both Matthew Henson and Frederick Cook, overwintering in order to make a Farthest North attempt in the spring.

These women are representative of female big-game hunters in many ways, but the very fact that they chose to write and publish narratives makes them anomalous among women who hunted. Their books are thus by definition atypical, but that does not mean that they had little influence. On the contrary, all these books were extremely popular. Seton's books were widely read and often appeared on "recommended reading" lists for male and female readers.[21] Herbert's safari account was praised on both sides of the Atlantic, the *New York Times* lauding it as "vividly described and very exciting" while the English *Spectator* described her as "the most genuine of sportsmen."[22] Sheldon singled out *My Arctic Journal* for its descriptions of hunting, and it enjoyed numerous reprints and remains in print today.[23] Popular with both women and men, these works may have been among the most read of big-game hunting narratives. Examining them closely reveals alternate connections among ideas of primacy of the will, gender, and the meaning of the hunt—connections that were apparently as acceptable to reviewers and to the reading public as those drawn by Van Dyke or Whitney.

Like men's narratives, women's hunting stories centered around the primacy of the will. This may at first seem counterintuitive, since that ideal had traditionally been connected both to performance in the workplace and to other characteristics associated with manliness—and every time those characteristics were called "the virile virtues," the rhetoric of willpower became more clearly gendered male. That connection was unstable, however, since willpower could also be demonstrated through sportsmanship, or through the controlled stalk of a dangerous animal. Moreover, primacy of the will was not only a male virtue. In turn-of-the-century America, women, too, could possess and demonstrate primacy of the will.

That ultimate self-mastery was not a quality that women were simply assumed to possess, however, and throughout the nineteenth century much of women's exclusion from public life was founded on beliefs in their inability to control themselves and their passions. But primacy of the will was not a given for men, either, rather a virtue gained and preserved through constant exercise, and, since its proof was in its demonstration, it was in theory possible for women to demonstrate willpower. As long as primacy of the will was mainly demonstrated in the workplace, however—and as long as success in that workplace was simply read backward as connoting the possession of willpower—women were largely excluded from taking part in such demonstrations. Moreover, the prevailing rhetoric of womanliness implied that they had little need for the will. Unlike men, their bodies and minds were not supposed to be battlegrounds of roiling passions. Instead, the Victorian ideal was of a woman sheltered and innocent, virtuous because of a lack of exposure to temptation, not due to an exercise of mental fortitude.[24]

By the late nineteenth century, however, a growing number of exceptions were beginning to test this rule: after all, it was only a small step of interpretation from a woman who was too pure to be subject to temptation to a woman whose self-control was so highly perfected that she simply shrugged it off. This conception of women's will seems to have gained in popularity in step with women's growing participation in recreational activities, lending itself to parallels between strengthening the body and developing willpower, and by the turn of the century stories of women attaining primacy of the will were appearing in popular magazines. In the short story "The Restoration of Helen," which appeared in *Outing* in 1906, Helen is a frumpy woman given to extravagant emotional displays, always weeping, clinging, and wailing; when her husband leaves her to study art in the big city, she collapses in despair. Her brother comes to Helen's aid, taking her running every day and encouraging her to work out with a punching bag. When her husband returns, he is amazed by Helen's new energy and attractiveness and approaches her, expecting her to fling herself into his arms. Instead, Helen turns away in silence: "her hardly won restraint had a strength that was new."[25] Her husband becomes jealous and uncertain of her love, and vows to give up the city and return to her. Here, Helen's physical training has helped her to develop self-restraint, and it is her control over her emotions that ultimately gives her control over her husband. Helen's goal, of course, is not political or economic power, but a better marriage, and this is also typical of how women's willpower was presented in such tales: as laudable and attainable, but directed toward success in the traditional areas of love and family.[26] Nevertheless, the story divorces both athleticism and emotional control from the rhetoric of manliness, nor would every woman writer feel the need to confine her display of willpower to the family sphere. Women big-game hunters, in particular, used the primacy of the will to claim status in the field.

Both Grace Seton and Agnes Herbert presented their experiences as meaningful in terms of self-mastery and the will. For that to work, those terms needed to be disconnected from the rhetoric of manliness, and in their narratives the women offer two alternate ways of imagining the role of the will in hunting. The first, most clearly articulated in Seton, is one in which the primacy of the will is presented as an internal struggle. Rather than battling animals and the landscape, the hunter's struggles in these narratives are with *herself*, following a pattern in which she is repeatedly filled with fear, overcomes it through an exercise of will, and emerges triumphant. The second, characteristic of Herbert, adopts the male sportsman-hunter's description of primacy of the will wholeheartedly but adapts it to a woman's point of view. In both types of writing the invocation of willpower remains central; seeking meaning for their hunting, these women drew on the still-hunter's valorization of self-mastery rather than striking out in an entirely new direction. At the same time, their use of the will was always tempered by a consciousness of gender, not only on the part of the hunter herself, but also as addressed to her reading audience. These hunters explicitly discussed the meaning of the will for *women* as they made meaning out of their hunts.

The first dynamic—of personal fear confronted and controlled—is perhaps the most common among women's narratives and powers both of Grace Seton's best-selling books. Seton repeatedly has to face down her own conviction that she cannot succeed—often, that she cannot succeed specifically because she is a woman—only to discover that, by controlling her fear, she controls the situation. At one point in *A Woman Tenderfoot*, she is crossing a mountain pass in the snow, trusting to her husband to pick out the safest way, when suddenly he is thrown from his horse and lies unmoving. "I could have screamed aloud; a great wave of soul destroying fear encompassed me—wild black fear. . . . For an instant I could not move. . . . But here was an emergency where I could do something besides blindly follow another's lead. I caught the frightened animal as it dashed out of the treacherous place . . . and [my husband] quickly recovered."[27] This dynamic appears again when she's about to participate in a roundup—"to be honest, I was exquisitely scared. Why scared? It is not for me to explain a woman's dread of the unknown and untried"—and presents itself in a different form in *Nimrod's Wife*, as she talks herself out of her own doubt as she faces a bear—"How the glory of it would ring down through the family annals.... Could I do it? For the sake of my descendants, I must try."[28] She tries, with both the bear and the roundup, and she masters them after first mastering herself. As her story unfolds, she learns and grows through these experiences, and at the conclusion of *A Woman Tenderfoot* she presents her narrative as outlining a personal journey that has changed her forever:

> I have pored in the morning over the big round footprints of a mountain lion where he had sneaked in hours of darkness, past my saddle pillowed head. I have hunted much, and killed a little, the wary, the beautiful, the fleet-footed big game. I have driven a four-in-hand over corduroy roads and ridden horseback over the pathless vasty wilds of the continent's backbone.... I know what it means to be a miner and a cowboy, and have risked my life when need be, *but*, best of all, I have felt the charm of the glorious freedom, the quick rushing blood, the bounding motion, of the wild life, the joy of the living and of the doing.... In short, though I am still a woman and may be tender, I am a Woman Tenderfoot no longer.[29]

Seton claims the experiences and virtues of both genders—she knows what it means to be a cowboy, and she is still a tender woman—and in claiming them she is transformed. This dynamic is markedly different from that in men's narratives, where the display of will reveals what already existed inside and is seldom presented as a journey from fear to courage. Instead, Seton's victory over her fears leads to her self-realization as a hunter and wilderness traveler.

This pattern of internal struggle is not unique to Seton. Mary Schaffer forces self-control on herself when, snow-blind, she faces a choice between a terrifying ride across a treacherous pass to a waiting food cache or making the entire party wait an extra day in camp while she recovers: "I confess to a huge lump in the throat ... but to whimper over a pair of eyes seemed weak indeed, with hunger as an alternative for the crowd. So there was nothing to do but to crawl up in the saddle and trust to getting down whole again."[30] This type of internal dialogue between fear and will gives these books an intimate and accessible feeling. That may have been a deliberate choice by the authors as they sought to connect with a female audience, inviting readers with no experience of horse trekking or bear shooting to imagine their feelings were they in the author's place, and to participate in her emotional journey toward confidence and mastery.

Agnes Herbert, on the other hand, offers a very different set of connections among being a woman, hunting, and the will. She suffers no self-doubt in print and her willpower is demonstrated primarily by the sportsmanlike stalk and the clean kill. Her cool under fire is unassailable. At one point, she is attacked by a lion, who claws at her legs as her cousin Cecily Baird runs up and shoots him point-blank; Herbert manages to say, "He will just do for that space in the billiard room," before she passes out. Facing the page bearing this account is a portrait of Baird in a gown, wearing a necklace, her hair swept up, the perfect Edwardian lady: hard to see, in that picture, the woman who, after bagging her first rhino, "had a great gash on her wrist . . . and the blood was running down her rifle. . . . She was too excited to speak, and there was no calming her down . . . I announced to her solemnly it was to be our last rhino shoot. The tension relaxed then, and she laughed at my serious face."[31] Coolness, courage, and the discipline to overcome the excitement of the hunt are all central to Herbert's depiction of willpower, and any display of sentiment is placed in that context. At one point Baird cries four tears, binding up Herbert's wrist (gashed open by an antelope's horns), "and I think four tears are allowable—I mean without showing any sort of cowardice or lack of courage—don't you?"[32]

Primacy of the will is on clear display here. At the same time, Herbert remains ever-conscious of her gender, constantly reminding readers that her demonstration is that of a woman, not a man. She frowns at her gunbearer when he urges her to kill a lioness with cubs, noting that "surely he had learned by this time that even a woman can be sporting," and attributes her fear of failing in front of her guides on the first day's shooting to her gender: "This is a woman all over. Try as she will she cannot rise superior to Public Opinion—even the opinion of a crowd of ignorant Somalis!"[33] Herbert, of course, performs superbly, and yet this is a markedly different dynamic than Seton's internal struggle: Herbert laughs at herself for her insecurity, but she never invites the reader to join her in doubt over whether she'll succeed.

In all these narratives the will continues to give the hunt its central meaning, even as it is disconnected from manliness and the virile virtues. Interestingly, men as well as women seem to have been willing to accept women's hunting in these terms. When Sheldon discusses his wife's coolness while bear hunting, or the *Spectator* calls Herbert a "sportsman," the language is identical to that used to praise men. Major Charles Radclyffe, hunting with Herbert and Baird in Alaska, watches the two women stalking walrus on a beach; Herbert bags her animal, but Baird holds fire as the rest of the herd rushes toward the water, unwilling to risk wounding a walrus that she might not be able to recover. He tells readers that he was struck by admiration, not only of the women's "well-planned stalk [involving a] long and arduous crawling process," but of Baird's restraint: "What force of will-power it required on her part to refrain from firing . . . she alone can tell, but it is on record in our memory to her everlasting credit that she did so."[34]

Despite men's willingness to praise women's sportsmanship in terms that could apply to either sex, however, women big-game hunters almost always presented their own experience as one defined by gender. For all these women the fact that they *are* women is part of the story they're telling, as meaningful and essential to the structure of their narratives as manliness is for men. Whether reading Seton's airy reassurance that she packed everything from "the essential powderpuff in my saddlebag to the unimportant food and bedding," or Herbert's acid observation that "I think steamer-travelling is most enjoyable—that is, unless one happens to be married, in which case there is no pleasure in it, or in much else for the matter of that," the story is always being told by a gendered narrator who constructs meaning for her performance partly by insisting that the lens placed before us shows a woman's point of view.[35] And the audience is constructed differently from that in men's narratives as well; there is often an assumption, implicit or explicit, that the reader is female. This is clearest in Seton's writing, where she offers advice and asides to "the-woman-who-goes-hunting-with-her-husband," even as she claims that identity for herself.[36]

It was not only the manly virtues that were disconnected from hunting in these narratives, however. Hunting as strenuous work simply vanishes in the writing of women. Instead, their experiences are almost always described in terms of leisure: the final line of Schaffer's *Old Indian Trails in the Rocky Mountains* is "*The last day's play was done!*"[37] Accompanying this is a dismissal of the pioneer past, no longer necessary to make leisured hunting into productive work; instead, women hunters consistently present their wilderness adventures as enjoyable escapes from domestic duties. Seton urges her readers to remember that they are not in the wilds to work: "Dear woman who goes hunting with her husband, be sure that you have it understood that you do no cooking, or dish washing. . . . You are taking a vacation."[38]

More than chores are being left behind by these women, however: so are other social expectations. Seton frames hunting as a release from the stifling life of high society, urging her reader to leave "the usual walk, the usual drive, the usual hop, the usual novel, the usual scandal,—in a word, the continual consciousness of self as related to dress, to manners, to position. . . . Do you not get enough of such life? . . . Enough; come with me and learn how to be vulgarly robust."[39] Such language marks a dramatic difference between women's narratives and men's. For Owen Wister and Caspar Whitney, the wilderness is a place for man's work and for getting in touch with the pioneer past, but they rarely celebrate being free of their houses, their friends, or social expectations in general. Nowhere in men's writing is there an equivalent to Herbert's fierce, exultant description of Somaliland:

> What a glorious country! Convention spelt with a little *c*, and originality—that most excellent of things—everywhere rife. No running of jungle affairs on the deadly tram-lines of tradition, and everything new looked on askance. Mrs. Grundy does not live in the wild. . . . Doesn't she regard originality very much in the light of a magazine of combustibles, and take care to lose all the match-boxes? But I—superior I—in Somaliland might strike, and strike, and strike.[40]

This reveling in the escape from domesticity and social pressures is framed as part of the appeal of this life for women, and that in turn makes it interesting that they invoked the primacy of the will at all. Uncoupled from its connections to work and manliness, it is still present, still makes women's hunting meaningful. But is it still the same discourse, still the same willpower, and how can we know? The answer lies in the elements of the discourse that women did not dismiss: sportsmanship, race, and class.

If primacy of the will powers women's narratives, sportsmanship is the most common secondary element invoked, as women hunter-writers insisted on their right to belong to the fraternity because they were performing according to the rules. This was one place where the sportsmen-hunters' anxiety about other men served women well. The opposite of the true sportsman, after all, was not a woman but rather a brute, a creature, the game hog, and female hunters could also reject associations with such a beast. Grace Seton draws on this dynamic repeatedly: she explains that she released a twelve-pound muscalongue because she had "no wish to be called by a little name of three letters that begins with *h* and ends with *g*," makes a point that she killed only one of each species of animal that she hunted, and reacts with horror when she suspects her friends Bobbie and Sallie of jacklighting a moose: "That either Sallie or Bobbie would kill a moose in that treacherous way, and that in close season, made it necessary for us to reconstruct our ideas of them, and was sadly depressing," she writes.[41] (The same type of parsing is occurring here as in men's narratives, with exactly the same implications about the revelation of character. Sallie and Bobbie had appeared to be of the right sort—a certain idea had been constructed of them—and how would the Setons ever have found out the truth about them without going hunting?) Nor was Seton alone in displaying her adherence to the rules. Herbert stalks two bull oryx but shoots only one—"I could have shot both, but as I was strong so was I merciful"—and is "ashamed" to have bagged a female Speke's gazelle, mistaking its sex.[42] Without invoking a language of manliness, these women still endorsed Van Dyke's ideals of honorable hunting. And Herbert sometimes went further, suggesting that women sportsmen might have their own reasons for following the rules. "I like not to war with feminine things," she writes, explaining why she passed up a shot at a female caribou. "They have enough to contend with as it is. Let her go, and my blessing with her."[43]

Nor was the idea that women could be sportsmanlike hunters confined to the big-game hunting narratives. The article "Miss Diana in the Adirondacks," which appeared in *Harper's Weekly*, describes Miss Diana's mountain adventures.[44] While the article's tone verges on satire, however, the accompanying illustration (figure 6.1) tells a different story: Miss Diana, clearly a member of the middle or upper classes, is just as clearly a sportsman, who waited to shoot until her impressive target had emerged from the water rather than bagging it while it swam. What is being challenged here, and in Seton's and Herbert's narratives, is the gendering of sportsmanship as exclusively male.

Sportsmanship was not the only basis of women's claim to parity, however. Look at Miss Diana again: every inch of her from her hat and hairstyle to her corseted waist and draped skirt tells us that she is a respectable lady of means. This image thus speaks to sportsmanship, but also to class and to race. Those were the other elements of the discourse consistently invoked in women's narratives as, shut out from claims to membership on the basis of gender, they mobilized class and race to claim equivalence with their male counterparts.

Earlier we saw Herbert's comment on "ignorant Somalis," but she does more than just comment. She also uses her encounters with Africans to demonstrate her own courage: when one Somali strikes at her with a spear

Figure 6.1. Cover illustration by W. A. Rogers for *Harper's Weekly*, August 25, 1883.

she describes herself as "frightfully annoyed" and has her shikári discipline the man immediately.[45] Africans are being used here, like the animals she hunts, as a means to display her coolness under pressure. Similarly, Seton proves herself not only by participating in roundups but by driving away a Mexican, a "dirty swarthy little man," who approaches her while she's alone in camp.[46] Josephine Peary contrasts herself to the Greenland natives, whom she describes as dirty, undisciplined children, and at one point, when Henson

**Diana's Own** 151

and Cook tell her that they are afraid the Greenlanders might mean them harm, she dismisses their fears with the comment, "The whole thing seemed very amusing to me, but both boys were evidently frightened."[47] Such moments in which hierarchy is drawn (with the narrator at the top) make an implicit argument that race and class, rather than gender, are the categories that matter most, and by which distinctions should be made among hunters. These women used their white skins and wealthy origins to make claims about the ways that their performances should be understood. Such claims also tied back into the overarching rhetoric of primacy of the will, since some of its associated virtues—especially prudence, self-control, and chastity—could also be invoked to differentiate white women of the "right" sort from women of other classes, races, and ethnicities.

Class and race were also made visible in employer-employee relationships, especially when it came to the question of who performed the servant's role in camp. Earlier we saw women hunter-writers urging their female readers to leave domestic chores behind, but someone still had to do that work, and on extended hunting trips working-class, often nonwhite, men were hired for that purpose. Most women hunters don't explicitly discuss who did the chores, but when they do they almost always conjure divisions of class and race. Seton is straightforward about this, telling her female readers that on expeditions they should insist that their guide do the cooking, assuring them that he "is used to it, and, anyway, is paid for it. He is earning his living."[48] Peary, more subtly, uses the division of labor to assert her status: she explains that, when her husband was ill, she left Matthew Henson to do the washing-up while she hunted to keep the camp in meat. Her relegation of Henson to the servant's role can be seen as a power play over her husband's confidant and companion, one that lets her frame their relationship in print as one of provider and dependent as well as of wife and servant.[49]

Scholars, especially those who have sought to valorize women adventurers from this period, have struggled with these moments. Dismay is the characteristic tone—that white women, victims of oppression themselves, should be so willing to pass it on to men and women of other classes and races—and it is in fact dismaying. Putting these stories into context with men's narratives, however, reveals a rationale for such moments, while serving as a reminder that gender is only one way through which people understand their own and others' behavior, and is never the whole of an identity. By claiming that class, race, and shared values were stronger determinants of inclusion than gender, women hunters aligned themselves with the hunter elite—men they knew, and married, and with whom they hunted and debated the meaning of those hunts. This claim to commonality is visible in the choice of will, sportsmanship, and the class-race dynamic as ways of structuring women's narratives, and perhaps also in the fact that so many women were hunting at all—because white, middle- and upper-class, Protestant men also seem to have perceived women's right to join them in the hunt as a function of what they shared in common. Like them, but not like them, Grace Gallatin Seton, Josephine Peary, Louisa Sheldon, Laura Sherman Gray, and countless others joined men in the field because they had more in common with their husbands than they ever had separating them.

At the same time, these claims existed in tension with men's narratives and the meanings that they had constructed for hunting, and that matters too. Men's and women's writing existed in a tangled interchange—both in the context of their appearances in *Harper's* and *Outing*, where readers encountered them side by side, and in the texts themselves. Two examples, one from Seton, the other from Peary, can illustrate such entanglements and the complexities they add to any reading. Tension is apparent in the very title of Seton's book *Nimrod's Wife*, which tells the story of a woman-who-went-hunting-with-her-husband—but Ernest Seton didn't hunt on that trip. He was no Nimrod. Instead, it was Grace who brought meat into camp and who was the Nimrod of the tale. The ambiguity lurking in the title is only reinforced by the illustrations, which sometimes undermine her narrative. At one point Seton describes herself as controlling a bucking horse on a steep slope; the accompanying drawing shows her hanging on the reins of a catatonic horse on flat ground (figure 6.2).[50]

This might well be attributed to artistic failings on the part of the illustrator, but Robert Peary performs much the same reinterpretation in his introduction to his wife's book. While Josephine presents herself in the text as roaming far afield, keeping the camp in meat while he is laid up with a broken leg, and coolly gunning down walrus, he assures the reader in the introduction that his two lasting images of his wife from this year were her watching faithfully by his side when his leg was broken, and sitting by him reloading *his* firearm as walrus approached.[51] Even in the texts themselves, then, women's readings could be disputed, and elements introduced that contradicted or undermined what they were saying.

This was hardly a one-way street, however. Women also critiqued men in their narratives—specific men, and also the entire story of hardship with which readers were familiar. Robert Peary was one of the foremost claimants

Figure 6.2. Illustration by E. M. Ashe, from Grace Gallatin Seton, *A Woman Tenderfoot*, 1900. Compare the image with Seton's description of the moment in the text: "Below us a thousand feet was a vicious looking torrent.... It was a shivery sight, but I started expecting the horse would follow. He, however, jerked back snorting... and I fell. Nothing but the happy chance of a tight grip on the reins kept me from sliding down that dreadful bank, over the rock into the water, and so into eternity.... [My horse] now plunged forward upon the sliding rock.... I could not keep away from his hoofs. ... I lost my balance again while dodging away from him as he plunged and balked, but managed to grab his mane and we both slid a horrible distance.... Such an ominous rolling and tumbling of stones and tons of earth sliding down over the low precipice into the water!" (306–308).

of primacy of the will, filling his books with descriptions of traveling through storms, battling frostbite, and suffering on the ice. Such moments work oddly with this dry note by Josephine near the end of *My Arctic Journal*: "As for [the Arctic experience being one of] cold, hardship, and hunger, that is nonsense. Of course, if I feel so inclined, I can go out and sit on an iceberg until I freeze to it, and let the wind and snow beat upon me, even starve myself; but my tastes do not run in that direction."[52] This cavalier dismissal of hardship seems directed right at her faithless and self-dramatizing husband, but, while the specificity of the target is unusual, the sentiment isn't. Grace Seton, describing her horse's uncontrolled slide down a shale slope, ambiguously notes that "not being a man, I don't pretend to having enjoyed that experience" and at one point explains, tongue firmly in cheek, that she is about to tell "how I killed my antelope. (If you wish to be proper, always use the possessive for animals you have killed. It is a Western abbreviation in great favor.)"[53] If women chose to depict their hunts as play, they were not above implying that it was play for men as well, despite the rhetoric of agonized effort; if they adopted parts of the sportsman-hunter discourse, it was sometimes with a conscious acknowledgment of the form. The exchanges over what these narratives meant, and what they said about women, men, and their relationships with one another, were a matter of bracketed comments and contradictions, sly asides, and ironic observations, a game in which the elements of discourse were mobilized against and around one another. So often partnered in the hunts they undertook, the interpretations they chose, and the narratives they produced, women and men negotiated the meaning of the hunt with one another, in plain view of the reading audience.[54]

These differences might seem to imply rupture, but they can also be understood as an integral part of the life of a discourse. The sportsman-hunter narratives had never been direct relations of the experience of hunting, but rather placed the hunt at the center of a constellation of meanings and associations that bore no inherent, essential relationship to events on the ground. Women big-game hunters came to that web of associations and rewove it, cutting away some elements and reinforcing others, while allowing the sportsmanlike still-hunt to retain its central importance. Their rearrangement of the discourse serves as a reminder that the meanings surrounding the hunt offered options rather than dictating outcomes. If the hunt was not *inherently* connected to manliness, if it had no natural and obvious meanings except those created for it, then the sportsmanlike hunt could be about self-control or self-discovery, could be about work or exultant freedom, could be about the hunter's gender or about her race, class, and social position. This variety was made possible by the separations among the elements that made up the discourse, the way that no connections existed among them except those created through narrative: what seemed like a seamless story was in fact nothing but seams, waiting to be split apart and reconfigured.[55] Women hunter-writers did that. They illustrate how it could be done.

In doing so, however, they also illuminate both the appeal and the flexibility that gave the sportsman-hunter discourse such lasting power. The allure of the associations given to still-hunting had always reached well beyond the founding group of elite men, appealing to new hunters taking up the sport as well as to editors, publishers, and readers. Women big-game hunters clearly found something in the sportsman-hunter discourse that spoke to them, so much so that they looked past the seemingly exclusionary languages of "manly sport with the rifle" and "the virile virtues" to find other elements that could help them interpret their hunting to themselves and to a readership made up of women as well as men. And the discourse was open enough to take them in: there was space for them to elide, disown, or gently mock rhetorics of manliness and strenuous work, even as they strengthened the connections among willpower, sportsmanship, race, and class. If they challenged some elements of the discourse, they reinforced other associations within it. This flexibility, the complex and sometimes contradictory meanings that the discourse could contain within itself, in turn helps to explain why this story remained so dominant for decades, able to accommodate some new meanings—and some new writers—even as the Gilded Age gave way to the first decades of the twentieth century.

# CHAPTER 7

# Sportsmen of the Breed
## British and American Hunters

*It is true that there is no big game left in Britain; but if the game is not British, its hunters are . . . out of every ten rifleman wandering about the world at present . . . nine are of the Anglo-Saxon breed.*
—Clive Phillipps-Wolley

*For my part, I have no patience with [English] society's nonsensical standards. . . . Thank God for America, where every man stands on his merits, if he has any.*
—William Hornaday

Women were not the only writers complicating the discourse created by American sportsmen-hunters. British big-game hunting narratives were also in circulation in the United States and also tremendously popular. Published by the same companies and in many of the same periodicals as American hunting tales, British narratives competed for the attention of middle-class reading audiences while offering those readers a fundamentally different interpretation of the hunt. British narratives would have a greater impact on American men's hunting tales than women's narratives did, however, for two reasons.

One was that the British narratives came first, preceding Van Dyke's invention of the manly still-hunter. As noted in the first chapter, British hunters and travelers were publishing on both sides of the Atlantic by the middle of the nineteenth century, and their writing linked big-game hunting to leisure, the mass slaughter of animals, and the wealthy play of aristocrats. They unquestionably influenced the emergence of American leisured big-game hunting, but such associations with the British came to pose a challenge for Americans as the sportsman-hunter discourse emerged. Van Dyke and his ilk sought to disassociate their hunting from lazy pleasure and aristocratic display, and they were successful as far as narratives by American hunters were concerned: by 1900 an entirely new set of associations surrounded the still-hunt. But British hunter-writers were still present, still publishing, and telling a very different story, one that celebrated aristocracy and leisure as well as the reach and power of the British Empire. British narratives thus always had the potential to undermine the American story of manly sport, if only by reminding readers that, not very long before, elite Americans had been celebrating "Millionaires' Hunting Clubs."

The other reason that British hunting had such an impact on American narratives was that, as big-game animals became ever scarcer in the continental United States, American hunters began to travel overseas to hunt in the British Empire. The beginning of the twentieth century marks a moment when the American hunter elite joined their British counterparts in pursuing game across four continents and disseminating their stories through a shared transatlantic publishing network. This presented new challenges for American sportsmen-hunters, ones that they solved in tandem with British writers, because in print both British and American hunters insisted to readers that hunting was most meaningful if understood in a *national* context. For the British, that was the context of imperialism and empire. For Americans, it remained the story of the self-reliant man of character revealing his true self in the wilderness. As that wilderness moved from frontier to empire, however, a new way of talking about "American" hunting began to emerge: no longer just associated with the pioneers, now American hunting was also being defined in relationship to British hunting and to British narratives. In the process, new layers of meaning were added to the sportsman-hunter discourse, ones that identified what it meant to hunt like an American in an international context, whether that related to racial exclusivity, the rules of sportsmanship, or the connections among violence, war, hunting, and empire.

Those meanings emerged in dialogue with British hunter-writers, both on the ground and on the page, and understanding that context requires a close examination of British hunters and the ways they described their actions in print. Every American reader of hunting tales would have been familiar with these narratives; they were hugely popular in the United States, despite offering a very different interpretation of hunting than that found in *The Still-Hunter*. How the British experienced and represented hunting is thus an essential part of the history of the turn-of-the-century big-game hunting narrative, even from an American perspective, and the first half of this chapter focuses on British hunters and their writing. The second half explores the response of the American sportsmen-hunters as they engaged with the British in person, in print, and, more and more often as the new century began, on the hunting grounds of the British Empire.

There were divisions between the two from the beginning, because British hunting had a radically different chronology from that of American hunting. By the nineteenth century there was no real wilderness sport to be had in the British Isles. Instead, hunting in Britain mainly consisted of shooting game birds and chasing fox and deer on private lands in England, or on the Scottish and Irish holdings of English aristocrats. Harsh laws punished those who trespassed on these elite hunting grounds.[1] As a result, Englishmen of the lower classes did not hunt for pleasure and subsistence in the way that many working-class Americans did, and even Englishmen of the middling classes often found themselves without access to such sport.[2]

Big-game hunting was another story altogether, one deeply rooted in Britain's imperial ascendancy. While American big-game hunters usually had their first experiences in their own country, Englishmen pursuing big game usually did so in India, the Malay Peninsula, and eastern and southern Africa. Often men hunting either to support their expeditions or to make their fortunes opened the way for British expansion, while pleasure hunters followed in the wake of territorial seizure, so that hunting both led to and followed the formal acquisition of new lands.[3] By the mid-nineteenth century Britain already had famous big-game hunters such as Roualeyn Gordon Cumming, William Cotton Oswell, and Sir Samuel Baker, whose narratives were consumed at home by avid readers; Baker also became governor of Sri Lanka, and in 1879 spent three years on a round-the-world hunting trip that included North America.[4] Such patterns were typical of British big-game hunters, who often played formal roles in the empire's expansion and who exported their experiences back to England in the form of adventure stories with imperial significance.

Hunting overseas for the British was thus an experience mediated both by their own understanding of empire and by hunting restrictions in England itself. In the context of British education and culture, hunting "out there" was inextricably associated with the imperial "out there." Boys were raised to think of soldiering and hunting as linked to the British territorial grasp and became men who went forth, armed, into the empire. From metropole to colony, the diaspora of eager hunters, public servants, and second sons was an emigration of men who would find "the wilderness," "the colony," and "the empire" inseparable concepts.[5] Some of them were aristocrats who found hunting lions and tigers a congenial change from riding to hounds. Others, especially British Army officers, discovered in hunting abroad a pastime denied them at home, one that had the pleasures and status associated with England's elite. Those hunters lived in Africa, India, or the Malay Peninsula and traveled easily among the three. For them, by 1900, the world was their hunting ground.

The nuances of the British imperial hunt have been well documented by historians, who have explored the links among hunting, imperialism, and British elites in far more depth than I can essay here. Leading the way has been John MacKenzie, who pioneered the study of British imperial hunting.[6] In his book *The Empire of Nature*, he shows that such hunting was marked by a "progressive restriction of social access" in which subsistence hunting was replaced by what he calls "the Hunt," sport defined by both rules of procedure and symbolic meaning. He describes the Hunt as the property of "an imperial and largely masculine elite [that] attempted to reserve for itself access to hunting, adopted and transformed the concept of the Hunt as a ritual of prestige and dominance, and set about the separation of the human and animal worlds to promote 'preservation' (later 'conservation') as a continuing justification of its monopoly."[7] This argument is part of MacKenzie's larger body of work on British hunting and imperialism, and overall he is absolutely correct: in the British Empire the big-game hunt was often conducted as a ritualized activity pursued by what might be defined as an elite. Despite that, however, it was very different in kind from both American hunting and American elites. There was never a single dominant way of pursuing game among the British, for one thing, nor was the British hunting elite a homogenous one, either economically or socially.[8] Overall, in fact, it seems that there was far *more* heterogeneity among British big-game hunters than there was among the American hunter elite in the same period.

(It's vital to note, though, that MacKenzie's hunters were definitely a *colonial* elite. Certainly from the point of view of colonized peoples who encountered British hunters, it mattered little whether or not the man trampling their crops had a title back home. Occasionally, however, historians other than MacKenzie have depicted English hunters as an elite in American terms.[9] Most British hunters in Africa and India were pursuing recreation unavailable to them at home, however, and are not an elite in that sense.)

British big-game hunters can be divided roughly into three types: aristocrats, traders and settlers, and British Army officers. The aristocrats are the best known now, England's lords and peers traveling abroad to bag a few heads for the billiard room. Lord North Buxton is one example, and his classic book *Short Stalks* takes readers from Africa to Norway to the Rocky Mountains as he wanders the globe in search of trophies.[10] Hunters like Buxton were born and raised in England and lived there most of their lives, while indulging in leisurely trips abroad.

The second group of hunters were traders, especially ivory traders, and settlers, men who typically became planters in British East Africa, Rhodesia, South Africa, or Malaya. These men were usually of the middling classes or, if they had aristocratic connections, had no fortunes to go with them, and the colonies became the places where they lived, built their homes, and raised their families. Moreover, for some of them, colonial settlement offered an opportunity to re-create an aristocratic system with themselves at the top, most famously in British East Africa.[11]

The final group, and by far the most numerous among the British hunter-writers, were British Army officers. Stationed for the most part in India, these men were drawn from a variety of middling- and upper-class social backgrounds, often depended on army pay, and might spend their entire adult lives abroad. Due to the army's liberal long leave policy, these soldiers had ample opportunity to take advantage of hunting, not only throughout the subcontinent but in Africa as well, in such numbers that Hindustani was often learned by African safari workers hoping for employment. Such hunters were for the most part young, single, and engaged with the romance of empire as much as with its practice—for the army held forth the promise that young men might become heroes of empire, although that promise was seldom fulfilled.[12]

These three groups were never completely stable, however, for many Englishmen shifted from imperial business to private pleasure and back again, as aristocratic hunters became colonial administrators or settlers temporarily joined the armed forces. These groups, especially the latter two, are thus best understood as fluid categories, and two quick examples can help to illustrate that.

Army officer Harald Swayne, author of *Seventeen Trips through Somaliland: A Record of Exploration and Big Game Shooting*, first visited Somaliland on long leave to hunt, but not all of his seventeen trips were taken for pleasure. In 1891 he was sent from Mandalay to Somaliland to reconnoiter African trade routes for the army, and in 1897 he represented the government of India on a mission, via Somaliland, to the King of Abyssinia. Swayne's vivid account reveals a world where pleasure hunting and the work of empire were intertwined, and where a twenty-five-year-old could be assigned to treat with tribal leaders on behalf of his government because of the knowledge he had derived from his leisure-time hunting.[13]

A parallel can be found in John Patterson's hunting classic *The Man-Eaters of Tsavo*, which has the distinction of being one of the only big-game hunting books to be made into a movie—not once, but twice (the classic B-movie *Bwana Devil* in 1952, starring Robert Stack, and the truly forgettable 1996 *The Ghost and the Darkness* with Val Kilmer). Patterson was an army officer commissioned to direct the building of a bridge for the Ugandan railway in 1898. Instead, he found himself confronting two man-eating lions who killed approximately 140 railway workers in nine months, bringing work on the railway to a standstill.[14] Patterson spends several chapters describing how he matches wit and will against the lions and finally manages to kill one of them. Appended to his own account is a description of the moment from the *Spectator*, whose reporter was covering the events for readers at home:

> As the shout went on from camp to camp that the first lion was dead, as the hurrying crowds fell prostrate in the midnight forest, laying their heads on his feet, and the Africans danced savage and ceremonial dances of thanksgiving, Mr. Patterson must have realised in no common way what it was to have been a hero and deliverer in the days when man was not yet undisputed lord of the creation, and might pass at any moment under the savage dominion of the beasts.[15]

This description positions Patterson as a kind of white savior, although it seems likely that the reporter was exaggerating the response of the men, who were mostly Indian, who were on strike at the time, and who at one point tried to kill Patterson. Indeed, Patterson himself spends almost as much time in his narrative describing the workers' mutiny as he does his encounters with the lions, placing Indians and Africans in the same category as the Tsavo man-eaters—as obstacles to the railroad that must be dominated and disciplined in order that civilization may progress. His book concludes with his return to East Africa on a pleasure hunting trip and his visit to the Tsavo bridge: "I looked on it as a child of mine, brought up through stress and danger and troubles of all kinds."[16] Those troubles are the troubles of empire; without watchful white men to guard its outposts, lions and colonized peoples alike might endanger the forward momentum of imperialism and return the British Empire to the "dominion of the beasts." Combining his roles as hunter, soldier, and engineer, Patterson crafted a hunting classic that took its meaning entirely from the context of its production, by a worker for and in empire.[17]

These conflations of experience created a complex but complementary set of meanings for British hunting, both in the lives of the hunters and in the narratives that they published. Their hunting was presented as meaningful because it familiarized them with local peoples and unexplored places, honed their skills at shooting, riding, and tactical maneuvering, and demonstrated the reach of the British Empire both to colonial subjects and to readers in England. It was also a necessary adjunct to the continued domination of the landscape, whether that consisted of expanding trade routes, conducting diplomatic missions, or building railway bridges.

This impression of British hunting as an activity pursued in different ways by men of varying backgrounds, yet never entirely separable from empire, is only further underlined by the experiences of army officers living in India. Historian Mary Ann Procida has characterized sport in British India as an "obsession" that blurred the lines among work, leisure, and duty. Hunting and other sports were used to demonstrate the prowess of the British to their colonial subjects, while providing the main source of recreation for many Anglo-Indian communities. Both men and women hunted and rode and were expected to do so well; failure to participate could harm professional advancement. For these people, hunting and shooting were both a way to engage with empire and, for women in particular, a taste of freedoms unacceptable at home.[18]

Despite the participation of women and older men, however, the vast majority of British hunters in India were young army officers with free time on their hands. For the Raj, hunting was seen as a way to keep these bored young men with guns busy and occupied (occupied, that is, with something other than sex and liquor, the two other standbys of bored young soldiers). Robert Baden-Powell credited the administration's promotion of polo and pig-sticking with replacing "the drinking and betting habits of the former generation [with] healthy exercise which also has its moral attributes."[19] Hunting in India could thus be about imperialism, and/or community, and/or professional advancement, but it was also a way to regulate the behavior of young men in empire.

Those men were not necessarily members of the aristocracy: although some of them came from privileged backgrounds, many were sons of the middling classes who had never hunted at home. Their narratives paint a picture of young men risking life and limb on a daily basis for the joy of risk itself. No better example of this élan exists than the immensely popular sport of pig-sticking. Pig-sticking consisted of flushing out wild boar—no domesticated pig, a prime boar could weigh up to three hundred pounds with nine-inch tusks—and chasing him on horseback with a spear.[20] The chase itself provided most of the danger, usually pursued across uncertain ground, the boar's speed requiring the successful hunter to risk, as the phrase had it, "neck or nothing." (One 1903 pig-sticking club log includes notes such as "this extraordinary pig must have run about five miles before he was bagged, and accounted for no less than six falls among his five hunters" and "indeed a merry day. Eight falls and only two pigs ridden.") When the boar turned at bay, it would often attempt to gut the horse in a maneuver known as the jink—essentially the ability to change direction on a dime—and pig-stickers spent enormous amounts of time training their horses to avoid such attacks (indeed, the camaraderie between man and horse was seen as one of the best features of the sport and as invaluable training for cavalrymen).[21] The pig-sticker then attempted to stab the boar; if the strike was not fatal, the boar might well pull the spear away from the pig-sticker, who would be honor-bound to maneuver his horse into position to recapture the weapon. These rules, which went to elaborate lengths to make pig-sticking as dangerous as possible, were played out by individual hunters and pig-sticking clubs throughout India and culminated in an annual championship match known as the Kadir Cup. The Kadir was open to both army officers and Indian aristocrats and ran every year from the 1860s into the 1930s (with hiatuses for the Afghan and Great Wars). The winner achieved fame throughout the British Empire.[22]

By 1900 an entire culture had grown up around the sport. There were pig-sticking dinners, pig-sticking reunions in England, a pig-sticking magazine (the *Hog-Hunter's Annual*), even songs of pig-sticking ("He's a true-bred 'un, none of your jinking,/Straight across country, no time for thinking;/There's a nullah in front, but a boar as well,/So hang the nullah, and ride like Hell").[23] The main purpose of these elaborate regulations does not seem to have been to restrict participation but rather to make a relatively easy sport more dangerous and thus more fun, and it was open not only to wealthy Indians and Englishmen but also to any soldier who could scrape together the money for a pony.[24] (Women also performed as pig-stickers, although the clubs tended to be exclusively masculine and women did not compete for the Kadir.) Alexander Wardrop, who wrote one of the great books on

Figure 7.1. Illustration by Sir Robert Baden-Powell, *Pigsticking; or, Hoghunting: A Complete Account for Sportsmen, and Others*, 1888.

pig-sticking, gives an idea of both himself and the game: "For myself I can only say that I have been in India for twenty-one years, and that all my leave (sufficient) and all my money (less) have been spent with spear or rifle.... I am no good, but I love the sport."[25] He describes how instructive it was to watch a friend in the Dragoon Guards leaping headfirst over a billiard-room sofa to demonstrate the correct way to fall off a horse, and summarizes the dangers of British Army hunting, and service, in India as follows:

> I have ... been "laid out" one way or another thirteen times. This includes, however, being twice mauled (panther only). It is by no means a heavy average ... my friend Major E. H. Phillips, D.S.O., later killed in action, had two bullets through him, was twice hit by poisoned arrows, was severely mauled by a tiger, and in a single season's hunting at home had over ninety

falls. As regards this last, however, he always claimed he was since then a wiser if not a better horseman.[26]

This elaboration of British hunting was about danger, high spirits, competition, and bored young men on India postings, and, like many forms of imperial hunting, it generated its own legends, romances, narratives, and nostalgia.

These legends were of course being promoted in print as much as they were in clubs and competitions: in Wardrop's book, complete with music and lyrics for those who might want to sing songs of pig-sticking, and in Baden-Powell's handbook, which offered advice to hunters while arguing that pig-sticking had "Value as a School for Soldiers," both as training for war and as a diversion from less salubrious pursuits ("So long as there was pig-sticking to be got one never wanted to go away to the usual poodle-faking at the hill-stations").[27] As with Swayne and Patterson, these texts linked together the genuine work of soldiering, the holding of imperial possessions, the play of sport, and the act of writing for an audience divided between the colonies and home—that is, England.

It was this orientation toward empire that united the British hunting narratives. British big-game hunters were more diverse, economically, socially, and in terms of where they made their homes and livelihoods than the American sportsmen-hunters were, and they partook of many styles of hunting for a wide variety of reasons. Their texts reflected that variety, ranging from memoirs of growing up in India, to anthologies like Wardrop's, to books that simply described all the animals shot in a single trip. These tales all had one thing in common, however. Lacking the quest narrative of manly display that characterized so many American hunting tales, and viewing their disparate landscapes through the common lens of empire, British hunters produced accounts in which the hunt itself was not necessarily meaningful as anything other than a diversion, but in which it always testified in some way to the more serious work of empire.[28]

Some did so very explicitly, interweaving imperial work with pleasure hunting, as in Swayne and Patterson. Some linked hunting to soldiering skills, as with pig-sticking, or in Chauncey Stigand's notorious *Hunting the Elephant in Africa*, which cheerfully inserted a chapter entitled "Stalking the African" between the chapters "Camp Hints" and "Hunting the Bongo."[29] (The chapter on stalking Africans is about organizing military expeditions and is a rarity in a book focused on hunting.) Many other writers, however, made the link implicitly. This is true even in the most common type of British hunting book, in which, in each chapter, the author sallies out, kills something, and comes back to camp. Such tales have a rather inescapable What-I-Shot-on-My-Summer-Vacation feeling to them, and yet they function at a more subtle level as evidence of the control these hunters exercise over the landscape. C. J. Melliss's rather scattered *Lion-Hunting in Somali-Land*, for example, seems at first glance to be a simple report of animals hunted and slain on a soldier's vacation—but even so innocuous an image as Melliss leaping up in the middle of the night on hearing a hyena's laugh and riding out after it in his pajamas, rifle clutched in one eager hand, is telling a story that depends for its very existence on the imperial power that allows Melliss to venture out without a second thought, either to his safety or to his right to hunt game in a foreign land. Nor is this separable from Melliss's identity as a soldier, one whose shooting and riding skills are on full and reassuring display to English readers at home.[30]

These narratives could serve other imperial purposes as well, for among their readers were the men who ruled the empire. Historian Angela Thompsell, examining hunting in Africa, has persuasively argued that both hunters and their narratives were of particular interest to colonial administrators because, unlike explorers who were simply passing through, hunters often needed to negotiate at length with local leaders in order to obtain hunting privileges, and as a result gained an understanding of the political structures of the various tribes they encountered. She suggests that this is one of the reasons that so many British hunters in Africa were recruited to colonial administration or to lead expeditions of negotiation or conquest (as Swayne did).[31] This was also in some ways an extension of already established uses of the hunt in India, where, as MacKenzie points out, administrators often used hunting trips as excuses to "appear in remote areas, check on subordinates, and gather intelligence."[32]

Of course, most British narratives did not lead directly to conquest, but even as frivolous an image as the one conjured by Melliss, of the world as imperial playground, was underscored by the constant elaboration of both regulations and infrastructure development throughout the British Empire in the late Victorian period. This was particularly true in Africa. Elephant and other big game were becoming scarce as early as the 1880s in some areas (mainly due to ivory hunters). By the first decade of the twentieth century, game reserves began to appear, requiring licenses for visiting white hunters while barring native Africans from the subsistence hunting on which they had traditionally depended.[33] Accompanying these changes was the development of extensive transportation networks, and British hunting narratives often described these changes to the landscape. For many, especially novice hunters like the young Winston Churchill, this was part of the point of the trip: seeing East Africa meant killing some animals and checking out the Ugandan railway, "one slender thread of scientific civilization, of order, authority, and arrangement, drawn across the primeval chaos of the world."[34] For other British hunters, such changes were cause for regret. William Cotton Oswell recalled with nostalgia "the feeling as you lay under your caross that you were looking at the stars from a point on the earth whence no other European had ever seen them ... [now] houses stand where we once shot elephants, and the railway train will soon be whistling and screaming through all hunting-fields south of the Zambesi."[35] This is as far from the ur-wilderness of the American narratives as can be imagined. Instead, whether in regret or approval, such writing conjured the image of a powerful and ever-expanding empire, one reassuringly controlled and exploited by Englishmen.[36]

Nor was that the only contrast with the American sportsman-hunter discourse. British hunters and their narratives were also rooted in a radically different framework of interpretation than that embraced by American hunter-writers. Authorial personae that shifted between formal and informal service to the empire, hunting described both as an adjunct to military training and as a bit of fun, and landscapes that became meaningful by being conquered, built on, and regulated were all consistent themes in the British narratives. These links to imperialism were forged in print and in the lives and identities of the writers, and that brings us to the sine qua non of British hunting, Frederick Courteney Selous. Selous's example shows how hunting, writing, and imperialism could shape and change a life—could, in fact, produce the most famous big-game hunter of all, whether in Europe or North America.

Selous was born in England in 1851 to a family that was comfortable, but not wealthy, leaving him to find a way to make his living: he wrote to his sister, "I must make a little money, but how? not by scribbling away on a three-legged stool in a dingy office in London." In 1870 the nineteen-year-old struck off into the empire. He spent ten years as an elephant hunter in southern Africa, but by 1880 elephant had become so scarce that it wasn't paying, and Selous decided to try writing a book: he wrote to a friend that, after all, "people have got good sums for writing bad books on Africa, full of lies, though I do not know if a true book will sell well." *A Hunter's Wanderings in Africa, Being a Narrative of Nine Years Spent among the Game of the Far Interior of South Africa* was a smash hit. Selous quickly found himself in demand as a guide while doing a lively side business in museum commissions. It didn't hurt that four years later his friend H. Rider Haggard published his enduring adventure tale *King Solomon's Mines* to acclaim on both sides of the Atlantic (everyone knew that Alan Quatermain was based on Selous). Selous also carried out a scientific survey of Mashunaland, publishing his observations in 1889 in the *Journal of the Royal Geographical Society*. The difference between such work and the "science" engaged in by American hunters was only emphasized by Selous's next step: he pitched the idea of a road connecting Mashunaland with South Africa to Cecil Rhodes and gained Rhodes's backing. In 1890 he pushed the road through (the Selous Road, it was called for a while).

More best-selling books followed, including *Travel and Adventure in South-East Africa, the Narrative of the Last Eleven Years Spent by the Author on the Zambesi and Its Tributaries: With an Account of the Colonisation of the Mashunaland and the Progress of the Gold Industry in That Country*. (The title gives a clear idea of the ways that British hunting narratives intertwined adventure, imperialism, colonization, and development.) In 1893 Selous was about to leave England for the United States on a book tour when he received news of the first Matabele uprising; he immediately canceled the tour and signed up as a soldier, for the first time. Later he wrote a book about it, *Sunshine and Storm in Rhodesia*, which proved as popular with readers as his hunting books.

By 1895 he had enough fame and money to lead a more leisured life and to focus on natural history, at which he excelled. He wrote an authoritative study on the African lion and donated his collection of African trophies, the finest in the world, to a natural history museum. He became a planter in Rhodesia while maintaining a house in England (managed for him during his absences by Rowland Ward, the taxidermy firm). He also became a friend and correspondent of Roosevelt's and Sheldon's, traveled repeatedly to North America to hunt, and in England played on the Big-Game Hunters Cricket Team.

When war came in 1914, Selous once again joined the armed forces. By 1915 he was in Mombasa, where, on parade with his men, he found himself being inspected by big-game hunter and friend Richard Meinertzhagen, who recalls that "[we] were soon deep in the question of the validity of the Nakuru Hartebeest and the breeding of the Harlequin Duck in Iceland. We both forgot that we were on parade, much to the amusement of Selous' platoon, who still stood rigidly to attention throughout the discussion." Two years later, at the age of sixty-five, he was shot and killed leading his company against a German force four times their strength. Selous was at various times a professional and a leisure-time hunter, a soldier, a writer, and a natural historian, a penniless son of empire and a darling of the patrician elite. As his friend John Millais noted, he was also a man who, for a generation of Englishmen, "stood for all that was best in romance and high adventure."[37]

That romance was a very different one than that which Ernest Thompson Seton had found on the Arctic prairies, or that Roosevelt had located in the West among his spurious wilderness ancestors (although in some ways it looks like a life Roosevelt might have aspired to). Far from being a vacationing hunter with a real job waiting back in a city, Selous's involvement with hunting was part of a lifelong project involving a multitude of professions, linked by an unwavering devotion to the project of empire. His hunting always took its meaning, not from any display of inner character *specific to the hunt itself*, but rather from its role in the wider story he was telling about British imperial reach, martial prowess, and patriotism.

Along with hundreds of other British hunter-writers, then, Selous offered audiences a meaning for hunting that was radically different from the tale American hunters were telling. Moreover, the British interpretation had *preceded* the creation of the American sportsman-hunter discourse and had always been widely available to American readers due to the transatlantic nature of the Anglophone press. Most major publishing houses had branches in both New York and London, and books by British and American hunters sold briskly on both sides of the Atlantic. Like Americans, British hunter-writers were also deeply involved in the periodical market, their tales often appearing first in serialized form: Churchill's *My African Journey* originally appeared in the *Strand*, for example, while Grinnell's correspondence at *Forest and Stream* shows him being approached by British hunter-writers hoping to break into the American market.[38] American and British writers also wrote introductions for one another's books and gave each other advice on publishing (Selous and Roosevelt, for instance, both encouraged Patterson to publish *The Man-Eaters of Tsavo*).[39]

The relationships among these hunters were not only textual, however; they were also closely connected by the experience of traveling to hunt. British and American sportsmen had been encountering one another, and visiting each other's hunting grounds, in ever-increasing numbers since the end of the American Civil War, and the beginning of the twentieth century was marked by a massive increase in this kind of international hunting tourism by Americans in particular.

The main reason for this was that by 1900 the continental United States was rapidly being hunted out.[40] Big-game animals were becoming ever scarcer, with some species moving close to extinction: in 1908 Kermit Roosevelt made the front page of the *New York Times* by refusing to shoot a bison, explaining that he feared it might be the last one.[41] At the same time, ongoing improvements to transportation were making travel ever cheaper and easier, while hunting grounds ranging from Alaska to British East Africa were developing infrastructures to support visiting hunters. All this meant that Americans seeking big game at the beginning of the twentieth century most often either headed up, to the Canadian Rockies and Alaska, or out, to try their hand on the imperial hunting grounds of South Asia and Africa.

Wherever they went in the British Empire, they found Englishmen and the apparatus of empire ready to assist them. In 1893, American William Lord Smith (it's a middle name, not a title) began his African shooting adventure by traveling from Boston to London, where he bought guns and provisions. Arriving in Aden, he ran into "an English officer, Captain Swayne, who gave [me] many valuable hints"—this was very likely the Swayne of *Seventeen Trips*—and then took a steamer down the coast. On landing, he was "most kindly received by the English resident . . . and, after a few days of preparation, he sent us off into the jungle."[42]

Smith's experience was typical. American hunters were frequently given advice and even taken hunting by friendly Englishmen—pig-sticking in India was always on offer, but Elliott Roosevelt was assisted in tiger hunting in India by British Army officers, while Whitney, seeking seladang in Malaya, found himself the guest of "the British Resident . . . a fine specimen of that clear-eyed, upstanding, intelligent class of young men whose common sense and uncorrupted rule have been the upbuilding of British Malaya."[43] Other Americans simply found themselves following already-blazed British trails. Prentiss Gray, traveling via the Pacific to Africa to photograph animals for the Academy of Natural Sciences of Philadelphia, ran into the Harvard Solar Eclipse expedition on his ship, and together they all went on a tiger hunt in Singapore arranged for them by the Sultan of Jahore.[44] These connections ran both ways, and British hunters visiting North America often found themselves welcome guests: Charles Sheldon invited Selous to go hunting with him in the Yukon, while British hunter Claude Cane, wishing to bring more trophies home with him from Alaska than the law allowed, enlisted the help of C. Hart Merriam to win him an exception from the government (and thanked Merriam in print for his assistance).[45]

There had always been significant rifts between American and British interpretations of the hunt, however, and these only became more visible as Americans moved out into the British Empire. One of the greatest differences is clear just from the names of their exclusive hunting clubs. For Americans, invoking Boone and Crockett linked the vanishing frontier to the sport of the hunter elite. The British, on the other hand, had no original wilderness to invoke: the British equivalent of the Boone and Crockett Club was the Shikári Club. The word derives from the Persian for "hunter" and was first used by Anglo-Indians to indicate British big-game hunters specifically, but by 1900 it was being regularly used in the literature to describe both British hunters and African gunbearers. Naming their exclusive organization the Shikári Club linked them to the global networks and colonial appropriations typical of the empire: the British hunter elite were reaching around the world, not back into a vanishing past.

This allowed them to celebrate—or mourn—the empire's growing infrastructure, but in either case they could acknowledge it as they pleased. Americans venturing into the British Empire, on the other hand, were facing a challenge both on the ground and on the printed page. In 1893 William Lord Smith could launch himself away from the English resident and into the jungle at a certain point in his narrative. Such separations were becoming harder to negotiate by 1900, however, as what wilderness was left in British territories was rapidly giving way to regulated game preserves and developing colonial landscapes. Subtle disjunctions began to appear in and among the printed narratives, especially among those by British and American hunters that lent themselves to comparison. Sheldon and Selous, for example, went hunting together in western Canada, but their narratives conjured different images of where they were: Sheldon's book was called *The Wilderness of the Upper Yukon*, Selous's *Hunting Trips in British North America*. This might seem a small difference, but there are different lineages here, as Sheldon's book aligns naturally with his *Wilderness of the North Pacific Coast Islands*, linking the wildernesses of the American Northwest, while Selous follows his works on Rhodesia and southern Africa with a trip to British North America—a colonial tour.

Disjunctions were also appearing in the ways that hunters assigned meaning to their experiences and in how they described the places to which they traveled. For American hunter Percy Madeira, the African veldt is the most untamed of landscapes: "The innocent-looking rock lying in the grass twenty or thirty yards from you may become a pugnacious rhinoceros; the silently stalking buffalo that has watched your approach, unseen by you, may suddenly charge out from the shadow of a tree; a lion may start up from the cover of a bunch of grass or a bush just ahead of you."[46] This landscape is a wilderness indeed, one ready to erupt into danger, in which Madeira's very presence is proof of his valor. He's not alone on the veldt, however; although they didn't hunt together, his visit was contemporaneous with Winston Churchill's. Churchill was delighted to find the Ugandan railway always handy and offers this description of staging out of the town of Masindi: "There are avenues of planted trees, delicious banks of flowers, a prepared breakfast, *cold*, not cool, drinks, a telegraph office, and a file of the *Times*. What more could an explorer desire?"[47]

Churchill, writing for the *Strand*, is offering British readers assurance that the empire is flourishing and that Englishmen traveling abroad will find all the comforts of home. Madeira's adventure, on the other hand, derives its meaning from the hunter imposing his own order over the perilous African landscape. It's a matter of emphasis, of course—Churchill could have been charged by a lion as easily as Madeira could have picked up some nice cooling drinks—but only Madeira's story depends on *concealing* some of the traces of British rule. The American sportsman-hunter could only bear so many railways, roads, and telegraph lines in his narrative before his wilderness started to look like the game preserve it in fact was. And, in the process, the American sportsman-hunter discourse was becoming a guide to *editing* the hunter's experience as it was converted into text.

What is happening here? Not duplicity, not repression, not some kind of vast hunter-based conspiracy—we know this because readers and reviewers appear to have consumed both British and American narratives without any perception of falsehood, nor did hunters point fingers at one another for producing delusional representations of Africa. Instead, side by side, readers are being given an Africa that is populated and empty, well-administered yet perilous, marked with bridges and water towers that, viewed from the correct angle (through the sights of a Winchester, for example), simply become invisible.

This had always been one of the major differences between British and American hunting narratives—one organized around empire, the other clinging to a formative myth about wilderness—and it continued to shape both genres even as British and American hunters explored each other's hunting grounds and aided each other's journeys. Comments on the differences between the two points of view were rare in the literature, however. The majority of British and American hunters, if they mentioned each other at all, did so only in passing. There were a few Americans, however, who explored the relationship in more depth—in particular, the most prolific writers, including Caspar Whitney, William Hornaday, and Theodore Roosevelt. And there were also certain themes that show British and American writers engaging across national lines in an ongoing, published conversation that offers insight into the interconnections and dissonances provoked by these two very different ways of interpreting the hunt.

Three themes in particular stand out. The first is the use of the term "Anglo-Saxon" as a racial and, sometimes, a class designation; the second is the role of sportsmanship in the hunt. Both are places where American and British hunters engaged in dialogue with each other, either through direct reference or by using a shared rhetoric that made it easy for readers to make connections across narratives. The third theme, the connection of war and military training to hunting, is central to many British narratives but conspicuously absent from American ones, creating a dissonance between the two, an absence of conversation. Together, these three themes illuminate the connections and disjunctions between British and American hunting narratives as they must have been experienced by readers at the time.

The language of Anglo-Saxonism permeated turn-of-the-century Anglophone culture. Historians have explored its many cultural uses as well as its transnational implications: Paul Kramer has shown how Anglo-American networks in this era were reinforced by the publishing explosion, which created "common affiliations and reference points" for literate people throughout the English-speaking world.[48] Big-game hunting narratives constituted such reference points, and both British and American hunter-writers used the term "Anglo-Saxon" freely to denote both ethnic exclusions and transatlantic solidarities, a process that often resulted in elaborate hierarchies of distinction. Lord North Buxton, for instance, classifies himself and Roosevelt as "Anglo-Saxons," while the American packers and guides he meets in the Rocky Mountains are depicted as rough colonials, an excusable result of the "struggle for existence . . . in a new country." His Moroccan gunbearer, on the other hand, who goes on strike for higher wages, is simply a "native" who is not "teachable"; Buxton fires him on the spot.[49] Similar parsing occurs in Hornaday's *Two Years in the Jungle*, where he explains that "I have no patience with [English] society's nonsensical standards. . . . Thank God for America, where every man stands on his merits, if he has any." Such divisions between Americans and their British compatriots collapse, however, when he opposes himself to a Dyak tribesman he meets: "the only difference between [us] is that he is a Dyak and I am an Anglo-Saxon—which makes all the difference in the world."[50]

The appearance of "Anglo-Saxon" here is no coincidence and the way Hornaday uses it offers a glimpse into the complexities of the term. Earlier he had expressed doubts about English standards; later in the book he praises the

> simple honesty and manly independence of the Dyak [who] are yet free from the grovelling idolatry and abominable religious fanaticism of the Hindoos, the sordid avarice of the Chinese, the deceit, treachery, and licentiousness of the Malays, and the brandy-and-sodaism of the Europeans. . . . Their morals are as much superior to ours as our intelligence is beyond theirs.[51]

At first glance it may appear that Hornaday has had some sort of conversion experience, but he is following a tradition that dates back at least to Montaigne, that of praising the noble savage in order to critique modern society. That praise may seem to sit oddly with his comment that being Anglo-Saxon makes all the difference, but it illuminates one use of the term. If Hornaday had just used "white" to describe himself, that wouldn't have parsed between him and the Europeans whose morals he suspects (nor, possibly, the Irish whom he openly despised).[52] "Anglo-Saxon," on the other hand, connects Hornaday to elite hunters on both sides of the Atlantic while delineating a racial identity that can be used to oppose "European" as well as "Dyak." It offers a more *precise* identity for him.

This precision allowed hunters to claim racial and cultural solidarity with one another, connecting the "right" men of North America to those of the British Empire. Sir Henry Seton-Karr dedicated his book *My Sporting Holidays* to "My Brother Sportsmen of the Anglo-Saxon Race," while British hunter Clive Phillipps-Wolley, mourning the fact that big game had vanished in Britain, assured his readers that "if the game is not British, its hunters are . . . nine [of every ten sportsmen] are of the Anglo-Saxon breed." These men hunt non-British game, including boar that "fight like a drunken Irishman"—a fitting target for Saxon rifles.[53] Americans also used this language freely: Poultney Bigelow celebrated the fact that there "are yet men of the Anglo-Saxon race who protest against its being surrendered to any other breed—African, Hebrew or Hibernian."[54] The number of slaps at the Irish becomes even more interesting when one notes that very few of these writers actually encountered the Irish while big-game hunting. Slighting comments and comparisons are common, however, and this suggests again that "Anglo-Saxon" is doing work that the term "white" could not, or could not do as well.

Certainly, as an assertion of friendship, the term connoted a closer relationship than just common descent. Elite British and American big-game hunters often seem to have felt that they had more in common with each other than they did with men of other *classes* in their own countries, and that "Anglo-Saxon" could convey that concisely. Nowhere is this dynamic better illustrated than by Buxton and Roosevelt, who had separate but similar encounters in the American West with an incompetent bandit named Cris. After talking his way onto Buxton's Western hunting trip, Cris attempted to hold Buxton up (Buxton's son knocked him unconscious); he then went on to be the bandit whom Roosevelt tracked across snowbound North Dakota and whose capture formed part of the basis of the Roosevelt legend. This shows what a small world the West was at that point in time, but it was also made clear in print that Roosevelt and Buxton had far more in common with each another than either did with the remarkably unsuccessful outlaw. "Without endorsing Mr. Smalley's opinion that for high breeding the best Americans beat the best Englishmen," Buxton tells us of Roosevelt's capture of Cris, "it must be admitted that, for humanity combined with pluck, this feat is calculated to make an Anglo-Saxon proud."[55] All indications are that Cris was also Anglo-Saxon, but Buxton is not just talking about racial heritage here. In moving easily from the "best" Americans and Englishmen to "Anglo-Saxon," he is using a language that connects men of a certain class across national boundaries.

Of course, religious, ethnic, and racial parsing also occurred in many narratives without using the term "Anglo-Saxon." One of the more unpleasant examples of this occurs in Robert Dunn's *Shameless Diary of an Explorer*, where Dunn finds himself, to his horror, accompanied to Mount McKinley not only by Jack, an Irish wrangler, but by a Jewish expedition member named Simon. "I splashed Jack, and he cursed me for five minutes. He's Irish, so it doesn't mean much," Dunn comments. "Simon said on the trail to-day that Jack wouldn't stick with us, 'because he's Irish.' 'Think so?' said I nastily remembering what Simon is."[56] Dunn's assertion of hierarchy through opposition (and Simon's attempt to do so, for that matter) are typical of such narratives: Owen Wister does it as well when he contrasts the amusement of himself and his "brother American" to "two Jew drummers" who panic when their carriage tips on a Western road.[57] The common appearance of such exclusionary line drawing in American narratives only lent itself to the use of "Anglo-Saxon" as yet another method of parsing among men, one that could reach across national borders while reinforcing already existing exclusions.

Invoking Anglo-Saxonism could thus serve to construct hierarchies of race, religion, ethnicity, and class, even as it created a bridge between elites of different nations. That bridge was made up of shades of meaning in which the connections between some Americans and their British counterparts could be based in common descent, or on class as well as common descent, or in the shared language and experiences that led these hunters to assist one another in the wilds and to read one another's narratives. The term was also part of wider cultural conversations in which the invocation of Anglo-Saxonism could be linked to imperial arguments about the "White Man's Burden," but it was not always used that way: Hornaday is making no such claim on the Dyak, but rather switching between ideas of national and racial superiority as it suits him. However it was utilized, this promotion of racial solidarity was part of both British and American culture in this era, and some American hunter-writers made it an integral part of their narratives, weaving it into the exclusions that were already part of the sportsman-hunter discourse.

Sportsmanship was another matter entirely. Always part of the story that American sportsmen-hunters were telling, the image of the self-controlled still-hunter stood in clear *opposition* to the British narratives. Here the contrast with the British opened the way for American hunter-writers to make statements about national identity while separating themselves from some of the more negative associations that surrounded American perceptions of British hunting.

The idea of restricting hunting on private lands had long been a contentious topic in the United States. Middling- and working-class Englishmen emigrating to America vehemently opposed the development of the type of private game ownership so common in their home country, and their insistence on a hunting commons had long shaped American game law and tradition.[58] The dislike of English laws appears to have been both popular and widespread: one Englishman who emigrated to Kansas in 1872 later recalled that the Americans he talked to "passed jokes and condemnation on the game laws of England, and often railed me on the subject, saying no country had a right to impose such restrictions on its inhabitants."[59] When the sportsmen-hunters emerged in the 1880s, they aligned themselves with these long-standing currents of thought, even as they fought to disconnect their own hunting from associations with aristocracy and wealthy leisure.

It's no surprise, then, that British hunting, especially in privately owned preserves, came in for a great deal of critique from American hunter-writers. Roosevelt told readers that "shooting in a private game preserve is but a dismal parody; the manliest and healthiest features of the sport are lost with the change of conditions," while Whitney noted that "sitting behind battues and having your game driven to you seems, from an American point of view, to savor more of 'pot hunting' than sport."[60] This image of British sport seems to have been so familiar that some writers simply invoke it in passing as an easy contrast: American H. A. Bryden writes of his day's shooting in Africa that "compared with a big English partridge drive ... [our] figures are modest enough; yet we had always the satisfaction of feeling that our sport was thoroughly and essentially wild ... and that, to our own exertions ... were the results of our day's sport entirely due."[61] This comment mobilizes familiar elements from the sportsman-hunter discourse, including wild sport, self-restraint, and the exertion required by the right kind of hunting, and the British hunt slides into the discourse here as an antagonist, as what American sport is *not*, even when pursued in Africa. Over time, sportsmanship became the most common basis for critique of the British, in the same way that Anglo-Saxonism became the language of connection.

Among the British, sportsmanship had never been a *necessary* part of the story that they were telling. There were prominent British hunters who called for sportsmanship and bag limits, including Buxton, Selous, and Hesketh Prichard, but many British hunters also routinely and publicly violated those ideals (including Selous in his early days as a professional hunter). Such violations might take place at home in massive pheasant shoots on landed estates or out in the empire, where such practices as the "tiger ring" remained popular well into the twentieth century. It is in fact difficult to find any single group among the British that hewed to the rules of sportsmanship as Americans understood them. This partly reflects the many roles that a British hunter might play over a lifetime: Selous explains that *A Hunter's Wanderings in Africa* might appear "a dreadful record of slaughter" but reminds readers that he was hunting, not for pleasure, but to support his expeditions.[62] It also reflects the greater heterogeneity among British authors: for every one who wanted to be a moderate sportsman, another would see potting every animal he came across as part of the pleasures of empire. Nor were British hunters always sanguine about being asked to obey game laws in what they regarded as the colonies: William Baillie-Grohman complained bitterly in print about the "pettifogging meanness" of being expected to follow Canadian game laws.[63]

For American sportsmen-hunters, on the other hand, sportsmanship had always been central to their narratives: even as their sport needed to be wild, so did their hunting need to be self-restrained. This in turn worked as a constant counterbalance to any admiration they might profess for the English. "Unhealthy" was the word Roosevelt most often used for English hunting: their predilection toward the shooting of huge bags "are symptoms of a spirit which is most unhealthy from every standpoint," he told readers of *The Deer Family*.[64] (This may seem particularly ironic coming from Roosevelt, whose performances in the field were so egregiously bloody that they drew the ire of some British sportsmen, but in printed discussions Roosevelt consistently linked healthy sport to self-restraint and to American, not British, hunting.) Nor was Roosevelt alone in condemning the British. Whitney concurred. "The American sportsman, who declines to shoot a doe . . . finds it hard to bring himself in touch with this side of the British sportsman," he told readers of *A Sporting Pilgrimage*; he later stated more bluntly that the "American sportsman has nothing to learn from the English sportsman."[65] For their part, the English seem to have been aware that, when it came to sportsmanship, they were the bête noire of their Anglo-Saxon brethren. "In America we, from the other side of the Atlantic, are not generally given credit for moderation," Claude Cane noted regretfully.[66]

These differences in attitude are visible in accounts of individual hunting as well. Selous's first book describes his experiences as a professional ivory hunter; this helps to explain the focus on killing animals, but the presentation is also very different from that of American narratives. "We came across a black rhinoceros cow . . . and, as we wanted meat for ourselves and our boys, shot her," Selous writes, adding that "we got some very good meat from her ribs, which was probably due to the fact that she was within a few days of calving."[67] (Compare this to the American who "declines to shoot a doe.") When it comes to elephant in particular, Selous is all business, beginning by harassing the animals from horseback, "our object being to tire them before we commenced fire. . . . [I] gave a young bull a bullet behind the shoulder as he came broadside past me. He only ran about 100 yards, and then fell dead. After this I quickly killed two more with five shots—a fine cow and another young bull. The fourth I tackled [was] a bull with tusks . . ."[68] This listing of kills is typical for British narratives. Selous also posted his kill numbers in the back of the book and they help to explain why elephant were becoming scarce in the area by 1880. Contrast this to American Winthrop Chanler, hunting for pleasure in East Africa. He and his friend George are surprised by a group of elephant and shoot, not only hitting a cow but missing the kill shot and breaking her leg. Together they watch in horror as the herd attempts to lift the wounded cow to her feet. "With our bad marksmanship it would have been (to say the least) brutal to blaze away at the gallant little herd," he writes, leaving the reader to decide if this is a punishment imposed by the hunters on themselves (no shooting unless you can hit your target) or intended as a testament to the elephants' valor. He and George retreat in shame, but Chanler returns to end the cow's suffering once the herd has given up and moved off.[69]

Americans thus brought their focus on sportsmanship with them as they began hunting in the British Empire. Selous, along with Melliss and his fellow soldier-hunters, might list all the animals they encountered and shot, but American narratives remained focused on the man, the stalk, and the singular performance, whether Bryden celebrating his modest kill count or Madeira tracking lions on foot across the veldt. This allowed Americans to transfer the discourse of the manly still-hunter from wild North America to the British Empire without losing any of the associations that they had worked so hard to construct. Instead, the central tenets of self-control and sportsmanship were thrown into sharp relief in contrast to the British hunt as the sportsmanlike stalk took on yet another meaning: defining what it meant to hunt like an American while traveling abroad.

All these conversations took place across and among published narratives, visible to readers on both sides of the Atlantic. The final theme of these narratives that I want to discuss, however, is far more elusive, because it has to do with something that American hunters did *not* write about: hunting as a training ground for war.

The British hunting narratives were saturated with military connections, partly because so many of the authors were soldiers, partly because the link to soldiering was often made explicit: Baden-Powell assured readers that "the hunting-field has been described by the best authorities as the training school for the cavalry officer."[70] Americans seem to have eschewed this idea completely, however: with the single exception of Theodore Roosevelt, none of the American sportsmen-hunters I've read have cited hunting as a training ground for war.[71] Since Van Dyke the American hunter-writers had presented their hunting as useful because it inculcated the manly virtues of the workplace, not of the battlefield. It might be argued that this was a politic move on their part, since their reading audience appears to have been deeply ambivalent about American imperialism overseas, but one would expect such a motivation to result in an ambivalent mix of stories. Instead, references to soldiering, war, and fighting seem to have been *not part* of the sportsman-hunter genre in the most profound sense: that of an absolute absence.[72]

This is all the more interesting because, of course, there were American hunter-soldiers—mainly Army officers stationed in the American West—and because, a generation earlier, soldiers like Custer had earned fame as big-game hunters. There are almost no published accounts of big-game hunting by American soldiers by the turn of the century, however; they appear for the most part to have been too poor to engage in prolonged hunts.[73] One notable exception was army officer, hunter, and explorer Lieutenant Frederick Schwatka, who wrote several popular books about his adventures, including *Nimrod in the North* and *A Summer in Alaska*; his narratives present hunting as a pleasure and as a way to feed his survey camps, however, rather than as intimately connected to the skills of soldiering.[74] Overall the association of martial prowess with hunting does not appear in the post-1880 American big-game hunting narratives (again, with the exception of Roosevelt).

The fundamental importance of manliness to the story the sportsmen-hunters were telling may have influenced them to avoid such associations; perhaps the aggressiveness associated with soldiering aligned too closely with violence, primitive masculinity, and atavism, all of which were elements of American culture that had been excluded from their narratives since Van Dyke. Moreover, unlike the narratives of British hunters, who tended to be forthright about the violence that accompanied imperial rule ("Stalking the African"), American hunter-writers had consistently elided the violence that had come with western expansion, and, when they pictured themselves having a frontier experience, it was usually in a wilderness populated only by animals. War had never been part of the story they had been telling, and violence had never been a constituent of manly character. Instead the central challenge to which they were responding was the threat posed by the Second Industrial Revolution to the nineteenth-century workplace virtues. Their hunting was never a lesson for colonized peoples abroad, but rather a display for middle- and upper-class readers at home.

This may actually have helped to smooth the way as more Americans began to hunt in the British Empire. The Englishman in Somaliland or Kumaon was very often a soldier, and hunting allowed him to gain practical knowledge of peoples and places that might someday come under British rule. As a result, where he was hunting mattered, because it was a real place—one that had been conquered or was about to be, marked perhaps by uprisings in the past or unrest in the present. American Percy Madeira, picking up his rifle and worrying about whether that shadowy rock is actually a rhino, makes no such connections, nor needs to. The meaning of his hunt is about his own performance, and, in the process, the East African veldt becomes just another stage. It can in fact be anywhere, and that allows both the history of the land, and the growing infrastructure of empire that so fascinated Churchill, to vanish without jarring the reader unduly. It's not about the stage. It's about the actor.

In the process, the realities of hunting in the British Empire faded from view. The elements of the sportsman-hunter discourse that were most strongly connected to an American exceptionalist story—hunting as work rather than as aristocratic leisure, the sportsmanlike stalk that displayed willpower and self-restraint, the pioneer heritage of "thoroughly and essentially wild" sport—were all accentuated through contrast with the British, and with what Americans at home thought about British hunting. Confronted in the British narratives with an alternate and very popular interpretation of the meaning of the hunt, American sportsmen-hunters engaged enthusiastically with some elements, publicly rejected others, and greeted still other associations with a resounding silence. In the process they strengthened already existing lines of exclusion while insisting that there was a single recognizably American way to hunt, whether in the Rocky Mountains or on the plains of East Africa.

The term "transnational" is most often deployed by those writing history from the bottom up, not by those studying fervent servants of empire or American elites, but in some ways it applies well to the connections between British and American big-game hunters.[75] Certainly those relationships were more than simply transatlantic, acted out as they were across continents and colonies, in languages of racial solidarity, and on the pages of international publications. Some of these connections were defined by friendship or by the exchanges between guest and host, while others existed entirely in print, in introductions and forewords or in shared publishing houses. And as they traveled across the same landscapes, hired the same guides, and were published in the same periodicals, British and American hunter-writers became ever more entangled, in person and in print.

Despite this, however, their hunting was always interpreted in their narratives and presented to their audiences in relentlessly national terms. Just as the writing of Churchill, Wardrop, and Selous offered British readers images of adventure, romance, and a world colonized and civilized by England, so American hunter-writers insisted that their hunting be understood as manly sport in the wilderness, a test that demonstrated sportsmanship and character. They used their readers' familiarity with British hunting to emphasize what was different about their own experiences and to talk about what it meant to be both American and an American sportsman. The need to take into account how hunter-writers understood and interpreted their own actions disrupts any reading of British and American hunting as straightforwardly transnational. Nationalism served a very real function in the narratives, one that reached beyond rhetoric to shape expectations and experiences alike. Although embedded in the shared contexts of international travel and transatlantic publishing, British and American hunters insisted to readers on both sides of the Atlantic that national identity was essential to understanding the meaning of the hunt.

And what did readers make of all this? Due to the transatlantic publishing trade, both American and British readers could move easily between Selous and Sheldon, Churchill and Madeira, between different translations of essentially identical hunts—and I can't be the first to wonder about where Churchill's railway fit into Madeira's wild savannah experience. Did readers of the time notice the disjunctions among these narratives? There is little direct evidence with which to answer that question, but it seems unlikely that there was a single nationalist reaction among the audiences for these stories. Readers had the materials available to choose among a variety of narratives, and some of them may have engaged in a dynamic of selection and translation similar to that performed by the hunters themselves. This was all the more likely because the narratives seldom stood alone. Offered in newspapers, magazines, and anthologies that put divergent tales side by side, or that bracketed stories of self-reliant sport with advertisements for railway packages and professional guide services, the reading experience as a whole always had the potential to undermine the discourse that surrounded American wilderness hunting.

That discourse had proven both flexible and resilient, however, adding strength with each new challenge. As women took up hunting—and as readers took up their narratives—they offered an alternative to "manly sport with a rifle," one that reinforced the connections among still-hunting, sportsmanship, and the race and class of the hunter. The British posed a more profound challenge, and American hunter-writers responded by comparing and contrasting themselves to their Anglo-Saxon brethren, emphasizing hierarchies of class and race while giving a new dimension to their allegiance to sportsmanship: now it meant hunting, not like an Englishman, but like an American, even when overseas. These changes helped to keep the story of the still-hunt relevant to turn-of-the-century American culture. In an era when men and women were hunting together in increasing numbers, hunting narratives suggested how such companionship could be understood. In a period when many Americans were debating the meaning of imperialism for their nation, the narratives became part of wider conversations about what it meant to hunt like an American—what it meant to *be* an American, whether at home or abroad.

Fissures were beginning to appear, however. The ever-growing popularity of the big-game hunt, and the changes to transportation that allowed hunters to pursue game globally, were not just challenges to narrative. They were having very real impacts on both animal populations and wilderness areas. American hunters had already contorted the story they were telling to adapt to hunting in the British Empire. Soon they would confront the need to negotiate not only railway stations and water towers but also regulated guiding, tourist infrastructures, and conservation laws. In response, they adapted once again; those adaptations form the final part of this story.

# Part Three
# Discourse and Consequences

CHAPTER 8

# Stories of Guides and Gunbearers

"... and yet how jolly they look," John Millais writes of his Micmac guides (figure 8.1)—but at this distance it is difficult to discern how he meant that comment to be read. Is he surprised, picturing his own reaction if he were asked to carry this much weight? Is he complacent, even smug, reassuring himself and his readers that he has not asked too much of his workers? Or is he impressed? Is his tone one of admiration? Any of these readings is possible. Many hunters wrote about their guides and admiration for their hard work abounds, but so too do denigrating comments, descriptions of conflict on the trail, and ugly moments of judgment based on class or race. Such stories filled hunters' narratives and overflowed into their photographs, and that raises questions: why were there so many ways of talking about the role of guides on these trips? How can moments of both praise and denigration be understood, especially considering that these narratives were written for white middle-class reading audiences? And why are discussions of guides and gunbearers so prevalent in the first place?

These questions don't form a useful starting place, however, because the answers make little sense without first understanding who guides were. Where did guides and gunbearers come from? What work did they do, why did they do it, and how did they understand the big-game hunt? Hinx and Bernard are engaged in performances of their own, but their relationship to the hunt is radically different from Millais's. They are carrying the packs for wages, which they will use to support themselves and their families, and from their perspective the photograph and its caption can be seen as free advertising: creating a chance for future work, perhaps, with another visiting hunter who has read Millais's book and wants jolly employees. They were no less entangled than was Millais in the global expansion of big-game hunting, but for them its fundamental meaning was economic. Any attempt to

MICMAC INDIANS PACKING
John Hinx and Steve Bernard are seen carrying over 120 lbs. a-piece, and yet how jolly they look. With such a weight they will tramp all day.

Figure 8.1. From John Millais, *Newfoundland and Its Untrodden Ways*, 1907.

understand the stories that hunter-writers told about their guides thus has to begin with the basics: with who guides were and how they related to the turn-of-the-century big-game hunt.

## I. GUIDES AND GUIDE ECONOMIES

The term "guide" is a remarkably flexible one. The only thing that connected all guides was that they were paid employees hired by a hunter. That hunter needed a variety of kinds of assistance, ranging from finding his way over unfamiliar ground and tracking animals, to skinning and preserving trophies, to having help with domestic camp duties such as tending the fire, washing clothes, and preparing meals. Depending on the trip's length he might also need assistance carrying supplies or handling pack animals. East Africa's safari system offered the most elaborate version of this, with hunters usually setting off with porters and grooms as well as with tentboys who did the cooking and cleaning, a headman who organized the safari, and one or more gunbearers and trackers. (The tentboy/headman distinction appears to have been an African one, rather than a racist imposition, and probably reflects the fact that the tentboys were doing what was traditionally women's rather than men's work.[1]) In other places, a hunter making a short trip into the wilds might hire only one or two guides. It's unusual to find visiting hunters venturing out without assistance of some kind, however, even if that help was just a local man who could point out where the mountain sheep liked to graze.

Even that was less straightforward than it might seem, however, because there was nothing intuitive about the interests and desires of big-game hunters. Historians focused solely on Western guides on the Great Plains have seen them as teaching their clients about hunting, but when it came to the art of the still-hunt, and looking at guiding worldwide, the reverse was clearly the case.[2] Major George Evans, hiring villagers to assist him in Burma, had one stalk after another spoiled by his helpers, who would yell suggestions to him as he crawled through the brush toward the animals, or frighten the game away by standing on the highest point they could find to watch the action. He suggests three sentences that every big-game hunter should learn in the native language where he is hunting: "Don't speak," "If you see the [animal], don't point," and "Sit here, don't move."[3] The focus on male animals and trophy heads was also new to many men hired as guides: Whitney ran into this, and he was hardly alone. Evans notes that "it must be remembered that your Burmans want meat. They don't care a brass farthing about the head, and would really rather you shot a cow than otherwise, the meat being more tender, and the animal itself less likely to charge than a bull."[4]

The biggest problem that hunters seem to have faced with guides, however, was preventing them from doing the shooting. Again and again in the narratives, hunters struggled to control their employees, who either thought of themselves as partners in the hunt or simply didn't care about their employer's experience once they were in the field. There was no easy way to handle this problem unless the sportsman was skilled enough to hunt without a guide. Charles Sheldon, after one bad experience, made it a policy to leave his men at camp to keep the coffee warm while he went hunting by himself, but not everyone was competent enough to choose this option.[5] Instead, many hunters arrived at their destination knowing that they needed a guide but uncertain of how to pick a good one. Warnings to such neophytes abound in the narratives. Horace Vachell notes "the unwisdom of engaging scouts and guides on no recommendation save their own.... Your honest trapper is in the woods, not lounging about a saloon or hotel.... Pay him well, and let it be plainly understood between you that he is not to shoot without orders."[6]

The "shoot *without orders*" matters, because it introduces yet another complication to the relationship between hunting and guiding: many guides and gunbearers were expected to hunt at various points during their trips. Expeditions needed to be fed, and the handful of trophy animals taken by sportsmen seldom provided enough meat for a hunting party over days or weeks. African gunbearers, as well as guides in Asia and North America, were often expected to supplement expeditions by fishing, hunting game birds, and, sometimes, shooting land animals for meat. Such day-to-day hunting is almost always invisible in the published narratives, but it is the reason that African gunbearers and white hunters were both referred to by the same term, "shikári" (hunter), and also explains why so many hunter-writers were able to comment knowledgeably on their guides' hunting abilities. When Samuel Davis notes that his Newfoundland guide could "not be excelled" as a still-hunter, or Agnes Herbert explains that some native Alaskans "are excellent still-hunters—though none of them, in my opinion, come up to the black shikári," both writers are revealing that they have seen their employees not only hunting but specifically stalking game, even as they stake out positions of expert judgment for themselves.[7] Employing guides who were competent hunters themselves could thus resolve thorny logistical issues, even as it created other problems: the possibility of employing a guide who shot without orders, for instance, and who competed with the sportsman for the trophy.

What sportsmen-hunters needed were employees who understood the point of the stalk and the need for a trophy head, who knew when to lead and when to follow, who understood which animals they were allowed to shoot and which were off-limits to them, and who offered skills ranging from speaking a variety of languages to knowing how to preserve a trophy: in other words, specialists. As more and more big-game hunters traveled out from the American East Coast, the demand for such specialists only increased, and the result was the emergence of a class of professional hunting guides. As guiding grew as a profession, in turn, it became both systematized and regulated, part of a modernizing tourist economy that eventually reached around the world.

An examination of guiding in Alaska at the end of the nineteenth century reveals that guides shared common patterns that linked mobility, opportunity, and skill. Men who chose to work as guides usually held other jobs as well while hunting for their own subsistence and pleasure. They achieved recognition, and sometimes renown, for their guiding work, and they seem to have been more concerned with licensing laws, game regulations, and career opportunities than with writing accounts of their experiences for *Outing* or *Forest and Stream*.

The experiences of the man known as "Alaska's #1 Guide" were typical in many ways (although not in the level of fame he eventually achieved). Andrew Berg was a Finn who emigrated to Alaska in 1888 and settled on the Kenai Peninsula. At various times he worked as a trapper, fisherman, and miner, but within a few years of arriving he also began to participate in the market for moose antlers (exported south to be sold for interior decoration purposes).[8] In 1898 sportsman Dall DeWeese, headed to the Kenai for a hunting trip, saw Berg's trophies on sale in Tacoma and, on arrival in Alaska, sought him out. "He said he would go with me if he could get off from the cannery," DeWeese told readers in a *Field and Stream* article describing the trip. "I went to the superintendent, Capt. Wetherbee, who very kindly arranged for his release."[9]

This method of finding a guide in the late nineteenth century—as well as the impression of rather haphazard pre-planning on DeWeese's part—was dictated by circumstance: DeWeese was the first wealthy sportsman to hunt the Kenai, and so there was no system in place to help him organize his trip before he arrived in Alaska. His experience seems to have been typical of the period. A young Prentiss Gray, visiting Alaska in 1904 with his college roommate to do some shooting, ran into a native man, "Indian Johnny," leading a pack train; when Johnny told the boys that he had some hunting experience, they promptly hired him to guide them. (Gray noted that "he had been Andrew Stone's guide and we found later that he bore a splendid reputation as a hunter."[10]) Arriving, then finding a guide, also seems to have been the pattern across the border in the Canadian Rockies, although beginning a bit earlier: 1887 is the date for the first big-game hunting party sallying out of Banff (two English sportsmen guided by Tom Wilson, who soon established himself as the guide officially recommended by the Canadian Pacific Railway).[11] In areas where the Hudson Bay Company held sway things were slightly different, because sportsmen could appeal to the HBC factors to recommend a guide. This was how Whitney found Beniah, and how Leonidas Hubbard and Dillon Wallace found George Elson: they simply wrote to the HBC man in James Bay, asking him to send them a native guide to take to Labrador.[12]

Indian Johnny, Berg, Elson, and Wilson were all pulled into guiding out of other occupations by the demands of sportsmen for assistance, local knowledge, and, sometimes, simply the need to have one member of the party who knew what he was doing in the woods. All these guides had held myriad other jobs and, although this is difficult to quantify, seem to have been characterized by wanderlust; at any rate, it's surprising how many of them were already on the move. Some were immigrants—Berg, for example, but also Mary Schaffer's guide Billy Warren, an Englishman who, after fighting in the Boer War, came to the Rockies seeking some type of work that didn't require him to sit in an office all day.[13] Other guides traveled far from home at different points. Elson had worked on the railways before achieving fame as a guide to Labrador, while James Tyrrell was guided on his expedition into the Canadian North by three Iroquois brothers from Quebec, one of whom had fought with Wolesley in Egypt.[14] Far from being just local men who happened to fall in with hunters, professional guides were thus often well traveled, sometimes across continents and oceans, and had a variety of work and life experiences that they brought to the job.

Guiding offered them a chance to participate in a hunting trip for cash wages, as well as the lure of spending time outdoors. Billy Warren embraced guiding for these reasons, and Edward House's guide in the Canadian Rockies (who owned a ranch in the area) also saw it as a chance to enjoy hunting and camping and be paid for it.[15] Hunters' narratives are full of accounts of pleasant nights spent by campfires listening to their guides tell hunting stories, or of guides and hunters shaking hands over a particularly satisfying trophy, and there is no reason to imagine that guides did not sometimes enjoy such trips or feel a sense of accomplishment over their successes. Pride in performance appears to have run very deep indeed, sometimes: George Elson, looking down on the Labrador lake that was the goal of his expedition, leaves us the stark comment in his journal, "Your joy no man taketh from you."[16]

Working as a guide could also enhance men's reputations within their communities. Berg became well known enough to merit newspaper coverage in Alaska when he arrived in a new town, while Roosevelt tells us that, shortly after becoming vice president, he went hunting in the West with guide Johnny Goff and was very full of himself—until he found out the locals referred to him simply as "Johnny Goff's tourist."[17] Of course, from the locals' point of view, it was the guide who was the stable factor and whose work helped to bring sportsmen into town, where they also spent money on lodging, equipment, and supplies, and hired cooks, packers, and wranglers.

Over time, guides also began to receive recognition from sportsmen-hunters, in part because of the growing popularity of hunting narratives. John Burnham mentions running into a hunting party and immediately recognizing their guide, Captain Hubrick, from pictures in sportsmen's magazines, while Agnes Herbert, hunting in Alaska, was happy to have hired guide Pitka Charley after being told that his skills "rivalled the celebrated Andrew Berg, most renowned of Alaskan hunters."[18] Such recognition mattered from the guide's point of view because it represented free advertising. Hunters recommended guides to one another personally, but they also promoted them by name in books, articles, and captioned photographs. Samuel Davis hired his Newfoundland guide, Richard LeBuffe, on another sportsman's recommendation and then included LeBuffe's mailing address in his own narrative of the trip, while another Newfoundlander, Bob Saunders, met Frederick Selous by coincidence, guided him twice, and then was recommended by him to John Millais, who discussed his skills at length in *Newfoundland and Its Untrodden Ways*.[19] Guides also enthusiastically promoted themselves, placing advertisements in local and national publications, giving away souvenir calendars, and jockeying to become the "official" guides recommended by railways and tourist hotels.[20]

The evidence left by these guides is very different from that of a hunting narrative published in *Outing*. Roosevelt wrote at length about his ranch in Medora, and histories of Medora have been written since, but finding out how much the Marquis of Medora paid to keep a guide permanently on staff can only be discovered by going there and taking the house tour. *Ranch Life and the Hunting Trail* has a weight in the hand; guide traces are mostly ephemera. This is clear even in the historiography, where two of the best books on guiding in this period—Hart's *Diamond Hitch* and Cassidy and Titus's *Alaska's No. 1 Guide*—are peppered with sidebars and illustrations that display photographs, letters, newspaper clippings, and bills. Such evidence tells a tale in which the financial relationship between guide and client, not the manly stalk, was the central meaning of the hunt. Even in hunters' own narratives such assessments occasionally become visible: Hesketh Prichard, talking to his guides about less sportsmanlike hunters for whom they had worked, records one guide's comment that "[a hunter like that] don't deserve no consideration, though his dollars is sound money to us."[21] This is as much a judgment of what constitutes proper hunting, and of what type of hunter deserves respect, as any overheated statement from Whitney's View-Point, and yet it couldn't be more different, because dollars are absolutely part of the equation.

Even as the sportsmen-hunters created one story about the still-hunt in their narratives, another way of understanding what they were doing was appearing among populations in the big-game hunting areas. That meaning was made visible in bills and advertisements, in the emergence of entire economies around visiting hunters, and occasionally in the reports of sportsmen who found that guides had their own motives for participating in the hunt. At one point House discovered that he had employed a guide intent on stocking his family's larder with moose meat, even if doing so ruined House's sport.[22] Other hunters found that paying up front had its drawbacks: Frank Russell arrived in the Barren Grounds having been warned that his guide would probably "be quite willing to lead me through the swamps as long as his pay was continued, and . . . if he found moose he would probably guide me away from them. Why should he give me a moose that he could come next day and kill for himself?"[23] Guides were also capable of negotiating their work conditions on the trail, directly or indirectly. A guide taken far from camp and forced to carry back a large trophy might easily damage it beyond repair in the act of skinning it, for example, forcing the hunter to leave it where it lay, and at least one sportsman discovered that, if he jumped into an icy stream to help his employees haul the boat, they would be happy to ease off and let him do all the pulling.[24] This was hunting as part of a tourist economy, where hunter-employers and their employees negotiated to try to find an outcome satisfactory to both, and where the hunter's first rule was not "manly sport with the rifle" but rather caveat emptor.[25]

Over time, guides became part of larger systems that I'm going to call "guide economies." A guide economy functions, not through random contacts such as Berg and DeWeese's, but rather by the laws of supply and demand: as more hunters arrive willing to pay for guides, more and more men take up guiding. Over time, guiding becomes regulated and licensed. Legislation begins to appear that deals specifically with the guide's role, not as part of a fantasy of manly sport, but in terms of local and state economies. Such changes were also part of wider modernizing tourist economies, which included the development of hotels, outfitters, and livery stables, as well as national and international advertising of hunting grounds and of the amenities available to visiting hunters.

Such a system emerged in Alaska within only a few years of the arrival of the first sportsman-hunter, and in the Canadian West even earlier than that. The Union Pacific was arranging railway packages for sportsmen as early as the 1880s, and some railroads published guidebooks for traveling hunters, listing hotels and giving the names and addresses of individual guides.[26] There was a considerable demand for this kind of guide economy and it expanded enormously in the first decade of the twentieth century. By then, hunters were coming to Alaska and the Canadian Rockies from all over North America. In 1907, heading up to the Cassiars from Seattle, Edward House found that on his boat alone there were twenty-three sportsmen: five from New York, two from Boston, two from Philadelphia, three from Pittsburgh, one from Chicago, four from Colorado Springs, one from Vancouver, and three hunters from England, two of them accompanied by their wives.[27] This increase in traffic had an effect not only because of the growing numbers of sportsmen but also because so many of them were neophytes. The haphazard approach of Dall DeWeese and Prentiss Gray was made necessary partly because of the lack of a guide economy, but both men were capable of hunting on their own if need be. As more and more sportsmen came north to bag big game, however, the number of inexperienced clients—and the lure of all that cash—meant that an entire apparatus came into being around them, so that would-be hunters could arrange their guides ahead of time through the railways and could book their hotel and outfitter by mail before arrival. Guides participated wholeheartedly in this and many branched out, becoming owners or part-owners of stables, outfitting companies, and, in rare cases, hotels.[28]

Legislation related to guiding attests to the speed with which the influx of visiting hunters became an important part of state economies. In 1910 Alaskan governor Walter Clark issued regulations for the licensing and compensation of guides and packers. Clark distinguished between first-class and second-class guides, with the first-class guides being white citizens and the second-class guides mixed-race or native, and set prices for guide licenses (first-class licenses were three times more expensive to purchase than second-class ones). According to the regulations, all guides, first or second class, could charge $5–10 a day for their services, and all out-of-state hunters were *required* to hire a guide for each hunter in the party.[29] This was an extension of a set of regulations originally created in Maine and known as the Maine system of guides, which ensured that out-of-state hunters would pour money into local economies by hiring local workers and by purchasing hunting and fishing licenses.[30] Such regulations framed visiting hunters as meaningful because of the dollars they had to spend and provide evidence of the economic importance of guiding to legislators and local communities alike. They also represent a massive alteration to hunting. In 1898 Dall DeWeese could simply walk into a cannery and emerge with a guide. Twelve years later, such insouciance would have resulted in a fine at the very least.

Hunting thus changed rapidly in Alaska and guides were at the heart of it. Andrew Berg's later career reveals him swiftly adapting to these changes. He had been a market hunter plucked from cannery work by DeWeese, but by 1910 his reputation as a guide was such that he was chosen to be licensed first in recognition of his pioneering role, which had won him folk-hero status that continues to this day in Alaska. In later years he also supplemented his guiding with work as a game warden and fish warden, new jobs that emerged with the spread of licensing and regulation. Neither he nor anyone else appears to have seen such work as incompatible with his roles as guide and hunter. In 1914 he wrote to the governor to clarify the rule about one guide per hunter in the case of married couples hunting together, while the next year he wrote again to suggest a prohibition on the sale of game meat, since market hunters were taking too high a toll on the animal population.[31] Quite a change from the newly arrived Finn hunting moose in order to hawk their antlers in Tacoma, but Berg was a man who moved with his times.

There was nothing unique about any of this. It occurred everywhere that hunters traveled—including in British East Africa, the other mecca of big-game hunters. Most historians who have studied the African safari have examined it in the contexts of British imperialism and racial oppression rather than in comparison with North American guide economies, but hunters' needs, and the laws of supply and demand, were much the same in both places. Increasing numbers of Americans were also traveling to Africa to hunt at the turn of the century. There they would find guide economies that were in some ways remarkably similar to those in North America and that developed in parallel ways over time. Examining the evolution of the safari can thus help to illuminate the global nature of the economies centered around big-game hunting, even as it offers a different approach to thinking about African workers and their relationship to the hunt.

As in Alaska, hunting in East Africa in the late nineteenth century was a matter of doing-it-yourself.[32] When A. Donaldson Smith left Philadelphia in 1893 to go on a trip to Lake Rudolf, he had to assemble his safari on arrival, a painstaking challenge. The hunting literature overflows with advice on the potential pitfalls of such an experience and how to avoid them. Most important, it seems, was making sure that your workers were from different villages and, if possible, of different tribes, which made it less likely that they would collectively (and repeatedly) strike for higher wages. It was also highly recommended that the neophyte hunter, if possible, employ a Somali as headman.[33] (The Somalis enjoyed a fearsome reputation among both white hunters and, it appears, other Africans. Part of that reputation was that, once having taken money and given their word, they could be counted on to carry out their side of a bargain: safaris with Somali headmen did not suffer from strikes. This benefit was offset, however, by the need to provide halal meat for all Somali workers and by their absolute refusal to have anything to do with pig-sticking—if the hunter wanted boar, he would have to track, kill, and dress his own trophy.[34]) The successful hunter thus needed to be knowledgeable about topics ranging from African tribal identities to Muslim dietary practices, and that was before he even started hiring. From the first moments, he was making decisions that could determine the outcome of his hunt—and he would be going farther into the wilds, and with far more kit, than would any similar hunter in Alaska or the Canadian Rockies.

That may be why change came even more quickly to British East Africa than it did to Alaska, fueled by the influx both of American sportsmen and of hundreds of British tourists, settlers, and soldiers on long leave. With this came a stabilization of the safari system, which soon developed its own economy and hierarchy. At the top of the ladder in any safari was the headman, who organized the other workers and took care of logistics, and the gunbearers and trackers who assisted the hunter in pursuit of game. Below them came camp servants, then grooms for the pack animals, and lastly porters. Percy Madeira describes the pay scale for these workers as of 1907: seventy-five rupees a day for the headman, trackers, and gunbearers, fifty for camp servants, twenty for grooms, and four rupees a day for porters.[35]

The extreme gulf between porter pay and gunbearer pay is very suggestive: it looks like the sort of pay scale found in any system where people are ranked in a hierarchy based on increasing skill and experience, and the safari system appears to have worked exactly that way. In *Seventeen Trips through Somaliland*, Swayne sums up the trajectory for his readers: as you pass through a village a boy leaves home to join your caravan; he hangs about until he can take the place of a porter who deserts; by his fourth or fifth expedition he's worked his way up to become a gunbearer or headman; and within a few more years he's settled in Aden as a merchant, trading with tribes he originally met by guiding sportsmen on safari. This finale may be unexpected, but it indicates that the safari system functioned within a wider realm of social and economic options for Africans.[36]

This advancement seems to have been a more formal process than in North America, based on letters of recommendation given to safari workers at the end of each trip. There are numerous accounts of African men meeting ships from England and India at the Aden docks, displaying recommendations from previous trips and competing to offer the widest set of skills to the inexperienced white hunters disembarking. Even as they tried to persuade potential employers to hire them, however, African workers, like North American guides, seem to have been making their own judgments: Swayne notes that the first English phrase that most Africans in Aden learned was the term "damn fool passengers."[37]

Hiring the right gunbearer, and being employed by the right hunter, mattered hugely because much of Africa's big game was dangerous to hunt.[38] The hunter and gunbearer needed to trust one another to be cool and competent under pressure. The ideal gunbearer stayed "at your elbow with the barrel of one rifle pressed against your leg that you may know that he is there," but there were hunters who crept up to game only to find their gunbearer (and their guns) hanging back in the brush.[39] Far more perilous was the gunbearer who panicked at the moment of the animal's charge. Evans notes the danger of being shot by a panicked gunbearer or of losing your gun as the man runs away, while other hunters, waiting for a clean shot, report being pushed or shaken by their frightened employee.[40] Fear could also distract a gunbearer at a crucial moment: Selous was permanently scarred when his gunbearer unthinkingly doubled the charge in his gun, causing it to explode in his face.[41]

A gunbearer could just as easily be endangered by an incompetent hunter. Winthrop Chanler describes wounding an African buffalo, which retreats into the bush. He is beginning to follow it in when his gunbearer, he tells us, murmurs the words "Mr. Dawnay" in his ear—the name of a white hunter who had been killed just four months earlier, by a wounded buffalo, in brush. Chanler hesitates, and as he does he hears the rest of the buffalo's herd moving toward him. "My nerves did not assume that steelly quality I had imagined always resulted from a sudden danger," Chanler writes. "I began to understand why buffalo shooting in the bush has always been considered unsafe, and began to regret that the road back to the open plain was not a shorter one." He and his gunbearer beat a hasty retreat.[42] In this case, the hunter was about to make a dangerously bad decision, and his gunbearer

Juma Yohari with Nilotic bushbuck
*From a photograph by Kermit Roosevelt*

Figures 8.2 and 8.3. Professional gunbearers. Figure 8.2 shows Juma Yohari on Roosevelt's 1909 safari. Roosevelt describes him in *African Game Trails* as "a coal-black Swahili Moslem.... [The gunbearers] were capital men for their special work" (390). Figure 8.3 is Jerramani, who also worked on Roosevelt's safaris, although he is not mentioned as a gunbearer; he may have been employed lower in the safari hierarchy. Twelve years later, in 1921 when this picture was taken, he was still in safari work, serving as Martin and Osa Johnson's headman and Martin's gunbearer. (Information on Jerramani from Pascal and Eileen Imperato, *They Married Adventure*, 100. Photograph by Martin Johnson, courtesy of the Martin and Osa Johnson Museum.)

knows, not only how foolish it is, but also how to dissuade his employer from continuing. He may very well have saved Chanler's life. White hunters did die in Africa, the unfortunate Dawnay among them, although it appears not to have happened often. Selous is one of the few writers to discuss the death of a white hunter at length, and he put the blame on the man's refusal to follow the good advice of his gunbearer. Considering Selous's popularity, that story would have been well known to neophyte hunters assembling a safari in Aden or Nairobi.[43]

This is why letters of recommendation mattered so much, because a competent and experienced gunbearer could save a hunter's life. By the same token, Africans wanted to know who was hiring them, and, the more skilled they were, the more likely they were to have the power to select among possible employers. In a how-to article entitled "The Caravan, Headman, Gun-Bearers Etc." Sir Frederick Jackson explained to readers that, to employ the best of the African gunbearers, a white hunter had to arrive with his own letter of recommendation from another hunter that these guides had worked for and respected.[44] This safari elite included men such as Karscho Aden, whom W. F. Whitehouse describes as "a man of great reputation in Somaliland [who] had been with William Astor Chanler in East Africa, and . . . had served a short time, with credit, with the British in the Somali war." This is clearly the same man as Donaldson Smith's "Karsha," who accompanies Smith's expedition to find a new route across Somaliland to Lake Rudolf, and whom Smith mentions as both having hunted with Astor Chanler and having originally discovered Lake Rudolf with Count Teleki's expedition.[45] Like a select number of his compatriots, Karscho Aden was a guide and explorer at the peak of his profession, renowned both in Somaliland and among the international set of sportsmen-hunters.

The safari thus linked employers and employees in a system of evaluation and selection even as it developed an internal system of promotion based on skill and experience. As in Alaska, the East African guide economy also offered opportunities for social and economic advancement, even as it became ever more regulated and organized over time, the better to accommodate the neophyte hunters arriving in droves. In 1893 Donaldson Smith needed to put in a great deal of effort in order to ensure a successful trip: before setting off for Africa, he read everything he could find on organizing safaris, solicited advice from Swayne and William Lord Smith, and stopped off in London in order to take a course from the map curator of the Royal Geographic Society. Just fourteen years later in 1907, however, Percy Madeira was able to take a very different path to safari success. First he wrote to Rowland Ward's, the London taxidermist, asking where the best bag in Africa had been secured that year. Told that it was in East Africa, he wrote to the Army & Navy Stores in London for an estimate of an outfit for a three-month trip for him and his wife including everything but clothes, guns, and ammunition, price including delivery at Nairobi; at the same time he contacted a safari outfitters in Nairobi. The Madeiras arrived in Nairobi and left for their safari within forty-eight hours: safari-by-mail.[46]

This systematization of the safari must have been a massive relief to many hunters (and to some African workers). In one stroke it moved the most difficult decisions out of the hunter's hands, reduced the likelihood of employees striking or proving incompetent in the field, and standardized pay and employment terms for the workers themselves. In 1910, when John McCutcheon described the safari pay scale in the *Chicago Tribune* (unchanged from Madeira's description), he added that he was also required by law to provide a blanket, sweater, and water bottle for each porter, while other expedition workers received those things as well as uniforms and shoes. The regulations don't seem to have fazed McCutcheon, who praises the ease of it all: "Newland and Tarlton is the firm that outfits most of the shooting parties that start out from Nairobi. . . . If you wish them to do so, they will get your complete outfit, so you need not bring anything with you but a suitcase."[47] He doesn't discuss how Africans were hired under this system, but probably the process of gaining experience had not changed much. McCutcheon notes that a number of young boys "stowed away" on his trip and emerged over time to work, and one of his photographs shows a worker carrying a child of perhaps five, suggesting that some fathers may have brought their sons along.[48]

Not all the changes were positive, however. In Africa especially there were devastating results, often intertwined with imperial rule. John MacKenzie has detailed the ways that British game regulations preserved game for white hunters while preserving it from Africans, many of whom depended on hunting for sustenance during times of crop failure. There was also a clear ceiling on economic advancement within the safari system as it became more systematized, because safari companies were always owned and operated by whites. Africans performed as skilled and sometimes highly paid employees within that system, but to attain economic independence they needed to make a lateral move to become traders or merchants. Finally, just as white hunters ran risks on safari, so did African workers. Some of them died, killed by wild animals or struck down by disease. Agnes Herbert lost one of her men to a rhino: "The death of the poor hunter could not, strictly speaking, be ascribed to me. I might so easily have been the victim myself, but the horror of it all and a pity of it bothered me as I suppose it would not have done a real sportsman.... I wept and wept." Although it happened early in the trip, she concludes her book with her visit to the man's family.[49] This was part of the darker side of the safari and much of it was connected to British imperial rule—but not all of it.[50] It was also the result of a tourist economy that promised dangerous thrills for wealthy visitors while offering an unmatched opportunity to earn cash wages to poorer local inhabitants, in a pattern that continues in some parts of the world to this day.[51]

That victimization occurred is thus a certainty and yet to see African gunbearers—or for that matter Alaskan guides—solely as victims runs counter to much of the evidence in the sources. When we look at guiding anywhere we see first and foremost skilled workers, capable of striking or otherwise destroying a hunt, negotiating for wages, jockeying for social mobility, traveling widely, and sometimes acquiring fame, wealth, and power in their own communities. Guides used visiting hunters for their own purposes and often turned the boom in hunting to their own account. It is the speed of adaptation to the rise of big-game hunting that one takes away first from these accounts—how quickly guides and gunbearers, in any country, latched onto the haphazard big-game hunt, tamed it into an organized economy, and then milked it for everything they could. This in turn dovetailed with the growth of systematization and, soon after, regulation, whether in Alaska or British East Africa.

The growing professionalization of guiding in turn made organizing a trip ever easier for neophyte hunters who had read stories of big-game hunting and wanted to try it themselves. Such hunters, no matter how inexperienced, wanted to return with a trophy head, and guides were being paid to make sure that their clients were successful. Such help could take a variety of forms. Claude Cane, finding that he and his guide were each licensed to kill two moose on the trip, made it part of their written contract that he could shoot all four himself in his quest for the perfect trophy, while his guide would refrain from killing any.[52] Other guides, however, found themselves employed by incompetent hunters who needed them to do the shooting, bagging trophies that the client could then pass off as his own. There seems to have been a healthy market for this kind of assistance. One guide placed an ad that promised that he "undertakes to show gentlemen and sportsmen wild goats. Success certain. It is always *your* goat."[53]

For some hunters, then, the promise that the guide would do the shooting if it was necessary (and would keep his mouth shut afterward) was part of what they were purchasing. Guides seem to have been more or less sanguine about this aspect of their profession. Prichard sums it up, in a quote of which we have already seen part:

> those who buy heads in this fashion are generally rich parvenus or so-called sportsmen, who, having started for the woods with the same publicity which pervades their lives, do not relish returning to their native towns without a trophy. What manner of man it can be who is thus content to buy and to lie is a difficult question. Certainly . . . as one of my hunters said, "He don't deserve no consideration, though his dollars is sound money to us."[54]

Sportsmen who do not follow the rules are framed here as either nouveaux or "so-called," expelled from the fraternity, but, to underscore their worthlessness, Prichard calls on the testimony of his guides. These men would receive extra pay for providing the trophies their clients would claim to have shot, although they did not necessarily approve of the hunters who consumed their product.

That product was not only being provided to visiting sportsmen, however. Trophies had long been popular commodities in the British Empire, and by the late nineteenth century a similar market was emerging in North America.[55] Many guides, like Andrew Berg, started out bagging trophies for this market and were hired by sportsmen because of this evidence that they knew how to find game, but, as the market expanded, the trophy trade also became both systematized and global. Prichard notes that by 1907 interlocked caribou horns (done artificially, but the implication was that the caribou had died in combat) were bringing in as much as $50 in Seattle, moose heads in eastern Canada were selling for £20–50, and taxidermists offered him $200 for the fifty-two-inch trophy head he brought out of the Newfoundland bogs. The same taxidermists also brought groups of recreational sportsmen out to intercept the caribou migration at a railway junction called Howley, charging $200 for a packaged trip including transport, room, board, and mounting of the finest heads, and they also armed groups of local hunters and sent them into the bush to bring back heads that could be sold in New York and London.[56] Clive Phillipps-Wolley reports that in Canada every upcountry trader had a list of prices for trophies according to length and span of antlers, while Evans notes that the Indians and Burmese who violated game laws were often in the employ of a taxidermist, selling him the skin and horns and saving the meat for their families.[57] Local hunters, taxidermists, international markets, and those who yearned for a trophy head, for whatever reason, were all being linked together through the extension of transportation networks and the globalization of the trophy trade. Eventually, it would encompass six continents.

The commoditization of the trophy was a logical outcome of both the rise of big-game hunting and the business of narrative. The popular tales published by the sportsmen-hunters were often illustrated with pictures of their trophies. Those in turn helped to create the demand that taxidermists were meeting by making trophy display a sign of status, whether as proof of manliness or simply through association with famous names like Roosevelt and Selous. This seems to have been an unintentional result from the point of view of the sportsmen-hunters, and they greeted it with a combination of contempt and complete bewilderment. After all, for them taking trophies had a twofold purpose: the heads served as proof of the success of their manly hunt and as a goad to recollection. No one waxes more poetic on this point than Phillipps-Wolley: "*He* shot the beasts whose spoils are round him, and in the doing of it scenes were graven on his memory which can never be effaced; mental and physical qualities which, but for these silent witnesses, Age the doubter would persuade him that he never possessed, were tried and not found wanting."[58] In this reading, the mounted head is functioning as a sort of cross between a trophy cup and a vacation slide, and in that context the idea of hanging a trophy you haven't actually shot seems peculiar, like showing vacation slides of a place you didn't actually visit. Phillipps-Wolley notes that "as to the men who *buy* such trophies, they are not of our guild, nor is it easy to comprehend them or their motives."[59]

The expanding market in trophies offers another example of the complex economics that underlay both hunt and hunting narrative. Sportsmen-hunters lauded the still-hunt, insisted that the successful stalk testified to character, and condemned the market in trophies while feeding demand for it through their own status displays. For local hunters, however, things were simpler. From their point of view, trophy taking, like guiding, was primarily an opportunity to make money.

The gulf between these ways of understanding the meaning of the trophy is wonderfully illustrated by a conversation reported by Hesketh Prichard. One night in Newfoundland he is approached in camp by an Indian hoping to sell him caribou antlers for five dollars. Misreading Prichard's hesitation, the Indian points out that no one will ever know that Prichard didn't shoot the caribou himself. Prichard replies that there will be one person who will know, "however hard I tried to deceive him, and that he happened to be a person of some importance to me. 'Your guide?' suggested the Indian. After I had explained that I meant myself, he stared at me stolidly for a moment, then said he would take the horns . . . and sell them at the railway."[60] The Indian has not the slightest idea what Prichard is getting at. This visiting tourist is about to fling himself into Newfoundland's blackfly-infested bogs in order to bag a trophy: surely it would make more sense just to buy it? And he probably did find a taker down at the railway, some visitor who never planned to go anywhere near the caribou hunting grounds—nor to spend any money on hiring guides.

This was no small point, and it adds one final layer of complexity to the interactions among local communities, guide economies, tourism, and the trophy trade, because the growth of the global market in trophies brought market hunters into direct conflict with *guides* in some parts of the world. For men making their living by taking sportsmen into the wilds, a dearth of trophy heads could mean a dearth of visiting hunters, and that in turn could have an economic impact on businesses ranging from hotels to livery stables. Andrew Berg's trajectory from supplying heads and horns in the late nineteenth century to working as a game warden in the twentieth makes sense in this context: by 1910 he was making far more money as a licensed guide than he ever would have selling antlers in Tacoma. In fact, by 1910 guides were regularly allying with sportsmen to support game regulations and conservation measures that set them in opposition to other kinds of working-class hunters. The best of the guides and gunbearers had always been specialists with a marketable and highly desirable set of skills. They had nothing to gain, in the end, by allowing other working-class men from their communities to bag trophy heads for cash, but the reasons they supported conservation remained primarily economic, part of a fundamentally different story about the meaning of the hunt and the importance of trophy heads than the one that their clients were telling.

Both guiding and the trophy market illuminate the complex mixture of marketing and meaning that coalesced around big-game hunting at the turn of the century. Guides, who were increasingly licensed professionals, understood themselves to be employees; to them the hunt and the trophy were commodities bought and paid for. That was not the story big-game hunters were trying to tell, however, even as the presence of guides on their trips raised the specter that any sportsman's hunt might not really be his own, that, having left town to fanfare, he was coming back as something else—as someone who had bought a trophy, and bought a story. Even more troubling, of course, was that the manly, self-reliant wilderness hunter needed a guide in the first place. All these problems were only exacerbated by the rise of guiding as part of a global tourist economy, even as the expanding trophy market undermined the value of the trophy as proof of a successful stalk. As they sat down to write up their hunts, the sportsmen-hunters had to come to terms with all these things. In particular, the troubling issue of the guide who did the shooting for his client would become central to the construction of the sportsman-hunter narrative.

## II. STORIES OF GUIDES AND GUNBEARERS

In 1907 Whelan Townsend wrote an article entitled "The Sportsman and His Guide" for *Outdoor Life*. He began by posing a startling question: "Why is it that the average sportsman is held in such contempt by the guides and hunters of the backwoods?"[61] His answer calls into play many of the elements of the sportsman-hunter discourse. Townsend explains that guides' disdain resulted from being hired by the sportsman

> to pitch his tent, to cook for him . . . to carry his rifle, to show him the game—and, only too often, to kill his trophies for him. In doing this he virtually acknowledges . . . that he is a weakling come to play at a life which calls for only strong men. . . . This is being nursed; it is not . . . exploring, wilderness hunting. . . . The sportsman should live the life he has temporarily chosen in the proper way. He goes to rough it, to emulate those backwoodsmen of the past who made the white man's trail across this continent. To me, a trip without the hard work . . . is not worth the doing.[62]

There was, by 1907, a "proper way" to experience the wilds, not like a middle-class tourist, but rather like a wilderness hunter. The right kind of hunter steps "temporarily" out of one persona and into the other, but Townsend's weakling fails to commit to the role. Instead, he behaves as if he is a tourist visiting the woods for pleasure, with paid employees he has hired to make the experience as easy as possible.

For Townsend, such an experience is entirely artificial and without meaning, yielding no gains to character and no connection to the pioneer past. Worse yet, incompetent hunters might give in to their darker natures: he describes meeting a sportsman shipping his trophy heads back East, and then the man's guides, who cheerfully admit to Townsend that the kills were in fact theirs. This is the commercial aspect of guiding at its most naked, but it's not what the hunt is supposed to be about, and Townsend shifts from material to moral values in a breath. "Never allow your guide to fire at your game," he instructs readers, "your trophies are of no value unless the result of your individual skill."[63] And instead of concluding the article by discussing how to win your guide's esteem (a conclusion that would reflect the opening question), Townsend presents a list of the other benefits that will accrue to the man who hunts in the right way: "he will learn lessons of endurance, perseverance and self reliance which will stand him in good stead in his life avocation."[64] From 1907, Townsend has twisted around to gaze back at the nineteenth-century manly virtues. For him the problematic element is not the guide's disdain so much as the hunter's character: his veracity, his reliability, whether the sportsmanship he displays is real or a veneer. It's a familiar question: how can you tell who a man really is? Townsend is explaining what the role of the guide needs to be in order for the hunt to be read as a meaningful performance.

Townsend's article is far less about winning the esteem of guides than it is about the threats posed by their presence. The sportsman-hunter discourse functioned partly by hiding from view some possible readings of the meaning of the hunt—as a display of leisure and luxury, for instance, or as a commodity bought and paid for—but guides could bring those readings back into play simply by being there, even as they cast a shadow over the display of self-reliance and autonomous action that lay at the heart of the still-hunt. Their presence always raised the possibility that the sportsman's performance might not have been an unmediated demonstration of manliness.

Almost every big-game hunter hired guides. That meant that almost every narrative had to deal with the threats posed by their presence, as well as the problematic questions raised by the tourist economies in which they functioned. No single way of describing guides ever emerged in response, however, and that makes sense, since hunters were reporting their personal experiences with other individuals over weeks or months of contact. Then, as now, sharing the experience of camping and wilderness adventure seems sometimes to have created close bonds between people of otherwise very different backgrounds—and then, as now, when those people did not get along, the trip had the potential to erupt into conflict. And such variety of experience only became more complicated as it was converted into narrative, because almost all the hunters who discussed their guides also used them in some way at the level of storytelling. Whether as foils for the protagonist, as characters in their own right, or as subjects of observation and discussion, guides and gunbearers proved useful to hunters as they sat down to write their narratives, working for them on the page as well as in the field.

This is where the value of framing these narratives, not as transparent reports of actual experience, but as deliberately crafted stories, becomes useful and explanatory. At one extreme, hunters wrote narratives in which their guides became part of their wider quests. At the other, they reported facts about their guides, and yet even the baldest statement can still be seen as making implicit claims about the writer's authority and expertise. Thinking about how these narratives functioned as *stories* can help to explain the many ways that the relationships between guides and their employers are presented in the narratives—whether through factual description, words of praise, or explosive depictions of conflict.

We have seen a fair amount of praise of guides already: Gray's description of Indian Johnny, for example, and Herbert's comment on the hunting skills of the black shikári. Harvard graduate William Lord Smith begins his 1897 narrative "An African Shooting Trip" by telling readers: "One is first impressed on starting into the jungle by the ability of his followers. With a good head-man, everybody from the head shikári, or hunter, down to the camel-men [will] do his share of the work."[65] As noted earlier, Somalis in particular seem to have commanded respect from their employers: McCutcheon explains that Somali gunbearers are "the aristocrats of Africa and demand large salaries. . . . [The Somali] will never desert in time of danger."[66] Sometimes praise occurred through comparison: Herbert, hiring guides in Alaska, notes that the "all-round capability of the average African head-man is non-existent in any follower one may acquire in Alaska [although some of them are] excellent still-hunters."[67] Some hunters also shared credit for their successes with their companions. Swayne dedicated *Seventeen Trips through Somaliland* to "my brave and intelligent Somali followers," while hunter Percy Etherton told readers that "I cannot close this Preface without a tribute of praise to my Garhwali Orderly, Rifleman Giyan Sing Pharswan, who accompanied me throughout the journey . . ."[68] Such tributes have not always been fully recognized in the historiography, particularly in that of the safari, which has sometimes assumed that the position of white employers toward their employees was one of unvaried contempt.[69] The narratives suggest otherwise.

These comments dovetail well with exposures of the workings of guide economies, with Swayne reporting on Africans in Aden muttering "damn fool passengers" and Jackson describing how the recommendation system functioned. Readers who enjoy footnotes will already have noticed how much of the information on guides here is actually drawn from the hunting narratives, and, without minimizing the genuine feeling that appears to have animated many moments of praise, I think that much of this writing also served a secondary purpose in print: to advance claims about the hunter and his ability to conduct an orderly and disciplined expedition, in part by establishing him as knowledgeable to his reading audience. Swayne, describing the Africans muttering "damn fool passengers," also makes it clear that he is not one, not with his seventeen trips through Somaliland, his role in turning village boys into successful merchants. Smith may be impressed by his followers' abilities, but there is a claim to competence buried in his comment: he knows how to pick a good headman and the result is the orderly safari he describes. Nowhere is this type of description clearer than in McCutcheon's comments on his safari's headman, "a young Somali, named Abdi. . . . He was strikingly handsome, efficient, and ruled the native porters firmly and kindly. Each day we patted ourselves on the back because of Abdi."[70] Even the most factual of descriptions could serve such a function. Jackson, describing the African elite who demanded letters of recommendation written by white hunters they knew and respected, also lets readers know that he is one of those respected hunters; it is there in the content of his text and in the fact of the text itself, in Jackson's ability to write an article entitled "The Caravan, Headman . . . Etc." and to have it published in a prestigious Badminton Library anthology. In making claims about the pitfalls to be avoided by other hunters (pitfalls they themselves had not fallen into), and by displaying their knowledge of guide economies, these hunters were advancing claims about their own authority and expertise. In talking about their guides, they were also talking about themselves.

Recognizing the dual function of such discussions can be useful to historians, in part because it helps to confirm the accuracy of the information. An author whose goal is to publicly demonstrate his intimate knowledge of the workings of the safari, and who has successfully marketed that display of expertise to the editors of an anthology on the subject, is probably invested in offering an accurate representation. It can also help to explain why these writers exposed so much information on guide economies, wage requirements, and the very real abilities of their employees: such displays of knowledge bolstered the authors' own claims of authority and expertise.

Not all discussions of guiding served this particular function, however; some of the narratives that praised guides did so primarily through anecdote instead. Herbert, for instance, takes to the field with a Somali gunbearer who had previously worked for other British sportsmen. She tells readers that she is worried that she will not perform well enough on her first day of shooting to impress him, and, when she does, she reports his reaction as proof of her abilities.[71] (There is a gender as well as a racial dynamic at play here, of course: she's talking about herself, her gunbearer, and the English men he has worked for, while placing him in the interesting position of passing judgment on all his employers.) In a somewhat similar situation in the Canadian Rockies, William Hornaday describes how, although told by his guide Charlie Smith that he is not a good enough shot to kill a distant goat, he insists on shooting anyway. Smith warns, "Well, if you don't hit him, I'll kick you down this ridge!" When Hornaday makes the shot, Smith warmly shakes his hand and his admiration—that of an expert witness—is offered to the reader as proof of Hornaday's prowess.[72] Here guides and gunbearers are being presented in a positive light, but now they are functioning to direct interpretation of the hunter's performance and to assure readers that the author is capable in the field. The guide is the surprised and pleased witness, even as it is made clear that these hunters don't really need him, that they are perfectly capable of taking their trophies on their own.

Considering the ways that guides could be used at the level of storytelling can also help to explain the ways that conflict is most often depicted in the narratives. Descriptions of conflict are common, sometimes fleeting, sometimes quite dramatic—and in many of them the hunter does not immediately appear to conquer all. C. J. Melliss, for example, is lion hunting in Somaliland when he insists, against their advice, that his porters build a small hide in which he and his gunbearer can wait out the night with a staked goat. It turns out to be a bad idea: it's too dark to see anything, and then it begins to rain. Melliss calls to his followers to come out of their enclave and fetch him and his gunbearer: "The reply we got was that no one cared about coming outside on such a dark night, with the lion probably prowling about; this accompanied with a good deal of laughter, which I felt was at our expense."[73] Melliss made his bed (or rather made others build it for him); now he must lie in it, at least until he resorts to offering additional money for their trouble. Melliss's employees can be seen here as negotiating their work conditions (and having some fun at the expense of both their employer and his highly paid gunbearer), but there are instances that present more serious challenges. Herbert explains how one of her porters, given a heavy gun to carry, couldn't seem to remember not to point it at her and so was given a lighter load, while Caspar Whitney never did manage to control Beniah and his men once musk-ox came into view.[74] Such moments certainly reveal something about guides' attitudes toward their employers, but they are extremely odd if we consider the narratives, not as transparent accounts of what happened, but as a result of authors' deliberate choices. Why would hunters choose to tell these stories on themselves, in print, for the consumption of white reading audiences at home?

If we think about the narratives primarily as stories rather than as factual accounts, such moments begin to take on a very specific meaning and function that is not readily apparent at the level of anecdote. Most importantly, in the trajectory of the tale as a whole, such moments don't stop the hunter from reaching his goal. Melliss spends an uncomfortable night, but he bags his lion in the end. Whitney reaches the musk-ox first. Herbert finds someone willing to carry the heavy gun. In the hunting narrative as a story, with a beginning, middle, and end, these instances of defiance become collected in the text as moments in which something happens besides the hunt, something that obstructs the hunter's pursuit of that goal, even as it plumps up the word count for authors being paid on that basis.

Such moments of conflict can be serious and somewhat sour, as in Whitney or Melliss, but they can also be presented as amusing, to the point that sometimes incidents that must have been threatening to the hunter at the time are played off for laughs in the narratives. At one point on his Greenland trip, hunter Harry Whitney asks his guide Tukshu to cover him with a rifle while he approaches a bull musk-ox with a camera, but as soon as he takes the picture the bull charges. "I had no further business in that immediate vicinity and proceeded to establish a sprinting record in the opposite direction," Whitney writes. "Tukshu held his fire much longer than I thought necessary under the circumstances. Perhaps he was interested in my performance. Finally, however, he did fire."[75] The experience cannot have been a pleasant one at the time, but the humor with which the anecdote is presented is what strikes the casual reader. It's funny; it's one of the reasons that, a century later, Harry Whitney's book is still a good read. However it may have seemed to the participants at the time, this moment takes its larger meaning in the narrative from the entertainment value it offers to Whitney's readers.

Moments of discord could also serve other literary purposes. At one point during his safari Winthrop Chanler insists on traveling across a lake on a creaky raft. As the raft moved out, he writes, his men lined the shores, and "shouted cheering words to us, such as, 'Look out for the crocodiles!' 'If master dies, who'll pay us.' These cries, added to the dismal chill of the air and my boatman's only too apparent dislike of his job, almost caused me to turn back; but, of course, that was out of the question."[76] Why is it out of the question? Chanler doesn't feel the need to explain that; it is out of the question because he has come to Africa to hunt, he is writing a narrative that is about his hunting, and he is on public display in that story, showing off his courage and perseverance. In this context, his African workers become a Greek chorus of doom, telling the reading audience how perilous Chanler's trip over the lake is. Such descriptions allow us to watch others watching the hunter, saying, "he can't do that, it's too dangerous," so that we know what it means when he succeeds. This is the flip side of having your shooting praised by your guide, but it serves much the same function. Chanler is talking about himself by talking about his employees.

At the same time, Chanler is altering the connections made by the act of the hunt itself. On the ground, the hunter-employer and his employees worked together against the challenges of landscape and prey in order to succeed. By grouping his workers as obstacles and challenges on the way to success, the hunter-writer changed that relationship, placing himself on one side and the guides, landscape, and wild game on the other, in a vast textual diorama, disciplined and organized through the presence of the sportsman-hunter. And in that process, in the conversion to representation, the very real power of guides and gunbearers to make or break a hunt becomes no power at all.

Considering these narratives as literary works can thus help to explain what is happening in such moments, both in the narratives themselves and in their appeal to readers. It also suggests that narrative depictions of guides, their employers, and their experiences together were primarily driven by issues of authority, expertise, and performance, whether in positive or negative descriptions. (This can also help to explain how both can occur in the same narrative, as in Herbert's and Chanler's writing.) And this approach is particularly explanatory when applied to the ugliest moments in the big-game hunting narratives: those hunter-writers who chose to display their autonomy and authority by disciplining their guides in the field and/or denigrating them in print. I'm not suggesting that such moments are easily distinguishable from the use of guides as part of a storyline, but they do reveal most nakedly the issues of autonomy, control, and singular performance by the hunter that underlie much of the writing about guides and gunbearers.

Those hunter-writers who chose to minimize their guides' abilities often did so by using language that denied them independence of action. The third chapter showed how James Kidder elided his guides' hard work through his use of the possessive case and the passive voice—"our natives were kept constantly on the lookout"—while taking full credit for the results of the hunt—"My success with the white sheep had come only with the hardest kind of work." There was no doubt, in the context of his narrative, that the work in question was not the guides', but rather Kidder's—his work "stalking [game] in a sportsmanlike manner" as well as his work controlling and monitoring his employees.[77] American middle-class society had long associated wage service with unmanly dependence, in iterations that stretched from early republican associations between autonomy and manliness, through the nineteenth-century ideal of the self-made man, and into an industrial era in which white-collar managers routinely took credit for the work of the manual laborers they directed.[78] By adopting this rhetoric, hunters could attribute their guides' actions to the disciplining influence of the hunter's will, while the guide himself became, in William Brooks Cabot's phrase, just the "service member of a party."[79] Interestingly, such descriptions almost never directly invoked the wage relationship: Kidder never states that his guides do what he says because he pays them, but instead uses a language of control, possession, and dependence to claim credit for the outcome of the hunt.

When dealing with nonwhite or mixed-race guides, some hunter-writers also downplayed their employees' hard-earned skills by ascribing them to race. Robert Peary describes facing a storm "through which none but an Eskimo, and a very good one at that, could have kept the trail for five minutes."[80] Here, being able to find the trail is equated with actually *being* an Eskimo, the hard work that it took to acquire such skill is completely concealed, and Peary's inability to find the trail himself is entirely excused. Cabot makes a similar move when describing Scots Cree guide George Elson's heroic rescue of his hapless employer Dillon Wallace, reminding readers that "[Elson's] gift was almost wholly an inherited one."[81]

Such essentializing comments on race could feed smoothly into the language of service and dependence, linked by popular conceptions of nonwhites as impulsive, undisciplined, and childlike—in other words, as lacking primacy of the will. Invoking such connections allowed narrators to combine the familial role of the patriarch and the masterful role of the still-hunter with a racial role in which nonwhites were positioned as dependent children: Roosevelt calls his African employees "children of the wilderness," while Peary's hunters are "my little brown children of the ice."[82] This language let the writer conceal the wage relationship by making the guide a child in the family of the hunt. Any time that a nonwhite worker displayed impulsiveness could thus be used to contrast his childishness with the mature will of the hunter: Ernest Thompson Seton tells readers that, when his Indian guide shot a caribou without permission, "I scolded [him] angrily, and he looked glum . . . like a naughty little boy caught in some indiscretion which he cannot understand."[83]

Narratives like Seton's concealed guides' hard work, acquired skills, and position in modernizing tourist economies by mobilizing ideas of race and of the meaning of service that reinforced one another. They positioned guides below hunters on a number of hierarchies, so that "the guide" became associated with "the passions," "the child," "the immature races," and "the servant," while the sportsman asserted himself as the opposite of all those things: the white native-born man of character. This reassured readers that such hierarchies were valid, while countering any doubts they might harbor about the sportsman's control over the hunt. Kidder's guides function only as extensions of his will, and his demotion of their work helps to frame his efforts stalking mountain sheep as his alone. Seton's guide may have bagged a caribou, but Seton is clearly not the kind of man who takes credit for his guide's hunting: instead he exposes it in the narrative even as he disciplines his guide, assuring readers in the process that the "wrong" kind of hunting won't be happening on his trip.

Disciplining the trigger-happy guide, and in the process making it clear that one's guides were not allowed to do any of the trophy hunting, is in fact one of the most common tropes in the narratives. Peary, hunting with his "children," tells readers that on one trip he left them behind because he was short of ammunition and did not trust them to shoot with the necessary self-control (control that Peary evidently has).[84] And this is where we come full circle, both to the performance of manliness that was the point of the still-hunt and to the ways that guides could threaten that performance. Such threats operated on several levels, the most basic being the problematic question of why the manly, self-reliant hunter needed a guide in the first place. A superlative hunter like Sheldon might be able to leave his "guides" in camp, but most visiting hunters needed their guides to help them find the animal. And some of them needed more, needed the guide to lead them right up to the animal—sometimes, needed the guide to shoot the animal for them.

As we saw earlier, the lurking possibility that the guide and not the hunter might have been responsible for the kill was a constant source of unease to the hunter elite, and this had been true from the earliest days of the sportsman-hunter discourse. Van Dyke, who didn't use guides, had nothing but contempt for the "tenderfoot" who depended on one, and in *The Deer Family* he critiques the pairing as endangering sportsmanship: "the tenderfoot and his murderous guide," he calls them.[85] Roosevelt also sees the hunter dependent on his guide as part of an ugly dyad, "the average tourist-sportsman, the city-hunter-with-a-guide."[86] That hunter is no longer a wilderness hunter and as a result the dreaded appellation "tourist" has crept into the hyphenate. Nor were Americans the only ones who worried about the guide's role. Sir Henry Seton-Karr tells readers that a hunter should "not, like an obedient dog, crawl . . . at the heels of a professional native. Better far to bungle a few stalks . . . than to be brought, automaton-like, within easy shot by a paid expert."[87] This is a heady mix of analogies. The professional native, and the English hunter reduced to the status of his cur, would have been a startling image for a British reading audience, but it is counterpoised immediately by a far more modern metaphor, that of "paid expert" and "automaton." The sportsman was supposed to be repudiating both images, demonstrating his manly self-reliance as well as his superiority to a modern system that reduced men to cogs in an industrial machine. Improper use of a guide could compromise that demonstration and, with it, the meaning of the hunt. These hunters' comments are both instructive and cautionary. They represent another attempt to distinguish among types of men, even as they wrestle with the possibility that *any* hunter accompanied by a guide might not be of the right sort.

In this context, scenes in which hunters disciplined guides offered a wealth of information to readers. Such moments delineated a power relationship, often framed as a racial one, but their main purpose was to testify to the hunter's insistence on doing his own stalking and shooting. If the guide had fired at the game because he was of a childlike, impulsive nature, then that just provided further exculpatory evidence: it wasn't that the guide thought the hunter had hired him to bag the trophy, it was that he knew better but was incapable of controlling himself.

Depicting guides this way thus solved a number of problems for the hunter, and yet there were always other ways to solve those problems. The decision to invoke race, to minimize a guide's abilities, or to portray the relationship as one of antagonism and control remained up to the individual writer, and that in turn reveals something about Seton, Peary, and Roosevelt. As we've seen, hunters could stake out claims to authority just as easily through positive words and praise. Edward House, who seems to have liked his guides, describes a hunt in which he stalks a rhino, only to discover her to be female and accompanied by her calf. Unwilling to shoot her, he spends an hour or so creeping about in the tall grass trying to avoid her as she rather lazily stalks him; in the end, everyone escapes unscathed. Later that night, hearing gales of laughter from the campfire, he emerges from his tent to find his gunbearer doing a very credible imitation of his contortions in the grass, to the amusement of the entire African workforce. House laughs too. His readers would not have been left in any more doubt than were Seton's about his commitment to sportsmanship, or that he did his own hunting while his gunbearer watched from a distance. There was always more than one way to make such claims, nor were hunters confined to using only one type of anecdote in their narratives. They built books out of these moments.

Hunters sitting down to craft a narrative thus had to deal with their guides on a literary level and had a wide array of models of how they could do that. They also had to contend with ever-increasing regulation and ever-expanding guide economies; those were far more likely to be concealed completely, however, leaving the books unbalanced at best, carefully edited snapshots of the world in which these writers were hunting. I want to conclude with a final example of what was included, and what left out, of Harry Whitney's popular *Hunting with the Eskimos: The Unique Record of a Sportsman's Year among the Northernmost Tribe—the Big Game Hunting, the Native Life, and the Battle for Existence through the Long Arctic Night*. It's clear even from the title how much of the book draws its substance from discussion of the native Greenlanders, and Whitney describes them in many different ways over the course of the narrative. He praises them at times, summing them up as "kindly, honest, upright in their dealings, considerate of the comfort of others, self-sacrificing, and most hospitable," while adding that, "when they are treated properly, Eskimos are the most hospitable people in the world"; since they put Whitney up for a year, the implication is that he knows how to treat them properly, an authority claim on display for readers.[88] It's clear from the text that the Greenlanders go to great lengths to take Whitney hunting and to keep him alive, and like many hunter-writers Whitney chooses not to downplay this. At one point he manages to fall off his sled, forcing the driver behind him to turn his own sled over "at the risk of killing himself and family ... to save me ... an exhibition of quick thinking, quick acting, wonderful nerve and high heroism."[89]

At the same time, however, the Greenlanders don't seem to have seen themselves as hired to sit back and let Whitney do the shooting. Whitney consistently frames such moments by attributing childish qualities to his companions, whether hunting musk-oxen ("When I saw them getting their guns out ... I told them very forcibly ... that I alone must shoot all the musk-oxen. They were very sulky at first, but finally replaced their guns in the cases") or narwhal ("The Eskimos ... were nearly beside themselves with excitement and every one of them who had a rifle tried to get a shot at the narwhal. After a time I succeeded in quieting the men down and then with my 30-40 rifle put three bullets in it and killed it"). When he insists that they only shoot male narwhal, "the Eskimos at once began to sulk.... They were as contrary as a lot of children."[90] No one reading the book would doubt his control over the hunt, his devotion to sportsmanship, or that his trophies were his own. Moreover, the introduction was written by Dillon Wallace (of lost-in-Labrador-twice fame), who tells readers that he laid "down the manuscript with reluctance ... sorry to say farewell to the excitable Tukshu and Sipsu, and the other notable ones of the tribe whom one cannot fail to like and respect."[91] This rather ambiguous piece of praise notes specifically the "excitability" of Tukshu, and yet this is the same guide who appears to have been not quite excitable *enough* when Whitney was being chased by the bull musk-ox. Praise, denigration, respect, and control combine in this book to create a complex picture of the Greenlanders, but a far simpler one of the author: the man always in control of his hunt.

None of this would seem to position Harry Whitney as engaged in a form of modern tourism and yet he was, in this case a very specific kind of tourist recruitment. Robert Peary raised money for some of his expeditions by selling berths to those who wanted to go north with him, and he did so by running very professional ads. AN UNUSUAL OPPORTUNITY WHICH WILL STIR THE PULSE OF ANY MAN WITH AN OUNCE OF SPORTING BLOOD, ran the banner on one advertisement, illustrated by a stylized image of a ship silhouetted in black against a rising (or setting) orange sun. Peary's proposal called on "true sportsmen, scientists and tourists" to apply for a ride north. "For the sportsman, the attraction of the voyage will be the certainty of bagging walrus (the lion of the North), reindeer, hare, foxes, ptarmigan and sea-birds, with even chances of getting musk-oxen and polar bears."[92] Harry Whitney answered this ad, although he spent a full year with the Greenlanders rather than just traveling there-and-back-again on the boat. He lingers over Peary's heroism in his book, but not the work that went into the advertisement, the money raised by it, or what it meant that the Greenlanders were clearly unsurprised by having Peary dump tourists into their midst. Greenland certainly did not have a modernizing guide economy on the scale of Alaska or British East Africa, but neither did Harry Whitney come there through chance alone. And how (or whether) the Greenlanders were compensated for hosting him remains a mystery as well. His work reveals all the different ways of describing guides, as well as what was concealed or omitted, as he told his tale of manly sport with the rifle in the far North.

## CODA

We thus have discourse and employment, representation and reality, and an established story about the still-hunt that had to contend with a swiftly changing world in which guides and their employers were both caught up in the process of modernization. The hunt as commodity was always a central truth for guides, but not for hunter-writers, who had crafted a literary meaning for it that insisted on the hunter's self-reliance and authority. The differences between these two ways of understanding the hunt, the gulf that lay between them, and the fact that it was widening by the minute at the beginning of the twentieth century had numerous consequences.

One of those consequences was the reinforcement of racial and class prejudices. Some of the sportsman-hunter narratives invoked hierarchies of race and class that would have been very familiar to white middle-class readers. Narratives such as Seton's, Peary's, and those by the two Whitneys depicted a world in which working-class and nonwhite peoples required both guidance and discipline while functioning as extensions of middle- and upper-class whites. Describing the work of guides this way obscured both wage relationships and tourist economies by using rhetorics of race, maturity, and dependence, concepts that some sportsmen imported into the wilderness with them and then exported back out to their readers in the form of narrative.

It seems worth wondering once again, however, whether all these stories fell neatly into place for readers over time, especially since there were always other ways to interpret what was happening in the field. Did every reader find it a seamless transition from Roosevelt's "children of the forest" to Swayne's "brave and intelligent Somali followers"? Did any of them find it strange that Harry Whitney's companions couldn't hit a narwhal only a few feet from them, but were perfectly capable of dropping a running musk-ox bull at a distance to protect a fleeing man? For every invocation of racial hierarchy as a way of asserting the autonomy of the hunter, there was a narrative that praised guides and gunbearers—including those who were nonwhite or mixed race—and the skills that they brought to the hunt.

This variety was made possible because the core narrative for the sportsmen-hunters centered, not on race and class, but on the display of willpower, authority, and expertise. Depictions of guides and gunbearers, whether positive or negative, were primarily driven by the need to negotiate issues of leisure, problems of hunters' dependence, and the disconnect between the "manly virtues" and the increasingly commercialized landscape of big-game hunting. The central issue was always control, of the hunt, of the guides, and of the self, as hunter-writers struggled to interpret for their readership the meaning of hunting in a tourist economy, with employees who had their own motivations for being there.

Keeping such control was becoming increasingly difficult, however, as the experience of hunting moved ever further away from the foundational story of the manly wilderness hunter. Far from stepping off a train and trusting to luck and their own skill with a rifle, sportsmen increasingly found themselves arranging their hunts by mail, completing masses of paperwork, and paying standardized wages for a regimented wilderness experience. Some hunters responded by discussing those experiences in their narratives, furthering their own claims of authority in the process. Others focused narrowly on the experience of the hunt alone, using the entry into the wilderness as a boundary edge that sliced off all connections to livery stables, hotels, railway lines, and advertising. This often made for a better story, but it bore less and less relation to the experiences of Americans traveling away from home, even as more Americans were beginning to do just that.

Sportsmen-hunters had generated an idea about hunting. This idea did not conform to anything that had ever really existed. Instead, it was created and then applied to a world where traveling hunters needed practical help from time to time and had to pay for it. In fact, everything that hunters needed—guides, gunbearers, porters, weapons, pemmican, boots, coffeepots, compasses—and all the things they wanted—champagne and cognac, mounted trophies, cameras and film—had to be purchased. They claimed in print that they wanted to escape the modern world, but they had to buy that escape, and the modern world turned out to be more than happy to sell it to them. They couldn't get away from money without spending lots of it, and they couldn't slide out of commercial economies without creating new ones in the process. Attempting to preserve the values of a vanishing nineteenth-century workplace, the sportsmen-hunters found themselves fueling a publishing explosion, a modernizing worldwide tourist economy, and a global market in trophies. This last in particular seems to have mystified them, because they don't seem to have seen themselves as purchasing their trophies, only everything it took to bag them: they were buying the process, not the product, a subtle difference that made a world of sense to Hesketh Prichard and none at all to the Indian he encountered in Newfoundland. The hunter-writers could control what happened in their narratives, but not what was happening in the world outside their texts, nor how their texts were being understood by their reading audiences. Their intent may have tended one way, but the system in which they had to operate in order to make that intent a reality became something else entirely. It operated on its own nondiscursive rules of supply, demand, publicity, and advertising, and it just kept growing.

As it grew, it would create yet another meaning for the hunt, one that was new in terms of its connection to modernizing tourist economies, but that revived an older set of associations as well: the vacation hunt as leisured play, as purchased pleasure. Guides had always seen the visiting hunter's experience in these terms, but by 1910 it was becoming visible to others as well, including nonhunting tourists, neophyte hunters encountering bureaucracy on their way to the wilds, and armchair travelers consuming tales of leisured holiday jaunts side by side with hunting narratives. This was a new challenge. The logic of the story the hunter-writers had constructed meant that they could not tell a tale in which they were tourists. The logic of the economic systems emerging around big-game hunting insisted that they were. This would prove to be a problem without a solution.

**CHAPTER 9**

# Dreaming of Howley
## Conservation and the Uses of Discourse

*As an explorer in the West in the early '70s, a man hunting in the game regions for successive seasons, and as one who has been personally interested and actively engaged in game protection, I myself have witnessed the whole course of these changing conditions. Perhaps no other fact so well illustrates the rapidity of the change as does this, that it may be described by one who has seen it all.*
—George Bird Grinnell

*Let us educate where we may and punish where we must—and lose no time about it.*
—Caspar Whitney

The year is 1897; the place, Howley, a railway junction in Newfoundland. A man carrying a rifle steps off the train and surveys the scene. Already men are lining up along the tracks. Some carry one weapon, some two; some have food hampers with them; some have bottles of whiskey. Many have brought chairs and are setting them up along the tree line. The man with the rifle has come from New York and he is setting foot on Newfoundland's soil for only the second time; the first was when he stepped off the steamship and walked to the train waiting to take him here. Now he hears both French and English being spoken. The air smells of whiskey and sweat. Soon the caribou will be coming. Their migration will bring them across this railway line and they will face a gauntlet of weapons fire that will slaughter them by the hundreds. Some of their heads will be taken by the waiting hunters, some by employees of St. John's taxidermists, and the rest will be left to rot. That will come later, though. Now, the man steps away from the train, finds an unclaimed spot, and begins introducing himself to his neighbors.

The scene at Howley is part of the modernization of hunting. It is one place among hundreds at the turn of the century where the confluence of ease of transportation, growing leisure time in which to travel, the increasing popularity of hunting and trophy heads, and improvements in weaponry came together to create a place of slaughter. Howley is also one place among hundreds where the sportsmen-hunters' battle for conservation became visible: "The Horror of Howley," they called it, mocking it and condemning it, instructing readers on why hunting this way was shameful and should not be supported. This should not be a surprise. Since John Reiger's fine work in the 1970s, historians have known that sportsmen were in the vanguard of conservation, and yet that fact remains counterintuitive (at least to nonhunters). How did hunters come to play a leading role in helping to *restrict* hunting? And why did they do it in the ways they did?

This chapter and the next make two related arguments about hunters, conservation, and the media. The first, highlighted here, is that, having created a new use for wilderness in the 1880s, the sportsmen-hunters had created a new argument for preserving it. That argument was emotionally based and rooted in the sportsman-hunter discourse. It shaped what, over time, became a powerful two-pronged approach to conservation, in which the hunter elite mobilized their social and political connections on behalf of the cause while using the national media to justify their actions to their readers. The second argument, explored in the next chapter, is that it was the powerful position that these hunters had previously established in the national press that made them so effective in promoting their vision of conservation, and eventually allowed them to impose their own unique view of hunting on hundreds of different groups of local and regional hunters. The sportsmen-hunters didn't begin publishing narratives of the still-hunt in order to change the politics of their times, but, as conservation became increasingly central to their discourse, their social and political power and their control of the published conversation helped to define the shape of American conservation.

At the end of the nineteenth century many hunters were already being forced to travel outside the continental United States to find big game, and by 1900 hunting hotspots across North America were passing legislation in a desperate attempt to keep their own wild areas from being hunted out. British Columbia consolidated its various ordinances into a Game Protection Act in 1898, a mere eleven years after the first group of big-game hunting tourists staged out of Banff, while in 1902 the Alaska Game Law set restrictions on both recreational hunting and trading in animal goods throughout the territory.¹ Sportsmen's embrace of conservation was thus only one of many responses to the very real crisis facing both game and wilderness at the turn of the century—a crisis that stemmed in part from hunting, but that was rooted in the changes brought on by industrialization.

By 1900, hunters were placing ever-increasing pressure on both game and wilderness. Many were professional market hunters, ranging from those employed by restaurants to the plume hunters who specialized in slaughtering egrets and the little owls favored for women's hats. Others were subsistence hunters trying to put meat on their own tables or to supply their communities with food. Such hunting took many forms, from freed slaves claiming the right to hunt and fish on publicly held land in the South, to native Alaskans bagging moose to feed their families over the winter, to Italian immigrants pursuing songbirds with nets and shotguns. These hunters have drawn the sympathy of many historians, but their impact on game is not always reducible just to an attempt to feed a hungry family, because local hunters increasingly had access to national and even global networks.² The subsistence hunter who fed his family on locally killed meat one day might slaughter two dozen elk for their teeth the next, or kill a thousand ducks to ship to diners in a neighboring state where the birds were officially out of season. (If that number seems ridiculously large, consider that it's possible to mount a Gatling gun in a rowboat—and some hunters did.) Sometimes such hunters availed themselves of interstate or national markets, sometimes they simply took advantage of local opportunities, as when Dawson's booming population during the Alaskan gold rush inspired hunters to kill fifteen hundred caribou to sell to the hungry miners.³

That subsistence hunters were perfectly capable of killing for the market created endless complications, especially when it came to legislation. The Alaska Game Law, for instance, trying to accommodate the need for year-round hunting by indigenous peoples, permitted "the killing [at any time] of any game animal or bird for food or clothing by native Indians or Eskimo." This well-intentioned loophole meant that indigenous hunters could focus entirely on profitable market hunting in open seasons, knowing that they could hunt for subsistence during the rest of the year: guide Andrew Berg summed up the problem in a letter to Alaska's governor, pointing out that "those who go out and shoot game for market early [in the] open season still have to live and will kill more game during [the] winter."⁴ Overall it seems that thousands of hunters existed somewhere between professional hunting and just killing for the table, always with an eye out for opportunity, their connection to wider markets made possible by a nearby railhead or canal. The same changes in transportation, communication, and industry that had made it possible for big-game hunting to emerge as a popular vacation pastime also complicated the idea of the "local" by connecting working-class men with the world, and it is difficult, now, to look at the kill counts posted by these hunters without feeling amazed that any American game survived the onslaught.

It was not only subsistence and market hunters who were slaughtering game, however. Recreational hunters were also putting pressure on game populations. Some of them were locals hunting for fun, such as the Texan who cheerfully reported that he showed six friends the "pleasure" of shooting robins by torchlight: they killed over ten thousand in two hours, and his friends were so impressed that he was "invited to command-in-chief" the group on their next foray "in search of large game."[5] There were also many hunters with the means to travel who had no interest in the ethics of sportsmanship, including the men who paid $200 for travel, room, board, and mounting of their best heads at Howley, while the example of Theodore Roosevelt shows that even members of the elite could post obscene kill counts and, despite private condemnation from other hunters, have it publicly overlooked.[6] Even those hunters who hewed faithfully to the code of sportsmanship could have an impact on game populations, however, for by 1900 there were thousands of them. Subsistence hunters, market hunters, sportsmanlike and unsportsmanlike hunters: by the turn of the century, it was becoming clear that there were not enough game animals to fill all their needs.

Individual hunters were not the real problem, however. The massive expansion of capital in the late nineteenth century was the main reason that hunters were able to drive so many species close to (or into) extinction. That expansion drove the changes that put wilderness areas within the reach of thousands who had not previously had such access. It facilitated interstate shipping so that, in the absence of comprehensive federal game laws, hunters could take advantage of uncoordinated state hunting seasons to provide restaurants with game killed over state lines. It drove the globalization of the market in meat, feathers, and trophies. And it was responsible for less obvious pressures as well: habitat loss as railways and agribusiness expanded, the pollution of rivers and destruction of watersheds by industry (especially mills and logging), the ongoing privatization of what had once been wild areas. The depredations of market hunters were facilitated by the presence of railways and canals, but the market also consumed wildlife habitat at a fantastic rate, converting dirt into farming soil, trees into lumber, mountain passes into railway cuts, owls into hats. In 1900, an ever-diminishing American wilderness had all these claims made on it at once.

This meant that no easy lines could be drawn between local and national or between subsistence and market hunting. No one stood outside this web of capital and consequences. Certainly the hunter elite were part of these changes, in their hunts and in their narratives, in their links to the publishing industry and in the popularization of hunting to which they had lent themselves so assiduously. The complexities of their position have been explored in earlier chapters: their enthusiastic embrace of the business of narrative, their ambivalent negotiations with emerging guide economies, and their unwilling entanglement in the international trophy market.

One final element remains to be added to the picture, however: the idea of conservation.

The idea that the government should intervene to protect wild game and wild places emerged from many sources in this period and took many forms, ranging from the sentimental animal fantasies of Ernest Thompson Seton to the preservationist pleas of John Muir to the language of scientific efficiency associated with Gifford Pinchot. Following the lead of Samuel Hays, historians have often framed the last as *the* language of conservation, but science and sentiment, efficiency and emotion, often mixed together in the voices of men and women interested in game protection.[7] Among the sportsmen-hunters there were also many ways to call for such protection and many reasons for doing so. In addition, sportsmen's interest in preserving some hunting grounds had preceded the emergence of conservation on the national agenda: leagues for game protection can be found as early as the 1870s, often but not always locally based.[8] Some members of the elite were also early converts to the cause. George Bird Grinnell is the best-known of this group, addressing the need for game preservation in *Forest and Stream* beginning in the late 1870s. He was initially focused on saving the American bison, but as time passed he adopted a wide range of conservationist causes, while pleading in his editorials for hunters to conduct themselves in a sportsmanlike manner.

Despite these antecedents, however, conservation seems to have become part of the story that the majority of sportsmen-hunters were telling only at the very end of the nineteenth century—the moment when the loss of both habitat and big-game animals was becoming an insurmountable problem in the continental United States. Perhaps because of this, some hunters seem to have perceived the idea of conservation as something created around the turn of the century. Anthony Dimock commented in 1915 that he was embarrassed to think back on his kill counts from the 1870s, "but conservation had not then been invented." In a similar vein, Prentiss Gray describes sitting up at a lick in 1896 with a shotgun, waiting for his first deer, then adds, "Later I came to learn that waiting at a lick was not sport."[9] Such perceptions made sense from the point of view of turn-of-the-century hunters. As noted earlier, while *Forest and Stream* and other early periodicals certainly discussed conservation, the fact that their content was provided mainly by reader submissions meant that they could never offer one single, focused position. Perhaps more importantly, before the publishing explosion and the emergence of the big-game hunting narrative as a literary genre, there was no obvious venue in which to connect conservation directly to a hunter's performance in the field. Conservation concerns could only become part of the self-controlled still-hunt, or of "manly sport with the rifle," after those terms had become meaningful to both hunters and readers in the 1880s. And conservation's popularity with hunters grew in step with that of the narratives themselves, as the publishing explosion allowed conservation-minded hunters to find print more frequently in the expanding national media.

For the younger generation of sportsmen-hunters, then, those born in the decade after the Civil War and including Caspar Whitney and Charles Sheldon, conservation came into focus as a meaningful cause near the end of the nineteenth century. It was a moment when the crisis facing wildlife was becoming a national concern, but after the national media had established the sportsman-hunter discourse as the dominant way in which individual hunters described their performances in the field. This meant that when men like Sheldon, Whitney, Gray, and Dimock adopted the idea of conservation, they would do so in a very different form from that of John Muir or even Gifford Pinchot. They would incorporate it into the sportsman-hunter discourse.

Conservation was in many ways a natural fit to the discourse. It married particularly well with the emphasis on will and self-control as displayed through sportsmanship—the public refusal by men like John Phillips and William Hornaday to take more than their share. Such refusal could easily segue into a discussion of how obeying game laws spoke to character. Grant LaFarge explained to readers of *Atlantic Monthly* that he went without a trophy head on one trip because he had reached the end of the season: "to-morrow the law would stand between our rifles and the game—no obstacle, perhaps, save to a sportsman's conscience."[10] Obeying the law here becomes linked to a public display of conscientious self-denial. At times sportsmen-hunters also deployed languages of efficiency and management, or invoked romantic views of the wilds, but accompanying those rhetorics, complementing and sometimes driving them, were the associations that hunter-writers had already drawn among the manly virtues, the display of character, and the meaningful hunt.

This can be seen most explicitly among those hunter-writers who argued for conservation because it answered the need for a place to pursue manly sport and to develop and display character. In 1893, Arnold Hague explained that sportsmen should support the protection of wapiti in Yellowstone because it would create a reservoir that would spill over the park's borders, offering continued "opportunities for healthy, manly sport to the ambitious hunter during the shooting-season."[11] This argument appeared repeatedly in writing by the sportsmen-hunters, with little change over time. In 1925 Charles Sheldon organized a National Recreation Conference, attended by President Calvin Coolidge, several congressmen, and a variety of outdoor enthusiasts. Sheldon called on the attendees to support the protection of game animals and their habitats because outdoor recreation "has a direct beneficial influence on the formation of sturdy character by developing . . . qualities of self-control, endurance under hardship, reliance on self."[12]

Sportsmen-hunters also argued that hunting mattered to future generations. This was the motive that Grinnell identified as the source of his and Roosevelt's interest in conservation: "We wanted the game preserved . . . in order that there might be good hunting which should last for generations."[13] This sense of what the next generation was losing was also expressed privately. Roosevelt told Selous in one 1897 letter, "I feel rather melancholy to think that my own four small boys will practically see no hunting on this side [of the Atlantic] at all. . . . I was just in time to see the last of the real wilderness life and real wilderness hunting."[14]

Those boys would not only miss seeing "real" wilderness hunting, however; they would also be losing a vital connection to the pioneer past. This was another way in which conservation was promoted, as hunter-writers argued that preserving wild areas and game would allow future generations to revisit the manly pioneer experience. Owen Wister told *Outing* readers a story about a little boy in the woods playing at being Meriwether Lewis, but the tale grows darker when Wister considers the future. "As I think of him . . . I cannot help feeling sorry for his children when they shall grow up. They, too, will read tales of Meriwether Lewis. . . . But what are they going to do[?]"

They will be unable to find wild places in which to act out their connection to their heritage, Wister thinks; they will find nothing recognizable in the feats of Lewis and Clark. He brushes away objections that there is no need to worry about this yet. "[You may] say that it is our grandchildren who will not find much trout fishing.... But bear in mind that men not yet forty have seen the buffalo like armies along the banks."[15]

These readings emerged from the sportsman-hunter discourse. Having framed the wilds as a place in which to develop and display the manly virtues and to connect with the pioneer past, sportsmen-hunters described the loss of wilderness as the defeat of generations as yet unborn. They themselves formed the link between the pioneer past and this barren future—they were the men in the middle, standing between Meriwether Lewis and the grandchildren Wister was envisioning—and that in turn placed responsibility on them. Hornaday's stationery for the Permanent Wild Life Protection Fund was embossed with a quote that read in part: "*The wild life of to-day is not wholly ours, to dispose of as we please. It has been given to us IN TRUST. We must account for it to those who come after us and audit our records.*"[16] While the sentiment was common among this group, the rather chilly language of accountancy was not. More typical was Madison Grant's comment on "what a mission and opportunity the Boone and Crockett Club has in these closing days of the century in its efforts to preserve the game and the forests; in short, to preserve to future generations some remnant of the heritage which was our fathers'."[17] Those "fathers" are both biological and cultural, and their patrimony belongs to native-born, Protestant, Anglo-Saxon men. The sportsmen-hunters had long argued that wilderness hunting could link the right kind of men to the values of a vanishing world. In constructing this role for wilderness, they had constructed an argument for saving it.

Once it was taken up into the discourse, conservation could also be linked to any of its other elements: Americanism, for instance, or manliness. We can see this process happening as a whole if we return for a moment to Caspar Whitney. Whitney had not been particularly preachy about conservation during his tenure at *Harper's*, and it's hard to know if he was familiar with the term during his early days there. By 1900 he was conversant with it, however, and in *Outing*'s View-Point he repeatedly wove conservation into the web of meaning constructed around the still-hunt. There was nothing inherently American about conservation, for instance, but Whitney easily and vaguely married the two, telling readers that "Mr. Pinchot needs help which his rangers cannot give him; and you and all of us can give the very help he wants....

Patriotism isn't confined, you know, to shouldering a gun." He noted in another column that "a man of some education [can hardly] fail of being wholly in sympathy with game protection" and in yet another described senators with anticonservation views as a "rapacious gang of un-American Americans."[18] At the same time, he had no words low enough for the man who turned his back on conservation. *"The man who keeps on killing so long as there is a bird in sight, or a cartridge in his gun, is the man who answers the prayer for support of forest preservation with the selfish sophistry that the trees will last as long as he lives,"* Whitney told readers in a passage that we have already seen—because this is yet another sign of the man of whom you need beware in business and social dealings, the one who is not *"an honorable sportsman—a man."*[19] Whitney urged men to identify themselves to others through their support of conservation policies, while explaining that "every woman can do her share . . . by refusing to purchase a feather-trimmed hat."[20] Conservation is not being supported here by a single coherent argument, but is being tied into a set of familiar associations diffused throughout the Sportsman's View-Point. Linked into the discourse, it slid easily into the story Whitney had always been telling readers about themselves.

Although the endorsement of conservation was a late addition to the discourse, over time it became one of the most recognizable tropes invoked by hunter-writers. This was in part a reflection of practical circumstance, since hunters heading into the field after 1900 were faced with both diminishing game and ever more elaborate regulations surrounding hunting. Public discussion about the way things used to be and the need to protect what was left may thus have been a natural move for many hunter-writers, but such conversations also offered a new angle of attack on some of the societal changes that they disliked the most, particularly the expansion of capital and all that came with it. Both British and American hunters decried this aspect of their era. Clive Phillipps-Wolley noted that "in this practical money-grubbing age it does not do to lament the good old days, unless you want to be laughed at; but it is hard, nevertheless, to look on the ocean of grassland . . . and not regret the great waves of animal life which used to sweep over it."[21] It's the "money-grubbing" that draws attention here, opposed to that telling phrase, "the good old days," and it stood for everything that sportsmen had been trying to escape when they entered the wilderness in the first place.

Attacks on market hunters could also be framed as part of a larger critique of the role of capital. Grinnell explained that "while many market hunters were just as good sportsmen as ever pulled trigger, the fact that they made merchandise of the game . . . made them very destructive," while Prichard phrased the problem with market hunting as being "the wandering and masterless men who invade the woods. Such would turn everything that lives into dollars."[22] This critique is a familiar one: Whitney's curse of "money, money, money" pulling everything into the marketplace, putting a price on everything (and admitting no value to anything without a price tag). At the same time, Prichard exposes another side of the argument with his use of the term "masterless men." Without masters, working-class men cannot be expected to resist the lure of money; Prichard is critiquing the market here, but he is also subtly promoting the need for "masters," socially and politically. Whitney invoked a similar divide when he wrote of conservation, "Let us educate where we may and punish where we must . . ."[23]

Such rhetoric sketched out a role for the sportsman-hunter, as well as enemies for him to confront, familiar ones in the context of the Progressive Era: unrestrained greed on the one hand and working-class men on the other. Capital was the real engine driving the cogs in the shape of market hunters: there would be no mass market in meat and trophies, tempting the poor to slaughter vast amounts of game, if there weren't wealthy private interests hungry to consume those things. Linking conservation and capital this way brought the hunter-writers full circle, back to the pressures from above and below, the social anxieties that had shaped their pursuit of manly sport from the beginning.

These concerns were not theirs alone. Their anxieties had always reflected the wider worries of the middle-class public. The attack on unrestrained capital, in particular, targeted an enemy who was one of the most visible and widely hated of all Progressive-Era bogeymen, appearing as "the trust," "the monopoly," "selfish private interests," reviled in presidential speeches, exposed in the muckraking press, and even starring as the villain in novels by the popular Frank Norris, in which it destroyed individuals in its guises as railways (in *The Octopus*) and the international market (in *The Pit*). As they condemned capital and promoted conservation, the sportsmen-hunters were thus drawing on rhetoric familiar to middle-class American readers—in particular the condemnation of individual selfishness linked to concerns about the unrestrained market—that could be turned against game hogs just as easily as it could be aimed at market hunters. The terms they used were drawn from their own anxieties, but spoke to the wider concerns of a national Progressive-Era reading audience.

Historians have long recognized the political influence of East Coast elites when it came to conservation, but it was in the marriage of that influence with their reach in the national press that the sportsmen-hunters had their greatest impact. The hunter elite in particular almost always accompanied their political power plays on behalf of conservation with writing that interpreted their actions to the public. This was in some ways an extension of the strategy that they had used to promote the still-hunt: having used the media to control and direct interpretation of their hunting, when they moved as a force for conservation they continued to write about what they were doing. The tremendous influence of these hunters as a conservation lobby derived in large part from this two-pronged approach, as they worked in the media to promote conservation, and in government to shape the practical forms that it would take.

The influence that they exerted with this approach was massive. The achievements of conservationist hunters in this period, especially the members of the Boone and Crockett Club, have been examined at length by historians (especially John Reiger, Thomas Dunlap, and James Trefethen), but for readers unfamiliar with that history it might be helpful to have a brief overview of what hunters accomplished in the Progressive Era. Most obvious are Roosevelt's myriad accomplishments, some achieved single-handedly as president: hugely increasing the number of forest reserves and federal bird reservations, passing the Antiquities Act which in turn allowed him to create eighteen national monuments (including Grand Canyon and Muir Woods), and creating national parks at Wind Cave, Crater Lake, and Mesa Verde. Being Roosevelt, he accompanied all this activity with an equally impressive volume of publishing and speechmaking, drafting proclamations for each national monument and addressing groups ranging from the Society of American Foresters to a Conference of Governors convened specifically to focus on conservation.[24] Nor was Roosevelt alone in creating parks. Both George Bird Grinnell and Charles Sheldon proposed new national parks—Grinnell Glacier, Sheldon Denali—and appealed to the public to make them realities, in their books, in the Boone and Crockett anthologies, and in *Forest and Stream* and *National Geographic*.[25] Both also drew on the social and political power of the club, Grinnell to the point that the creation of Glacier National Park was presented as a club achievement in one Boone and Crockett book.[26] Grinnell was also the leading force behind the landmark 1894 Yellowstone Game Protection Act, which he promoted through numerous editorials and petitions in *Forest and Stream*, while Sheldon secretly advised the National Geographic Society, which was attempting to create Katmai National Monument in Alaska, on where to fix boundaries that would protect the bear population in the area (the secrecy was necessary because bear protection was so unpopular at the time). Boone and Crockett members also created a national plan for game refuges in coordination with the Biological Survey, worked to ban jacklighting and driving deer with hounds in the Adirondacks, and designed a plan to protect the elephant seals of Guadalupe Island. They participated on the committee whose report was partly responsible for creating thirteen western forest reserves, rallied to defeat legislation that would have expanded market hunting in Alaska, and were the driving force, in alliance with the Audubon Society, behind the historic 1913 Weeks-McLean Act protecting migratory birds.[27] All these activities (with the exception of Sheldon's secret bear work) were supported by references to ancestry and to patriotism, by Whitney's columns and Roosevelt's speeches, and by articles in the Boone and Crockett anthologies arguing that club members had no choice but to promote conservation. "No sooner had the Club been organized," Grinnell explained to readers, "than it became apparent that on all hands the selfishness of individuals was rapidly doing away with all the natural things of this country."[28]

The club was certainly not the only force behind conservation, nor were hunters the only members of social and/or political elites who promoted the cause. Such advocates often found themselves drawn into the orbit of either the club itself or its members, however, and gained both political support and media influence from those connections. John Lacey, a Civil War veteran and congressman from Iowa, worked closely with Grinnell on the 1894 Yellowstone Game Protection Act; the Boone and Crockett Club responded by promptly inducting him as an associate member. Lacey went on to sponsor a number of other bills, including what became known as the Lacey Act of 1900, which banned traffic in any wildlife or plants taken illegally. It was the first federal law protecting wildlife.[29] *Forest and Stream* ran numerous articles lauding Lacey's endeavors, including publishing a letter from one reader supporting the Lacey Act that was so long it had to be spread over two issues (this in a magazine whose average printed letter was four paragraphs long).[30] Charles Sheldon's endeavors to create Denali National Park also included reaching beyond Boone and Crockett boundaries as he courted judge and famed Alaskan mountaineer James Wickersham. Their friendship included several invitations for Wickersham to attend Boone and Crockett dinners, creating political connections that were advantageous on all sides when he became Alaska's territorial delegate to Congress in 1909. Wickersham did his part to convince fellow Alaskans that the proposed park would bring in tourists, but national reach was necessary to make Denali a reality—reach achieved through Sheldon's wide-ranging friendships and political connections and through the recruitment of *National Geographic* to the park's cause.[31] Horace Albright, one of the founders of the National Park Service, later claimed that "it was really only the forceful work of the Boone and Crockett Club ... that brought [Denali] enough recognition to make it a park."[32]

Other members of the hunter elite created effective conservation organizations of their own, mixing elements of the sportsman-hunter discourse with wider Progressive-Era rhetorics as they went. In 1918, for instance, Madison Grant launched the Redwoods Protection League together with Sierra Club head Stephen Mather and scientists (and Boone and Crockett members) John C. Merriam and Henry Fairfield Osborn. In support of the League, Grant published articles as well as a book that called on "patriotic Californians" to donate funds, reminding them that the redwoods were caught in the "competition between the growing enlightenment of the people and the forces of destruction." Destroying redwoods, he told readers, was the equivalent of breaking up "one's grandfather's clock" for kindling.[33] No reader familiar with the sportsman-hunter discourse would have been confused by the rather loose associations among patriotism, one's ancestral clock, and the "enlightened" segment of the public.

William Hornaday also became an influential figure in his own right. Along with establishing the Permanent Wild Life Protection Fund, he headed the New York Zoological Society (originally a branch of the Boone and Crockett Club), and, when the Society threw its support behind the Weeks-McLean Act, Hornaday persuaded it to fund publication of a book he wrote, *Our Vanishing Wild Life*, which was given away to every member of Congress as part of the lobbying effort.[34] He was also one of the founders of the American Bison Society, which repeatedly petitioned Congress for the reintroduction of bison onto the Plains and accomplished it in 1907—the first animal reintroduction in North America.[35] The ABS produced handsome bulletins for its members, filled with lavish images of shaggy bison; Hornaday described his lobbying efforts in one issue, noting that "the Society's overtures were received by Congress in a friendly ... spirit," while reminding members that it was "the duty of the American people to do something more for ... the bison."[36] The language of work and duty seems to have been infectious: when the *New York Times* reported on the society's work, its reporter singled out "Dr. HORNADAY's patriotic labor" for praise.[37]

Over time, hunters' rhetorics and activities on behalf of conservation created myriad areas of overlap where related crusades could support one another both in action and in print. The Boy Scouts, for example, were the focus of much Progressive-Era anxiety about raising manly boys in an industrial era: as noted earlier, libraries issued lists of books for the organization that were intended to model "manly self-reliance," while the Scouts themselves announced their dedication to inculcating "modest manliness."[38] Small wonder that they drew interest from both Hornaday and Ernest Thompson Seton. Hornaday created a Wildlife Protection Medal, originally available to anyone but used exclusively within the Scouts organization by 1922 (and renamed for Hornaday after his death).[39] Seton wrote *The Book of Woodcraft and Indian Lore* specifically for the Boy Scouts Association, urging boys toward "an ideal that is . . . clean, manly [and] self-controlled" and including a chapter entitled "Still-Hunting the Buck; or, the Deer Hunt," which introduced a new generation of self-controlled, manly boys to the proper way to hunt.[40] Meanwhile, Grant's Redwoods League inspired the California Federation of Women's Clubs to form their own, very effective Save the Redwoods League in Humboldt County.[41] The president of the national Federation of Women's Clubs, Mary Sherman, wrote an article for *Better Homes and Gardens* in 1925 explaining why women's clubs should advocate for conservation, reminding mothers that contact with nature helped to make "your boys manly and your girls gentle."[42] That article appeared in the same year that Charles Sheldon told President Coolidge that hunting and wilderness recreation were essential to building "sturdy character . . . qualities of self-control [and] reliance on self."

This constantly overlapping rhetoric among purely conservationist projects, other Progressive causes, and hunters' writing reflected the wider social anxieties and interests from which the sportsman-hunter discourse had emerged in the first place. This made it easy for hunters to exchange ideas and rhetoric with other elements of middle-class culture in this period, and those connections in turn produced real-world results. Rhetorics of manliness fed into action, as every timber baron hoping to chop down a Humboldt County redwood or Boy Scout who found himself still-hunting a sawhorse "deer" could testify. Mobilizing a discourse that was recognizably their own but that could trade elements with the rhetorics of other reform groups, the sportsmen-hunters had a massive influence on the turn-of-the-century

A Dream of Howley, by One Who Has Never Been There

Figure 9.1. Illustration by John Millais, *Newfoundland and Its Untrodden Ways*, 1907.

conservation movement. They also promoted their own particular version of it to an international reading audience that by 1905 numbered in the hundreds of thousands.

Those readers, for the most part, never went to Howley. They knew it, not as a great place to pick up a trophy, but through John Millais's sketch (figure 9.1), which offered readers a scene of dogs and men running amok while a magnificent horned caribou stands silhouetted against the skyline, suggesting the true sport to be had beyond the horizon. They knew it through Millais's description of how, in 1897, one man with a Winchester seated on the railway line killed 28 caribou without ever standing up, and left all but one on the ground to rot.[43] They knew that Frederick Selous, taken to Howley by his guide, refused to hunt there—they knew because Selous wrote to Whitney about it and Whitney featured the letter in the View-Point, adding a note that few of the hunters described by Selous appeared to be Americans, "Heaven be praised for the fewness."[44] The government of Newfoundland eventually came under so much public pressure that it invited Madison Grant to collaborate with legislators to create a strict game law that, among other things,

**Dreaming of Howley** 235

forbade the shooting of caribou on or beside a railway line. Millais gave the public outcry, both within and beyond Newfoundland, credit for the law's passage.[45]

When the sportsmen-hunters set off the fad in trophies, they did so unintentionally through a combination of social influence and published narrative. When they moved as conservationists, they used the same language and the same techniques deliberately. They shut down hunting at Howley using political pressure and the popular media, editorial columns and satiric illustration. In doing so, they showed how public support could be rallied to the conservation cause through a combination of political maneuvering and published rhetoric. Robert Sterling Yard, one of the founders of the Wilderness Society, would later write of these years that, while many "popular organizations to conserve forest, wild life, scenery, and natural resources of many kinds, sprang into existence in every corner of the country," they all "followed the leadership of the Boone and Crockett club, the pathfinder and pioneer."[46]

In the 1880s the sportsmen-hunters had created a new set of uses for wilderness: as a stage for the performance of the manly virtues, as a site for the development of character, and as a connection to the vanishing American past. In creating new uses for wilderness, they had created new reasons to preserve it. The forms that such preservation took would never be separable from the discourse of which it was part, however. The next chapter considers the limits that the sportsman-hunter discourse set both on the hunter elite's vision of conservation and, in the end, on hunting itself.

Mr. Phillips Regrets the Impending Extinction of the Grizzly Bear

Figure 9.2. This photograph appears in William Hornaday's *Camp-fires in the Canadian Rockies*. To modern audiences, the caption ("Mr. Phillips Regrets the Impending Extinction of the Grizzly Bear") is counterintuitive enough to be humorous. In 1906, however, the combination made perfect sense to ardent conservationists like Phillips and Hornaday. They sometimes doubted whether anything could prevent the extinction of big-game animals, but in the end their conservation work made a tremendous difference to the grizzly and many other species.

CHAPTER 10

# The End of the Hunt
## Conservation and the Limits of Discourse

The previous chapter showed how the sportsmen-hunters integrated conservation into their narratives and used it to rally public support against unsportsmanlike hunting in places like Howley. Howley *was* a horror, and I suspect that few of my readers feel deeply sorry for the men who were barred from shooting there, and yet it is worth a final look. The sportsmen-hunters were successful in barring lazy hunters from shooting at Howley. They also barred hunters who went to Howley because it was the only place that they had the time and money to reach before their vacations ended; after all, Millais, Prichard, and Selous all bagged caribou in Newfoundland, they just didn't do it on a railway line. Nor were recreational hunters the only ones whose hunting at Howley ended. So did that of the working-class Newfoundlanders employed by taxidermists, who would have to make up the wages they lost from easy shooting at Howley by risking their lives hunting seals on the treacherous ice or fishing off the Grand Banks—then, as now, one of the most dangerous jobs in North America.

Nor was Howley exceptional. Every protection was also by definition a restriction. Historian Karl Jacoby pointed out that new laws create new crimes in his phenomenal study *Crimes against Nature*, and that was the case here; every one of the conservationists' successes can be reframed as someone else's loss.[1] The Blackfeet lost the right to use the land that became Glacier National Park; Havasupai Indians were excluded from their traditional hunting grounds at the Grand Canyon; market hunters and restaurateurs found their economic activities restricted by federal protection of migratory birds; tourists seeking to sample the pleasures of jacklighting in the Adirondacks had to change their holiday plans. Some of these exclusions were more momentous than others—some of those placed on Native Americans, in particular, had devastating cultural and economic impacts—but every conservationist success excluded someone.² After all, if there was no one seeking to consume these places and animals, there would be no need for protection. Every time conservationists acted, they limited or closed off access to some people and not others, to some uses and not others. And the hunter elite were more effective at this than any other conservation group, for good reason.

Having mobilized as a group for reform, the sportsmen-hunters did not start from a clean slate. Instead they drew on the assumptions, motivations, and rhetorics that they had associated with hunting since the 1880s. Mobilized to protect wildlife, they did so from the discourse most familiar to them, one that accepted only one form of hunting and one "proper" use of wilderness while ruthlessly excluding all others. In the 1970s and 1980s historians praised sportsmen's contribution to conservation; from the 1990s to the present day they have focused on the ways that conservation laws discriminated along lines of race and class; but both the best and the worst things the sportsmen-hunters did flowed from the same source: their construction of the meaning of the hunt.³ The sportsmen-hunters came to conservation out of a certain way of conceiving of the importance of wilderness that was heavily freighted with their own anxieties and desires. The power they deployed flowed along those lines of meaning. Understanding how they conceptualized the meaning of their hunting can illuminate the reasons behind their actions.

It can also help to explain why their particular vision of conservation drew the support of a middle-class audience numbering in the hundreds of thousands. When the sportsmen-hunters began to embrace conservation at the end of the nineteenth century, they were already positioned at the nexus of the New York publishing industry, in large part because of the popularity of their hunting narratives. Having come to dominate the recreational press for reasons that originally bore no relationship to conservation, at the beginning of the twentieth century hunter-writers found themselves with ready access both to political power and to a national media platform from which to explain, direct, and (to some degree) control interpretation of their actions.

This is the reason why the hunter elite matters so much, and it distinguishes them from the hundreds of varieties of local hunting that existed across North America in this period. Mobilizing their considerable social and political power in Washington and New York, and using their already established dominance of the recreational press to persuade their readers to support what they were doing, sportsmen-hunters helped to shape conservation at the turn of the century. Over time they were joined by a wide variety of other constituencies, ranging from working-class guides to powerful groups such as the Audubon Society. They would also be supported by, and sometimes directly engaged by, their reading audiences, who were far from passive and who saw in the national media a way to promote their own concerns. Exploring the ways in which writers, editors, and readers used the media to shape America's wilderness reveals both the importance of the hunter elite's legacy and the reasons that it took the forms it did.

This is a rather different approach to understanding the sportsman-hunter stance on hunting restriction than is usually taken—one that tries to see what it was that they *thought* they were doing, rather than focusing on the consequences of their actions for others. It is worth pursuing because it holds the answer to a related question: why their strategy *worked*. As shown in the last chapter, the sportsmen-hunters were tremendously effective, and that surprised some observers even at the time: British hunter William Baillie-Grohman commented on the widespread support he found for game legislation among Americans in 1900, adding that he did not believe such laws would have been accepted even twenty years earlier. But why did so many Americans agree to support such obvious class legislation as that barring market hunters from jacklighting deer in the Adirondacks or shooting bison in Yellowstone, especially considering the long-standing American opposition to restricting hunting? And why did it happen so quickly?[4]

The answer lies in part in the realm of rhetoric, in the languages that had traditionally been used to oppose game legislation and the ways that those languages had been defused or deconstructed by the sportsmen-hunters. Throughout most of the nineteenth century, there seems to have been a widespread perception that game laws were elitist, designed to favor hunters who had privilege, wealth, and leisure. In 1859, Carolina planter William Elliott blamed local opposition to game laws on the fact that "the preservation of game is . . . associated [with] ideas of aristocracy . . . and oppression toward the poor." Ten years later, in his account of his leisurely hunting trip through the Adirondacks, Murray noted, "I am not in favor of 'game laws,' passed for the most part in the interest of the few and the rich, to the deprivation of the poor and the many. . . . I do not look at the Wilderness as belonging to sportsmen or any other class; it belongs to the country at large."[5]

In the process of giving meaning to the still-hunt, the sportsmen-hunters had attacked both Elliott's and Murray's versions of what hunting could mean. They had done so in order to disconnect their hunting from associations with aristocracy and idle leisure, but, when it came to conservation, those deconstructions proved invaluable. Historians studying hunting restriction in this period have often focused on how such laws affected both white working-class and nonwhite hunters, but from the point of view of the hunter elite those were two very different categories. Restricting the hunting of nonwhite men did not present an insurmountable hurdle in terms of provoking political resistance: white Americans in this era were notably unconcerned both by Indian dispossession and by laws that restricted the rights of people of color. Rather, the sportsmen-hunters recognized that the primary battle was going to be about restricting the hunting of native-born white men, whether those men were hunting for sport, the market, or subsistence—and American opposition to those types of game laws ran very deep indeed. From the earliest days of *The Still-Hunter*, however, the sportsmen-hunters had disconnected their own hunting from rhetorics of aristocracy and elitism. As they took up conservation, they focused on a new and far more consequential disconnection: breaking the long-standing associations in American culture between game laws and unjust class legislation.

By connecting conservation to ideals of Americanism, patriotism, and opposition to selfish private interests, the hunter elite could claim that their advocacy of game laws was being undertaken for the common good. As early as 1881, Grinnell was arguing in the pages of *Forest and Stream* that "the rich man can travel to distant fields where game is plenty. . . . With the poor man it is not so. . . . It is, therefore, the man of modest means who is or should be interested in game preservation even more than he whose fortune is ample." This was a theme with Grinnell: in a later editorial titled "We, the People," he stressed that "laws prohibiting the destruction of game in its breeding season . . . are not for the advantage of any narrow clique. They are for the good of us, the people."[6] This argument was repeated by many different conservationists. Charles E. Whitehead, counsel for the Society for the Preservation of Game, published an article explaining that the difference between European and American game laws was that European laws protected game for a class, while American laws preserved it for everyone.[7] Roosevelt sounded the same message on every possible occasion, telling readers that, while European game laws had unquestionably been administered "in the selfish interest of one class," it would be "utterly foolish to regard proper game laws as undemocratic, unrepublican."[8]

Here market and/or subsistence hunters are being linked, through their desire to use game for their own ends, to all those who act in their own selfish interests, who are lining their pockets at the people's expense—and

Figure 10.1. The ever-enthusiastic Theodore Roosevelt arrives at Yellowstone National Park in 1903. Laying the cornerstone for the triumphal arch at its northern entrance, he praised the park for "its essential democracy" and called on "the people as a whole" to assume "ownership in the name of the nation" and to "jealously safeguard . . . the scenery, the forests, and the wild creatures." Photograph courtesy of Houghton Library, Harvard University.

that group of malefactors explicitly crossed class boundaries. Whitehead explained that people in the West actually wanted game regulations and that it was the market men of Chicago who were seeking to permit the year-round sale of game, imposing their will on the speechless masses.[9] Roosevelt proclaimed, "Most emphatically, wild game not on private property *does* belong to the people, and the only way in which the people can secure their ownership is by protecting it in the interest of all against the vandal few."[10] To the sportsmen-hunters this was the division that mattered most when it came to conservation, one that grouped a handful of people of different classes together on the side of selfishness and greed, opposed to the needs of the American Everyman.

This did not mean that nativist sentiments and racial hierarchies did not play a role. The sportsman-hunter discourse had always been open to those elements, although not all hunters invoked them, and when it came to conservation some writers linked unscrupulous hunting to rhetorics of race and ethnicity. William Hornaday devotes a full chapter in *Our Vanishing Wild Life* to decrying songbird hunting by Italian immigrants, calling for hunting prohibitions specifically aimed at "aliens" and wondering if it will "require blows and kicks and fines to remove from Antonio's head the idea that . . . killing song-birds for food is right!" His discussions of Italians and, later, "Southern Negroes," draw on some of the ugliest nativist and racial rhetorics of his time, but he takes aim at other targets as well. Taxidermists and restaurateurs draw his fire, as do both "well-gowned women and ladies' maids" who buy feathered hats. He also condemns the subsistence hunter who "sordidly shoot[s] for the frying-pan,—to save bacon and beef at the expense of the public," "THE GAME HOG," and every sportsman who shoots to the full extent of the legal limit, since his actions reveal a "savage desire to kill . . . in men [who should show] a very different spirit."[11] Nativism and race play important roles in how the working classes are being depicted here, but that is not the full story. Native-born subsistence hunters take their place as well, as does the wealthy woman in her feathered hat, the haberdasher who sold it to her, and the gentleman who is concealing his secretly savage nature, all linked by the market and by their desire to take more than their fair share.

It is in fact rare to find any sportsman-hunter condemning *only* working-class hunters in print. Madison Grant, discussing the need for a federal law restricting market hunting in Alaska, enumerates the opponents to game laws, the enemies he sees arrayed against "the people of the United States." One is

Alaska's governor, Walter Clark, who fought the Boone and Crockett Club to block the legislation and lost. After condemning Clark, Grant goes on:

> The destruction of game is far more often effected by local residents than it is by visiting sportsmen, but the chief evildoer, and the public enemy of all classes, is the professional hunter, either Indian or white, who kills for the market. Worse still, perhaps, is the professional dealer in heads and antlers, who employs such hunters to provide game heads for the decoration of the banquet halls of the growing class of would-be sportsmen, who enjoy the suggestion of hunting prowess conferred by a selected collection of purchased heads.[12]

Here they are, the rogues gallery of the sportsmen-hunters: local hunters, professional market hunters, trophy dealers, politicians who condone the trade, and "would-be" sportsmen willing "to buy and to lie." (Like Whitney, Grant always directed his greatest ire, not at working-class men, but at those who "desire to pose as sportsmen [but] have not the strength or skill to hunt themselves."[13]) The list sprawls across class lines but the antipathy goes back to the origins of the sportsman-hunter discourse: most of these types were being derided by the hunter-writers long before conservation entered the mix.

What is new in this formulation is Grant's solution to the problem: federal legislation. "It is peculiarly the duty of the Federal Government," he explains, "to preserve and control the wild game of this national domain, because the people of the United States as a whole are the ones most interested in its preservation. It is to Congress, rather than to the residents of Alaska, that we must look for the enactment and enforcement of suitable laws."[14] Only federal legislation, passed on behalf of the people, can restrain the appetites of all these special interests. This argument both defuses any straightforward identification of game laws with class legislation and connects conservation to the wider trends that characterized Progressive-Era reform. It also helps to direct readers' interpretations of Grant's motives, not only in writing the article, but in helping to write and pass the law.

Whitney's attacks on those who opposed game laws also escape any simple class-based categorization. "**National Forests [Are] Held in Trust for Us All**," he explains to readers; those who labor for forest conservation are "a handful of patriots working unselfishly for the multitude, cursed by the corrupt, misunderstood by the unintelligent *as is usual in reform movements*."[15] In the View-Point the enemies of game preservation range from "un-American" senators working "for a handful of pirates at Washington" to the "persevering native-on-the-spot" who sells trophy heads at the train station.[16] Senator and native may be separated by race and class lines, but they are linked by their desire to use the game selfishly, while those who oppose them are presented as unselfish patriots. After all, as Whitney points out, game legislation is a "common and vital interest ... the effective protection of wild bird and animal and fish life [matters to us] irrespective of class, trade or residence." "Be a sportsman!" he urges readers, "Be a good American."[17]

Whitney also sometimes *attacked* game regulations when he thought that they were unfair, and the language he uses is interesting. In one editorial, he decries the idea of prohibiting *all* sale of game. "Prohibition Is Class Legislation," runs Whitney's headline. "There must be fairness in game legislation otherwise it will fail, and deserves to fail," he explains. "No class more than another has a God-given right to enjoy the game of this country."[18] *Outing*'s readership was middle and upper class, and yet from his phrasing Whitney seems sure that they would be ready to oppose any legislation that stank of class favoritism. This suggests that middle-class Americans may not have entirely overcome their antipathy to class-based game legislation. Instead, that antipathy may have been partially defused by the ongoing, public, and published insistence of the national recreational press that class legislation was precisely what well-written game laws were *not*.

This in turn offers a new line of approach to issues of import to the current historiography. There, conservation legislation—especially that promoted by elites—has been redefined in large part as class legislation. Exploring the impact of conservation on regional groups of working-class and nonwhite men, Jacoby and other historians have revised the triumphal tale of turn-of-the-century conservation, positioning it instead as part of a process in which Native Americans were driven from ancestral lands, rural whites were barred from subsistence use of traditional commons, and "local" hunters across the continent found themselves imposed upon by legislation from the top down.[19] This new, more critical perspective on conservation history has been hugely influential, and for good reason.

One important question remains, however. There is no doubt that in 1900 white native-born middle-class Americans had little sympathy for either poor rural whites or professional market hunters, but it is difficult to find a time when they *did*; prejudice alone cannot explain the timing of conservation legislation. Middle-class Americans had also opposed game laws in the past, but suddenly many of them did not anymore. And reading these stories and editorials—reading Grinnell's "We, the People" or Whitney's "Game Legislation Is Class Legislation"—challenges us to ask whether "class legislation" is the most useful term to use. It certainly must sometimes have looked like class legislation to those being legislated *against*, but, as Jacoby has shown, even working-class communities sometimes lacked consensus when it came to opposing game laws (this seems to have been especially true in those areas where guiding was bringing in tourist dollars). And I think that there comes a point where the terms of "class" do not seem to be getting us closer to explaining what is happening.

A different way of approaching such a problem is suggested by political theorist Adam Przeworski:

> Social differences acquire the status of cleavage as an outcome of ideological and political struggles.... Is the society composed of classes or of individuals with harmonious interests? ... What are the classes? Which class represents interests more general than its own? Which constitute a majority? Which are capable of leading the entire society? ... The ideological struggle is a struggle *about* class before it is a struggle *among* classes.[20]

This offers a provocative and useful way to think about conservation legislation at the turn of the century, one that unites this story with the current historiography to yield a new reading. The sportsmen-hunters persistently refused class—refused to admit that still-hunting was about class-based values rather than being about "manliness," or that conservation legislation was class discrimination. Instead they argued that they represented the interests of society as a whole. They spoke for their pioneer forefathers, for thousands of American readers, for generations as yet unborn, and as part of the Progressive reform movement. They claimed that conservation wasn't about class and, promoting that claim through the national media, they won that struggle first. Working-class hunters didn't just get oppressed by clear class legislation; first, they lost the battle over whether it would be understood as class legislation at all.

The previous chapter discussed how conservation was incorporated into the sportsman-hunter discourse while appealing to wider Progressive-Era reform rhetorics, but rhetoric is not just talk. By connecting hunting with writing about hunting—a move that they made, not in order to promote any particular political policy, but rather to give meaning to the still-hunt—the sportsmen-hunters secured a foothold in the emerging national media that, over time, became a powerful and established presence. The discourse they presented was always contested, but for forty years it remained the central way in which the meaning of big-game hunting was interpreted in print for a national middle-class reading audience. Once conservation was integrated into that discourse, the hunter-writers' dominant position in the media offered them a site from which to persuade the public to support their political agenda, as well as a way to direct interpretation of their political actions. It provided them with a pulpit from which to make their argument. It gave them a voice with which no other single group of hunters could compete.

This was not something they had planned when the big-game hunting narrative first rose to popularity in the early 1880s, but, as they became more and more politically active on behalf of conservation, it was something they could *use*. They used it to tell readers why wilderness needed to be preserved and to insist that conservation legislation was *not* class legislation, that instead the proper terms of the argument were those of democracy opposed to selfish private interests. And it must have seemed natural to them to explain, interpret, and argue for their political choices using the media. As they had made "writing about hunting" seem like an inevitable result of the decision to hunt, so they made "writing about conservation" a seamless part of their lobbying for that cause.

Moreover, as they reached out to wider reform movements they found other constituencies reaching out to them. By defining the terms of the argument as one in which all those invested in conservation, of any class, stood against the vandal few, the sportsmen-hunters did more than just disparage their enemies; they also signaled their availability as allies to other groups interested in conservation. Not all of those groups were independent of the hunter elite. Historian Jonathan Spiro has done a painstaking job of parsing the tremendous overlap in membership among leading conservation groups of the day (at one point, eleven of the twelve core members of the National Audubon Society were also Boone and Crockett members).[21] The sportsmen-hunters found themselves engaging across class lines as well, however, approached by or approaching fishermen, farmers, and Western or Canadian conservation groups. Each time this happened, it further reinforced both their public argument that conservation was not the province of one special interest group, and their own perception that this was true.

Perhaps the best-known example of the alliances that sportsmen forged is the progression of the Weeks-McLean Act. In 1912, conservation forces introduced several separate bills into Congress intended to protect migratory game birds by creating national shooting seasons for them, including the

Weeks Act and the McLean Act. The Weeks Act was the first to be reviewed in committee but was not passed to the floor. In response, a group quickly convened to revise the McLean Act before it came up for review. The group included Boone and Crockett members Hornaday, Grant, Osborn, Grinnell, and Charles Davison (although only the last two were specifically representing the club's interest in the bill). Joining them was T. Gilbert Pearson of the Audubon Society, who suggested that the act be rewritten to include *all* migratory birds, including insectivorous birds (to attract support from farmers) and songbirds (to rally women's groups to the cause). Once this was accomplished, the act also gained the powerful support of the agricultural industry—and no longer looked as if it represented only the interests of leisured sportsmen. In 1913 the revised Weeks-McLean Act passed into law.[22] Confronted with a bill that looked too much like the work of a special interest group, sportsmen responded by expanding the groups to which the legislation appealed, forming alliances that erased obvious class lines from view even as they successfully restricted market hunting across the country.

The Weeks-McLean Act is only one among many examples of the complex alliances forged by conservationists during this period. Some were locally based but crossed class lines in order to effect regulation. Historian Richard Judd has described how a coalition of small businessmen, guides, camp owners, and aesthetes in Maine called on rhetorics of health-giving sport while forging practical alliances with sportsmen in an effort to block industrial development of the Androscoggin River.[23] Some of the hunting clubs that mobilized for conservation were also constituted across class lines: Alaska's Interlocked Moose Horns Club included packers and guides as well as sportsmen, and it was managed not by a member of the elite but by a game warden.[24] Nor was there ever a single national consensus among the working class when it came to restricting market or even subsistence hunting: especially in communities where visiting hunters brought in hard cash, local entrepreneurs had every reason to ally themselves with sportsmen. Guides in particular appear to have reached out to sportsmen, both in supporting game legislation and in mobilizing alliances with sportsmen's groups to help push regulations through, and letters from guides regarding game protection appeared in *Forest and Stream* and even in *Outing* (albeit paraphrased by Whitney). The sportsmen-hunters' argument that conservation legislation was not class legislation was thus constantly reinforced by the construction of practical cross-class alliances among groups aimed at the same goal. Every time the hunter elite found such allies, whether guides seeking to preserve good trophy hunting in order to remain employed or Audubon members fighting to save songbirds, they strengthened their claim to speak for wider constituencies, both in their own eyes and in those of the American reading public.

Conservation came in many forms besides this one and was promoted for various reasons by myriad groups in this period. The sportsmen-hunters had an impressive impact on the terms of the debate, however, in part due to their control over magazines and presses, their contributions to contemporary booklists, and their connections to publishers. Just the sheer dominance of their view of conservation in the recreational periodical press, especially in the nexus of *Recreation*, *Outing*, and the editorial columns of *Forest and Stream*, must have had an influence on readers.

The impact of publication reached far beyond simple instruction, however. It's one thing to write, another to be read. Subscribing to a periodical like *Outing* or buying a book like *The Still-Hunter* could signal a reader's participation in a national community. Over time, those readers became ever more engaged, especially once they were mobilized as a nationwide lobby for game protection. Their choices illuminate both the importance of the sportsmen-hunters' control of the media and how readers themselves perceived that media's influence in their own communities.

At the most basic level, readers supported the hunter-writers by consuming their products. By purchasing *Forest and Stream*, *Outing*, or the Boone and Crockett anthologies, readers helped to fund both hunter-writers and the media in which their narratives appeared. By the end of the nineteenth century, however, readers were also being recruited to take action for conservation causes. *Forest and Stream* called on every man "who has his country's good at heart" to copy the magazine's petition in support of the Yellowstone Game Protection Act, to circulate it among his friends, and then to send it to his congressional representatives, with the promise of publication in the magazine of the names of those who signed.[25] (Grinnell also reached beyond the recreational press, publishing a long letter in the *New York Times* laying out his argument for the Protection Act.[26]) Whitney ran similar campaigns, asking readers to write to their state legislatures and to their senators in Washington about conservation laws, as well as to the Newfoundland government about Howley (which they did in enough numbers to influence the ban on hunting there).[27] Flowing out across North America from the publishing nexus in New York, hunter-writers not only instructed their audiences but engaged with them—and those audiences responded.

The media's insistence that educated Americans supported conservation, and that opposition arose only from a selfish few, also offered assurance to readers with conservationist proclivities that they were not alone—that, while they might feel as if they were a minority in their own community, they were part of an American majority. As a result some readers seem to have perceived the national media as an ally in their attempts to effect change in their local communities. This process is most visible, not in *Outing*, but in *Recreation* under George Oliver Shields's editorship. Non-elite readers may have attempted to use *Outing* to instigate change—someone wrote to Whitney about the Triton Club's sneaky snowcrusting—but his habit of only printing letters from those with names worth mentioning obscures the degree to which he was interacting with everyday readers. Shields, however, ran an open letters column where readers could interact with the wider national community of sportsmen, sometimes to great effect.

Readers often used the forum of *Recreation* to condemn members of their own communities who violated the rules of sportsmanship. In 1903, two readers from Worcester, Massachusetts, wrote a letter tattling on their neighbor S. E. Hanson, who in their opinion had behaved as a game hog by taking over one thousand pounds of fish in one day. "Lay it on thick," they urged Shields, "[teach him] to see himself as others see him." Shields obliged, explaining that the value of such exposure was not to reform Hanson, but rather for the moral example he provided: "all young boys and men who look on him will be inspired with a wholesome contempt."[28] Hanson may or may not have been embarrassed by his neighbors' actions, but it's telling that they reached out to a publication in New York in an attempt to shame a man they knew in their own community.

That man was certainly not a member of the hunter elite—*Recreation* appears to have catered to those who identified as sportsmen, but who were of lower-middle- or middle-class backgrounds—and yet, as with Whitney, this is about hunters targeting their own kind. Class was seldom explicitly discussed in *Recreation*, but at one point a hunter in Sheboygan wrote in to argue that a law barring hunting on Sundays was unfair to working men. A fellow New Yorker, signing himself "Buckskin George," responded in the following issue:

> Your correspondent . . . forgets the real purpose of laws. They are created not for any one class but for the good of all. It is true many are able to enjoy more privileges than others. This, however, is not in consequence of game laws nor class legislation. It is merely the outgrowth of conditions

that have characterized all civil life.... I am not a capitalist, but a poor devil hanging over a desk many long hours a day.²⁹

This is a different perspective from that of Madison Grant. Here is a fellow sufferer (or at least someone who claims to be such) taking up the refrain that game legislation is not class legislation, even if he follows that line of thought through to a rather disconsolate fatalism.

Most interesting are those correspondents who tried to use *Recreation* to restrict hunting in their local communities. Sometimes that was done by attempting a general call to arms: one writer from Idaho used *Recreation* to ask that "if there be any game wardens or deputy sheriffs in Idaho one should be posted at the deer licks on Sulphur creek near Bear valley. [When we] reached there August we found the hundreds of deer that were always there before had been killed or run out."³⁰ It's hard to tell the purpose of making this appeal via a monthly periodical; perhaps it was simply to publicize the attitude of the writer, M. W. Miner, or perhaps he truly felt that this was the most effective way to reach sympathetic members of Idaho law enforcement.

Dr. J. J. Bush of El Paso, however, staged an entire campaign with *Recreation* as an integral part of his strategy, with the clear intent of bringing public pressure to bear. He began by explaining that, "becoming disgusted at the open violation of the game laws around El Paso, a few of us sportsmen joined the L.A.S. [League of American Sportsmen] about 18 months ago. We at once served notice on the marketmen and express companies that violators would be punished. Result: Not a carcass to be seen last winter." Some hunters were still bringing in massive kill counts from Mexico, however, so Bush and his allies petitioned railway officials to increase international freight rates on game to eight times the normal rate in order to discourage them. "We first wrote RECREATION, then Governor Otero," Bush explained. "The El Paso daily papers took up the cause in the meantime." His campaign was successful: he and his friends shut down the trade from Mexico, and then, on a report from New Mexico, got an ineffective game warden fired and replaced by a more dedicated man. "Thus the L.A.S. becomes a power in the land," Bush noted solemnly, and "RECREATION is on sale at all the news stands in El Paso."³¹ Linking *Recreation*'s circulation, local papers, and local politics, Dr. Bush and his friends promoted sportsmanlike hunting and hindered other hunters from pursuing game (including those who were hunting within legal limits in Mexico), while looking to a New York publication for legitimacy and a sense of community that reached far beyond hometown borders.

All these writers were engaged in some way in the business of narrative, whether they were being compensated for their writing (as Hornaday and Grant often were) or were offering both free content and free publicity to an editor like Shields. *Recreation* and *Outing* also assured Dr. Bush and M. W. Miner that they weren't alone, even as their letters fed into the claims of authority being made by the recreational press. Whitney is the prime exemplar here: whether publishing letters on conservation from famous names such as Hornaday and Selous, or describing for his readers what "President Roosevelt said [about conservation] the other night at the Boone & Crockett annual dinner," he supported conservation while reminding his audience that he was speaking from a position of expertise and authority.[32] Mention in Whitney's column could also carry one's political agenda before thousands of readers, and throughout the decade influential members of conservation and hunting organizations appealed through him to *Outing*'s audience, even as those without famous names wisely chose the more letter-friendly route of *Recreation*.[33]

Even as the sportsmen-hunters found a new use for their readers, then—no longer just as consumers of tales of manly sport, but also as a constituency that could bring political pressure to bear—so too did their readers find new uses for them. This constant interaction among sportsmen-hunters, the media they dominated, and their reading audiences was at work in the creation of Denali National Park, the passage of federal game laws, the replacement of ineffective game wardens, and the shaming of Mr. Hanson on the streets of Worcester. And each new iteration further complicates any idea of straightforward class legislation or class prejudice, even as it testifies to the power of this media and its editors, writers, and readers.

In refusing class, sportsmen-hunters had created a language that could be mobilized successfully by a wide variety of constituencies. This was not necessarily always a good thing, especially for those on the opposing side; it was, however, a powerful thing. It reinforced the claims of sportsmen-hunters that game legislation was not class legislation, and helped to conceal the limitations that such rules often placed on subsistence hunters, through a language of public good versus private interest. It defined the entire debate in terms that promoted middle-class standards by first refusing to consider that they might *be* class standards. And it succeeded in this because of the personal and political connections of the sportsmen-hunters and their domination of the national recreational media. All these things emerged out of the business of narrative and from the discourse of the still-hunt, although that discourse had not originally been created for this purpose. Always complicated, wide-reaching, and unpredictable in its consequences, the sportsman-hunter discourse became a fundamental part of how conservation was constructed at the beginning of the twentieth century.

～

Big-game hunters thus did a great deal to promote conservation; conservation, however, would eventually prove to be a challenge to the continuation of big-game hunting. While at first it had fit well with the other elements of the sportsman-hunter discourse, over time conservation became more and more difficult to reconcile with "manly sport with the rifle." By 1910, throughout much of the world, big-game hunting required licenses and, eventually, lotteries, as well as a knowledge of local, state, and national laws. Change took more dramatic forms as well, as many of the hunting grounds that the sportsmen-hunters most valued—and the big-game animals they most prized—were put off-limits for years, for decades, or, in the case of the national parks, permanently.

Most of the legislation that the hunter elite supported managed to find a middle ground, limiting but not eliminating hunting, but I want to conclude by looking at two examples located at the extremes: the hunter elite's role in the creation of national parks, in which all hunting was banned, and the Boone and Crockett Club's embrace of moratoriums on their own hunting. Supported as always by rhetoric in the press, and underwritten by both the popular media and congressional legislation, both of these endeavors were logical extensions of the sportsman-hunter discourse—and, in the case of hunters limiting their own hunting, only explicable through reference to that discourse. They also challenge any easy categorization of these men as motivated solely by prejudice based on race or class. Nevertheless, while linked through the discourse, the two stand apart from one another. The national parks remain the most visible public legacy left by the hunter elite. Their conversations about their responsibilities as hunters offer a window into the most personal decisions they made about the role of the hunt in their own lives. In the end, having linked conservation to manliness, sportsmanship, and the primacy of the will, sportsmen-hunters would find that the discourse they had created around the still-hunt committed them to opposing the hunt itself.

If you have visited a national park, then you've enjoyed the foremost legacy of the sportsmen-hunters. The hunter elite, with their scientific aspirations, had always understood the importance of preserving habitat in order to preserve animals, and Roosevelt, Grinnell, Grant, and Sheldon in particular insisted that the country needed both parks and hunting grounds. It's there in the creation of Glacier, Denali, and the 1894 Yellowstone Game Protection Act, and also in the range of conservation issues pursued by these men: saving bison and bears, but also redwoods, songbirds, and elephant seals, along with rivers, watersheds, and wetlands. The discourse surrounding hunting opened out into these causes, so that Hornaday could frame the reintroduction of the bison to the Plains as a patriotic duty and Grant could appeal to save the redwoods as part of his "heritage."

The hunter elite also had a profound influence on the entire idea of what national parks should look like, of what a park should be. This was largely due to Grinnell's passionate support of the 1894 Yellowstone Game Protection Act. When Yellowstone was created in 1872, it was unclear at first whether it was the land that was protected or also the animals on that land—and equally unclear what "protected" might mean in terms of logging and mining. It wasn't until 1894 that both hunting and out-of-season fishing in the park were definitively prohibited by the Protection Act, along with any activity that would cause "injury or spoilation of timber, mineral deposits, natural curiosities or wonderful objects within said park."[34]

This was a tremendous victory for the hunter elite, one that protected Yellowstone while offering a new idea of what national parks were for and how they should be used. Many parks created in the United States after 1894 followed Yellowstone's (and Grinnell's) lead by protecting game, although that was only one among many options—some new parks, notably Mount Rainier and Denali, permitted hunting as well as activities such as mining.[35] It was not until 1918 that the National Park Service considered the patchwork of policies in place across the country and chose one: "Hunting will not be permitted in any national park."[36] (Commercial logging in parks was banned at the same time, but mining remained problematic for years to come.) Historically speaking, there was never anything obvious, intuitive, or sacrosanct about the American national park model. All its elements—the forms that parks took, which activities were allowed in them, the legislation that shaped and protected them—emerged from decades-long negotiations among multiple constituencies. The hunter elite brought passion and conviction as well as political pull and massive cultural influence to that fight. They created a number of parks, but, perhaps more importantly, they conceived of, wrote about, and garnered public support for park legislation that protected animals and habitat while radically restricting human activity. And they did this decades ahead of the emergence of a unified federal policy in the United States or of similar legislation in other countries (Canada, for instance, did not pass a federal-level national parks act until 1930).[37]

The sportsmen-hunters' contributions to the national parks were thus not just about creation but also about use—in particular about finding the balance among use, management, and policing necessary to preserve these places in a form that seemed untouched. This may seem like a contradiction in terms, but it made perfect sense from the point of view of the Progressive-Era hunter-writers.[38] From the very first moments of the sportsman-hunter discourse, although they continually invoked the "frontier," the wilderness that they sought was never a frontier. Frontiers are zones of transition, populated spaces. The sportsmen-hunters' wilderness, on the other hand, was an empty stage waiting for the vacationing hunter to arrive, a static bubble of time in which Meriwether Lewis's America remained frozen even as the world moved on around it. This wilderness was imagined as pristine in state and yet it demanded management, since hunters wanted it protected from some uses and open to others, stocked with some animals but not others, with only certain props allowed (cameras, for example, but not Gatling guns). This vision of wilderness was highly flexible in some ways, for the standard it was held to was a shifting one: it only needed to be like Lewis's wilderness, however that was imagined to have been.

In other ways, however, this vision was markedly inflexible, in particular in its resistance to allowing other claims to be made on it. This was not true of some other uses of wilderness and game: railways passing through forests did not preclude local people from bagging deer for dinner there, and subsistence and market hunters sometimes shared the field—indeed, were sometimes the same person. If the wilderness was to be preserved as the setting for an experience that allowed the visitor to feel as if he were Lewis or Boone, however, it could not serve any of these other purposes as well. The vision of American parks as pristine, primeval places has repeatedly been called into question by historians, but they usually situate their discussions within wider intellectual histories of the wilderness, not of the frontier.[39] That may be in part because the history of the frontier is now associated with violence, especially against indigenous peoples, but the sportsmen-hunters had constructed connections between the frontier and the wilderness that refused both violence and the presence of Native Americans. Their ideal was a wilderness emptied of Indians but available to middle- and upper-class Anglo-Saxons, people with limited vacation time but some means to spend on travel, who should feel as though they were the first people to arrive in that place, even as their pioneer forefathers had.[40] Preserving that experience for future generations of American men and boys meant creating wilderness areas where "man is only a visitor"—Edens that had never been inhabited, and never would be.

In the national parks, the sportsmen-hunters thus replaced hunters with tourists—but then, by 1910, hunting and tourism were beginning to look remarkably similar. Neophyte hunters and camera-toting tourists shared guides, hotels, railway cars, and livery stables, and also organized trips by mail, arrived with certain expectations of what their wilderness experience should be like, and clamored to see wapiti and bison and (eventually) bears. Sharing these desires in common, hunters and tourists occupied many of the same spaces, even as tourism began to overtake hunting both as a source of income for many local communities and as the way in which many middle-class Americans were choosing to experience "wilderness."

That change was part of a wider transformation, one that was inevitable—not in the form that it took, which was shaped by the context of the times, but in the fact of change itself, as the Second Industrial Revolution forever altered the concept of a local hunting ground. That big-game animals represented both a meaningful link to the nation's past and current-day national property was a vision promoted by the sportsmen-hunters as they insisted that no single group of people had the right to kill off all the game to which they had access. That vision was caught up in the tides of Progressive reform and also in wider movements, from local place out into global market, from the world actually inhabited by Boone and Crockett to a new world of wage work and consumerism. Local communities were changing in character and the cultural basis of property was shifting too—how people imagined what it meant to own something, how public property was defined. Barred from hunting Yellowstone bison so that they would be available for gaping tourists from San Francisco and Boston, local hunters found legislation regulating their behavior in accordance with a national community that could now affect and be affected by them through the combination of revolutions in industry, transportation, and communication. It was the ability to bring tourists from New York to Yellowstone so that they could see bison and wapiti that gave those animals value, even as the increasing power of the federal government enabled potential visitors to exercise power from New York and Washington to police them as national property.[41]

This would have happened anyway. It was essentially a modern change, one that depended on all the things that had made both big-game hunting and its narratives possible and popular—an America made accessible through print descriptions, illustrations, and photographs, through railways and steamer travel (and, soon, the automobile), and through increasing leisure time that let people actually visit these places. The sportsmen-hunters had a role in this, both politically and because they promoted wild areas through photographs and loving description, and yet the creation of the national parks seems so very far from where Van Dyke started when he wrote *The Still-Hunter.* Caught up in the national press and vended to thousands, the sportsmen-hunters' vision of the importance of wilderness to Americans became a contributor, not to a return to the pioneer past, but to a rush into modern tourism.

The hunter elite must have known this would happen. Certainly those who made public cases for the parks—Sheldon and Grinnell in particular—used both photographs and lavish written descriptions to make the case for the beauty and grandeur of these places, while carefully editing out any elements that might discourage tourists (e.g., large bear populations). The sportsmen-hunters had also struggled for years with the growth of tourist economies surrounding the hunt and had seen their published narratives bracketed by bird-watching tales and tourist travelogues. They must have been aware of the degree to which tourism would fill the gaps left by hunters. And they helped to make that happen: having successfully commodified the story of the hunt, they used the same forum—their published narratives—to *de-*commodify game and wilderness by creating a value for some animals and places that transcended the monetary. Charles Sheldon knew that tourists visiting Denali would never experience it the way he had, living off the land, building a house with his own hands in which to live alone through the winter, and discovering a new species of sheep on the way. But he also knew that such an experience had to become impossible if Denali was to be preserved at all.[42]

Having created a new use for wilderness, the hunter elite had created a new reason to preserve it. They had also conceived of a new way to imagine what "wilderness" should look like, and of its importance as a stage, that helped to direct the ways in which it was preserved. Wapiti would be part of the Yellowstone stage set, for instance, while wolves would be eradicated; Native Americans would have little presence in the rewritten histories of the parks, in the same way that they had been so conspicuously absent from sportsman-hunter narratives set in the West. The parks themselves would become beacons to Wister's Anglo-Saxon, "forever homesick for the out-of-doors." Even today the parks are popularly described as "American Edens" and even identified with actually *being* a real American, although their visitorship remains overwhelming Anglo and middle- or upper-class.[43] They are American wilderness as imagined by the hunter elite, ahistorical, carefully managed, and rhetorically associated with a certain kind of exceptional American experience.

At the same time, the sportsmen-hunters themselves were also changing, in large part because of their endorsement of conservation, which in the end acted to limit their hunting. And this is, in many ways, the oddest part of what has been a very odd story—that, in the end, big-game hunters themselves led the way in helping to legislate big-game hunting close to extinction in the continental United States.

That so many hunters worked so hard to make hunting impossible for themselves has puzzled historians. James Tober suggests that "the very constituencies that sportsmen had rallied in their battle for control over wildlife policy were now expressing demands that conflicted with their own."[44] This is a common argument: that, having mobilized the public as a conservation juggernaut, hunters were unable to get out of its path in time. This explanation does not fully take into account the key role of hunters in the creation of national parks, however, nor in calling for permanent moratoriums on the hunting of certain animals. It doesn't explain Charles Sheldon at all. To understand why so many hunters turned away from hunting, we need to return one final time to the sportsman-hunter discourse. There is no better place to see the explanatory power of this approach, or the importance of taking their writing seriously, than in their own published conversations with each other and with their readers about the reasons that the big-game hunt must end.[45]

Praising self-control and self-restraint had been part of the still-hunt since Van Dyke, and sportsmen from Kidder to Hornaday had boasted of setting self-imposed limits on their hunting. It was a way of demonstrating their self-control, part of the display of manly character that was the point of still-hunting (and of writing about still-hunting). At first game legislation seemed to fit naturally into this story and married easily with the goals of the sportsman-hunter. His declared disinterest in large kill counts, and his construction of hunting as a test of will, meant that the restrictions imposed by regulations could be seamlessly incorporated into the story he was telling, so that obeying the law provided additional evidence of his self-control and sportsmanship. From Harry Whitney's scramble to buy a postdated game license in order to conform to a law he had just learned about ("Never have I willingly poached," he assured readers), to Grant LaFarge's insistence that respecting close seasons was a testament to a hunter's conscience, the sportsmen-hunters consistently turned obedience to the law into moments of meaningful drama in their narratives.[46]

As pressures on game increased, however, it slowly became clear that merely obeying game laws would not be enough. In many cases big-game hunters were faced with a choice: to continue hunting, even as many animals were being pushed to the edge of extinction, or to preserve game by choosing *not to hunt*. If big-game hunting became incompatible with self-restraint, duty, and the common good, then hunting itself, for the gentleman sportsman, must prove to be expendable. Either that, or the entire discourse would need to be dismantled and a new meaning created for the still-hunt.

How did the sportsmen-hunters respond to this challenge and how did they explain it to readers? This question can be answered by turning a final time to the Boone and Crockett books. In the thirty-two years stretching from 1893 to 1925, the club published six anthologies. Following the series over time offers a guide to the ways that the hunter elite publicly presented their changing understandings of the relationships among manly sport, conservation, and the impacts of habitat loss and overhunting on American wilderness and game. Taken as a whole, the anthologies provide a history of manly sport with the rifle from its inception, through its years of greatest popularity, to the end of the hunt.

The first Boone and Crockett anthology, *American Big-Game Hunting*, appeared in 1893 and was edited by Roosevelt and Grinnell. It opens with an article ostensibly by the editors (but clearly by Roosevelt—his voice is absolutely distinctive) that sets forth the club's aims. "The Club," Roosevelt explains, "is organized primarily to promote manly sport with the rifle among the large game of the wilderness, to encourage travel and exploration in little-known regions of our country, and to work for game and forest preservation."[47] Note the order of priorities, as well as the fact that, in 1893, there were still big-game animals to hunt and little-known regions to explore. Most of the articles are straightforward hunting tales set in the continental United States ("A Day with the Elk," "Nights with the Grizzlies"), although Arnold Hague argues for Yellowstone's role as a breeding ground for game and Roosevelt writes about forest reserves. He also calls on sportsmen to "[discourage] all unsportsmanlike proceedings and all needless slaughter," condemning snowcrusting and jacklighting specifically.[48] All this is exactly what one would predict, based on the ideals that Van Dyke had laid out a decade earlier and that Roosevelt reiterates in his aims: the sportsmanlike stalking of big game is being defined for club members and the reading public alike as "manly sport with the rifle."

The next book, *Hunting in Many Lands*, appeared two years later and followed the same formula as its predecessor, save that the hunting tales were set abroad for the most part (although Whitney's man-eating cougars managed to claw their way into the book). It included two articles describing the club's advocacy for the Yellowstone Game Protection Act but otherwise offered little discussion of conservation goals. Two years after that, however, in 1897, *Trail and Camp-fire* included an article by Madison Grant entitled "The Origins of the New York Zoological Society" (the society functioned for years as an organ of the club). The article offers grim predictions for game. Grant explains that zoos are necessary because animals are vanishing: within twenty-five years, he predicts, African fauna will have been destroyed by "rinderpest and the repeating rifle" and "game in India and North America in a wild state will almost have ceased to exist." He concludes with a quote that we have already seen, describing "what a mission and opportunity the Boone and Crockett Club has . . . to preserve to future generations some remnant of the heritage which was our fathers'."[49] Here, conservation is being yoked to an invocation of the past as well as to the duty owed to future generations—a seamless incorporation of game preservation into the sportsman-hunter discourse. It is also the first hint of the possibility of animal extinction that appears in a Boone and Crockett book.

In 1904, *American Big Game in Its Haunts* introduced a change in the purpose of the club itself. Grinnell's explanation is worth repeating verbatim:

> Since the inception of the Boone and Crockett Club its plans and purposes have changed not a little. Originally organized for social purposes, for the encouragement of big-game hunting . . . it has, little by little, come to be devoted to the broader object of benefiting this and succeeding generations by preserving a stock of large game. It is still made up of enthusiastic riflemen, and their love of the chase has not abated. But, since the Club's formation . . . [the] extraordinary development of the whole Western country, with the inevitable contraction of the range of all big game, and the absolute reduction in the numbers of the game consequent on its destruction by skin hunters, head hunters and tooth hunters, has obliged

the Boone and Crockett Club, in absolute self-defense, and in the hope that its efforts may save some of the species threatened with extinction, to turn its attention more and more to game protection.[50]

There is no better place in which to see articulated the changes that have occurred in the continental United States since Roosevelt penned his cheerful aims eleven years earlier. In just a little more than a decade, the club has altered from a social club invested in "manly sport" to an organization lobbying for hunting restrictions. Grinnell points to the reasons: habitat loss, amplified by the destruction caused by market hunters. The club's response is "absolute self-defense," a fascinating phrase: the defense of their own style of hunting, or of places to pursue it, or of the game itself? With the sympathetic Roosevelt in the White House, Grinnell had never had a better time to push this agenda.

He was the sole editor of this book and it offered a far more varied selection of articles than its predecessors: tales of hunting, naturally, but also amateur writing on science ("Distribution of the Moose") and six articles on conservation—almost half of the contributions to the anthology. For readers familiar with previous volumes, this signaled the growing importance of conservation to the hunter elite. One of those articles was the text of the address given at that year's annual dinner meeting, Henry Fairfield Osborn's "Preservation of the Wild Animals of North America." There is no clearer indication of the growing incongruity of the position that the sportsmen-hunters found themselves in: how strange that the annual address to a hunting club would focus on animal preservation.

Almost ten years passed before the next Boone and Crockett book, *Hunting at High Altitudes*, appeared in 1913. Offering only five hunting articles (two of those memoirs from the early 1880s), the book revealed a more formal reorientation of the club's mission. That change was not due solely to the arrival of Charles Sheldon as a member, but he quickly became central to the active lobbying for game preservation. (It's worth noting, by the way, that the changes to the club were not the result of an influx of new members. The membership was remarkably stable. Instead, Roosevelt, Grant, Whitney, and the rest appear to have altered direction in response to the times.) In an article entitled "The Game Preservation Committee," an anonymous author (probably editor Grinnell) explained that in 1911 the club had formed a special committee to explore practical ways to contribute to conservation. In 1912 Sheldon became its chairman. The committee then joined forces with the Biological Survey to create a comprehensive plan of national game refuges, while calling on the club to lend its "name and influence" to worthy conservation projects that were not focused on big game, including those intended to protect birds and fish. (The timeline here parallels the club's legislative work on the Weeks-McLean Act and its alliance with the Audubon Society.)[51]

Most strikingly, the committee's report for 1912, included in the anthology, expresses what can only be described as ambivalence toward hunting. "We believe that to discourage the sportsman will destroy the most effective force now working for game protection," the report states. "But the sportsman must conduct his sport like a gentleman; he should be the first to refrain from shooting animals in places where they are so diminished in numbers that the killing of them will tend toward their extermination, or even endanger their increase."[52] Hunting "like a gentleman" had always meant displaying self-restraint, but now that implies, not just choosing to master the still-hunt, but also recognizing that some game animals should not be hunted at all. The report calls for a total prohibition on hunting mountain sheep and grizzly bears in the continental United States, while noting that "from the present outlook it seems that the antelope should never again be molested by the sportsman."[53] That placing animals permanently off-limits is an odd goal for a hunting club seems to have been recognized by the author of the report (technically the full committee, but clearly Sheldon):

> Whenever possible, the Game Committee seeks to restore big game animals to areas where they can increase and afford sport. Since some of our animals are on the verge of extinction, they can never again serve that purpose, but must if possible be permanently preserved. We desire to hand down to future generations opportunities for sport as well as the animals that we have hunted, but the sport must be consistent with the effective preservation of the animals.[54]

Forced to decide between hunting and saving animals, the Boone and Crockett Game Preservation Committee chose the latter.

Grinnell offered an implicit explanation for this change—for how a club devoted to hunting could come to work for its prohibition—in his accompanying "Brief History of the Boone and Crockett Club." Manly sport, *then* exploration, *then* preservation:

> Such were the purposes of the Club when it was formed.... Gradually, however, the settlement of the country and the sweep of population to the westward made it more and more difficult to carry out the two

first-named, while the same causes magnified the importance of the third. ... The Boone and Crockett Club, organized as an association of hunting riflemen, to promote manly sport with the rifle, and to investigate the wild and unknown portions of the country, can no longer do either of these things within the limits of the United States. Little hunting trips may be made, and occasionally a head or two of game killed, but the old wild frontier of the limitless prairies and of the steep and rugged unknown mountains is gone forever.[55]

Manly sport with the rifle is no longer possible in the continental United States, according to Grinnell.

In the 1880s Van Dyke never could have imagined this possibility. Neither, in all likelihood, did Whitney, Grinnell, or even Sheldon when they first included conservation in the sportsman-hunter discourse—not that it would lead to total prohibition, to one species after another being placed completely off-limits to big-game hunters. And it wasn't the hunters' fault that the animals were so reduced: that was about capital and expansion, about diminishing habitat, not about any individual's willpower or lack thereof. In the logic of the story they had been telling, however, conservation had become linked to the display of manly character, and that was defined by self-restraint. Being a manly hunter had once meant refraining from jacklighting or refusing to shoot at Howley; now it demanded abstinence. No more antelope, or mountain sheep, or grizzly bear in the Rockies: Sheldon made it clear in print that the club members needed to commit themselves to this with the same passion that they had brought to still-hunting in the first place. As we see them willingly locking themselves into this change, it gives us an idea of how the discourse they had created had in turn changed them. It had constructed a meaning for the hunt that made it completely logical that they should take this next step: not hunting at all.

Twelve years would pass before the publication of the next Boone and Crockett book in 1925. The Progressive Era was over by then; a great war and an influenza epidemic had swept the world; Roosevelt was six years in his grave. Sheldon took Roosevelt's place at Grinnell's side as co-editor and the pairing was reflected in the title of the book, *Hunting and Conservation*. In the preface readers were told that while these "two aspects of outdoor life ... to the uninformed, may seem opposed. ... There is no conflict between [them] ... the Boone and Crockett Club ... has changed with changing conditions, so that now it is devoted chiefly to setting better standards in conservation."[56] Grinnell repeated his death-knell for hunting: "For most of us the old-time use of the hunting-rifle in the United States has passed, never to return."[57] Madison Grant echoed the sentiment, noting that the club had transformed from a hunting club to a conservation club as America had been transformed from frontier to "almost old world conditions."[58]

Very little of the book was devoted to hunting. Instead, readers were offered John C. Phillips's "Conservation of Our Birds and Mammals," Grinnell's "American Game Protection," and Grant's "Saving the Redwoods," as well as his discussion of the creation of McKinley and Glacier National Parks. There were only three hunting articles and two of them were memoirs, including Sheldon's "The Big Game of Chihuahua, Mexico [1898–1902]." In a voice as recognizable in its own way as Roosevelt's, Sheldon reminisces about traveling the desert with the vaqueros who "were my companions, or really good, well-tested friends. . . . [I would awake to] coffee already prepared. . . . After their cheerful words wishing me good luck" he would set off to hunt for antelope.[59]

> I can recall many delightful trips, riding for days over wide areas in search of these interesting animals, not all successful in finding and killing game, yet not one of them disappointing to him who had learned to love the desert. . . . I have been reliably informed that it is now so difficult to find them that it is not worth while to make a hunt for them. Nobody who loves wild life would now care to kill one. A hunter with the right feeling can never enjoy an antelope hunt for sport again.[60]

In a world of limited wilderness, limited resources, and a powerful moral configuration centered on manly self-restraint, the sportsmen-hunters had helped to legislate their own hunting out of existence.

# Afterword

Of course, that world was not gone forever—not least because of decades of effort by the sportsmen-hunters themselves. Their most dire predictions did not come to pass. Some animals were lost to extinction, but reserves and parks have often functioned as Grinnell, Sheldon, and Grant had hoped, preserving animals while creating reservoirs that provide good hunting beyond protected boundaries. Elephants still roam East Africa, including in the massive Selous Game Reserve, while bison can be found in Yellowstone and grizzlies and caribou wander Sheldon's beloved Denali. Big-game hunting also continues, for both subsistence and sport, and it remains economically meaningful, with every state's Fish and Wildlife Service financed by the sale of permits and licenses and by excise taxes on recreational equipment. And guiding as a business continues as well: in 2012, guided hunting supported over twenty-two hundred jobs and brought an estimated $51 million into Alaska's economy.[1]

While the world in which big-game animals survived for the use of future generations became a reality, however, the nexus of events that made that reality possible vanished into history. The big-game hunting narrative as middle-class reading pleasure did not survive the cultural upheavals following the Great War. Its meanings lingered on, its languages of self-reliance and manliness part of American culture well into the 1920s, and hunting stories continued to be published in the recreational press, but the successors to *Scribner's* and *Collier's* were finished with hunting. After being an integral part of American culture, and American conservation, for four decades, the narrative of manly sport with the rifle, as written for generalist middle-class readers, died out.

There were many reasons for this. The national media was changing, and magazines were being joined by other forms of mass communication. Tastes were changing as well, as were the needs that drove them: the virtuous, self-restrained nineteenth-century man who sought somewhere to reveal his true character seems to have lost much of his appeal by the late 1920s, at least in the generalist periodical market. Many of the younger sportsmen-hunters continued to still-hunt and to teach their sons and daughters the sport, but they stopped publishing in the generalist press—and whether they decided that writing was no longer a necessary part of their display, or whether those periodicals were no longer interested in purchasing their stories, was a process of interaction over years.[2]

Contributing to this change was the continuing *expansion* of hunters attracted to some of the central elements of the sportsman-hunter discourse. Historian Louis Warren has described how some Italian American hunters in the 1930s adopted sportsmanship as part of making their hunting "American," and that association was in large part due to the sportsmen-hunters, who had worked very hard indeed to make sure that American hunting was identified with sportsmanship rather than with pot-hunting songbirds.[3] (Certainly Grant and Hornaday hadn't intended that immigrants could simply prove themselves of the "right sort" by embracing sportsmanship, but they and others had left that reading wide open, a door that female hunters had already walked through.) These new hunters enthusiastically demonstrated their American sportsmanship in club rules, but they fit it into their own set of associations around hunting, and those didn't include writing stories about the hunt. This had an impact on the narratives as well, as elements of the sportsman-hunter discourse were embraced by those who did not write about hunting, who saw no market for it, who didn't see themselves as authors at all. Sportsmanlike American hunting survived—survives, to the current day—but its narratives did not make the journey from *Harper's*, the *New Yorker* of its day, to the *New Yorker* of ours.

Hunters still sometimes caught the public imagination, but by the 1920s they were often using newer forms of media to do so, even as they returned the leisured big-game hunt to one of its former incarnations, as one part of wider stories about journeys to distant and exotic lands. Martin and Osa Johnson included big-game hunting in their best-selling books, including Martin's *Camera Trails in East Africa* and Osa's enduring *I Married Adventure*, but always as part of more sweeping travelogues, even as they offered audiences photographs and film footage as well as narratives. Carl Akeley also discovered that filming lions attracted larger audiences than simply writing about them, enough so that he was inspired to design his own 35mm motion picture camera.[4] In turn, movie cameras made living animals worth more than dead ones, even as improvements to the telephoto lens increased a hunter's odds of taking close-up photographs of live lions without being eaten in the process.

All these changes underline the uniqueness and historical contingency of the big-game hunting narrative as middle-class reading pleasure. During the late nineteenth century, changes to work and leisure, the emergence of a national print media, and the desires of a handful of white, native-born, Protestant, middle- and upper-class, college-educated men from the urban Northeast converged to create a new story about the meaning of one kind of American big-game hunting. This new story did not emerge from the history of hunting as much as from the history of work, class, and manliness. It rewrote the stalk as the single proper way to hunt by framing it as a display of willpower and the manly virtues, consistently rejected any links between such hunting and either violence or luxury, and created a new use for leisure in the process. Displayed on the printed page as much as in the field, it rode the shockwave of the publishing explosion across North America and the Atlantic Ocean. By publishing, the hunter-writers accrued social power; they dominated the emerging literature, for a time, but for long enough. When they mobilized as advocates for conservation, they had a platform with which no one else could compete, and they used it, as did their readers, to change hunting forever—including, finally, their own, as they linked the crisis facing game and wilderness to their own commitment to self-restraint and self-denial in the hunt.

All this was about far more than just shooting animals and would never have happened without the impact of the Second Industrial Revolution, which opened up hunting grounds and revolutionized publishing even as it compromised traditional sites of male display and performance. The anxieties and opportunities of this period gave power to the new meaning of the still-hunt, ensuring its appeal to a vast reading audience struggling with the same social transformations. The turn-of-the-century American big-game hunting narrative was a product of its times, unique to its moment, but that very groundedness made it hugely consequential. It spoke clearly to its readers, giving them reasons to save wilderness as well as persuasive arguments about the forms that protection should take; it attached meanings to hunting, to wild places, and to people, that made sense of the world for hunters and readers alike; and it gained strength even in its contests with women and with British hunters, widening its meanings and its audiences, as readers sought to understand how to judge manliness and reliability, what conservation might look like in their local communities, and what it meant to be an American in the new century.

The sportsmen-hunters built a cultural hegemony without (for the most part) the intent to use it for political ends. When conflicts over the uses of animals and wild places became part of their lives, however, that access gave them power. They were more historically important than other American hunters in this era because they shaped the outcome of so many conflicts over nature. And if Adam Przeworski is right, if fights over class are struggles first over whether they are about class at all, then their impact was even greater than they are sometimes given credit for. Although there were always other forces at work promoting conservation, the hunter elite's relentless insistence that game legislation was not class legislation played a central role in building a national consensus around both hunting restrictions and the ways wilderness was protected, in the United States as well as in Canada and Newfoundland.[5] Disassociating their hunting from the leisured play of aristocrats and from primitivism and violence served them well in their own time. Disassociating game laws from class injustice changed the shape of North American wilderness.

This helps to illuminate the importance of media access in struggles over nature, but it also suggests that such access can be about culture as well as about power. Market and subsistence hunters and, for the most part, working- and middle-class casual sport hunters don't seem to have thought that publishing was a relevant part of hunting in the first place; taking the history of hunting as a whole, the fluorescence of writing about it by this one specific group of hunters is what stands out as odd, rather than the dearth of other voices. This is about more than just who had connections in the media, although that was important. It's also about how the still-hunt's meaning was constructed in the first place, why some people displayed their hunting through writing while others felt no such compulsion, and the looping ways in which yet other men and women were attracted by and recruited into the connections between hunting and writing over time—the creation of a constituency out of an ever-expanding community of hunters, writers, editors, and readers.

This looping effect complicates the sources as well. If a group of texts are deliberately crafted by individuals and published somewhere like *Harper's* or *Outing*, then they can never be taken as straightforward accounts of what actually happened. There are always other considerations in play. What happened in the hunt, how the writer understood those events, the wider frameworks within which discourses are constructed, the literary conventions to which the writer conforms, the writer's understanding of what will sell based on earlier examples, the expectations and influence of editors, even the enticements of being paid by the word—all these have to be taken into account.[6] Pioneers like Van Dyke reveal clear connections to the culture from which they emerge, but writers contributing to an already established genre provide evidence of literary conventions and marketing decisions as much as they do any consistency of experience over time. This is clear from looking at Caspar Whitney. Watching him choose big-game hunting as a means of social and professional advancement, and then disseminate its meanings as he rode the emergence of the expert editor into living rooms across America, shows both why someone would choose to define himself personally through the still-hunt and how that story became so dominant in the national media. His rise doesn't make sense without the *business* of publishing; compared to the old-fashioned clutter of *Forest and Stream*, Whitney's *Outing* was a recognizably twentieth-century product, his editorial control and unmistakable voice marking him as part of the generation that redefined the American periodical. He was not groundbreaking so much as he was a relentless cultural amplifier, but it was the changing role of the editor, and the publishing explosion, that helped to make him so loud.

Positioning these sources as consciously crafted commodities also opens the way to move between experience and narrative with flexibility, using story arc to give context to anecdotes where guides successfully defied their employers, for instance, while using the history of the workplace to explain the manly still-hunt when its literary precursors prove impossible to locate. Taking literary production into account can also help to answer questions about influence and power, revealing, for example, how conservation lobbying in Washington, and local struggles to impose restrictions on fellow hunters, met and strengthened each other in the nexus of the recreational press. And seeing publishing as a business also makes the market visible in places where it might otherwise be concealed. The proof for what market hunters were doing at the turn of the century was measured in carcasses, meat, and feathers, in empty skies and devastated forests. The representational practice of what they were doing was written by their enemies, by Hornaday and Grant and Whitney, and told a story of selfishness and greed, not of need, and certainly not of class—and yet that was also a kind of commodity. Plume hunters made money selling feathers for women's hats, but Whitney made money selling *Outing*—and, if *Outing* was consumed by enough readers, it could change the meaning of purchasing that feathered hat. Meaning drives consumption. In seeking to alter how animals and wilderness were commodified, the hunter-writers used a new market, and a different kind of commodity, to effect change.

Those changes remain with us, although some are barely visible. The idea that the story of the national parks is about the selfless protection of uninhabited wilderness remains part of mainstream American culture, even as the National Park Service is beginning to incorporate indigenous peoples back into park histories. The idea that leisured men on vacation in the wilds are getting in touch with some kind of primal male experience, and that this is an agreed-upon reading in any era, has enough cultural power that it still has an impact on readings of Roosevelt in particular, as if he lived that story rather than creating it as he went. And Roosevelt himself continues to have a ridiculously disproportionate impact on our understandings of Progressive-Era hunting. He published a lot, and that unquestionably speaks to influence, but, in discussing the meanings given to hunting by hundreds of authors over forty years, is any one writer, however prolix, a reasonable sample?

That mistake has mattered, and not just because Roosevelt has given an erroneous impression of the connections between American big-game hunting and masculinity, imperialism, violence, and war. Hidden in his long shadow are the refusal by hundreds of his compatriots to associate their hunting with violence; the fight to construct a meaning for American sportsmanship by explicitly *opposing* it to that of British soldiers and aristocrats; Charles Sheldon and Edward House and the many other hunters who liked and respected their guides; and the big-game hunting women who found a place for themselves in the field and, sometimes, in print, aided and attracted by a discourse that disavowed violence and valorized self-control. Some of their stories have already been brought to light, especially by women's historians, but these men and women, and their guides, most often hunted together, and understanding them means seeing them whole, in their interconnections as well as in their individuality. It also means looking beyond rhetorics of the frontier to globalizing tourist economies and transatlantic publishing houses, recognizing the very real skills displayed by both still-hunters and their guides, and seeing that hunting has a history made up of the meanings it is given by people—meanings that change over time, just as people do.

That brings this story full circle, because, while cultural history has not yet taken full account of the hunter elite, there has always been one place that didn't lose sight of them: American hunting culture. It's rare to find a modern magazine or book for hunters that mentions conservation without discussing the hunter elite's contributions, although the ever-present Roosevelt often gets most of the credit.[7] And while the sportsman-hunter discourse itself is gone, some of its elements also survive. No one hunts now exactly like the hunter elite did—they can't, because the world that the sportsmen-hunters came from is gone—but, like every culturally constructed activity, hunting draws on what came before through a process of selective memory in the creation of a usable past. Continuity remains, not least because hunting is so often a family tradition, one shared by parents with their sons and daughters.[8] And some of those traditions, even now, center around a remarkably recognizable version of the still-hunt.

In the mid-nineteenth century Frank Forester told readers that the still-hunt was a boring waste of time, but Van Dyke rewrote its meaning when he framed it as a test of self-restraint and willpower. His belief that the character of boys and men could be developed and revealed through the hunt was taken up and repeated thousands of times, by Grant and Hornaday, by Roosevelt and Whitney. In 1925 Charles Sheldon told the president that hunting taught "self-reliance," even as he reminded readers of *Hunting and Conservation* that men with "the right feeling" thought carefully about hunting and refrained from shooting when it was the wrong thing to do.

Every US state but one requires hunters to take an education class before they can receive their first license, and in some of those classes students encounter a pocket-sized book by Jim Posewitz called *Beyond Fair Chase: The Ethic and Tradition of Hunting*. It opens with an anecdote about a boy who has just received his first license to take an antlered bull elk. He sets off, accompanied by his father. The stalk is arduous, through thigh-deep snow, but, when the boy finally sights an elk, it's in a thicket and he can't see if it has antlers. Although excited and impatient, he holds fire and is seeking a better view when the elk races away, revealing its mighty antlers as it goes. Far from being disappointed, the father is proud. "To pass up the chance to kill your first [elk] because of a small doubt about whether or not everything is absolutely right remains the teacher's trophy," Posewitz explains. Although understandably disappointed, the boy comes to agree. "In time he would realize that the hunt had already been fulfilled. . . . It was a great hunt, and it remains a cherished memory."[9]

Charles Sheldon left a greater legacy than just Denali.

# Acknowledgments

To my mother, Carol Kelly: this is as much your book as mine. From introducing me to *Great Mud*, to being the world's best research assistant, to snarky (but oh so accurate) critique, I couldn't have asked for a better or more sympathetic collaborator. You always believed someday I would publish a book—we did it!! Profound thanks to my high school history teacher, Kevin O'Reilly, who taught me to think like a historian and to love the complexity of conflicting sources. And to him, as well as to Richard Aieta and Elizabeth Moon: I didn't tell you when you were my teachers what a difference you made to me, but I hope you knew.

This book has undergone quite an evolution from its beginnings as a little dissertation. Ronald Walters oversaw those early days and, like all his students, I appreciate having had such a kind and genial advisor. To Paul Kramer, who valiantly read a full draft over a holiday weekend, and to my press readers, Gregory Dehler, Phoebe Young, and Anonymous1: thank you all for your time, effort, and generosity in engaging with my work and offering such useful and supportive critique (and to Greg in particular for all his help with the devilish William Hornaday). Catherine Jones, Bonnie Miller, and Katherine Moran gave thoughtful feedback on individual chapters, and over the years Bonnie has also generously shared her work with me, including her publishing proposal (on which I modelled mine): thank you!

Part of the postdoctoral research for this book was conducted on a Mayer Fellowship at the Huntington Library; I am very grateful to have had the opportunity. I happily had access to Harvard's wonderful library system, including the Theodore Roosevelt Collection (a sunny and welcoming place to work) and the fabulously quirky Zoological Library, and to their wonderful librarians. The librarians at Enoch Pratt Free Library in Baltimore cheerfully trekked down to the vaults to find innumerable hunting books for me, all last checked out sometime around the Roaring Twenties, while Durham County Library's investment in ebooks kept me in fiction even when I was trapped at home with my manuscript. North Carolina State University's incredibly helpful Carl Piraneo and the friendly staff at Harvard's Houghton Library and at the Boston Public Library helped me transform images into TIFFs at the eleventh hour. (Forget the national parks: libraries are *definitely* America's best idea.) I also received kindly assistance from the BPL's Jessy Wheeler, from Alaska's Wildlife Information Center, and from Conrad Froehlich, director of the Martin and Osa Johnson Museum, who filled me in on the fascinating background of the Johnsons' headman Jerramani.

Over the years I floated many of the ideas here at conferences, and I want to thank everyone who took the time to let me know that this project was worthwhile, whether by accepting my papers or through kind words and helpful critique. In my years as adjunct or (glorious term) "contingent faculty," conferences were often my only touchstone for professional encouragement of any kind, and I enjoyed hearing about the work of colleagues and sharing mine more than I can say. My students at Hopkins, Emmanuel, and Duke were also enthusiastic reminders that the choice to teach did not make me contingent in their eyes. The opportunities you gave me to help you, and your kindness to me and to each other, were what made my decision to teach worthwhile. I will take those memories (as well as having been part of the SEIU's against-all-odds victory) with me as I go.

In 1942, adventurer Caroline Mytinger wrote, "A woman's destiny is not fulfilled until she holds in her arms her own little book." To everyone at the University Press of Kansas who helped to bring that book into being and announce it to the world, thank you all so very much—including, and especially, Editor Kim Hogeland for her incisive critique and brilliant choice of readers.

Last but never least, I want to acknowledge Barbara Boisseau, our beloved family friend, and Matthew Arnold, who was a source of unexpected hope on a very dark day. My grandparents, though gone, remain a constant inspiration, so to George and Belle Kane, and Patrick and Alice Kelly: from baseball to my Newfie roots to baking a damn good apple pie, I am what you helped make me, and I love you. Finally, I want to thank those powers who have watched over me and mine—in them is my trust, until I am relieved of their trust in me. This book represents fifteen years of my life and I have done the best I can with it; may it be *amalgata*.

# Notes

**INTRODUCTION**

1. Charles Sheldon, "The Big Game of Chihuahua, Mexico," in *Hunting and Conservation*, George Bird Grinnell and Charles Sheldon, eds. (New Haven, CT: Yale University Press, 1925), 163–164.

2. This is a summary of the argument; the evidence for these assertions is presented in the following chapters, while the second half of the introduction discusses the connections to the historiography.

3. The rise of hypermasculinity is discussed in many cultural histories including T. J. Jackson Lears's foundational *No Place of Grace: Antimodernism and the Transformation of American Culture 1880–1920* (New York: Pantheon Books, 1981). Men's historians have located it as a reaction against modernity: E. Anthony Rotundo, *American Manhood: Transformations in Masculinity from the Revolution to the Modern Era* (New York: BasicBooks, 1993), and John Kasson, *Houdini, Tarzan, and the Perfect Man: The White Male Body and the Challenge of Modernity in America* (New York: Hill & Wang, 2001); and/or the perceived growing power of women: Michael Kimmel, *Manhood in America: A Cultural History* (New York: Free Press, 1996).

4. Lears and Rotundo in particular offer complex analyses (see note 3 above); my objection is not to anyone's argument per se but rather to the use of hunting as evidence of atavistic violence. Lears explores the ways the strenuous life could become a "cult of violence" (118) connected to a "careful primitivism" (108), which I would agree was true of imperialism but less so of hunting. Rotundo traces the urge to primitivism in this period; see 230–234. John Pettigrew claims that "Post–Civil War hunters . . . took up the sport to reconnect to a fundamental precivilized violent existence." *Brutes in Suits: Male Sensibility in America 1890–1920* (Baltimore: Johns Hopkins University Press, 2007), 88. Karen R. Jones in *Epiphany in the Wilderness: Hunting, Nature, and Performance in the Nineteenth-Century American West* (Boulder: University Press of Colorado, 2015) positions sport hunting by both British and Americans as a response to a long-standing "crisis of masculinity" that she dates all the way back to 1855 with the publication of Elisha Lewis's book (37).

5. Gail Bederman, *Manliness and Civilization* (Chicago: University of Chicago Press, 1995), uses Roosevelt to link hypermasculinity and hunting, while Sarah Watts in *Rough Rider in the White House: Theodore Roosevelt and the Politics of Desire* (Chicago: University of Chicago Press, 2003) sees him as encouraging "spontaneous

primitivism" (191). Jones cites him as giving an "essentially martial quality to the game trail experience" (41) while Pettigrew points to Roosevelt as evidence that there was a "moral blurring between hunting and war" at the turn of the century (83).

6. Some of Roosevelt's compatriots produced literature with violent and/or exceptionalist images of the frontier, but Roosevelt was unusual in importing it into nonfiction hunting narratives. For associations between the frontier and violence, see Richard Slotkin's *The Fatal Environment: The Myth of the Frontier in the Age of Industrialization 1800–1890* (New York: Atheneum, 1985) and *Gunfighter Nation: The Myth of the Frontier in Twentieth Century America* (New York: HarperPerennial, 1993), especially his discussion of the "aristocracy of violence," 158–182. Bederman, focusing on Roosevelt, connects hunting, violence, the frontier, and Anglo-American imperial fantasy; see also Jones, 37–38, and Amy Kaplan's "Romancing the Empire: The Embodiment of American Masculinity in the Popular Historical Novel of the 1890s," *American Literary History* 2 (4) (Winter 1990), 659–690.

7. Recent work focused on British hunting in North America includes Greg Gillespie's *Hunting for Empire: Narratives of Sport in Rupert's Land, 1840–70* (Vancouver: University of British Columbia Press, 2008) and Monica Rico's *Nature's Noblemen: Transatlantic Masculinities and the Nineteenth-Century American West* (New Haven, CT: Yale University Press, 2013).

8. Watts draws on psychologists' claims that all hunting "produc[es] alternately a lurid fascination with the violence at hand and the exquisite pleasure of sadistic emotional release" (175). Pettigrew argues for both a single meaning and a single narrative for hunting, claiming that there is a "psychic regenerative pleasure provided by the actual act of killing animals" (87) and that "the American hunting story—formulized well before Roosevelt's writing—turn[ed] on the psychic rewards of violence and killing" (91). Simon Harrison in *Dark Trophies: Hunting and the Enemy Body in Modern War* (New York: Berghahn Books, 2012) also frames all hunting as violence, claiming for instance that Southern hunting and lynching were linked, "speak[ing] a single narrative" with a "single moral purpose" (114).

9. Perhaps because of a lack of Roosevelt, historians of British and Canadian hunting have considered elite hunting a constructed activity well worth exploring: for Canada, see, for instance, George Colpitts, *Game in the Garden: A Human History of Wildlife in Western Canada to 1940* (Vancouver: University of British Columbia Press, 2002), and Jean Manore and Dale Miner, eds., *The Culture of Hunting in Canada* (Vancouver: University of British Columbia Press, 2007). John MacKenzie has been exploring hunting in the British Empire for decades; good recent work includes Angela Thompsell, *Hunting Africa: British Sport, African Knowledge and the Nature of Empire* (London: Palgrave Macmillan UK, 2015). Historians of women's hunting have always framed it as culturally constructed: see Kenneth Czech, *With Rifle and Petticoat: Women as Big Game Hunters, 1880–1940* (Lanham, NY: Derrydale, 2002), and Mary Zeiss Stange, *Woman the Hunter* (Boston: Beacon, 1997).

10. Many environmental historians have analyzed regional types of hunting: see Karl Jacoby, *Crimes against Nature: Squatters, Poachers, Thieves, and the Hidden History of American Conservation* (Berkeley: University of California Press, 2001); Louis

Warren, *The Hunter's Game: Poachers and Conservationists in Twentieth-Century America* (New Haven, CT: Yale University Press, 1997); Steve Hahn, "Hunting, Fishing, and Foraging: Common Rights and Class Relations in the Postbellum South," *Radical History Review* 26 (1982), 37–64; and Richard Judd, "Reshaping Maine's Landscape: Rural Culture, Tourism, and Conservation, 1890–1929," *Journal of Forest History* 32 (4) (October 1988), 180–190.

11. Early histories of conservation paid close attention to the roles played by hunters and especially the Boone and Crockett Club, most notably John Reiger, *American Sportsmen and the Origins of Conservation* (New York: Winchester, 1975), James Tober, *Who Owns the Wildlife? The Political Economy of Conservation in Nineteenth-Century America* (Westport, CT: Greenwood, 1981), and Thomas Dunlap, *Saving America's Wildlife* (Princeton, NJ: Princeton University Press, 1988). When the defining works on anxiety, modernity, and the frontier emerged in the 1980s, however, these earlier conservation histories were not points of reference; rather, Roosevelt dominated the conversation.

12. Discussions of this change are offered in Reiger, Tober, Dunlap, and to some degree in Jacoby although his focus is more on the consequences.

13. Other scholars have taken this approach: Sara Mills has explored how literary conventions influenced female travel writers as they converted their diaries into published texts in *Discourses of Difference: An Analysis of Women's Travel Writing and Colonialism* (London: Routledge, 1991), while Gillespie has discussed the challenges this dynamic poses for historians seeking to use published narratives as sources (10–11).

## CHAPTER 1. "WHAT LUXURY IT IS": ELITE HUNTING ENTERS THE GILDED AGE

1. Theodore Roosevelt, *An Autobiography* ([1913] New York: Da Capo, 1985), 34.

2. George Bird Grinnell, "Climbing for White Goats," in *Hunting*, Archibald Rogers, ed. (New York: Charles Scribner's Sons, 1897), 119; on saying no, Caspar Whitney, Sportsman's View-Point, *Outing*, February 1907, 669; on sportsmen, Whitney, Sportsman's View-Point, *Outing*, October 1908, 110, original italicized, hereafter SVP.

3. This phrase is in the constitution of the Boone and Crockett Club, which can be found in the back of the club's anthologies, including Theodore Roosevelt and George Bird Grinnell, eds., *Hunting in Many Lands* (New York: Forest & Stream Publishing, 1895).

4. William H. H. Murray, *Adventures in the Wilderness; or, Camp-Life in the Adirondacks* ([1869] Syracuse, NY: Syracuse University Press, 1970), 19.

5. Articles on such gentlemen's activities as foxhunting and bird hunting were plentiful throughout the nineteenth century; when I am describing the limits on descriptions of hunting, I am referring to big-game hunting specifically. Herbert's two-volume work on *Field Sport* includes a brief discussion of moose and an anecdote about a bear, but it isn't until page 318 in the second volume that he mentions big-game hunting in the West, and then it is to admit that "with Western sport I have

no practical acquaintance": Henry William Herbert, *Frank Forester's Field Sports of the United States, and British Provinces, of North America*, vol. 2 (New York: Stringer & Townsend, 1849), 318.

6. Elisha J. Lewis, *The American Sportsman* ([1855] Philadelphia & London: J. B. Lippincott, 1906), 408.

7. Murray: on jacklighting, see ch. 9; quote, 18; cost, 25.

8. Australia and Antarctica have no big game; hunters occasionally sought jaguar and guanaco in South America, but such hunts are rare in the literature.

9. The American elk is misnamed (it is not actually related to the European elk) and turn-of-the-century hunters almost universally used its correct name, wapiti (a Shawnee word, pronounced "whoppity").

10. There were notable big-game hunters from the Continent in this period, but the hunters who engaged in the Grand Tour were predominantly British, probably owing to the reach of the British Empire.

11. Sir Henry Seton-Karr, *My Sporting Holidays* (London: Edward Arnold, 1904), 27.

12. For Baker, see Edgar Barclay, *Big Game Shooting Records: Together with Biographical Notes and Anecdotes on the Most Prominent Big Game Hunters of Ancient and Modern Times* (London: H. F. & G. Witherby, 1932), 56; for the Earl of Dunraven, ephemera collected during a visit to Estes Park, in the author's possession.

13. In *Epiphany in the Wilderness: Hunting, Nature, and Performance in the Nineteenth-Century American West* (Boulder: University Press of Colorado, 2015), Karen Jones describes hunting on the Plains between 1860 and 1890 as the "golden age" of sport hunting, but it's unclear why: Africa, Alaska, and the Canadian Rockies would eclipse the Plains as hunting grounds in short order, while the golden age of *writing* about hunting awaited the publishing explosion of the 1880s. Greg Gillespie also cautions against confusing leisured hunters traveling in the West and hunting for sport before the 1880s with the sport hunters who specifically traveled with the *goal* of hunting for recreation (and, I would add, of publishing tales about the hunt) in the final decades of the century: see *Hunting for Empire: Narratives of Sport in Rupert's Land, 1840–70* (Vancouver: University of British Columbia Press, 2008), 4, 115.

14. Henry Leavitt Ellsworth, *Washington Irving on the Prairie; or, A Narrative of a Tour of the Southwest in the Year 1832* (New York: American Book, 1937), 9. Spelling uncorrected from the original.

15. Richard Slotkin, *The Fatal Environment: The Myth of the Frontier in the Age of Industrialization 1800–1890* (New York: Atheneum, 1985): Custer, 407–409; Bennett, 409–411. "Millionaires' Hunting Club" in William F. Cody, *Buffalo Bill's Life Story: An Autobiography* (New York: Farrar & Rinehart, 1920), 137. For Davies, see Paul Andrew Hutton, introduction to Henry E. Davies, *Ten Days on the Plains* ([1871] Dallas: Southern Methodist University Press, 1985): 3–4, 19–20.

16. John Palliser, *The Solitary Hunter; or, Sporting Adventures in the Prairies* (New York: Routledge, 1856): salt lick, 29, jacklights, 31, dogs, 54; Joshua Fraser, *Three Months among the Moose: "A Winter's Tale" of the Northern Wilds of Canada* (Montreal: J. Lovell & Son, 1881), 9. This kind of sampling is common: see also S. H. Hammond,

*Wild Northern Scenes: Adventures in the Adirondacks with Rifle and Rod* ([1857] New York: Arno, 1967), where the hunters jacklight, kill game swimming in the water, and course with hounds.

17. Fraser, 38–39.

18. Herbert (1849): shooting moose, 237; Guards, 248–249.

19. Richard Irving Dodge, *The Hunting Grounds of the Great West: A Description of the Plains, Game, and Indians of the Great North American Desert* ([1877] London: Chatto & Windus, 1878), 118.

20. Ibid., 111.

21. Madison Grant, "A Canadian Moose Hunt," in *Hunting in Many Lands*, Theodore Roosevelt and George Bird Grinnell, eds. (New York: Forest & Stream Publishing, 1895), 84–106.

22. Herbert (1849), 274–275.

23. Michael Punke, *Last Stand: George Bird Grinnell, the Battle to Save the Bison, and the Birth of the New West* (Washington, DC: Smithsonian Books, 2007), 7, 62, 68.

24. For Grinnell, see Punke, esp. 128–129; for Hornaday and bison, see Gregory Dehler, *The Most Defiant Devil: William Temple Hornaday and His Controversial Crusade to Save American Wildlife* (Charlottesville: University of Virginia Press, 2013), esp. 64–64, also Punke, 136–137.

25. Henry William Herbert, *Frank Forester's Field Sports of the United States and the British Provinces of North America.* (n.p.: W. A. Townsend, 1864), 273.

26. The short-lived 1874 *Field and Stream* often gets confused with the influential *Field and Stream* founded in 1895, but they are unrelated. Thanks to Jessy Wheeler of the Boston Public Library for untangling the *Fields and Stream*s for me!

27. This is sometimes implied in cultural histories that move smoothly from frontier to elite big-game hunting; historians who draw the connection explicitly are usually working on Roosevelt. John Pettigrew sees a single American narrative about "violence and killing" that connects Roosevelt to qualities displayed by the pioneers in *Brutes in Suits: Male Sensibility in America 1890–1920* (Baltimore: Johns Hopkins University Press, 2007), 91, while Sarah Watts draws a line from "the bloodthirsty scalper" Crockett to the Boone and Crockett Club, which she claims encouraged patricians to "reclaim their primitive selves [in] a Darwinian struggle with nature": *Rough Rider in the White House: Theodore Roosevelt and the Politics of Desire* (Chicago: University of Chicago Press, 2003), 173.

28. Daniel Herman, *Hunting and the American Imagination* (Washington, DC: Smithsonian Institution, 2001).

29. Fraser: realities, 163; better employed, 167.

30. Elliott Roosevelt, *Hunting Big Game in the Eighties: The Letters of Elliott Roosevelt, Sportsman, Edited by His Daughter Anna Eleanor Roosevelt* (New York: Scribner, 1933), 22.

31. Ellsworth, 122–123. Italics in original.

32. Information on Van Dyke's life taken from Robert Wegner's foreword to the 2004 edition of *The Still-Hunter* (Mechanicsburg, PA: Stackpole Books), v–xi.

33. Clive Phillipps-Wolley, "On Big Game Shooting Generally," in *Big Game Shooting, from the Badminton Library of Sports and Pastimes*, vol. 1 ([1894] London: Longmans, Green, 1895), 20.

34. Theodore S. Van Dyke, *The Still-Hunter* ([1882] New York: Macmillan, 1923): brute heart, 13; manly sport, 28. "Scientific" here indicates sport that involves planning and methodical execution: see Kermit Roosevelt's description of a curious sheep that approached him by moving from one sheltering bush to another as stalking him "in a most scientific manner": Kermit Roosevelt, *The Happy Hunting-Grounds* ([1919] Farmingham, AL: Palladium, 2000), 96.

35. Van Dyke, *Still-Hunter*: pavement, viii; disappointment, 71; long quote, 98; buck-ague, 219; speed of fire, 308.

## CHAPTER 2. FALL OF THE WORKPLACE, RISE OF THE HUNT

1. "Books on Big Game," in *Trail and Camp-fire: The Book of the Boone and Crockett Club*, George Bird Grinnell and Theodore Roosevelt, eds. (New York: Forest & Stream Publishing, 1897), 332; Sheldon in John C. Phillips, ed., *American Game Mammals and Birds: A Catalogue of Books 1582 to 1925; Sport, Natural History, and Conservation* (Boston: Houghton Mifflin, 1930), alphabetically organized, see "Van Dyke."

2. Both quoted in Robert Wegner, forward to T. S. Van Dyke, *The Still-Hunter* (Mechanicsburg, PA: Stackpole Books, 2004), ix.

3. This description of manliness, work, and character draws on Anita Clair Fellman and Michael Fellman, "The Primacy of the Will in Late 19th-Century American Ideology of the Self," *Historical Reflections* 4 (1977), 27–44; Daniel Walker Howe, "American Victorianism as a Culture," *American Quarterly* 27 (5) (December 1975), 507–532; Daniel Rodgers, *The Work Ethic in Industrial America 1850–1920* (Chicago: University of Chicago Press, 1978); and E. Anthony Rotundo, *American Manhood: Transformations in Masculinity from the Revolution to the Modern Era* (New York: BasicBooks, 1993). In *Character Is Capital: Success Manuals and Manhood in Gilded Age America* (Chapel Hill: University of North Carolina Press, 1997), Judy Hilkey shows that success manuals framed willpower as "the most manly of all traits" (142).

4. On moral force of work and building character, see Rodgers, 11–17. Rotundo discusses the links between male performance and family position, 169–170, and the attribution of failure at work to poor character, 179. He also explores morality, religion, and manly character in "Body and Soul: Changing Ideals of American Middle Class Manhood, 1770–1920," *Journal of Social History* 16 (4) (Summer 1983), 25.

5. See Fellman and Fellman; also Rodgers, esp. 11–12. For discussions of character in the period, see for example Caspar Whitney, "What We Stand For," *Collier's Outdoor America* 42 (March 13, 1909), and Theodore Roosevelt, "Value of an Athletic Training," *Harper's Weekly*, December 23, 1893.

6. Most sources cited here discuss these exclusions; Rodgers considers fears of devolution, 11–12. Colleen McDannell in "'True Men as We Need Them': Catholicism and the Irish-American Male," *American Studies* 27 (2) (Fall 1986), 19–36, parses

the ethnic and cultural judgments underlying the assessment of certain activities as "manly."

7. Mary Ryan, *Cradle of the Middle Class: The Family in Oneida County, New York, 1790–1865* (New York: Cambridge University Press, 1981). On upper classes as producing classes, see Rodgers, 15–16; he argues that in the North especially idle gentlemen were rare owing to the triumph of middle-class standards. On elite identification and on the use of education as a filter that allowed some of the newly rich to join the elite, see Edward White, *The Eastern Establishment and the Western Experience: The West of Frederic Remington, Theodore Roosevelt, and Owen Wister* (New Haven, CT: Yale University Press, 1968), esp. 20–22; John G. Sproat, *"The Best Men": Liberal Reformers in the Gilded Age* (New York: Oxford University Press, 1968); and E. Digby Baltzell's books *Philadelphia Gentlemen: The Making of a National Upper Class* (Glencoe, IL: Free Press, 1958) and *The Protestant Establishment: Aristocracy and Caste in America* (New York: Random House, 1964).

8. These changes are described in John Higham's *Strangers in the Land: Patterns of American Nativism, 1870–1925* (New Brunswick, NJ: Rutgers University Press, 2002) and Alan Trachtenberg's *The Incorporation of America: Culture and Society in the Gilded Age* (New York: Hill & Wang, 1982); figure on population increase from Richard Hofstadter, *The Age of Reform* (New York: Vintage Books, 1955), 217. On one-third being immigrants, see Trachtenberg, 88. Class conflict and depressions are eloquently described in Higham's chapter "Crisis in the Eighties" (term "savage depression," 68) and Trachtenberg's chapter "Capital and Labor." The figure on wealth is from Nell Irwin Painter, *Standing at Armageddon: The United States, 1877–1919* (New York: W. W. Norton, 1987), xix–xx. On business failures in 1893, see Thomas Schlereth, *Victorian America: Transformations in Everyday Life, 1876–1915* (New York: HarperCollins, 1991), 33–34. On urbanization, see Trachtenberg, 114–116, and Hofstadter, 174–178.

9. The impact of this change on self-employed men can easily be overestimated: while the *proportion* of middle-class men who were self-employed dropped dramatically in this period, that had far more to do with new people entering the middle class than with changes to those already there. The actual number of self-employed men remained remarkably stable throughout the period: see Peter Filene, *Him/Her/Self: Sex Roles in Modern America* (New York: Harcourt Brace Jovanovich, 1975), 81–82.

10. The classic work on the impacts of this era's cultural transformations is T. J. Jackson Lears, *No Place of Grace: Antimodernism and the Transformation of American Culture 1880–1920* (New York: Pantheon Books, 1981).

11. Walter Lippmann, *Drift and Mastery: An Attempt to Diagnose the Current Unrest* ([1914] Madison: University of Wisconsin Press, 1985), 46. Rodgers describes how industrialization undermined links between work and economic success, 27–28, Hilkey the anxiety caused by this disconnect, 88–89, 123.

12. Poultney Bigelow, *Seventy Summers*, vol. 1 (New York: Longmans, Green, 1925), 160.

13. Foster Rhea Dulles, *Americans Abroad: Two Centuries of European Travel* (Ann Arbor: University of Michigan Press, 1964), 135. On elite revulsion against arrivistes, see Sproat, 148–149.

14. Richard Slotkin discusses class tensions as described in the media, especially in the chapters on the *Herald* in *The Fatal Environment: The Myth of the Frontier in the Age of Industrialization 1800–1890* (New York: Atheneum, 1985). On fears of wealthy provocation and retaliation by the dispossessed, see Clyde Griffen, "The Progressive Ethos," in *The Development of an American Culture*, Stanley Coben and Lorman Ratner, eds. (New York: St. Martin's, 1983), 144–180.

15. William Hornaday, *The Man Who Became a Savage: A Story of Our Own Times* (Buffalo, NY: Peter Paul, 1896), 264.

16. Sproat, Baltzell, and White all describe this crisis. On elite's sense of isolation, see Geoffrey Blodgett, "Reform Thought and the Genteel Tradition," in *The Gilded Age*, H. Wayne Morgan, ed. (Syracuse, NY: Syracuse University Press, 1970): 55–76.

17. For anxieties, see Hilkey, 91, and Rotundo, *American Manhood*, 250–251. Karen Halttunen's *Confidence Men and Painted Women: A Study of Middle-Class Culture in America, 1830–1870* (New Haven, CT: Yale University Press, 1982) is the classic examination of middle-class anxieties about social deception.

18. Miles Orvell's *The Real Thing: Imitation and Authenticity in American Culture, 1880–1940* (Chapel Hill: University of North Carolina Press, 1989) discusses these cultural responses in depth.

19. Richard Ohmann, *Selling Culture: Magazines, Markets, and Class at the Turn of the Century* (New York: Verso, 1996): Westerns, 334; short stories, 314.

20. James Tober explores the meaning of these changes for sport, local, and market hunters in *Who Owns the Wildlife? The Political Economy of Conservation in Nineteenth-Century America* (Westport, CT: Greenwood, 1981).

21. For travel time, see Frederic Irland, "Sporting in an Untouched American Wilderness," in *Hunting*, Archibald Rogers, ed. (New York: Charles Scribner's Sons, 1897), 132, and John Millais, *Newfoundland and Its Untrodden Ways* (London and New York: Longmans, Green, 1907), 337. Daniel Herman in *Hunting and the American Imagination* (Washington, DC: Smithsonian Institution, 2001) explores the links between the stalk's growing popularity and increasing leisure time, 156.

22. Samuel T. Davis, *Caribou Shooting in Newfoundland: With a History of England's Oldest Colony from 1001 to 1895* ([1895] Fort Myer, FL: Premier, 1997): *Harper's* and Holbertson, 92–93; cost, 107; diary, 194–195; "do likewise," 210. Italics in original.

23. Ibid., 15–16. The figure of $280 assumes virtue on Sundays.

24. Ibid., 186.

25. Frederic Remington, "Stubble and Slough in Dakota," *Harper's Monthly*, August 1894, 453.

26. Anthony W. Dimock, *Wall Street and the Wilds* (New York: Outing Publishing, 1915), 424.

27. Davis, 142.

28. Stowe is now Phillips Academy, Andover, which kindly allowed me to borrow their copy with Dimock's inscription.

29. Editorials and nonfiction articles sometimes discussed market hunting, often condemning it, while some travelogues included descriptions of how local people

hunted. In terms of market share, word count, and how hunters presented their own experiences, however, the sportsman-hunter narrative was dominant in the middle-class press.

30. Good biographical sources on Roosevelt include Edmund Morris's *The Rise of Theodore Roosevelt* (New York: Coward, McCann, & Geoghegan, 1979) and Kathleen Dalton's *Theodore Roosevelt: A Strenuous Life* (New York: Alfred A. Knopf, 2002).

31. Christopher Lasch, "The Moral and Intellectual Rehabilitation of the Ruling Class," in *The World of Nations: Reflections on American History, Politics, and Culture* (New York: Alfred A. Knopf, 1973), 83.

32. Bigelow, 282.

33. White notes that backwoods hunters ranked low on the social scale (32–33) and that the cowboy in particular was seen as vicious (50), while Herman traces American disdain for subsistence hunters back to colonial times. George Colpitts in *Game in the Garden: A Human History of Wildlife in Western Canada to 1940* (Vancouver: University of British Columbia Press, 2002) finds similar disdain in Canada, often linked to prejudice against indigenous and Métis hunters (41–43, 90).

34. Theodore Roosevelt, *Ranch Life and the Hunting-Trail* ([1888] New York: Readex Microprint: 1966), 55–56.

35. Ibid., 83.

36. Ibid., 186.

37. On patriarchal life and qualities, see Roosevelt, *Ranch-Life*, 164; on manliness, Roosevelt, *The Wilderness Hunter* (New York: G. P. Putnam's Sons, 1893), 329.

38. Roosevelt, *Ranch-Life*, 24, 100.

39. For "deities," see Theodore Roosevelt, "The Boone and Crockett Club," *Harper's Weekly* 37 (18 March 1893), 267. Membership requirements from the club's constitution.

40. Grinnell, "Climbing for White Goats," in *Hunting*, Archibald Rogers, ed. (Charles Scribner's Sons, 1897), 119; Arnold Hague, "The Yellowstone Park as a Game Reservation," in Theodore Roosevelt and George Bird Grinnell, eds., *American Big-Game Hunting* ([1893] New York: Forest and Stream Publishing, 1901), 257.

41. The founders of both the still-hunting genre and the club itself were older: Grinnell, for instance, was born in 1849. Even in the club, however, roughly two-thirds of the members were born after 1860, and when middle-class adherents of the still-hunt are included the numbers skew further toward a post–Civil War cohort. That the majority of sportsmen-hunters were born in the 1860s or early 1870s also places them in the cohort that felt the cultural impact of the Second Industrial Revolution most forcefully.

42. John Jay Chapman, *Memories and Milestones* (New York: Moffat, Yard: 1915), 184. Chapman did not hunt big game (to my knowledge), but he did marry the sister of Winthrop and William Astor Chanler, two leading Boone and Crockett members who will be making appearances later in this book. As usual with the elite, one degree of separation at most seems to be the rule.

## CHAPTER 3. MAKING MEANING OUT OF MOOSE: CONSTRUCTING THE HUNTING NARRATIVE

1. Harry Hale, "At St. Mary's," in *Hunting*, Archibald Rogers, ed. (New York: Charles Scribner's Sons, 1897), 265–300.

2. James Holmes at Alaska's Wildlife Information Center kindly forwarded my question about this to Kenai moose biologist John Crouse. He explained that moose have glands between their "digits," and as a result the hair there is indeed emerald green. I appreciate the time both men took to satisfy my (and, if you're reading this, your) curiosity!

3. Andrew J. Stone, "The Moose: Where It Lives and How It Lives," in *The Deer Family*, Caspar Whitney, ed. (New York: Macmillan, 1903): "green," 298.

4. This title is commonly given to Theodore Roosevelt, but Roosevelt was a famous man who also hunted big game. British hunter Frederick Selous was the most famous hunter known *for* his hunting, a household name in America and an imperial hero in England. Among American hunters famed for their hunting alone, and in terms of the hunter with the most respect from his peers, the title unquestionably belongs to Sheldon.

5. Charles Sheldon, *The Wilderness of the North Pacific Coast Islands: A Hunter's Experiences While Searching for Wapiti, Bears and Caribou on the Larger Coast Islands of British Columbia and Alaska* (New York: Charles Scribner's Sons, 1912): Merriam, 134; slop quote, 163. His affection for the islands seems to have been genuine; despite his own estimation that it rained 80 percent of the time, when he married Louisa Gulliver in 1909, he took her hunting there for their honeymoon.

6. See for instance Henry William Herbert, *Frank Forester's Field Sports of the United States and the British Provinces* (n.p.: W. A. Townsend, 1864), 273–278, for a prolonged description of a bear's suffering and slaughter.

7. Stone, 292.

8. Over the years readers (none of them hunters) have insisted that there must be a subconscious love of violence at work in hunting that I'm missing, one that might be unknown *even to the hunters themselves*. There's no evidence for that, however, just individual disdain for hunting on one side and a tremendously consistent interpretation of the still-hunt as being about self-control and self-discipline repeated in hundreds of sources from 1880 to 1920. Speaking professionally, I hope readers will respect my decision to analyze the evidence without straying into totally unsupported psychological speculation. (Speaking personally, I am only willing to accept this critique from vegans. Is there a purer expression of violence against and hatred for animals than the gestation crate? How anyone who eats factory-farmed meat can argue about *hunters'* hatred of animals with a straight face bewilders me.)

9. Percy C. Madeira, *Hunting in British East Africa* (Philadelphia & London: J. B. Lippincott, 1909), 9.

10. St. George Littledale, "Caucasian Aurochs," in *Big Game Shooting, from the Badminton Library of Sports and Pastimes*, vol. 2, Clive Phillipps-Wolley, ed. (London: Longmans, Green, 1895), 71.

11. The idea that the narratives constituted a kind of trophy was suggested to me by Professor Michael Johnson: many thanks!

12. William T. Hornaday, *Our Vanishing Wild Life: Its Extermination and Preservation* (New York: C. Scribner's Sons, 1913): savage desire, 49; true sportsmen, 54.

13. For historiography linking primitivism to big-game hunting, please see the discussion of hypermasculinity and especially footnote 4 from the introduction.

14. This description of "discourse" is based on Michel Foucault's explorations, particularly in *The Archaeology of Knowledge and the Discourse of Language* (New York: Pantheon Books, 1972): see the first section on discursive regularities, also pp. 103–108, and 118–125.

15. All quotes from "The Strenuous Life" sourced from Theodore Roosevelt, "The Strenuous Life," in *The Strenuous Life: Essays and Addresses* (New York: Century, 1901), http://www.bartleby.com/58/index.html.

16. In a keyword search for the term in the *New York Times* from 1900 to 1910, I found that the "strenuous life" was very seldom invoked in relation to imperialism; instead it seems to have been associated with boys' play, wealthy men's sport, manly displays in leisure, and above all Roosevelt himself.

17. George Bird Grinnell, "Climbing for White Goats," in *Hunting*, Archibald Rogers, ed. (New York: Charles Scribner's Sons, 1897), 119; James Kidder, "Big Game Shooting in Alaska," in *American Big Game in Its Haunts*, George Bird Grinnell, ed. (New York: Forest & Stream Publishing, 1904), 208; Caspar Whitney, "SVP," *Outing*, November 1906, 241.

18. Charles Sheldon, *The Wilderness of Denali: Explorations of a Hunter-Naturalist in Northern Alaska* ([edited journals from 1908] New York: Charles Scribner's Sons, 1930).

19. Kidder: "my natives," 108; bear, 153; stream, 179; lookout, 142; rain, 153.

20. Ibid., 110.

21. Caspar Whitney, "What We Stand For," *Collier's*, March 13, 1909, 15.

22. Caspar Whitney, SVP, *Outing*, July 1907, 491.

23. Kermit Roosevelt, *The Happy Hunting-Grounds* ([1919] Farmingham, AL: Palladium, 2000), 3; Robert Steed Dunn, *The Shameless Diary of an Explorer: A Story of Failure on Mount McKinley* ([1907] New York: Modern Library, 2001), 5.

24. George Bird Grinnell, "In Buffalo Days," in *American Big-Game Hunting*, Theodore Roosevelt and George Bird Grinnell, eds. ([1893] New York: Forest & Stream Publishing, 1901), 191.

25. Agnes Herbert and a Shikári, *Two Dianas in Alaska* ([1909] Mechanicsberg, PA: Stackpole Books, 2004), 61, 135.

26. Nicholas Proctor, *Bathed in Blood: Hunting and Mastery in the Old South* (Charlottesville: University Press of Virginia, 2002). Although there is little evidence of this type of alteration in behavior among the sportsmen-hunters, obeying the rules of sportsmanship unquestionably remained a way to signal membership in a social group; Daniel Herman points out that the Boone and Crockett rules served this purpose rather than simply being an end unto themselves in *Hunting and the American Imagination* (Washington, DC: Smithsonian Institution, 2001).

27. Daniel Elliott, "The Caribou," in *The Deer Family*, Caspar Whitney, ed. (New York: Macmillan, 1902), 275.

28. William Hornaday, *Two Years in the Jungle: The Experiences of a Hunter and Naturalist in India, Ceylon, the Malay Peninsula and Borneo* ([1885] New York: Charles Scribner's Sons, 1901): instruction, 248; Irish, 3; Hindoo, 183; elephant, 133.

29. William Hornaday, *Camp-fires in the Canadian Rockies* ([1906] New York: Charles Scribner's Sons, 1927).

30. Ibid., 158.

31. Ibid., 73. Italics in original.

32. Ibid., 31.

33. Lewis repeatedly describes these types as two entirely different kinds of people: "Of all the disagreeable characters that a well-bred sportsman is likely to be thrown in contact with, that of a *pot-hunter* is the most disgusting, the most selfish, the most unmanly": *The American Sportsman* ([1855] Philadelphia: J. B. Lippincott, 1906), 134–135). Note that "pot-hunters" are not subsistence hunters shooting *for* the pot, but rather any hunter who shoots game indiscriminately.

34. He may have been speaking to a more specific audience as well. In 1894 Hornaday was passed over for membership in the Boone and Crockett Club because his hunting had been, in Grinnell's words, "in a measure professional," and *Camp-fires* can also be seen as an assertion that Hornaday was now bagging game like a sportsmanlike gentleman: see Gregory Dehler, *The Most Defiant Devil: William Temple Hornaday and His Controversial Crusade to Save American Wildlife* (Charlottesville: University of Virginia Press, 2013), 154.

35. George Colpitts, *Game in the Garden: A Human History of Wildlife in Western Canada to 1940* (Vancouver: University of British Columbia Press, 2002), 133.

36. No author given, "Literature of American Big-Game Hunting," in *American Big-Game Hunting*, Theodore Roosevelt and George Bird Grinnell, eds. ([1893] New York: Forest & Stream Publishing, 1901), 321. Although no author is listed, Roosevelt's voice is always distinctive, and some of the material is lifted from other publications that appeared under his name.

37. Theodore Roosevelt, "The Boone and Crockett Club," *Harper's Weekly* 37 (March 18, 1893), 267.

38. Dillon Wallace, *The Lure of the Labrador Wild* ([1905] Halifax, NS: Nimbus, 1990), 2–3.

39. Caspar W. Whitney, *On Snow-shoes to the Barren Grounds: Twenty-Eight Hundred Miles after Musk-Oxen and Wood-Bison* (New York: Harper & Brothers, 1896), 12–13.

40. Ibid., 292.

41. Ernest Thompson Seton, *The Arctic Prairies* (New York: Charles Scribner's Sons, 1917), v.

42. This article is in the Dillon Wallace papers at Memorial University of Newfoundland; it bears no date but appears to be circa 1905.

43. Ben Merchant Vorpahl, *My Dear Wister: The Frederic Remington–Owen Wister Letters* (Palo Alto, CA: American West, 1972): Wister quote, 80.

44. See for example Madison Grant, "A Canadian Moose Hunt," in *Hunting in Many Lands*.

45. Frederick Jackson Turner, "The Significance of the Frontier in American History," at Primary Sources: Workshops in American History, accessed November 3, 2012, http://www.learner.org/workshops/primarysources/corporations/docs/turner.html.

46. Vorpahl, 80, 86.

47. Emerson Hough, *The Frontier Omnibus* (New York: Grosset & Dunlap, 1903), at Internet Archive, accessed October 18, 2012, http://archive.org/details/frontieromnibus00houggoog.

48. Dillon Wallace, "The Passing of Our Big Game," *Outing*, September 1910, 736.

49. Theodore Roosevelt, "Value of an Athletic Training," *Harper's Weekly*, December 23, 1893, 1236.

50. John Pettigrew, for instance, frames Roosevelt as aligning himself with a consistent hunting narrative that stretches back directly to the pioneers rather than as choosing among a number of different possible interpretations of western hunting by eastern elites: *Brutes in Suits: Male Sensibility in America 1890–1920* (Baltimore: The Johns Hopkins University Press, 2007), 91.

51. "Books on Big Game," in *Trail and Camp-fire: The Book of the Boone and Crockett Club*, George Bird Grinnell and Theodore Roosevelt, eds. (New York: Forest & Stream Publishing, 1897), 333–334. The article is unattributed but is by Roosevelt; a slightly different version, attributed to him, appears in *Fortnightly Review* 69 (April 1898).

52. Theodore Roosevelt, *Through the Brazilian Wilderness and Papers on Natural History* (New York: Charles Scribner's Sons, 1924), 332.

53. A. Donaldson Smith, *Through Unknown African Countries: The First Expedition from Somaliland to Lake Rudolf* (London: Edward Arnold, 1897), 290.

54. Dillon Wallace, *The Long Labrador Trail* (New York: Outing Publishing, 1906), 23.

55. I realize Hubbard starved to death, but it wasn't intended to be a trip with mortal stakes. They should have brought a gill-net.

56. Frederick Schwatka, *A Summer in Alaska in the 1880s: A Popular Account of an Alaska Exploring Expedition along the Great Yukon River, from Its Source to Its Mouth, in the British North-West Territory, and in The Territory of Alaska* ([1893] Secaucus, NY: Castle Books, 1988), 204; see also 178–179 for critique of "parlor map-makers." Some sportsmen also recognized there were reasons some places had not been visited: Percy Etherton rather plaintively describes how "I went on in the afternoon over the same vast plains, desolate and seemingly limitless . . . where man has never yet set foot, and presumably does not wish to": P. T. Etherton, *Across the Roof of the World: A Record of Sport and Travel through Kashmir, Gilgit, Hunza, the Pamirs, Chinese Turkistan, Mongolia and Siberia* (New York: Frederick A. Stokes, 1911), 160.

57. H. Hesketh Prichard, *Through Trackless Labrador* (New York: Sturgis & Walton, 1911), xv.

58. William Brooks Cabot, "Camp and Travel in the North-Country," in Harvard Travellers Club, *Handbook of Travel* (Cambridge, MA: Harvard University Press, 1917), 26.

59. Glover Allen, "Preface," in Harvard Travellers Club, *Handbook of Travel* (Cambridge, MA: Harvard University Press, 1917), n.p.

60. Sheldon, *Wilderness of the North Pacific Coast Islands*, 92.

61. Lt. Col. J. H. Patterson, *The Man-Eaters of Tsavo* ([1908] New York: St. Martin's, 1986), 321.

62. In *Outing*, December 1907, 373, Hornaday announces his collection, noting Britain's and Germany's national collections and urging Americans to prevent all the good heads from being taken out of the country by foreigners.

63. *Trail and Camp-fire*, for instance, contains five different authors' observations on bears presented in a single section, while Claude Cane discusses the proliferation of species, including James Kidder's *Ursus kidderi* and Andrew Stone's *Ursus merriami*: Claude Richard John Cane, *Summer and Fall in Western Alaska: The Record of a Trip to Cook's Inlet after Big Game* (London: H. Cox, 1903), 44.

64. Henry Fairfield Osborn, "Preservation of the Wild Animals of North America," in *American Big Game in Its Haunts*, George Bird Grinnell, ed. (New York: Forest & Stream Publishing, 1904), 352–353.

65. John Millais, *Newfoundland and Its Untrodden Ways* (London: Longmans, Green, 1907), 1.

66. Elmer Frank, "A Remarkable Adventure with Grizzly Bears," *Outing*, November 1901, quotes 149–150.

67. Theodore S. Van Dyke, *The Still-Hunter* ([1882] New York: Macmillan, 1923), 60.

68. Owen Wister, "The White Goat and His Ways," in *Musk-Ox, Bison, Sheep and Goat*, Caspar Whitney, ed. (New York: Macmillan, 1904), 260–261.

69. Examples abound; some of the best known are by George Oliver Shields (see below) and the section on "The Great American Trout-Swine" in Theodore S. Van Dyke's *Flirtation Camp; or, The Rifle, Rod, and Gun in California: A Sporting Romance* (New York: Fords, Howard, & Hubert, 1881); see also Grace Seton and William Hornaday's uses of the term in chs. 6 and 10 respectively.

70. Van Dyke, *Flirtation Camp*: trout-swine, 151; *porcus*, 154. For "old hog," George Shields, "Colorado Has One," *Recreation*, January 1902, 32; "Seattle swine," *Recreation*, March 1900, 196.

71. For Gardner, see "Colorado Has One"; C. P. White, "Letter," *Recreation*, March 1903, xxv.

72. Ernest Russell, "Moose Snaring in Nova Scotia," *Recreation*, January 1903, 3.

73. Caspar Whitney, SVP, *Outing*, October 1908, 110. Italics in original.

### CHAPTER 4. THE BUSINESS OF NARRATIVE

1. John C. Phillips, ed., *American Game Mammals and Birds: A Catalogue of Books 1582 to 1925: Sport, Natural History, and Conservation* (Boston: Houghton Mifflin, 1930), hereafter Sheldon, *Catalogue*. Information on the collection's intent and con-

tent is from the LOC's description of the book in its online catalogue; sadly, the librarians I contacted at Yale had no knowledge of the collection.

2. Sheldon, *Catalogue*. The catalogue is organized alphabetically by author's last name, so I will footnote a reference only if it has an unusual listing.

3. John C. Phillips, "Preface," in Sheldon, *Catalogue*, 4.

4. Much of this discussion of consumption and identity was influenced by Richard Ohmann's *Selling Culture: Magazines, Markets, and Class at the Turn of the Century* (New York: Verso, 1996).

5. See under "B" for "Boone and Crockett" in Sheldon, *Catalogue*.

6. Phillips, "Preface," 5–7.

7. Richard Ohmann, *Making and Selling Culture* (Middletown, CT: Wesleyan University Press, 1996), 230.

8. William Stowe argues that nineteenth-century male travel writers tried to give an aura of productive labor both to travel, usually associated with consumption, and to writing, a pursuit often condemned as effeminate. It's a small step to see this dynamic at work in hunting as well. William W. Stowe, *Going Abroad: European Travel in Nineteenth-Century American Culture* (Princeton, NJ: Princeton University Press, 1994): 10–11, 126–127, 159–160. In *The Labor of Words: Literary Professionalism in the Progressive Era*, Christopher Wilson analyzes the role of the "gentleman amateur" in American writing before the 1880s and its associations with leisure rather than with productive work (Athens: University of Georgia Press, 1985), 8–9.

9. Wallace gave this name to a chapter in *The Lure of the Labrador Wild* ([1905] Halifax, NS: Nimbus, 1990); Ernest Thompson Seton, *The Arctic Prairies* (New York: Charles Scribner's Sons, 1917), i.

10. "Books on Big Game," in *Trail and Camp-fire: The Book of the Boone and Crockett Club*, George Bird Grinnell and Theodore Roosevelt, eds. (New York: Forest & Stream Publishing, 1897), 341.

11. William Hornaday, *Camp-fires in the Canadian Rockies* ([1906] New York: Charles Scribner's Sons, 1927), 8.

12. See Daniel Walker Howe, "American Victorianism as Culture," *American Quarterly* 27 (5) (December 1975), 524–527.

13. Charles Sheldon, *The Wilderness of Denali: Explorations of a Hunter-Naturalist in Northern Alaska* ([edited journals from 1908] New York: Charles Scribner's Sons, 1930), 293.

14. This dynamic was identified by Thorstein Veblen at the time; he argued that elite hunters were trapped by "certain canons of good breeding . . . and those canons will not permit him, without blame, to seek contact with nature on other terms": *The Theory of the Leisure Class* ([1902] New York: Random House, 2001), 187.

15. Wallace's papers include clippings announcing these engagements (Wallace papers, Centre for Newfoundland Studies Archives, Memorial University of Newfoundland).

16. *Cleveland Plain-Dealer*, 7 November 1914.

17. Caspar Whitney, SVP, *Outing*, November 1905, 229–230.

18. Caspar Whitney to Albert Bigelow Paine, July 18, 1905, Albert Bigelow Paine letters, 1875–1934, Huntington Library.

19. Col. Roger D. Williams to George Bird Grinnell, February 2, 1905, George Bird Grinnell papers, 1879–1951, Huntington Library; for a more casual approach, see Chauncey Stigand to John P. Holman, June 16, 1919, also Grinnell papers.

20. Dillon Wallace, *The Long Labrador Trail* (New York: Outing Publishing, 1906): call to duty, 2; surrender, 90; plain duty, 114.

21. Owen Wister to Fernand Lungren, August 30, 1911, Fernand Lungren papers, 1897–1928, Huntington Library.

22. Charles Sheldon, *The Wilderness of the Upper Yukon: A Hunter's Explorations for Wild Sheep in Sub-Arctic Mountains* (New York: Charles Scribner's Sons, 1911), 46–47.

23. Frederick Selous, introduction to Percy Madeira, *Hunting in British East Africa* (Philadelphia & London: J. B. Lippincott, 1909).

24. The relationship between writers and the personae they inhabit has been widely discussed in histories of travel writing. Stowe notes travel writing "offered aspiring authors a ready-made form, a sure fire subject" (11) and a chance to "recast themselves as the kind of narrators, protagonists, and travelers they most wanted to be" (55).

25. For an overview see Frank Luther Mott, *A History of American Magazines 1885–1905* (Cambridge, MA: Belknap Press of Harvard University Press, 1957), still the standard work, esp. 4–5; Wilson, *Labor of Words*, argues for the importance of changes to copyright law, 74–82.

26. Thomas Schlereth, *Victorian America: Transformations in Everyday Life, 1876–1915* (New York: HarperCollins, 1991): books tripling, 177. On invention of bestseller, Wilson, *Labor of Words*, 79.

27. Mott, 5, 11.

28. On circulation, Ohmann, *Selling Culture*, 29; Christopher P. Wilson, "The Rhetoric of Consumption: Mass-Market Magazines and the Demise of the Gentle Reader, 1880–1920," in *The Culture of Consumption: Critical Essays in American History, 1880–1980*, Richard Wightman Fox and T. J. Jackson Lears, eds. (New York: Pantheon Books, 1983), 42.

29. On magazine topics, Mott; xiii–xv; on *Recreation*, Sheldon, *Catalogue*, under "R" in the periodicals section.

30. Description based on reading *Outing*, 1895–1909, and sampling *Forest and Stream* between 1878 and 1905.

31. Caspar Whitney to Jack London, November 13, 1905, Jack London papers, 1866–1977, Huntington Library.

32. From copyright information in the books.

33. Caspar Whitney to Jack London, November 30, 1906, Jack London papers.

34. Sidney Wright, *Adventures among Wild Beasts: Romantic Incidents and Perils of Travel, Sport, and Exploration throughout the World* (Philadelphia: J. B. Lippincott; London: Seeley, 1909).

35. Sheldon's *Catalogue* is invaluable for tracing these reprints; see under "B" for Bryant.

36. For prices paid, see Mott, 39–41.

37. These connections are clear in the published writing and private correspondence of many of these hunters; Mott details the social milieu of the publishing elite; for the history of a publishing family, see J. Henry Harper's *The House of Harper* (New York: Harper & Brothers, 1912).

38. Ben Merchant Vorpahl, *My Dear Wister: The Frederic Remington–Owen Wister Letters* (Palo Alto, CA: American West, 1972): on Bigelow, 21–22; musk-ox complaints, 168; Caspar W. Whitney, "The Cougar," in *Hunting in Many Lands*; Roosevelt filling in, see editorial note accompanying Theodore Roosevelt, "The Boone and Crockett Club," *Harper's Weekly* 37 (March 18, 1893), 267; Harper's involvement in *Outing*, see "Outing in New Hands: The Publication Purchased by Caspar Whitney and Ten Other Men," *New York Times*, February 15, 1900, 12; republication of *The Wilderness Hunter*, see entry under "Roosevelt" in Sheldon, *Catalogue*.

39. From copyright information in the books.

40. This paragraph is based on Ohmann's and Wilson's work; see Ohmann, *Selling Culture*, for middle-class identity of readers, 174; for magazine reading as cultural experience, 29.

41. Percentages based on research into membership list and errs, if at all, by *underestimating* the number of publications. Many thanks to research assistant C. A. K. for help with this!

### CHAPTER 5. WHITNEY RISING

1. Information on Whitney from several sources including the *National Cyclopedia of American Biography*, vol. 25 (New York: J. T. White, 1940), 284. Information on Cora's birthplace is from the 1900 US Census. The Internet offers a lot of unsourced or inaccurate information about Whitney and there is a rumor of a wife predating Cora, but I have been unable to find evidence for an earlier marriage in the census or New York State marriage records.

2. Whitney's birth year can be found given as 1861, 1862, 1863, and 1864; the 1861 date is the one that he gave most often in interviews, while the census has him born in 1862 (in 1890) and 1864 (in 1900). On his death in 1929, however, his obituaries all gave his age as 64, and working backward from this gives him yet another birth year: 1865.

3. Frank Luther Mott, *A History of American Magazines 1885–1905* (Cambridge, MA: Belknap Press of Harvard University Press, 1957), 368.

4. Michael Oriard, *Reading Football: How the Popular Press Created an American Spectacle* (Chapel Hill: University of North Carolina Press, 1993), 141.

5. Price Collier, "Sport's Place in the Nation's Well-Being," *Outing*, July 1898, 383. This division applied to middle- and upper-class East Coast boys, who had little chance to hunt without traveling. Many adults of this set participated in sports such as golf and lawn tennis, but those never attracted the same rhetoric as amateur sport for youth: they were not seen as building or revealing character.

6. On manly boys, see Caspar W. Whitney, *A Sporting Pilgrimage* (New York: Harper & Brothers, 1894), i. On tests, Collier, 384.

7. S. W. Pope in *Patriotic Games: Sporting Traditions in the American Imagination, 1876–1926* (New York: Oxford University Press, 1997) argues that amateurism emerged in reaction to professional sport and discusses Whitney's influence. Mark Dyreson in *Making the American Team: Sport, Culture, and the Olympic Experience* (Urbana: University of Illinois Press, 1998) shows how Whitney promoted the idea that athletics revealed national identity; see also his "Regulating the Body and the Body Politic: American Sport, Bourgeois Culture, and the Language of Progress, 1880–1920," in *The New American Sport History: Recent Approaches and Perspectives*, S. W. Pope, ed. (Urbana: University of Illinois Press, 1997), 121–145. In the same volume, Elliott Gorn describes the rise of amateurism in "Sports through the 19th Century," 33–57.

8. Whitney, Amateur Sport, *Harper's Weekly*, June 27, 1896, 646. Italics in original.

9. Whitney, Amateur Sport, *Harper's Weekly*, December 28, 1895, 1251.

10. See for example Roosevelt, "The Boone and Crockett Club," *Harper's Weekly*, March 18, 1893, 267.

11. Whitney, *Sporting Pilgrimage*, 281–282.

12. Whitney, Amateur Sport, *Harper's Weekly*, October 5, 1895, 954.

13. Whitney, Amateur Sport, *Harper's Weekly*, April 4, 1896, 333–334.

14. Whitney, Amateur Sport, *Harper's Weekly*, July 4, 1896, both quotes 669.

15. *Bookman*, December 1900, 361. Information on Whitney's star status is from myriad sources, including those on amateur sport cited above.

16. In 1895, for instance, Whitney denounced the University of Minnesota for fielding a "ringer." The university responded with an open letter denying the charge, which was widely reprinted in midwestern papers; Whitney reprinted the letter in *Harper's* and denounced everyone who signed it (Amateur Sport, *Harper's Weekly*, December 28, 1895).

17. No author given, "The Minister and Athletics: Mr. Caspar Whitney's Views," *Outlook* 55 (January 9, 1897), 181.

18. John A. Lucas, "Caspar Whitney," *Journal of Olympic History* 8 (2) (2000), 36.

19. Whitney, Amateur Sport, *Harper's Weekly*, July 4, 1896.

20. Theodore Roosevelt, *The Wilderness Hunter* (New York: G. P. Putnam's Sons, 1902), 323. TR states that he was at Harvard with Whitney, but Harvard maintains records of all those who attended, and Whitney is not listed. Whitney himself never claimed that he attended, only that he passed the entrance exams.

21. Caspar W. Whitney, "The Cougar," in *Hunting in Many Lands*, Theodore Roosevelt and George Bird Grinnell, eds. (New York: Forest & Stream Publishing, 1895), 238–254.

22. Caspar Whitney, *On Snow-shoes to the Barren Grounds: Twenty-Eight Hundred Miles after Musk-Oxen and Wood-Bison* (New York: Harper & Brothers, 1896), 18.

23. Ibid., 28.

24. Ibid., 12–13.

25. Ibid., 52.

26. Ibid., 56. I wonder what he was thinking too! We tried to mime this out over Christmas dinner last year and it raised a lot of questions: miming "I will kill you" turns out to be quite easy; the "if-then" clause, not so much.

27. Ernest Thompson Seton, *The Arctic Prairies* (New York: Charles Scribner's Sons, 1917), 6.

28. Whitney, *On Snow-shoes*, 208–209.

29. Ibid., 218. It's worth noting that what Whitney is doing is not technically snow-crusting, since the snow is hard and icy and the musk-ox don't break through it; as Whitney presents it, it's more of a slippery race.

30. Ibid., 135.

31. Hunter Frank Russell had exactly the same experience there a few years later, although he credited the Indians' behavior to avarice: he thought they were worried that his Winchester would damage their fur returns and also figured that, by killing all the musk-ox before he caught up, they could make extra money by selling him one. Frank Russell, "Hunting Musk-Ox with the Dog Ribs," in *Hunting*, Archibald Rogers, ed. (New York: Charles Scribner's Sons, 1897), 322; see also Russell's *Explorations in the Far North: Being the Report of an Expedition under the Auspices of the University of Iowa during the Years 1892, '93, and '94* (Iowa City: State University of Iowa, 1898).

32. Whitney, *On Show-Shoes*, 252–253.

33. Ibid., 304.

34. For Sheldon, see *American Game Mammals and Birds: A Catalogue of Books 1582 to 1925: Sport, Natural History, and Conservation*, John C. Phillips, ed. (Boston: Houghton Mifflin, 1930), hereafter Sheldon, *Catalogue*; *New York Sun* review reprinted in back of Lt. Col. John H. Patterson, *In the Grip of the Nyika: Further Adventures in British East Africa* (New York: Macmillan, 1909); for a similar review, see "Books and Authors," *Canadian Magazine*, October 1896, 581.

35. Caspar Whitney, "The Musk-Ox and Its Hunting," in *Musk-Ox, Bison, Sheep and Goat*, Caspar Whitney, ed. (New York: Macmillan, 1904), 18.

36. Ibid., 21.

37. Ibid., 25–27. This also serves as further evidence that Whitney was more interested in entertaining readers than in offering an accurate account of events. Despite his claim that this moment was unforgettable, it actually rated only two sentences in *Snow-shoes*: "I went straight on, keeping just under the top of the ridge, and when the two musk-oxen came opposite me it was within about 100 yards. I fired twice, scoring each time" (*Snow-shoes*, 259).

38. See for example David Young's dismissal of "Whitney, the American who wanted to segregate athletes by social class and called working-class athletes 'vermin'" in *The Olympic Myth of Greek Amateur Athletics* (Chicago: Ares, 1984), 73.

39. Whitney, *Sporting Pilgrimage*, 281.

40. Ibid.: putrefied limb, 288; polluted sea, 219; bower, 281. One might also phrase this as a series of images of the superego overwhelmed by the forces of the id, especially as represented by the fecal sea.

41. Ibid.: money, 113; purity, 219.

42. Whitney, SVP, *Outing*, February 1907, 669.

43. Caspar W. Whitney, *Jungle Trails and Jungle People* (New York: Macmillan, 1904), 296–297. The use of "man-eating" is not hyperbolic; in this case the tiger had eaten a child.

44. Most of this is based on Charles H. Brown's excellent *The Correspondents' War: Journalists in the Spanish-American War* (New York: Charles Scribner's Sons, 1967): Whitney in privileged group, 276–277, 313; Bigelow controversy, 231–232; Davis quote, 277. Bigelow's slightly differing version can be found in *Seventy Summers*, vol. 1 (New York: Longmans, Green, 1925), 286–287.

45. Whitney's articles appeared in *Harper's:* typical is "The Santiago Campaign," October 1898.

46. Lee quoted in Brown, 349.

47. Richard Harding Davis, "Our War Correspondents in Cuba and Puerto Rico," *Harper's Magazine*, May 1899, 945.

48. "Outing in New Hands: The Publication Purchased by Caspar Whitney and Ten Other Men," *New York Times*, February 15, 1900, 12.

49. "Caspar Whitney's Debt," *New York Times*, May 2, 1903, 11.

50. Sheldon's *Catalogue* has a complete history of *Outing* in the periodical section.

51. On Howland, see Mott, 633; Bigelow, 300–301.

52. *Harper's Magazine*, that is, which cost 35 cents; *Harper's Weekly* was quite a bit cheaper. Whitney wrote for both at various times.

53. See *Outing*, October 1894; for "A Jamestown Romance," March 1895; Lenz's disappearance, February 1895, complete with picture of a hopeful young man with bicycle and "*Outing*" on his cap. After Wallace published *The Lure of the Labrador Wild*, one of the *Outing* staff tried to talk him into completing Lenz's trip; Wallace wisely declined.

54. Charles Frederick Holder, "Big Sharks as Game," *Outing*, October 1900: sportsmanlike, 50; guillotine, 53.

55. Leonidas Hubbard, "The Doom of Michigan's Grayling," *Outing*, October 1900.

56. Edwin Sabin, "The Lost Ball," *Outing*, October 1900: quote, 61.

57. Whitney, SVP, *Outing*, June 1903, 385. Bold in original.

58. Whitney, SVP, *Outing*, August 1907, 623.

59. Whitney, SVP, *Outing*, April 1902, both 104.

60. Christopher P. Wilson, "The Rhetoric of Consumption: Mass-Market Magazines and the Demise of the Gentle Reader, 1880–1920," in *The Culture of Consumption: Critical Essays in American History, 1880–1980*, Richard Wightman Fox and T. J. Jackson Lears, eds. (New York: Pantheon Books, 1983), 56.

61. Quoted in Richard Ohmann, *Selling Culture: Magazines, Markets, and Class at the Turn of the Century* (New York: Verso, 1996), 288.

62. Christopher P. Wilson, *The Labor of Words: Literary Professionalism in the Progressive Era* (Athens: University of Georgia Press, 1985), 40.

63. Duck, "Bay Snipe at Currituck," *Forest and Stream*, October 16, 1890, 248; the same issue offers a letter-column debate about hounding deer in the Adirondacks, 249.

64. Oriard notes that "Whitney directed his deepest scorn at those from his own class who betrayed its values" (157–158).

65. Whitney, SVP, *Outing*, December 1900, 89.

66. Gene Stratton-Porter, "Photographing the Belted Kingfisher: Remarkable Photographs of This Shy Bird," *Outing*, November 1901, 190.

67. W. Cameron Forbes, "The Football Coach's Relation to the Players," *Outing*, December 1900, 339; Leonidas Hubbard, "Afoot in Nature's Game Preserves: The Adirondack Park Region," *Outing*, November 1900, 198.

68. Emerson Hough, "Daniel Boone," *Outing*, June 1903, 365.

69. Robert Steed Dunn, "On the Chase for Volcanoes IV: Veiled Craters and We Ourselves," *Outing*, May 1908, 155.

70. Col. Roger D. Williams to George Bird Grinnell, February 2, 1905, George Bird Grinnell papers, 1879–1951, Huntington Library.

71. Caspar Whitney, *The Flowing Road* (Philadelphia: J. B. Lippincott, 1913), 310.

72. Ibid., 115.

73. Ibid., 134, 137.

74. Ibid., 154.

75. Ibid., 156.

76. Ibid.: hair, 157; adventure, 160.

77. No author given, SVP, *Outing*, April 1906, 105.

78. No author given, "Exploring Unknown America," *Outing*, June 1906, 359.

79. No author given, SVP, *Outing*, April 1906, 105.

80. Whitney, SVP, *Outing*, November 1905, 229–230.

81. Ibid.

82. Zona Gale, "Editors of the Younger Generation," *Critic* 44 (April 1904), 318.

83. Mott, 637–638. I think Mott's circulation figures are incorrect. He claims *Outing* was at "ninety thousand, with some forty pages of advertising a month" in 1896, but there was no advertising and ninety thousand seems *very* high; Whitney puts the circulation at under twenty thousand when he took over in 1899. I have thus used Whitney's report for circulation rather than Mott's. (There are other small errors in Mott as well, especially in terms of the Hubbard expedition.)

84. On "thrilling," see H. E. Coblentz's review of *Jungle Trails* in *Dial*, December 1, 1905, 378; for "masterly," *Literary Digest* 45 (December 14, 1912), 1133.

85. Caspar Whitney to Jack London, September 12, 1905, Jack London papers, 1866–1977, Huntington Library; Caspar Whitney to Albert Bigelow Paine, February 8, 1905, and July 18, 1905, Albert Bigelow Paine letters, 1875–1934, Huntington Library.

86. Caspar Whitney to Jack London, August 24, 1905, and January 5, 1905, Jack London papers.

87. Caspar Whitney to Fernand Lungren, September 12, 1905, Fernand Lungren papers, 1897–1928, Huntington Library.

88. Steward Edward White to Fernand Lungren, September 30, 1905, Fernand Lungren papers.

89. To clarify: *Outing* generally paid less than *Harper's* per word but offered as much or more when it came to well-known authors like Paine and London.

90. See full discussion in final chapter.

91. "Mice, Said Bill of Fare," *New York Times*, November 15, 1905, 7.

92. For *Outing*'s misfortunes see "Knapp Banks Fail; Big Loan to *Outing*; Binghamton Trust Co. and Private Concerns Backed Magazine for about $700,000," *New York Times*, April 10, 1909, 1. Of Whitney's $36,157 in liabilities, $29,500 was a loan to *Outing* he had personally accepted from another of *Outing*'s owners, and $4,380 money owed to the Binghamton Trust Company ("Caspar Whitney Bankrupt," *New York Times*, September 15, 1910, 3).

93. The second Mrs. Whitney is presumed vivacious because of her active life: she was one of the organizers of the League of Women Voters, worked for war relief in France, and appears in the social columns regularly. Nor does she seem to have lessened her activities with his death: less than three months afterward, she was imploring a stationary company to get her black-bordered mourning stationary delivered as soon as possible since she was about to depart on a cruise for Bermuda.

94. Caspar Whitney, "What We Stand For," *Collier's*, March 13, 1909, 15.

95. "Caspar Whitney, 64, Explorer, Is Dead," *New York Times*, January 19, 1929, 11.

96. "Caspar Whitney's Will: War Correspondent Left Estate Put at $300,000 to Widow," *New York Times*, January 30, 1929, 4.

## CHAPTER 6. DIANA'S OWN: WOMEN AND THE BIG-GAME HUNT

1. Both Mary Zeiss Stange's *Woman the Hunter* (Boston: Beacon, 1997) and Kenneth P. Czech's *With Rifle and Petticoat: Women as Big Game Hunters, 1880–1940* (Lanham, NY: Derrydale, 2002) offer excellent reevaluations of women's hunting.

2. Andrea Smalley, "'Our Lady Sportsmen': Gender, Class, and Conservation in Sport Hunting Magazines, 1873–1920," *Journal of the Gilded Age and Progressive Era* 4 (4) (October 2005), 355–380, for all information except exhibition shooting, for which see Laura Browder, *Her Best Shot: Women and Guns in America* (Chapel Hill: University of North Carolina Press, 2006), 3–5.

3. Annie Peck, "Practical Mountain Climbing," *Outing*, August 1901, 700.

4. Lesley Glendower Peabody, "The Canoe and the Woman," *Outing*, August 1901, 533.

5. Adele Marie Shaw, "The Transformation of Arline Baird," *Outing*, February 1908, 617.

6. Jane E. Reid, *The Joys of the Long Trail: Three Women Adventure-Travellers in Canada at the Turn of the Century* (Ann Arbor, MI: UMI Dissertation Services, 1999), frames women as freed to travel by widowhood; Susan L. Blake, in "A Woman's Trek: What Difference Does Gender Make?," in *Western Women and Imperialism: Complicity and Resistance*, Nupur Chaudhuri and Margaret Strobel, eds. (Bloomington: Indiana University Press, 1992), claims that "women who had the freedom to travel were almost all single" (21). There are dissenting voices as well. In *Penelope Voyages: Women and Travel in the British Literary Tradition* (Ithaca, NY: Cornell University Press, 1994), Karen Lawrence points out the paradox of framing women's travel as an escape from patriarchal oppression while claiming men's travel as a flight from women (104), while Sara Mills in *Discourses of Difference: An Analysis of Women's*

*Travel Writing and Colonialism* (London: Routledge, 1991) argues against the portrayal of women travelers as exceptional or transgressive (32).

7. Joe Dubbert, "Progressivism and the Masculinity Crisis," in *The American Man*, Joseph Pleck and Elizabeth Pleck, eds. (Englewood Cliffs, NJ: Prentice-Hall, 1980), sees men as going to the woods to act out a yearning for "natural male fulfillment" (311). Michael Kimmel in *Manhood in America: A Cultural History* (New York: Free Press, 1996) characterizes some Progressive-Era men as escaping to "a more pristine earlier world where men were men and women virtually nonexistent" (188) while John Pettigrew in *Brutes in Suits: Male Sensibility in America 1890–1920* (Baltimore: Johns Hopkins University Press, 2007) claims that sport hunters "separated themselves from women" as part of their search for an experience they felt was "natural and essential to their masculine identity" (84).

8. Information from E. J. Hart, "Yahe-Weha—Mountain Woman: The Life and Travels of Mary Schaffer Warren, 1861–1939," in Mary T. S. Schaffer, *A Hunter of Peace: Mary T. S. Schaffer's Old Indian Trails of the Canadian Rockies* (Banff: Whyte Museum of the Canadian Rockies, 1980), 2–12.

9. Mary Schaffer, *Old Indian Trails: Incidents of Camp and Trail Life, Covering Two Years' Exploration through the Rocky Mountains of Canada* (New York: Knickerbocker, 1911), 106.

10. Prentiss N. Gray, *From the Peace to the Fraser: Newly Discovered North American Hunting and Exploration Journals 1900–1930* (Missoula, MT: Boone and Crockett Club, 1994), 106.

11. Margaret Marsh in "Suburban Men and Masculine Domesticity, 1870–1915," in *Meanings for Manhood: Constructions of Masculinity in Victorian America*, Mark Carnes and Clyde Griffen, eds. (Chicago: University of Chicago Press, 1990), 165–185, notes that many Progressive-Era men chose social options that couples could pursue together; it's possible that this dynamic was at play in big-game hunting as well.

12. St. George Littledale, for example, hunted in the Caucasus with his wife in 1891 and 1887; Lord North Buxton had ladies in his party in Norway; Percy Madeira's wife went on safari with him; Henry Fairfield Osborn took his daughter Josephine with him to the Canadian Rockies, naming a waterfall after her; further examples appear later in the chapter. Picture of Delamere's safari in Valerie Pakenham, *Out in the Noonday Sun: Edwardians in the Tropics* (New York: Random House, 1985), 74. On Mrs. G, see Lt. Col. F. W. Caton-Jones, "The Nagpur Hunt," in *Modern Pig-Sticking*, Lieutenant-General Sir A. E. Wardrop, ed. ([1914] London: Macmillan, 1930), 165.

13. Czech, esp. 62 for description of trophy book; Mary A. Procida in *Married to the Empire: Gender, Politics and Imperialism in India, 1883–1947* (Manchester: Manchester University Press, 2002) has a great chapter on British women and hunting, 137–157.

14. Quoted in Catherine Cassidy and Gary Titus, *Alaska's No. 1 Guide: The History and Journals of Andrew Berg 1869–1939* (Soldotna, AK: Spruce Tree, 2003), 22.

15. Charles Sheldon, *The Wilderness of the North Pacific Coast Islands: A Hunter's Experiences while Searching for Wapiti, Bears and Caribou on the Larger Coast Islands of British Columbia and Alaska* (New York: Charles Scribner's' Sons, 1912): rapids, 195–198; quote, 177.

16. Cassidy and Titus, 43.

17. Donald Simpson, *Dark Companions: The African Contributions to the European Exploration of Africa* (New York: Barnes & Noble Books, 1976), 17. As the safari became more regulated, African women seem to have been excluded, although Swayne recounts that a Somali woman joined his safari in order to travel between villages.

18. William Adolph Baillie-Grohman, "The Chamois," in *Big Game Shooting, from the Badminton Library of Sports and Pastimes*, vol. 2, Clive Phillipps-Wolley, ed. ([1894] London: Longmans, Green, 1895), 97.

19. Charles Sheldon, *The Wilderness of the Upper Yukon: A Hunter's Explorations for Wild Sheep in Sub-Arctic Mountains* (New York: Charles Scribner's Sons, 1911): Hosfalls, 180–182; otter, 295.

20. Information on Herbert from Mary Zeiss Stange's foreword to Agnes Herbert and a Shikári, *Two Dianas in Alaska* ([1909] Mechanicsburg, PA: Stackpole Books, 2004): v–xiv. The reader may be surprised to find an Englishwoman here, but it's a chicken-and-egg problem; the writing of American and English women often had more in common than that of American men and women; the next chapter examines American hunter-writers in contrast to English hunter-writers; neither chapter leads the other easily. That being so, I beg the reader's indulgence.

21. See for example Eugene Didier, "Holiday Books: Fifty of the Best Published since Last July—Another List of Fifty," *New York Times*, December 8, 1900, BR2.

22. "Women Hunters in Africa: Two Dianas in Somaliland," *New York Times*, November 9, 1907, BR270; "Current Literature," *Spectator*, November 16, 1907, 749–750.

23. For the book's popularity, see Robert M. Bryce's introduction to *My Arctic Journal*, by Josephine Peary (New York: Cooper Square, 2002): v–xxix; for Sheldon, see *Catalogue*.

24. Among the historical sources on women and the rhetorics used to deny them access to the public sphere, see for instance Nancy Isenberg's *Sex and Citizenship in Antebellum America* (Chapel Hill: University of North Carolina Press, 1998).

25. Adele Marie Shaw, "The Restoration of Helen," *Outing*, May 1906, 235.

26. This was a prevailing view of will for women: as Whitney put it in a column on Wellesley women's rowing: "the rowing, like . . . other games, is simply a means to the end . . . that she may fill her position in the world [with] most pleasure and satisfaction to herself, and—to perhaps one other." Caspar Whitney, Amateur Sport, *Harper's Weekly*, June 27, 1896, 645.

27. Grace Gallatin Seton, *A Woman Tenderfoot* (New York: Doubleday, Page, 1900), 105–107.

28. Ibid., 203; Grace Gallatin Seton, *Nimrod's Wife* (New York: Doubleday, Page, 1907), 139.

29. Seton, *Woman Tenderfoot*, 357–361.

30. Schaffer, *Old Indian Trails*, 158.

31. Agnes Herbert, *Two Dianas in Somaliland: The Record of a Shooting Trip* (London: John Lane, 1908): billiard room, 62–63; rhino, 231.

32. Ibid., 262.

33. Ibid.: sporting, 258; Somalis, 39.

34. Herbert and a Shikári, *Two Dianas in Alaska*, 176.

35. Seton, *Nimrod's Wife*, 83; Herbert, *Two Dianas in Somaliland*, 8.

36. This is how Seton addresses her reader throughout *A Woman Tenderfoot*—her version of "Constant reader."

37. Schaffer, *Old Indian Trails*, 360. Italics in original.

38. Seton, *Woman Tenderfoot*, 39–40.

39. Ibid., 20–22. This freedom was hardly unqualified; all these authors emphasized that they behaved and were treated as ladies.

40. Herbert, *Two Dianas in Somaliland*, 168–169.

41. Seton, *Nimrod's Wife*: h–g, 390; jacklighting, 38–39.

42. Herbert, *Two Dianas in Somaliland*: oryx, 109; gazelle, 49.

43. Herbert and a Shikári, *Two Dianas in Alaska*, 214.

44. W. A. Rogers, "Miss Diana in the Adirondacks—a Shot across the Lake," *Harper's Weekly*, August 25, 1883.

45. Herbert, *Two Dianas in Somaliland*, 287. "Shikar" is the Persian word for the hunt, and "shikári" means hunter; here Herbert is indicating her gunbearer.

46. Seton, *Nimrod's Wife*, 47.

47. Peary, 166.

48. Seton, *Woman Tenderfoot*, 39–40.

49. Ibid., 63, 81.

50. Seton, *Woman Tenderfoot*, 308.

51. Robert Peary, "Preface," in Josephine Peary, *Arctic Journal*, 4.

52. Josephine Peary, 178.

53. Seton, *Woman Tenderfoot*: pretending, 136; antelope, 145.

54. For a close reading of such negotiations in *Two Dianas in Alaska*, see Tara Kathleen Kelly, "Goddess and Leader: Conflict and Companionship in Agnes Herbert's Hunting Travelogues," in "Who Carries the Luggage? Gendered Discourses on Companionship in Travel Writing," Floris Means, ed., unpublished manuscript.

55. This is another reason that "discourse" is such a helpful way to frame the choices open to these writers. Roger Chartier notes that Foucault's idea that a discourse operates in a "field of strategic possibilities" means that those making choices within its confines can express contrary opinions: *On the Edge of the Cliff: History, Language, and Practices* (Baltimore: Johns Hopkins University Press, 1997), 57–58.

## CHAPTER 7. SPORTSMEN OF THE BREED: BRITISH AND AMERICAN HUNTERS

1. John MacKenzie, *The Empire of Nature: Hunting, Conservation and British Imperialism* (Manchester: Manchester University Press, 1988), 12–23.

2. I've been using " middle class" to describe a specific group of Americans and their value system centered on productive work and valorization of the will. In England those who might be considered, in terms of production, to belong to a middle

class had a different history, so I'm using "middling classes" to describe those British who were neither aristocrats nor working class.

3. The complex relationship of professional hunters, territorial expansion, and imperialism is examined in Valerie Pakenham's *Out in the Noonday Sun: Edwardians in the Tropics* (New York: Random House, 1985); for an account by one hunter who claimed territory only to come into conflict with the British colonial apparatus, see John L. Boyes, *A White King in East Africa: The Remarkable Adventures of John Boyes, Trader and Soldier of Fortune, Who Became King of the Savage Wa-Kikuyu, Written by Himself* (New York: McBride, Nast, 1912).

4. Edgar Barclay in *Big Game Shooting Records: Together with Biographical Notes and Anecdotes on the Most Prominent Big Game Hunters of Ancient and Modern Times* (London: H. F. & G. Witherby, 1932) discusses many of these men, including Baker, 56; William Cotton Oswell's charming article "South Africa Fifty Years Ago" appears in *Big Game Shooting, from the Badminton Library of Sports and Pastimes*, vol. 1, Clive Phillipps-Wolley, ed. (London: Longmans, Green, 1894), 26–87, with an introduction by Baker, who notes that "I have always regarded Oswell as the perfection of a Nimrod" (in "William Cotton Oswell: A Biographical Sketch," 28).

5. J. A. Mangan's *The Games Ethic and Imperialism: Aspects of the Diffusion of an Ideal* (New York: Viking, 1986) explores connections between British schooling and ideas of empire.

6. Besides John MacKenzie's *Empire of Nature*, see his "Chivalry, Social Darwinism and Ritualised Killing: The Hunting Ethos in Central Africa up to 1914," in *Conservation in Africa: People, Policies and Practice*, David Anderson and Richard Grove, eds. (Cambridge: Cambridge University Press, 1987), 41–61; "The Imperial Pioneer and Hunter and the British Masculine Stereotype in Late Victorian and Edwardian Times," in *Manliness and Morality: Middle-Class Masculinity in Britain and America 1800–1940*, J. A. Mangan and James Walvyn, eds. (New York: St. Martin's, 1987), 176–198; and his introduction to *Imperialism and the Natural World*, John MacKenzie, ed. (Manchester: Manchester University Press, 1990), 1–14.

7. MacKenzie, *Empire of Nature*, 22.

8. Many historians have noted this heterogeneity: see for example Angela Thompsell, *Hunting Africa: British Sport, African Knowledge and the Nature of Empire* (London: Palgrave Macmillan UK, 2015), esp. 35–36.

9. Matt Cartmill, for example, characterizes English hunters in Africa as "gentlemen [pursuing] a familiar recreation appropriate to their high station": *A View to a Death in the Morning: Hunting and Nature through History* (Cambridge, MA: Harvard University Press, 1993), 135. In context this might be read as applying only to administrators, but even they were not always familiar with hunting in England.

10. Lord Edward North Buxton, *Short Stalks; or, Hunting Camps North, South, East, and West* (New York: G. P. Putnam's Sons, 1892). Roosevelt ranked this book with *The Still-Hunter* in terms of impact, and it is an excellent introduction to the world of aristocratic British hunters.

11. See Pakenham's chapters "Settlers" and "Traders."

12. See Pakenham's chapter "Soldiers"; she discusses the romance of empire in "Administrators." Most primary sources used here are by British Army officers. Baden-Powell discusses army life and the leave system at length: Lieutenant General Sir Robert Baden-Powell, *Memories of India: Recollections of Soldiering and Sport* (Philadelphia: David McKay, n.d.). On Africans speaking Hindustani, see H. G. C. Swayne, *Seventeen Trips through Somaliland and a Visit to Abyssinia: A Record of Exploration and Big Game Shooting with Descriptive Notes on the Fauna of the Country* (London: Rowland Ward, 1900), 41–42.

13. Swayne details from *Seventeen Trips*.

14. While the idea of animals causing such devastation seems stunning now, it's actually a fairly low count for two man-eaters in close proximity to an unarmed human population; some of the man-eaters Jim Corbett killed in Kumaon had posted counts in the high hundreds. Scientists have hypothesized that the lions in the Tsavo area are more aggressive than the normal run of lions owing to higher testosterone levels; whether or not they constitute a subspecies is under investigation.

15. Lt. Col. J. H. Patterson, *The Man-Eaters of Tsavo* ([1908] New York: St. Martin's, 1986), *Spectator* quoted on 107.

16. Ibid., 300–301. The Mau-Mau blew the bridge up in the 1950s; perhaps they had read the book.

17. Its fame became such that John McCutcheon concludes his discussion of the Tsavo man-eaters with a weary remark: "No book on Africa seems complete unless this incident is mentioned somewhere within its pages." John T. McCutcheon, *In Africa: Hunting Adventures in the Big Game Country* (Indianapolis: Bobbs-Merrill, 1910), 36.

18. Mary A. Procida, *Married to the Empire: Gender, Politics and Imperialism in India, 1883–1947* (Manchester: Manchester University Press, 2002), esp. 137–157; "obsession," 141.

19. Baden-Powell, *Memories of India*, 31.

20. Lieutenant General Sir Robert Baden-Powell, *Pigsticking; or, Hoghunting: A Complete Account for Sportsmen, and Others* (1889] London: Wyman & Sons, 1924), 61–63.

21. Baden-Powell discusses the benefit for cavalrymen in *Pigsticking*, while "Maori" Hamilton-Browne offers this to readers: "A man may love a bow-wow, or a man may love a girl,/He may prate on points of pedigree, or rave about a curl,/But a trooper can love both of these, in a tiny way of course,/For most of his affections are lavished on his horse": G. Hamilton-Browne, *Camp Fire Yarns of the Lost Legion* (London: T. Werner Laurie, 1913), 124.

22. This description is drawn from Baden-Powell and the incomparable anthology *Modern Pig-Sticking* ([1914] London: Macmillan, 1930), edited and partly written by Alexander Wardrop: log quoted on 108; history of the Kadir in the appendices. MacKenzie discusses pig-sticking in *Empire of Nature*, 186–189. Pakenham notes that winning the Kadir in 1883 was the making of Baden-Powell's career (148). In her mystery *The Game*, Laurie King provides a gripping fictional account of the sport (for those who like their pig-sticking on the imaginative side).

23. Information from Wardrop: on *Hog Hunter's Annual* and social events, see introduction; "Songs of Pig-Sticking" are in appendix B. A "nullah" is an Indian term for a well-concealed gully or ditch.

24. And sometimes not even that; as in modern horseracing, in the Kadir outstanding riders were often mounted on horses not their own. Baden-Powell also notes that many men who could not afford to keep a horse year-round bought one at the beginning of pig-sticking season and sold it at the end (Baden-Powell, *Pigsticking*, 188).

25. Wardrop, 2.

26. Ibid., 235.

27. Baden-Powell, *Pigsticking*: "Value" in table of contents; poodle-faking, 34.

28. Historians might object, correctly, that this generalization glosses over tremendous discursive variations in depictions of the British Empire. In *Discourses of Difference: An Analysis of Women's Travel Writing and Colonialism* (London: Routledge, 1991), Sara Mills has shown that British depictions of colonial contexts are far from homogenous—that, for example, India and Africa were represented as having different histories and as requiring different colonial missions—and Thompsell and MacKenzie have also paid nuanced attention to such heterogeneity. In contrast to American narratives, however, and from the point of view of an English reader at home, I think it's fair to say that the reasons the hunters were there in the first place, the idea of *having* a colonial mission, and the sense of entitlement and ownership, however contextual, linked otherwise heterogeneous narratives to the overall workings of the empire.

29. Chauncey Stigand, *Hunting the Elephant in Africa and Other Recollections of Thirteen Years' Wanderings* (New York: Macmillan, 1913). MacKenzie in *Empire of Nature* carefully considers these implications and discusses the conflicts that arose between hunters and the colonized peoples on whose lands they pursued their sport (190).

30. C. J. Melliss, *Lion-Hunting in Somali-Land, Also, an Account of "Pigsticking" the African Wart-Hog* (London: Chapman & Hall, 1895).

31. Angela Thompsell, "The Expert Knowledge of Frederick Courteney Selous," paper presented at the Britain and the World conference, Austin, TX, March 29, 2013.

32. MacKenzie, *Empire of Nature*, 176.

33. MacKenzie explores the ways that conservation was used as a pretext for exclusion in *Empire of Nature*; see also Thomas P. Ofcansky's "A History of Game Preservation in British East Africa, 1895–1963" (PhD. diss., West Virginia University, 1981).

34. Winston Spencer Churchill, *My African Journey* (London: Hodder & Stoughton, 1908), 8. Churchill was supposed to be inspecting the railway but spent a great deal of time hunting animals and sneering at the Africans.

35. Oswell, 35.

36. For a very different reading of British hunting narratives that sees them as offering images of untamed wilderness, see Thompsell's *Hunting Africa*, esp. ch. 1.

37. Most of this information is from John Millais's *Life of Frederick Courtenay Selous, D.S.O.* (New York: Longmans, Green, 1919): office, 56; lies, 132; Mashunaland,

172–173; Selous Road, 179; Matabele Uprising, 197; lion monograph, 193; TR and hunting in West, 230–231; cricket team, 359; Shikári Club, 367; Meinertzhagen, 305; death, 345; romance, 359. On the popularity of Selous's books, see Pakenham, 150–152. Barclay has an excellent biographical sketch of Selous with an assessment of his importance as a collector. Millais spells Selous's middle name differently from all other sources; I don't know why.

38. See for instance Chauncey Stigand to George Bird Grinnell, January 7, 1919, George Bird Grinnell papers, 1879–1951, Huntington Library.

39. Millais, *Life of Frederick Courtenay Selous*, 222; their role is also described in Selous's introduction to *Man-Eaters of Tsavo*.

40. This change was discussed by American and British hunters; see for example Theodore Roosevelt to Frederick Selous, November 30, 1897, in Elting E. Morison, ed., *Letters of Theodore Roosevelt*, vol. 1 (Cambridge, MA: Harvard University Press, 1951).

41. "Kermit Balks at Buffaloes: President's Son Refuses to Shoot Game That Is Almost Extinct," *New York Times*, September 29, 1908, 1.

42. William Lord Smith, "An African Shooting Trip," in *Trail and Camp-fire: The Book of the Boone and Crockett Club*, George Bird Grinnell and Theodore Roosevelt, eds. (New York: Forest & Stream Publishing, 1897): 78–81, quote on 81.

43. Caspar W. Whitney, *Jungle Trails and Jungle People: Travel, Adventure and Observation in the Far East* (New York: Charles Scribner's Sons, 1905), 187.

44. Prentiss N. Gray, "Missing a Tiger and Shooting the Sun," in *Told at the Explorers Club*, Frederick Blossom, ed. (New York: A. & C. Boni, 1931), 142–143.

45. Claude Richard John Cane, *Summer and Fall in Western Alaska: The Record of a Trip to Cook's Inlet after Big Game* (London: H. Cox, 1903): trophy problem, 121; Merriam, 159.

46. Percy C. Madeira, *Hunting in British East Africa* (Philadelphia: J. B. Lippincott, 1909), 7.

47. Churchill, 150.

48. Paul A. Kramer, "Empires, Exceptions, and Anglo-Saxons: Race and Rule between the British and United States Empires, 1880–1910," *Journal of American History* 88 (March 2002), 1326.

49. Buxton: struggle for existence, 77; teachable, 139.

50. William Hornaday, *Two Years in the Jungle: The Experiences of a Hunter and Naturalist in India, Ceylon, the Malay Peninsula and Borneo* ([1885] New York: Charles Scribner's Sons, 1901): society, 295; tribesman, 417.

51. Ibid., 472.

52. Hornaday's comments on "the festive Home Ruler . . . on his native bog" leave no doubt as to his feelings about the Irish: *Two Years in the Jungle*, 3.

53. Sir Henry Seton-Karr, *My Sporting Holidays* (London: Edward Arnold, 1904), frontispiece. On Anglo-Saxon sportsmen, see Clive Phillipps-Wolley, "On Big Game Shooting Generally," in *Big Game Shooting, from the Badminton Library of Sports and Pastimes*, vol. 1, Clive Phillipps-Wolley, ed. (London: Longmans, Green, 1894), 1; on boar, see Clive Phillipps-Wolley, "The Caucasus," in *Big Game Shooting, from the*

*Badminton Library of Sports and Pastimes*, vol. 2, Clive Phillipps-Wolley, ed. ([1894] London: Longmans, Green, 1895), 35.

54. Poultney Bigelow, *Seventy Summers*, vol. 1 (New York: Longmans, Green, 1925), 226. For other anti-Irish comments, see for example William Adolph Baillie-Grohman, *Fifteen Years' Sport and Life in the Hunting Grounds of Western America and British Columbia* (London: Horace Cox, 1900), 230; Neville B. Craig, *Recollections of an Ill-Fated Expedition to the Headwaters of the Madeira River in Brazil* (Philadelphia: J. B. Lippincott, 1907), 377; and W. S. Rainsford, "Camping and Hunting in the Shoshone," in *Hunting*, Archibald Rogers, ed. (New York: Charles Scribner's Sons, 1897), 49.

55. Buxton: quote, 109; story of his and TR's encounters, 105–109.

56. Robert Steed Dunn, *The Shameless Diary of an Explorer: A Story of Failure on Mount McKinley* ([1907] New York: Modern Library, 2001), 33.

57. Owen Wister, "The White Goat and His Country," in *American Big-Game Hunting*, Theodore Roosevelt and George Bird Grinnell, eds. ([1893] New York: Forest & Stream Publishing, 1901), 29.

58. For the resistance of English immigrants to private game preserves and associations with unfair game laws, see James Tober, *Who Owns the Wildlife? The Political Economy of Conservation in Nineteenth-Century America* (Westport, CT: Greenwood, 1981), esp. 17–18, and Steve Hahn, "Hunting, Fishing, and Foraging: Common Rights and Class Relations in the Postbellum South," *Radical History Review* 26 (1982), 39–40.

59. W. L. Hartshorne, "Letter," *Recreation*, March 1903, 203–204.

60. Theodore Roosevelt, *The Wilderness Hunter* (New York: G. P. Putnam's Sons, 1893), 449; Caspar W. Whitney, *A Sporting Pilgrimage* (New York: Harper & Brothers, 1894), 21.

61. H. A. Bryden, "Game-Bird Shooting in South Africa," *Outing*, November 1900, 142.

62. Frederick Courteney Selous, *A Hunter's Wanderings in Africa: Being a Narrative of Nine Years Spent among the Game of the Far Interior of South Africa* ([1882] London: Macmillan, 1925), ix.

63. Baillie-Grohman, *Fifteen Years' Sport*, 33–35, quote from 33.

64. Theodore Roosevelt, "The Deer and Antelope of North America," in *The Deer Family*, Caspar Whitney, ed. (New York: Macmillan, 1902), 21.

65. Whitney, *Sporting Pilgrimage*, 21; Whitney, SVP, *Outing*, July 1907, 487.

66. Cane, 24. Yes, the same Cane who needed Merriam's intervention because he shot more animals than was legal.

67. Selous, *Hunter's Wanderings*, 381.

68. Ibid., 363.

69. Winthrop Chanler, "Hunting in East Africa," in *Hunting in Many Lands*, Theodore Roosevelt and George Bird Grinnell, eds. (New York: Forest & Stream Publishing, 1895), 52.

70. Baden-Powell, *Pigsticking*, 44.

71. The closest I came to finding a comment on hunting as preparation for soldier-

ing (outside, of course, of Roosevelt) is a quote from Xenophon that heads an essay in *Hunting and Conservation* and is not commented on in the text.

72. There were other writers extolling the martial virtues, most famously William James in "The Moral Equivalent of War," but they were not big-game hunters. Vast amusement may be derived from imagining, in as much detail as possible, William James stalking tiger on foot. Or, better yet, his brother Henry doing so.

73. Rainsford, 64, discusses soldiers being too poor to hunt.

74. Frederick Schwatka, *Nimrod in the North; or, Hunting and Fishing Adventures in the Arctic Regions* (New York: Cassell, 1885) and *A Summer in Alaska: A Popular Account of the Travels of an Alaska Exploring Expedition along the Great Yukon River, from Its Source to Its Mouth, in the British North-West Territory, and in The Territory of Alaska* ([1893] Secaucus, NY: Castle Books, 1988).

75. I received helpful feedback on these ideas at a conference hosted by the Victorian Studies Association of Western Canada.

### CHAPTER 8. STORIES OF GUIDES AND GUNBEARERS

1. Hunter-writers often seem to feel the need to explain the use of "tentboy," and they say that Africans taught it to them: typical is Agnes Herbert's description of her cook's assistants, "men of at least forty, who always referred to themselves as 'boys'": Agnes Herbert, *Two Dianas in Somaliland: The Record of a Shooting Trip* (London & New York: John Lane, 1908), 30. That this distinction was based on women's work is my best guess as to the term's origins.

2. For Plains guides, see Annie Gilbert Coleman, "The Rise of the House of Leisure: Outdoor Guides, Practical Knowledge, and Industrialization," *Western Historical Quarterly* 42 (4) (Winter 2011), 436–457.

3. Major G. P. Evans, *Big-Game Shooting in Upper Burma* (New York, Bombay, and Calcutta: Longmans, Green, 1911), 231. British and American hunters had very similar experiences with guides and gunbearers, so the evidence here is drawn from hunter-writers of both nationalities.

4. Evans, 169. Angela Thompsell in *Hunting Africa: British Sport, African Knowledge and the Nature of Empire* (London: Palgrave Macmillan UK, 2015) notes that Stigand had similar experiences with Africans guiding him to meaty elephants with disappointingly small tusks (56).

5. Charles Sheldon, *The Wilderness of the Upper Yukon: A Hunter's Explorations for Wild Sheep in Sub-Arctic Mountains* (New York: Charles Scribner's Sons, 1911), 257.

6. Horace Annesley Vachell, *Life and Sport on the Pacific Slope* (London: Hodder & Stoughton, 1900), 254.

7. Samuel T. Davis, *Caribou Shooting in Newfoundland: With a History of England's Oldest Colony from 1001 to 1895* ([1895] Fort Myers, FL: Premier, 1997), 142; Agnes Herbert and a Shikári, *Two Dianas in Alaska* ([1909] Mechanicsburg, PA: Stackpole Books, 2004), 61.

8. Information from Catherine Cassidy and Gary Titus, *Alaska's No. 1 Guide: The History and Journals of Andrew Berg 1869–1939* (Soldotna, AK: Spruce Tree, 2003), 1–9.

9. Quoted in Cassidy and Titus, 9.

10. Prentiss N. Gray, *From the Peace to the Fraser: Newly Discovered North American Hunting and Exploration Journals 1900–1930* (Missoula, MT: Boone and Crockett Club, 1994), 29.

11. E. J. Hart, *Diamond Hitch: The Early Outfitters and Guides of Banff and Jasper* (Banff: Summerthought, 1979), 8–11.

12. Dillon Wallace, *The Lure of the Labrador Wild* ([1905] Halifax, NS: Nimbus, 1990), 9–10.

13. E. J. Hart, "Yahe-Weha—Mountain Woman: The Life and Travels of Mary Schaffer Warren, 1861–1939," in Mary T. S. Schaffer, *A Hunter of Peace: Mary T. S. Schaffer's Old Indian Trails of the Canadian Rockies* (Banff: Whyte Museum of the Canadian Rockies, 1980), 7.

14. James Tyrrell, *Across the Sub-Arctics of Canada: A Journey of 3,200 Miles by Canoe and Snowshoe through the Hudson Bay Region* (Toronto: William Briggs, 1908), 170.

15. Edward J. House, *A Hunter's Camp-fires* (New York: Harper & Brothers, 1914), 238.

16. George Elson, *Diary of Mr. George Elson, 1905 (Chief Indian Guide): An Account of a Journey in Labrador* (Ottawa: National Archives of Canada Microfilm #R1648-0-6-E, copied from the private papers of Mrs. M. B. H. Ellis, 1953), August 2.

17. On Berg, see Cassidy and Titus, 34; Theodore Roosevelt, *An Autobiography* ([1913] New York: Da Capo, 1985), 41.

18. John Burnham, "Hunting in the Nutzotins," in *Hunting and Conservation*, George Bird Grinnell and Charles Sheldon, eds. (New Haven, CT: Yale University Press, 1925), 426; Herbert and a Shikári, *Two Dianas in Alaska*, 298.

19. Davis, 93; John Millais, *Newfoundland and Its Untrodden Ways* (London: Longmans, Green, 1907), 73–74.

20. Hart does a phenomenal job of tracing these connections in *Diamond Hitch*: see esp. his chapter "Contracts and Competition," 49–65.

21. H. Hesketh Prichard, *Hunting Camps in Wood and Wilderness* (New York: Sturgis & Walton, 1910), 200.

22. House, 296.

23. Frank Russell, *Explorations in the Far North: Being the Report of an Expedition under the Auspices of the University of Iowa during the Years 1892, '93, and '94* (Iowa City: State University of Iowa, 1898), 4.

24. On skinning, see Madison Grant, "A Canadian Moose Hunt," in *Hunting in Many Lands*, Theodore Roosevelt and George Bird Grinnell, eds. (New York: Forest & Stream Publishing, 1895), 97; on boats, Claude Richard John Cane, *Summer and Fall in Western Alaska: The Record of a Trip to Cook's Inlet after Big Game* (London: H. Cox, 1903), 78.

25. Tina Loo, examining guide-employer conflict in the Canadian Rockies, speculates that resistant indigenous guides may have called on a cultural "Trickster"

version of masculinity, but the fact that guide-employer conflict occurred across so many different cultures suggests that such resistance was the result of economic and social negotiation between classes rather than specific to any one group: "Of Moose and Men: Hunting for Masculinities in British Columbia 1880–1939," *Western Historical Quarterly* 32 (2001): 296–319.

26. See for example *Camping in the Rocky Mountains: A Guide to Colorado, Utah, and Mexico* (Denver, CO: Denver & Rio Grande Western Railroad, 1906) and Fred Clifford, *Haunts of the Hunted: Vacationers' Guide to Maine* (Bangor & Aroostook Railroad, 1903). On Union Pacific's railway packages, see advertisement in the back pages of George Oliver Shields, *Cruisings in the Cascades: A Narrative of Travel, Exploration, Amateur Photography, Hunting, and Fishing, Etc.* (London: Sampson Low, Marston, Searle, & Rivington, 1889).

27. House, 307–308.

28. Billy Warren, for example, ended up running a hotel in Banff (Hart, "Yahe-Weha," 12). Richard Patrick Roth in "The Adirondack Guide (1820–1919): Hewing Out an American Occupation" (PhD diss.: Syracuse University, 1990) discusses the entrepreneurial activities of Adirondack guides, 84–85, 105–107.

29. Cassidy and Titus, 33.

30. James Tober in *Who Owns the Wildlife? The Political Economy of Conservation in Nineteenth-Century America* (Westport, CT: Greenwood, 1981) has an excellent description of the system, 72.

31. Cassidy and Titus: #1 guide, 33; letters to governor, 41, 43. Folk-hero status clear from informal conversations with Alaskans, although admittedly mostly librarians.

32. "British East Africa" is being used loosely here: before 1900, most safaris were staging out of Aden, but around 1900 Nairobi became the focus.

33. Most of the books cited here offer such advice. Popular handbooks such as the British *Hints to Travellers* and the Harvard Travellers Club's *Handbook of Travel* also offered detailed advice: *Handbook of Travel*, for instance, includes the article "Foot Transport in East Africa" which has an entire section entitled "Tribes from Which to Choose" (the author recommends Somalis as "much more intelligent than the natives; polite, clean, and proud" [149]). John T. Coolidge Jr., "Foot Transport in East Africa," in Harvard Travellers Club, *Handbook of Travel* (Cambridge, MA: Harvard University Press, 1917); Douglas Freshfield and Captain W. J. L. Wharton, eds., *Hints to Travellers: Scientific and General*, 7th ed. (London: Royal Geographic Society, 1893).

34. No small demand, providing halal meat meant having the skill to shoot an animal in such a way as to cripple but not kill it, allowing one's Somali employees to approach it safely to cut its throat and bleed it correctly. See footnote above for sources on Somalis, also John T. McCutcheon, *In Africa: Hunting Adventures in the Big Game Country* (Indianapolis: Bobbs-Merrills, 1910), 350.

35. Percy Madeira, *Hunting in British East Africa* (Philadelphia & London: J. B. Lippincott, 1909), 17–20.

36. H. G. C. Swayne, *Seventeen Trips through Somaliland and a Visit to Abyssinia: A Record of Exploration and Big Game Shooting with Descriptive Notes on the Fauna of the Country* (London: Rowland Ward, 1900), 41–42.

37. Madeira and Swayne both discuss the recommendation system and the scene at Aden; on "damn fool passengers," see Swayne, 16.

38. And that danger did not come only from the animals. In an era before antibiotics, even a scratch from a thorn (never mind a gaping wound from a lion's claws) could prove fatal, especially on a safari days or weeks from the nearest medical care.

39. McCutcheon, 68.

40. Evans, 196; on being pushed, see Madeira, 215. Herbert misses a shot due to sudden pressure on her shoulder, only to discover that her guide thought he was helpfully "steadying" her: Agnes Herbert, *Casuals in the Caucasus: The Diary of a Sporting Holiday* (London: John Lane, 1912), 136.

41. John Millais, *Life of Frederick Courtenay Selous, D.S.O.* (New York: Longmans, Green, 1919), 158.

42. Winthrop Chanler, "Hunting in East Africa," in *Hunting in Many Lands*, Theodore Roosevelt and George Bird Grinnell, eds. (New York: Forest & Stream Publishing, 1895), 31–32.

43. Selous's friend French refused to listen to his gunbearer's advice when told he was striking off in the wrong direction and died after a few days' wandering; Selous attributed the death to French's being "terribly obstinate." Frederick Selous, *A Hunter's Wanderings in Africa: Being a Narrative of Nine Years Spent among the Game of the Far Interior of South Africa* ([1882] London: Macmillan, 1925), 400–401.

44. F. J. Jackson, "The Caravan, Headman, Gun-Bearers Etc.," in *Big Game Shooting, from the Badminton Library of Sports and Pastimes*, vol. 1, Clive Phillipps-Wolley, ed. (London: Longmans, Green, 1895), 183.

45. W. F. Whitehouse, "To Lake Rudolph and Beyond," in *Hunting and Conservation*, George Bird Grinnell and Charles Sheldon, eds. (New Haven, CT: Yale University Press, 1925), 281 (Whitehouse's safari took place in 1899); A. Donaldson Smith, *Through Unknown African Countries: The First Expedition from Somaliland to Lake Rudolf* (London: Edward Arnold, 1897), 170.

46. Madeira, 19–20.

47. McCutcheon, 68.

48. Ibid.: stowaways, 71; photograph, 110.

49. Herbert, *Two Dianas in Somaliland*: death, 233; visit, 306.

50. I haven't discussed violence against safari members in part because it was becoming ever rarer by the time most Americans were hunting in Africa, as well as being illegal in many areas; there was a great deal of violence associated with early safaris, however, most famously Stanley's.

51. Guide work in the Himalayas presents clear current-day parallels, including the mixture of competence and incompetence on the part of mountaineer/tourists, the financial and cultural conflicts on expeditions, and the way that the exploitation of guides and porters must be juxtaposed with their skill, their pride in their work, and their resistance to being reduced *only* to exploited workers, as some of them become celebrated mountaineers in their own right. The parallel also raises the question of whether overt racism was at work in the *consumption* of such tales by

turn-of-the-century readers; certainly many current-day Americans thrill to books and television shows about upper-class tourists thrashing about on Everest and K2 without considering the risks incurred by guides and porters.

52. Cane, 142.

53. Quoted in Vachell, 254. Italics in original.

54. Prichard, 200.

55. I'm focusing on the North American market in relation to the sportsmen-hunters; excellent discussions of the meaning of trophies in England can be found in John MacKenzie, *The Empire of Nature* (Manchester: Manchester University Press, 1988), 28–34, and Deborah Cohen, *Household Gods: The British and Their Possessions* (New Haven, CT: Yale University Press, 2009).

56. Prichard: interlocked horns, 120; moose and taxidermists, 200; Howley, 204.

57. Clive Phillipps-Wolley, "Hints on Taxidermy, Etc.," in *Big Game Shooting, from the Badminton Library of Sports and Pastimes*, vol. 2, Clive Phillipps-Wolley, ed. ([1894] London: Longmans, Green, 1895), 415; Evans, 154.

58. Phillipps-Wolley, "Hints on Taxidermy," 415.

59. Ibid., 413.

60. Prichard, 223.

61. Whelan Townsend, "The Sportsman and His Guide," *Outdoor Life* 19(2) (February 1907), 173.

62. Ibid., 173–174.

63. Ibid., 175.

64. Ibid., 176.

65. William Lord Smith, "An African Shooting Trip," in *Trail and Camp-fire: The Book of the Boone and Crockett Club*, George Bird Grinnell and Theodore Roosevelt, eds. (New York: Forest & Stream Publishing, 1897), 85–86.

66. McCutcheon, 350.

67. Herbert and a Shikári, *Two Dianas in Alaska*, 61.

68. P. T. Etherton, *Across the Roof of the World: A Record of Sport and Travel through Kashmir, Gilgit, Hunza, the Pamirs, Chinese Turkistan, Mongolia and Siberia* (New York: Frederick A. Stokes, 1911), xvi.

69. Cartmill, for instance, frames the safari as a relentlessly oppressive relationship between "local folk [sic] and their foreign conquerors" and, in criticizing white hunters, misses the real skill of safari workers: "[The hunter's] weapons were carried for him by a gunboy, who handed them [over] on demand like a caddy passing clubs to a golfer" (*A View to a Death in the Morning: Hunting and Nature through History* (Cambridge, MA: Harvard University Press, 1993), 135–136). Interestingly, Cartmill's sole primary source, William Rainsford, actually describes his gunbearer as a "good tracker, a splendid hunter, a self-sacrificing guardian, a heathen and a gentleman": W. S. Rainsford, *The Land of the Lion* (London: Heinemann, 1909), 46.

70. McCutcheon, 68.

71. Herbert, *Two Dianas in Somaliland*, 38–41.

72. William Hornaday, *Camp-fires in the Canadian Rockies* ([1906] New York: Charles Scribner's Sons, 1927), 164–166.

73. C. J. Melliss, *Lion-Hunting in Somali-Land, Also, an Account of "Pigsticking" the African Wart-Hog* (London: Chapman & Hall, 1895), 40.

74. Herbert, *Two Dianas in Somaliland*, 282.

75. Harry Whitney, *Hunting with the Eskimos: The Unique Record of a Sportsman's Year among the Northernmost Tribe—the Big Game Hunting, the Native Life, and the Battle for Existence through the Long Arctic Night* (New York: Century, 1910), 308.

76. Chanler, 16.

77. James Kidder, "Big Game Shooting in Alaska," in *American Big Game in Its Haunts*, George Bird Grinnell, ed. (New York: Forest & Stream Publishing, 1904), 208.

78. See Daniel Rodgers, *The Work Ethic in Industrial America 1850–1920* (Chicago: University of Chicago Press, 1978), 32–39.

79. William Brooks Cabot, "Camp and Travel in the North-Country," in Harvard Travellers Club, *Handbook of Travel* (Cambridge, MA: Harvard University Press, 1917), 18.

80. Robert Peary, *Nearest the Pole: A Narrative of the Polar Expedition of the Peary Arctic Club in the S.S. Roosevelt, 1905–1906* (New York: Doubleday, Page, 1907), 141.

81. Cabot, 25.

82. Theodore Roosevelt, *A Book-Lover's Holidays in the Open* ([1916] New York: Charles Scribner's Sons, 1926), 128; Peary, *Nearest the Pole*, 124.

83. Ernest Thompson Seton, *The Arctic Prairies* (New York: Charles Scribner's Sons, 1917), 210. This attitude appears in many forms: see for example William Brooks Cabot's comment that "such peoples as the Eskimo are ever children in the presence of advanced races. They are to be led when they can be led, restrained by a firm hand when for their good": *In Northern Labrador* (Boston: Gorham, 1912), 33.

84. Peary, *Nearest the Pole*, 155.

85. Theodore S. Van Dyke, "The Deer and the Elk of the Pacific Coast," in *The Deer Family*, Caspar Whitney, ed. (New York: Macmillan, 1903), 172.

86. Roosevelt, *Book-Lover's Holidays*, 16.

87. Sir Henry Seton-Karr, *My Sporting Holidays* (London: Edward Arnold, 1904), 45.

88. Whitney: kindly, 74; hospitable, 192.

89. Ibid., 197.

90. Ibid.: musk-oxen, 290–291; narwhal, 362; sulking, 368.

91. Dillon Wallace, introduction to Whitney, xiv.

92. Peary Arctic Expedition (1905–1906), Huntington Library.

**CHAPTER 9. DREAMING OF HOWLEY: CONSERVATION AND THE USES OF DISCOURSE**

1. On British Columbia, British Columbia Conservation Office Service, "110 Years of Service: The Beginning 1905–1918," accessed November 11, 2016, http://www2.gov.bc.ca/gov/content/environment/natural-resource-stewardship/natural-resource-law-enforcement/conservation-officer-service/about-the-cos/110-years-of-service; Alaska Game Law, see T. S. Palmer and H. W. Olds, *Game Laws for 1902: A Summary*

*of the Provisions Relating to Seasons, Shipment, Sale, and Licenses* (Washington, DC: UNT Digital Library), accessed November 6, 2016, http://digital.library.unt.edu/ark:/67531/metadc85555/.

2. I don't mean to imply that such sympathy is unwarranted: the story of hunting restriction is often one of blatant injustice. Louis S. Warren in *The Hunter's Game: Poachers and Conservationists in Twentieth-Century America* (New Haven, CT: Yale University Press, 1997) traces the explosion of trade that ended up threatening wildlife.

3. Frederick Selous, *Recent Hunting Trips in British North America* (New York: Charles Scribner's Sons, 1907), 307.

4. Alaska Game Law, see Palmer and Olds. Berg quoted in Catherine Cassidy and Gary Titus, *Alaska's No. 1 Guide: The History and Journals of Andrew Berg 1869–1939* (Soldotna, AK: Spruce Tree, 2003), 43.

5. F. L. Crow quoted in William Hornaday, *Our Vanishing Wild Life: Its Extermination and Preservation* (New York: C. Scribner's Sons, 1913), 106.

6. See for instance discussion of British reactions to Roosevelt's African safari in Angela Thompsell, *Hunting Africa: British Sport, African Knowledge and the Nature of Empire* (London: Palgrave Macmillan UK, 2015), 146.

7. Samuel P. Hays, *Conservation and the Gospel of Efficiency: The Progressive Conservation Movement, 1890–1920* (New York: Atheneum, 1969). This is especially the case in general histories of the era—see for example Robert H. Wiebe, *The Search for Order, 1877–1920* (Westport, CT: Greenwood, 1980)—while Char Miller in *Gifford Pinchot and the Making of Modern Environmentalism* (Washington, DC: Island/Shearwater Books, 2001) also frames Pinchot's approach as foundational, and for good reason.

8. James Tober discusses these leagues in *Who Owns the Wildlife? The Political Economy of Conservation in Nineteenth-Century America* (Westport, CT: Greenwood, 1981).

9. Anthony W. Dimock, *Wall Street and the Wilds* (New York: Outing Publishing, 1915), 238; Prentiss N. Gray, *From the Peace to the Fraser: Newly Discovered North American Hunting and Exploration Journals 1900–1930* (Missoula, MT: Boone and Crockett Club, 1994), 1–2.

10. C. Grant LaFarge, "Sintamaskin," originally published in *Atlantic Monthly*, quote taken from reprinting in *Trail and Camp-fire: The Book of the Boone and Crockett Club*, George Bird Grinnell and Theodore Roosevelt, eds. (New York: Forest & Stream Publishing, 1897), 131.

11. Arnold Hague, "The Yellowstone Park as a Game Reservation," in *American Big-Game Hunting*, Theodore Roosevelt and George Bird Grinnell, eds. ([1893] New York: Forest & Stream Publishing, 1901), 257.

12. Charles Sheldon quoted in George Bird Grinnell, "National Recreation Conference," in *Hunting and Conservation*, George Bird Grinnell and Charles Sheldon, eds. (New Haven, CT: Yale University Press, 1925), 478.

13. George Bird Grinnell, introduction to *The Works of Theodore Roosevelt*, vol. 1 (New York: Scribner's & Sons, 1923), xviii.

14. Theodore Roosevelt to Frederick Selous, November 30, 1897, in Elting E. Morison, ed., *Letters of Theodore Roosevelt*, vol. 1 (Cambridge, MA: Harvard University Press, 1951).

15. Owen Wister, "The Wilderness Hunter," *Outing*, December 1901, 251–252.

16. See Hornaday's stationery, for example William Hornaday to Ernest Ingersoll, May 14, 1915, George Bird Grinnell papers, 1879–1951, Huntington Library. Italics in original.

17. Madison Grant, "The Origins of the New York Zoological Society," in *Trail and Camp-fire: The Book of the Boone and Crockett Club*, George Bird Grinnell and Theodore Roosevelt, eds. (New York: Forest & Stream Publishing, 1897), 320.

18. Caspar Whitney, SVP, *Outing*: patriotism, November 1905, 230; man of education, December 1900, 358; gang, February 1908, 625.

19. Caspar Whitney, SVP, October 1908, 110. Italics in original.

20. Caspar Whitney, SVP, April 1901, 98.

21. Clive Phillipps-Wolley, "Big Game of North America," in *Big Game Shooting, from the Badminton Library of Sports and Pastimes*, vol. 1, Clive Phillipps-Wolley, ed. ([1894] London: Longmans, Green, 1895), 376.

22. George Bird Grinnell, "American Game Protection," in *Hunting and Conservation*, George Bird Grinnell and Charles Sheldon, eds. (New Haven, CT: Yale University Press, 1925), 230; H. Hesketh Prichard, *Hunting Camps in Wood and Wilderness* (New York: Sturgis & Walton, 1910), 201.

23. Caspar Whitney, SVP, *Outing*, October 1908, 120.

24. See for instance "At a Meeting of the Society of American Foresters Held at the Residence of Mr. Gifford Pinchot, Washington, D.C. March 26, 1903," in Theodore Roosevelt, *A Compilation of the Messages and Speeches of Theodore Roosevelt, 1901–1905*, Alfred Lewis, ed. (Washington, DC: Bureau of National Literature and Art, 1906), 208–209; *Conference of the Governors of the United States* (Washington, DC: GPO, 1909).

25. See Stephen Capps, "A Game Country without Rival in America: The Proposed Mount McKinley National Park," *National Geographic Magazine* 31 (January 1917): 69–84. While at the time Denali ended up becoming McKinley National Park, I am calling it by its current name because that was Sheldon's expressed preference: he felt it would be more respectful to the native peoples of the area.

26. Madison Grant, "The Beginnings of Glacier National Park," in *Hunting and Conservation*, George Bird Grinnell and Charles Sheldon, eds. (New Haven, CT: Yale University Press, 1925), 446–470.

27. The best brief summary of the club's accomplishments is Grinnell's "Brief History of the Boone and Crockett Club," in *Hunting at High Altitudes*, George Bird Grinnell, ed. (New York: Harper & Brothers, 1913), esp. 438–442; all information from there unless otherwise indicated; on Adirondacks, William Cary Sanger, "The Adirondack Deer Law," in *Trail and Camp-fire*, 264–278; on seals, Charles Townsend, "Elephant Seals of Guadalupe Island," in *Hunting at High Altitudes*, 406–420.

28. Grinnell, "Brief History," 490.

29. It could be argued that earlier laws including the Yellowstone Game Protection Act did so, but the Lacey Act marks the first time the federal government regulated interstate trade in order to protect wildlife.

30. For *Forest and Stream* support, see "Government Game Restoration," *Forest and Stream* 49 (9), July 10, 1897, 21; "The Lacey Game Bill," *Forest and Stream* 51 (26) (December 24, 1898), 509; two-part letter, Joseph B. Thompson, "The Lacey Act," *Forest and Stream* 55 (4–5) (July 28, 1900, and August 4, 1900).

31. On Sheldon and Wickersham, see Frank Norris, *Crown Jewel of the North: An Administrative History of Denali National Park and Preserve*, vol. 1 (Anchorage, AK: US Department of the Interior, 2006), http://www.nps.gov/dena/learn/history culture/park-history.htm, ch. 2, "Charles Sheldon's Vision," esp. 14–15. This does not mention that Wickersham was famous but the Wickersham Wall certainly is!

32. Horace Albright and Marian Albright Schenck, *Creating the National Park Service: The Missing Years* (Norman: University of Oklahoma Press, 1999), 300.

33. Madison Grant, *Saving the Redwoods* (New York: Zoological Society, 1919): road trip, 112–116; patriotic Californians, 110, 116; enlightenment, 118; clock, 112.

34. See "Report of the Executive Committee," *Eighteenth Annual Bulletin of the New York Zoological Society* (New York: Office of the Society, 1913), 43.

35. Jonathan Spiro, *Defending the Master Race: Conservation, Eugenics, and the Legacy of Madison Grant* (Burlington: University of Vermont Press, 2008), 67.

36. W. T. Hornaday, "Report of the President," in *Second Annual Report of the American Bison Society* (New York: American Bison Society, 1909): Congress, 9; duty, 2.

37. "The Bison Comes to Its Own," *New York Times*, May 28, 1908, 6. Capitalization in original.

38. Edward L. Sabin, "The Boy Scouts Movement," *Lippincott Magazine* 88 (1911), 256–257.

39. Boy Scouts of America, "William T. Hornaday Awards," Boy Scouts of America, accessed June 8, 2015, http://www.scouting.org/scoutsource/Awards/Hornaday Awards.aspx.

40. Ernest Thompson Seton, *The Book of Woodcraft and Indian Lore* (Garden City, NJ: Doubleday, Page, 1912): quote, 7–8; still-hunting, 283–286.

41. Cameron Binkley, "'No Better Heritage Than Living Trees': Women's Clubs and Early Conservation in Humboldt County," *Western Historical Quarterly* 33 (2) (Summer 2002), 194.

42. Mary Sherman, "Our Work for National Parks," *Better Homes and Gardens*, May 1925, 198.

43. John Millais, *Newfoundland and Its Untrodden Ways* (London: Longmans, Green, 1907), 324.

44. Whitney, SVP, *Outing*, January 1901, 476.

45. Millais, *Newfoundland*, 324.

46. Quoted in Spiro, 73.

## CHAPTER 10. THE END OF THE HUNT: CONSERVATION AND THE LIMITS OF DISCOURSE

1. Karl Jacoby, *Crimes against Nature: Squatters, Poachers, Thieves, and the Hidden History of American Conservation* (Berkeley: University of California Press, 2001).

2. For Havasupai, see Jacoby; for Blackfeet, Louis S. Warren, *The Hunter's Game: Poachers and Conservationists in Twentieth-Century America* (New Haven, CT: Yale University Press, 1997).

3. For the positive, see John F. Reiger, *American Sportsmen and the Origins of Conservation* (New York: Winchester, 1975); Thomas Dunlap, *Saving America's Wildlife* (Princeton, NJ: Princeton University Press, 1988); and James Trefethen, *An American Crusade for Wildlife* (New York: Winchester, 1975); for the negative, see Jacoby; Warren; and Mark David Spence, *Dispossessing the Wilderness: Indian Removal and the Making of the National Parks* (New York: Oxford University Press, 1999).

4. William Adolph Baillie-Grohman, *Fifteen Years' Sport and Life in the Hunting Grounds of Western America and British Columbia* (London: Horace Cox, 1900), 27.

5. Elliott quoted in Steve Hahn, "Hunting, Fishing, and Foraging: Common Rights and Class Relations in the Postbellum South," *Radical History Review* 26 (1982), 40; William H. H. Murray, *Adventures in the Wilderness; or, Camp-Life in the Adirondacks* ([1869] Syracuse, NY: Syracuse University Press, 1970), 20, 93.

6. George Bird Grinnell, "New Facts on Game Protection," *Forest and Stream* 15 (8) (March 24, 1881), 143, and "We, the People," *Forest and Stream* 17 (26) (January 26, 1882), 503.

7. Charles E. Whitehead, "Game Laws," in *Hunting in Many Lands*, Theodore Roosevelt and George Bird Grinnell, eds. (New York: Forest & Stream Publishing, 1895), 362.

8. Theodore Roosevelt, "The Deer and Antelope of North America," in *The Deer Family*, Caspar Whitney, ed. (New York: Macmillan, 1902): selfish interests, 63; unrepublican, 19.

9. Whitehead, 362.

10. Roosevelt, "Deer and Antelope," 62.

11. William Hornaday, *Our Vanishing Wild Life: Its Extermination and Preservation* (New York: C. Scribner's Sons, 1913): Italians, 100–101; women, 54; subsistence, 63; savage desire, 49.

12. Madison Grant, "The Condition of Wild Life in Alaska," in *Hunting at High Altitudes*, George Bird Grinnell, ed. (New York: Harper & Brothers, 1913), 371.

13. Madison Grant, "Distribution of the Moose," in *American Big Game in Its Haunts*, George Bird Grinnell, ed. (New York: Forest & Stream Publishing, 1904), 388; his article was reprinted from the *Seventh Annual Report of the Forest, Fish and Game Commission of the State of New York*.

14. Grant, "Condition of Wild Life," 374.

15. Whitney, SVP, *Outing*: forests, February 1908, 627, bold in original; patriots, November 1905, 230, italics mine.

16. Whitney, SVP, *Outing*: senators and pirates, February 1908, 625; native, December 1907, 376.

17. Whitney, SVP, *Outing*: common interest, May 1901, 217; sportsman/American, November 1906, 241.

18. Whitney, SVP, *Outing*, May 1901, 218.

19. See for example Jacoby; Warren; Hahn; and Spence.

20. Adam Przeworski, *Capitalism and Social Democracy* (Cambridge: Cambridge University Press, 1985), 101.

21. Jonathan Spiro, *Defending the Master Race: Conservation, Eugenics, and the Legacy of Madison Grant* (Burlington: University of Vermont Press, 2008), 392–393.

22. The full story of the battle for the act has been told in several sources, including Trefethen, 151–153. It had an even bumpier ride than this description allows, but my point (the blurring of class lines through alliance-making) stands.

23. Richard W. Judd, "Reshaping Maine's Landscape: Rural Culture, Tourism, and Conservation, 1890–1929," *Journal of Forest History* 32 (4) (October 1988), 180–190.

24. Catherine Cassidy and Gary Titus, *Alaska's No. 1 Guide: The History and Journals of Andrew Berg 1869–1939* (Soldotna, AK: Spruce Tree, 2003), 35.

25. "In Behalf of the Park," *Forest and Stream* 30 (7) (March 8, 1888), 121.

26. George Bird Grinnell, "Protection of the National Park," *New York Times*, January 29, 1885, 3.

27. See for instance Whitney, SVP, May 1901, 218.

28. George Oliver Shields, "A Massachusetts Fish Hog at Large," *Recreation*, March 1903, 277–278.

29. Buckskin George, "Letter," *Recreation*, February 1900, 120–121.

30. M. W. Miner, "Letter," *Recreation*, January 1900, 40.

31. J. J. Bush, "Letter," *Recreation*, February 1903, 144.

32. Whitney, SVP, March 1902, 724.

33. In October 1908, for example, Whitney praised the work of Hornaday's American Bison Society and gave the address to which readers could send donations, while in December 1907 he published an open letter to America's sportsmen from Grant, Hornaday, and John Phillips (SVP, *Outing*: 1908, 112; 1907, 373–376).

34. "Yellowstone Game Protection Act 1894," America's National Park System: The Critical Documents, 1994, accessed June 15, 2015, http://www.nps.gov/parkhistory/online_books/anps/anps_1f.htm.

35. Glacier and Mesa Verde, for instance, followed the Yellowstone model, while Crater Lake banned hunting but allowed mining, and Mount Rainier allowed hunting (information from respective National Park Acts). Frank Norris describes the struggles over hunting and mining in Denali in *Crown Jewel of the North: An Administrative History of Denali National Park and Preserve*, vol. 1 (Anchorage, AK: US Department of the Interior, 2006), http://www.nps.gov/dena/learn/historyculture/park-history.htm.

36. "Secretary Lane's Letter on National Park Management, 1918" in America's National Park System: The Critical Documents.

37. "Historic Chronology of National Parks," Parks Canada, accessed January 18, 2017, http://www.pc.gc.ca/APPS/CP-NR/release_e.asp?bgid=727&andor1=bg.

38. Many environmental historians have explored the contradictions of managing land perceived as "wild," ranging from Nancy Langston in *Forest Dreams, Forest Nightmares: The Paradox of Old Growth in the Inland West* (Seattle: University of Washington Press, 1995) to Jan Dizard's discussion of the Quabbin deer crisis in *Going Wild: Hunting, Animal Rights, and the Contested Meaning of Nature* (Amherst: University of Massachusetts Press, 1999).

39. The classic essay critiquing ideas of wilderness is William Cronon's "The Trouble with Wilderness; or, Getting Back to the Wrong Nature," *Environmental History* 1 (1996): 7–28.

40. Marguerite Shaffer in *See America First: Tourism and National Identity, 1880–1940* (Washington, DC: Smithsonian Institution Press, 2001) frames tourist landscapes as giving visitors the chance to star in an agreed-upon narrative (302) and notes that the national parks in particular offer a complex combination of outdoor experience and consumer culture (268).

41. Warren explores the transformation of local hunting areas into "national commons" during this period: see especially his epilogue "Localism, Nationalism, and Nature."

42. Sheldon and Grant's lobbying for the park was spurred by the building of a railway line from Seward to Fairbanks, which Sheldon realized would open up the area to market hunters who would annihilate the animals: see Norris for the (well-told) full story.

43. Both "American Edens" and the idea that you can't be a real American if you don't appreciate the national parks appear in the first ten minutes of Ken Burns, *The National Parks: America's Best Idea; A Film by Ken Burns*. dir. Ken Burns (Hollywood, CA: PBS Home Video, 2009, DVD). Visitor statistics from Myron Floyd, "Race, Ethnicity and Use of the National Park System," *Social Science Research Review* 1 (2) (Spring/Summer 1999), 1.

44. James Tober, *Who Owns the Wildlife? The Political Economy of Conservation in Nineteenth-Century America* (Westport, CT: Greenwood, 1981), 183.

45. There was never total unity over this, and bitter divisions appeared among some members of the hunter elite, but in periodicals and in the Boone and Crockett books in particular these differences of opinion were glossed over to the point of invisibility, while the trend toward total restriction on hunting some species was accurately reflected. Gregory Dehler in *The Most Defiant Devil: William Temple Hornaday and His Controversial Crusade to Save American Wildlife* (Charlottesville: University of Virginia Press, 2013) explores Hornaday's dissent from the group specifically as well as some of the other disagreements among the hunter elite.

46. Harry Whitney, *Hunting with the Eskimos: The Unique Record of a Sportsman's Year among the Northernmost Tribe—The Big Game Hunting, the Native Life, and the Battle for Existence through the Long Arctic Night* (New York: Century, 1910), 442.

47. Theodore Roosevelt and George Bird Grinnell, "The Boone and Crockett

Club," in *American Big-Game Hunting*, Theodore Roosevelt and George Bird Grinnell, eds. ([1893] New York: Forest & Stream Publishing, 1901), 10–11.

48. Ibid., 13–14.

49. Madison Grant, "The Origins of the New York Zoological Society," in *Trail and Camp-fire: The Book of the Boone and Crockett Club*, George Bird Grinnell and Theodore Roosevelt, eds. (New York: Forest & Stream Publishing, 1897), both quotes 320.

50. George Bird Grinnell, "Big Game Refuges," in *American Big Game in Its Haunts*, George Bird Grinnell, ed. (New York: Forest & Stream Publishing, 1904), 442.

51. "The Game Preservation Committee," in *Hunting at High Altitudes*, George Bird Grinnell, ed. (New York: Harper & Brothers, 1913): information 423–425, quote 424.

52. Ibid., 427.

53. Ibid., 429.

54. Ibid., 431–432.

55. George Bird Grinnell, "Brief History of the Boone and Crockett Club," in *Hunting at High Altitudes*, 437.

56. George Bird Grinnell and Charles Sheldon, preface to *Hunting and Conservation*, George Bird Grinnell and Charles Sheldon, eds. (New Haven, CT: Yale University Press, 1925), xi.

57. George Bird Grinnell, "American Game Protection," in *Hunting and Conservation*, 220.

58. Madison Grant, "The Establishment of Mt. McKinley National Park," in *Hunting and Conservation*, 438.

59. Charles Sheldon, "The Big Game of Chihuahua, Mexico," in *Hunting and Conservation*, 163–164.

60. Ibid., 158–159.

**AFTERWORD**

1. McDowell Group, *Economic Impacts of Guided Hunting* (Juneau, AK), accessed November 11, 2016, http://www.alaskaprohunter.org/Economic_Impacts_of_Guided_Hunting_Final.pdf.

2. Prentiss Gray, for instance, took his daughter Barbara hunting in Alaska in 1930 but only found print with a far more exotic story about hunting in Singapore: *From the Peace to the Fraser: Newly Discovered North American Hunting and Exploration Journals 1900–1930* (Missoula, MT: Boone & Crockett Club, 1994); "Missing a Tiger and Shooting the Sun," in *Told at the Explorers Club*, Frederick Blossom, ed. (New York: A. & C. Boni, 1931), 139–150.

3. Louis S. Warren, *The Hunter's Game: Poachers and Conservationists in Twentieth-Century America* (New Haven, CT: Yale University Press, 1997), 47.

4. Robert and John Ste. Marie, "The 'Akeley' 35mm Motion Picture Camera: No. 158," Green Mountain Camera (blog), September 18, 2017 (10:30 a.m.), http://www.gmcamera.com/blog/2011/08/the-akeley-35mm-motion-picture-camera-no-158/.

5. To clarify: conservation sentiment in the United States, as we've seen, had a direct effect on Newfoundland. Canada had its own elites (and influential recreational periodicals) supporting conservation, a story that lies beyond the scope of this book; nevertheless it's fair to say that US conservation and changing middle-class attitudes toward game laws had an impact on Canadian conservation as well.

6. As noted in the introduction, both Sara Mills and Greg Gillespie have explored these issues. Mills's analyses of female travel writers encompass lived experience and the influence of literary conventions on the conversion of diaries into published texts, while Gillespie discusses the challenges that published narratives about hunting and exploration pose for historians seeking to use them as sources: Mills, *Discourses of Difference: An Analysis of Women's Travel Writing and Colonialism* (London: Routledge, 1991); Gillespie, *Hunting for Empire: Narratives of Sport in Rupert's Land, 1840–70* (Vancouver: University of British Columbia Press, 2008), 10–11.

7. See for instance Chip Lohman, "The North American Model of Wildlife Conservation," *American Hunter*, July 2015, and Jim Posewitz, *Beyond Fair Chase: The Ethic and Tradition of Hunting* (Helena, MT: Falcon, 2002).

8. I have had female students who hunted, and women often appear in hunting magazines as well: see for example "A True Alaskan Prom Night," in which fifteen-year-old Cassidy bags her grizzly, skins and dresses it, and still makes it to prom on time: *American Hunter*, July 2015.

9. Posewitz, 2–4. Prevalence in hunting courses from personal communications and also visible in the book's Amazon reviews.

# Works Cited

**NEWSPAPERS AND PERIODICALS**

*Canadian*
*Dial*
*Forest and Stream*
*Harper's Magazine*
*Harper's Weekly*
*New York Times*
*Outing Magazine*
*Recreation*
*World Magazine*

**HUNTINGTON LIBRARY ARCHIVES, SAN MARINO, CA**

Albert Bigelow Paine letters, 1875–1934
Fernand Lungren papers, 1897–1928
George Bird Grinnell papers, 1879–1951
Jack London papers, 1866–1977
Peary Arctic Expedition (1905–1906)


Albright, Horace, and Marian Albright Schenck. *Creating the National Park Service: The Missing Years.* Norman: University of Oklahoma Press, 1999.
Allen, Glover. "Preface." In Harvard Travellers Club, *Handbook of Travel.* Cambridge, MA: Harvard University Press, 1917.
*America's National Park System: The Critical Documents*, edited by Lary Dilsaver. Washington, DC: 1997. Accessed June 15, 2015. http://www.nps.gov/parkhistory/online_books/anps/anps_1f.htm.
Baden-Powell, Lieutenant General Sir Robert. *Memories of India: Recollections of Soldiering and Sport.* Philadelphia: David McKay, n.d.
———. *Pigsticking; or, Hoghunting: A Complete Account for Sportsmen, and Others.* 1889. London: Wyman & Sons, 1924.

Baillie-Grohman, William Adolph. "The Chamois." In *Big Game Shooting, from the Badminton Library of Sports and Pastimes*, edited by Clive Phillipps-Wolley. Vol. 2. 1894. London: Longmans, Green, 1895, 77–111.

———. *Fifteen Years' Sport and Life in the Hunting Grounds of Western America and British Columbia*. London: Horace Cox, 1900.

Baker, Sir Samuel. "William Cotton Oswell: A Biographical Sketch." In *Big Game Shooting, from the Badminton Library of Sports and Pastimes*, edited by Clive Phillipps-Wolley. Vol. 1. 1894. London: Longmans, Green, 1895, 26–31.

Baltzell, E. Digby. *Philadelphia Gentlemen: The Making of a National Upper Class*. Glencoe, IL: Free Press, 1958.

———. *The Protestant Establishment: Aristocracy and Caste in America*. New York: Random House, 1964.

Barclay, Edgar. *Big Game Shooting Records: Together with Biographical Notes and Anecdotes on the Most Prominent Big Game Hunters of Ancient and Modern Times*. London: H. F. & G. Witherby, 1932.

Bederman, Gail. *Manliness and Civilization*. Chicago: University of Chicago Press, 1995.

Bigelow, Poultney. *Seventy Summers*. Vol. 1. New York: Longmans, Green, 1925.

Binkley, Cameron. "'No Better Heritage Than Living Trees': Women's Clubs and Early Conservation in Humboldt County." *Western Historical Quarterly* 33 (2) (Summer 2002): 179–203.

Blake, Susan L. "A Woman's Trek: What Difference Does Gender Make?" In *Western Women and Imperialism: Complicity and Resistance*, edited by Nupur Chaudhuri and Margaret Strobel. Bloomington: Indiana University Press, 1992, 347–355.

Blodgett, Geoffrey. "Reform Thought and the Genteel Tradition." In *The Gilded Age*, edited by H. Wayne Morgan. Syracuse, NY: Syracuse University Press, 1970, 55–76.

"Books on Big Game." In *Trail and Camp-fire: The Book of the Boone and Crockett Club*, edited by George Bird Grinnell and Theodore Roosevelt. New York: Forest & Stream Publishing, 1897, 321–325.

Boyes, John L. *A White King in East Africa: The Remarkable Adventures of John Boyes, Trader and Soldier of Fortune, Who Became King of the Savage Wa-Kikuyu, Written by Himself*. New York: McBride, Nast, 1912.

British Columbia Conservation Office Service. "110 Years of Service: The Beginning 1905–1918." Province of British Columbia. Accessed November 11, 2016. http://www2.gov.bc.ca/gov/content/environment/natural-resource-stewardship/natural-resource-law-enforcement/conservation-officer-service/about-the-cos/110-years-of-service.

Browder, Laura. *Her Best Shot: Women and Guns in America*. Chapel Hill: University of North Carolina Press, 2006.

Brown, Charles H. *The Correspondents' War: Journalists in the Spanish-American War*. New York: Charles Scribner's Sons, 1967.

Bryce, Robert M. Introduction to *My Arctic Journal*, by Josephine Peary. New York: Cooper Square, 2002, v–xxix.

Burnham, John. "Hunting in the Nutzotins." In *Hunting and Conservation*, edited by

George Bird Grinnell and Charles Sheldon. New Haven, CT: Yale University Press, 1925, 412–437.

Burns, Ken. *The National Parks: America's Best Idea; A Film by Ken Burns.* Directed by Ken Burns. Hollywood, CA: PBS Home Video. 2009. DVD.

Buxton, Lord Edward North. *Short Stalks; or, Hunting Camps North, South, East, and West.* New York: G. P. Putnam's Sons, 1892.

Cabot, William Brooks. "Camp and Travel in the North-Country." In Harvard Travellers Club, *Handbook of Travel.* Cambridge, MA: Harvard University Press, 1917, 3–69.

———. *In Northern Labrador.* Boston: Gorham, 1912.

*Camping in the Rocky Mountains: A Guide to Colorado, Utah, and Mexico.* Denver, CO: Denver & Rio Grande Western Railroad, 1906.

Cane, Claude Richard John. *Summer and Fall in Western Alaska: The Record of a Trip to Cook's Inlet after Big Game.* London: H. Cox, 1903.

Capps, Stephen. "A Game Country without Rival in America: The Proposed Mount McKinley National Park." *National Geographic Magazine* 31 (January 1917): 69–84.

Cartmill, Matt. *A View to a Death in the Morning: Hunting and Nature through History.* Cambridge, MA: Harvard University Press, 1993.

Cassidy, Catherine, and Gary Titus. *Alaska's No. 1 Guide: The History and Journals of Andrew Berg 1869–1939.* Soldotna, AK: Spruce Tree, 2003.

Caton-Jones, Lt. Col. F. W. "The Nagpur Hunt." In *Modern Pig-Sticking*, edited by Lieutenant-General Sir A. E. Wardrop. 1914. London: Macmillan, 1930, 158–173.

Chanler, Winthrop. "A Day with the Elk." In *American Big-Game Hunting*, edited by Theodore Roosevelt and George Bird Grinnell. 1893. New York: Forest & Stream Publishing, 1901, 61–73.

———. "Hunting in East Africa." In *Hunting in Many Lands*, edited by Theodore Roosevelt and George Bird Grinnell. New York: Forest & Stream Publishing, 1895, 13–54.

Chapman, John Jay. *Memories and Milestones.* New York: Moffat, Yard, 1915.

Chartier, Roger. *On the Edge of the Cliff: History, Language, and Practices.* Baltimore: Johns Hopkins University Press, 1997.

Churchill, Winston Spencer. *My African Journey.* London: Hodder & Stoughton, 1908.

Clifford, Fred. *Haunts of the Hunted: Vacationers' Guide to Maine.* Bangor, ME: Bangor and Aroostook Railroad, 1903.

Cody, William F. *Buffalo Bill's Life Story: An Autobiography.* New York: Farrar & Rinehart, 1920.

Cohen, Deborah. *Household Gods: The British and Their Possessions.* New Haven, CT: Yale University Press, 2009.

Coleman, Annie Gilbert. "The Rise of the House of Leisure: Outdoor Guides, Practical Knowledge, and Industrialization." *Western Historical Quarterly* 42 (4) (Winter 2011): 436–457.

Colpitts, George. *Game in the Garden: A Human History of Wildlife in Western Canada to 1940.* Vancouver: University of British Columbia Press, 2002.

*Conference of the Governors of the United States.* Washington, DC: GPO, 1909.

Coolidge, John T., Jr. "Foot Transport in East Africa." In Harvard Travellers Club, *Handbook of Travel*. Cambridge, MA: Harvard University Press, 1917, 147–155.

Craig, Neville B. *Recollections of an Ill-Fated Expedition to the Headwaters of the Madeira River in Brazil*. Philadelphia: J. B. Lippincott, 1907.

Cronon, William. "The Trouble with Wilderness; or, Getting Back to the Wrong Nature." *Environmental History* 1 (1996): 7–28.

Czech, Kenneth P. *With Rifle and Petticoat: Women as Big Game Hunters, 1880–1940*. Lanham, NY: Derrydale, 2002.

Dalton, Kathleen. *Theodore Roosevelt: A Strenuous Life*. New York: Alfred A. Knopf, 2002.

Davis, Samuel T. *Caribou Shooting in Newfoundland: With a History of England's Oldest Colony from 1001 to 1895*. 1895. Fort Myers, FL: Premier, 1997.

Dehler, Gregory. *The Most Defiant Devil: William Temple Hornaday and His Controversial Crusade to Save American Wildlife*. Charlottesville: University of Virginia Press, 2013.

Dimock, Anthony W. *Wall Street and the Wilds*. New York: Outing Publishing, 1915.

Dizard, Jan. *Going Wild: Hunting, Animal Rights, and the Contested Meaning of Nature*. Amherst: University of Massachusetts Press, 1999.

Dodge, Richard Irving. *The Hunting Grounds of the Great West: A Description of the Plains, Game, and Indians of the Great North American Desert*. 1877. London: Chatto & Windus, 1878.

Dubbert, Joe. "Progressivism and the Masculinity Crisis." In *The American Man*, edited by Joseph Pleck and Elizabeth Pleck. Englewood Cliffs, NJ: Prentice-Hall, 1980, 303–320.

Dulles, Foster Rhea. *Americans Abroad: Two Centuries of European Travel*. Ann Arbor: University of Michigan Press, 1964.

Dunlap, Thomas. *Saving America's Wildlife*. Princeton, NJ: Princeton University Press, 1988.

Dunn, Robert Steed. *The Shameless Diary of an Explorer: A Story of Failure on Mount McKinley*. 1907. New York: Modern Library, 2001.

Dyreson, Mark. *Making the American Team: Sport, Culture, and the Olympic Experience*. Urbana: University of Illinois Press, 1998.

———. "Regulating the Body and the Body Politic: American Sport, Bourgeois Culture, and the Language of Progress, 1880–1920." In *The New American Sport History: Recent Approaches and Perspectives*, edited by S. W. Pope. Urbana: University of Illinois Press, 1997, 121–145.

Elliott, Daniel. "The Caribou." In *The Deer Family*, edited by Caspar Whitney. New York: Macmillan, 1903, 257–288.

Ellsworth, Henry Leavitt. *Washington Irving on the Prairie; or, A Narrative of a Tour of the Southwest in the Year 1832*. New York: American Book, 1937.

Elson, George. *Diary of Mr. George Elson, 1905 (Chief Indian Guide): An Account of a Journey in Labrador*. Ottawa: National Archives of Canada Microfilm #R1648-0-6-E, copied from the private papers of Mrs. M. B. H. Ellis, 1953.

Etherton, P. T. *Across the Roof of the World: A Record of Sport and Travel through Kashmir, Gilgit, Hunza, the Pamirs, Chinese Turkistan, Mongolia and Siberia.* New York: Frederick A. Stokes, 1911.

Evans, Major G. P. *Big-Game Shooting in Upper Burma.* New York, Bombay, and Calcutta: Longmans, Green, 1911.

Fellman, Anita Clair, and Michael Fellman. "The Primacy of the Will in Late 19th-Century American Ideology of the Self." *Historical Reflections* 4 (1977): 27–44.

Filene, Peter. *Him/Her/Self: Sex Roles in Modern America.* New York: Harcourt Brace Jovanovich, 1975.

Floyd, Myron. "Race, Ethnicity and Use of the National Park System." *Social Science Research Review* 1 (2) (Spring/Summer 1999): 172–180.

Forester, Frank. See Herbert, William Henry.

Foucault, Michel. *The Archaeology of Knowledge and The Discourse on Language.* New York: Pantheon Books, 1972.

Fraser, Joshua. *Three Months among the Moose: "A Winter's Tale" of the Northern Wilds of Canada.* Montreal: J. Lovell & Son, 1881.

Freshfield, Douglas, and Captain W. J. L. Wharton, eds. *Hints to Travellers: Scientific and General.* 7th ed. London: Royal Geographic Society, 1893.

Gale, Zona. "Editors of the Younger Generation." *Critic* 44 (April 1904): 318–322.

"The Game Preservation Committee." In *Hunting at High Altitudes*, edited by George Bird Grinnell. New York: Harper & Brothers, 1913, 421–432.

Gillespie, Greg. *Hunting for Empire: Narratives of Sport in Rupert's Land, 1840–70.* Vancouver: University of British Columbia Press, 2008.

Gorn, Elliott. "Sports through the 19th Century." In *The New American Sport History: Recent Approaches and Perspectives*, edited by S. W. Pope. Urbana: University of Illinois Press, 1997, 33–57.

Grant, Madison. "The Beginnings of Glacier National Park." In *Hunting and Conservation*, edited by George Bird Grinnell and Charles Sheldon. New Haven, CT: Yale University Press, 1925, 446–470.

———. "A Canadian Moose Hunt." In *Hunting in Many Lands*, edited by Theodore Roosevelt and George Bird Grinnell. New York: Forest & Stream Publishing, 1895, 84–106.

———. "The Condition of Wild Life in Alaska." In *Hunting at High Altitudes*, edited by George Bird Grinnell. New York: Harper & Brothers, 1913, 367–392.

———. "Distribution of the Moose." In *American Big Game in Its Haunts*, edited by George Bird Grinnell. New York: Forest & Stream Publishing, 1904, 374–390.

———. "The Establishment of Mt. McKinley National Park." In *Hunting and Conservation*, edited by George Bird Grinnell and Charles Sheldon. New Haven, CT: Yale University Press, 1925, 438–445.

———. "The Origins of the New York Zoological Society." In *Trail and Camp-fire: The Book of the Boone and Crockett Club*, edited by George Bird Grinnell and Theodore Roosevelt. New York: Forest & Stream Publishing, 1897, 313–320.

———. *Saving the Redwoods.* New York: Zoological Society, 1919.

———. "Saving the Redwoods." In *Hunting and Conservation*, edited by George Bird Grinnell and Charles Sheldon. New Haven, CT: Yale University Press, 1925, 182–200.

Gray, Prentiss N. *From the Peace to the Fraser: Newly Discovered North American Hunting and Exploration Journals 1900–1930*. Missoula, MT: Boone & Crockett Club, 1994.

———. "Missing a Tiger and Shooting the Sun." In *Told at the Explorers Club*, edited by Frederick Blossom. New York: A. & C. Boni, 1931, 139–150.

Griffen, Clyde. "The Progressive Ethos." In *The Development of an American Culture*, edited by Stanley Coben and Lorman Ratner. New York: St. Martin's, 1983, 144–180.

———. "Reconstructing Masculinity." In *Meanings for Manhood: Constructions of Masculinity in Victorian America*, edited by Mark Carnes and Clyde Griffen. Chicago: University of Chicago Press, 1990, 183–204.

Grinnell, George Bird, ed. *American Big Game in Its Haunts*. New York: Forest & Stream Publishing, 1904.

———. "American Game Protection." In *Hunting and Conservation*, edited by George Bird Grinnell and Charles Sheldon. New Haven, CT: Yale University Press, 1925, 201–257.

———. "Big Game Refuges." In *American Big Game in Its Haunts*, edited by George Bird Grinnell. New York: Forest & Stream Publishing, 1904, 442–452.

———. "Brief History of the Boone and Crockett Club." In *Hunting at High Altitudes*, edited by George Bird Grinnell. New York: Harper & Brothers, 1913, 433–491.

———. "Climbing for White Goats." In *Hunting*, edited by Archibald Rogers. New York: Charles Scribner's Sons, 1897, 111–121.

———, ed. *Hunting at High Altitudes*. New York: Harper & Brothers, 1913, 421–432.

———. "In Buffalo Days." In *American Big-Game Hunting*, edited by Theodore Roosevelt and George Bird Grinnell. 1893. New York: Forest & Stream Publishing, 1901, 153–211.

———. Introduction to *The Works of Theodore Roosevelt*. Vol. 1. New York: Scribner's & Sons, 1923, 15–16.

———. "National Recreation Conference." In *Hunting and Conservation*, edited by George Bird Grinnell and Charles Sheldon. New Haven, CT: Yale University Press, 1925, 471–491.

Grinnell, George Bird, and Charles Sheldon, eds. *Hunting and Conservation*. New Haven, CT: Yale University Press, 1925.

Grinnell, George Bird, and Theodore Roosevelt, eds. *Trail and Camp-fire: The Book of the Boone and Crockett Club*. New York: Forest & Stream Publishing, 1897.

Hague, Arnold. "The Yellowstone Park as a Game Reservation." In *American Big-Game Hunting*, edited by Theodore Roosevelt and George Bird Grinnell. 1893. New York: Forest & Stream Publishing, 1901, 240–270.

Hahn, Steve. "Hunting, Fishing, and Foraging: Common Rights and Class Relations in the Postbellum South." *Radical History Review* 26 (1982): 37–64.

Hale, Harry. "At St. Mary's." In *Hunting*, edited by Archibald Rogers. New York: Charles Scribner's Sons, 1897, 265–300.

Halttunen, Karen. *Confidence Men and Painted Women: A Study of Middle-Class Culture in America, 1830–1870.* New Haven, CT: Yale University Press, 1982.

Hamilton-Browne, G. *Camp Fire Yarns of the Lost Legion.* London: T. Werner Laurie, 1913.

Hammond, S. H. *Wild Northern Scenes: Adventures in the Adirondacks with Rifle and Rod.* 1857. New York: Arno, 1967.

Harper, J. Henry. *The House of Harper.* New York: Harper & Brothers, 1912.

Harrison, Simon. *Dark Trophies: Hunting and the Enemy Body in Modern War.* New York: Berghahn Books, 2012.

Hart, E. J. *Diamond Hitch: The Early Outfitters and Guides of Banff and Jasper.* Banff: Summerthought, 1979.

———. "Yahe-Weha—Mountain Woman: The Life and Travels of Mary Schaffer Warren, 1861–1939." In *A Hunter of Peace: Mary T. S. Schaffer's Old Indian Trails of the Canadian Rockies,* by Mary T. S. Schaffer. Banff: Whyte Museum of the Canadian Rockies, 1980, 1–13.

Harvard Travellers Club. *Handbook of Travel.* Cambridge, MA: Harvard University Press, 1917.

Hays, Samuel P. *Conservation and the Gospel of Efficiency: The Progressive Conservation Movement, 1890–1920.* New York: Atheneum, 1969.

Herbert, Agnes. *Casuals in the Caucasus: The Diary of a Sporting Holiday.* London: John Lane, 1912.

———. *Two Dianas in Somaliland: The Record of a Shooting Trip.* London & New York: John Lane, 1908.

Herbert, Agnes, and a Shikári. *Two Dianas in Alaska.* 1909. Mechanicsburg, PA: Stackpole, 2004.

Herbert, Henry William. *Frank Forester's Field Sports of the United States, and British Provinces, of North America.* Vol. 2. New York: Stringer & Townsend, 1849.

———. *Frank Forester's Field Sports of the United States, and British Provinces, of North America.* Vol. 2. N.p.: W. A. Townsend, 1864.

Herman, Daniel. *Hunting and the American Imagination.* Washington, DC: Smithsonian Institution, 2001.

Higham, John. *Strangers in the Land: Patterns of American Nativism, 1870–1925.* New Brunswick, NJ: Rutgers University Press, 2002.

Hilkey, Judy. *Character Is Capital: Success Manuals and Manhood in Gilded Age America.* Chapel Hill: University of North Carolina Press, 1997.

"Historic Chronology of National Parks." Parks Canada. Accessed January 18, 2017. http://www.pc.gc.ca/APPS/CP-NR/release_e.asp?bgid=727&andor1=bg.

Hofstadter, Richard. *The Age of Reform.* New York: Vintage Books, 1955.

Hornaday, William. *Camp-fires in the Canadian Rockies.* 1906. New York: Charles Scribner's Sons, 1927.

———. *The Man Who Became a Savage: A Story of Our Own Times.* Buffalo, NY: Peter Paul, 1896.

———. *Our Vanishing Wild Life: Its Extermination and Preservation.* New York: C. Scribner's Sons, 1913.

———. "Report of the President." In *Second Annual Report of the American Bison Society.* New York: American Bison Society, 1909, 1–18.

———. *Two Years in the Jungle: The Experiences of a Hunter and Naturalist in India, Ceylon, the Malay Peninsula and Borneo.* 1885. New York: Charles Scribner's Sons, 1901.

Hough, Emerson. *The Frontier Omnibus.* New York: Grosset & Dunlap, 1903. Accessed October 18, 2012. http://archive.org/details/frontieromnibus00houggoog.

House, Edward J. *A Hunter's Camp-fires.* New York: Harper & Brothers, 1914.

Howe, Daniel Walker. "American Victorianism as Culture." *American Quarterly* 27 (5) (December 1975): 507–532.

Hutton, Paul Andrew. Introduction to *Ten Days on the Plains,* by Henry E. Davies. 1871. Dallas: Southern Methodist University Press, 1985.

Imperato, Pascal, and Eileen Imperato. *They Married Adventure: The Wandering Lives of Martin and Osa Johnson.* New Brunswick, NJ: Rutgers University Press, 1999.

Irland, Frederic. "Sport in an Untouched American Wilderness." In *Hunting,* edited by Archibald Rogers. New York: Charles Scribner's Sons, 1897, 131–166.

Isenberg, Nancy. *Sex and Citizenship in Antebellum America.* Chapel Hill: University of North Carolina Press, 1998.

Jackson, F. J. "The Caravan, Headman, Gun-Bearers Etc." In *Big Game Shooting, from the Badminton Library of Sports and Pastimes,* edited by Clive Phillipps-Wolley. Vol. 1. 1894. London: Longmans, Green, 1895, 176–184.

Jacoby, Karl. *Crimes against Nature: Squatters, Poachers, Thieves, and the Hidden History of American Conservation.* Berkeley: University of California Press, 2001.

Jones, Karen R. *Epiphany in the Wilderness: Hunting, Nature, and Performance in the Nineteenth-Century American West.* Boulder: University Press of Colorado, 2015.

Judd, Richard W. "Reshaping Maine's Landscape: Rural Culture, Tourism, and Conservation, 1890–1929." *Journal of Forest History* 32 (4) (October 1988): 180–190.

Kaplan, Amy. "Romancing the Empire: The Embodiment of American Masculinity in the Popular Historical Novel of the 1890s." *American Literary History* 2 (4) (Winter 1990): 659–690.

Kasson, John. *Houdini, Tarzan, and the Perfect Man: The White Male Body and the Challenge of Modernity in America.* New York: Hill & Wang, 2001.

Kelly, Tara Kathleen. "Goddess and Leader: Conflict and Companionship in the Alaskan Wilderness." In "Who Carries the Luggage? Gendered Discourses on Companionship in Travel Writing," edited by Floris Means. Unpublished manuscript.

Kidder, James. "Big Game Shooting in Alaska." In *American Big Game in Its Haunts,* edited by George Bird Grinnell. New York: Forest & Stream Publishing, 1904, 99–204.

Kimmel, Michael. *Manhood in America: A Cultural History.* New York: Free Press, 1996.

Kramer, Paul A. "Empires, Exceptions, and Anglo-Saxons: Race and Rule between the British and United States Empires, 1880–1910." *Journal of American History* 88 (March 2002): 1315–1353.

LaFarge, C. Grant. "Sintamaskin." In *Trail and Camp-fire: The Book of the Boone and Crockett Club*, edited by George Bird Grinnell and Theodore Roosevelt. New York: Forest & Stream Publishing, 1897, 124–151.

Langston, Nancy. *Forest Dreams, Forest Nightmares: The Paradox of Old Growth in the Inland West*. Seattle: University of Washington Press, 1995.

Lasch, Christopher. "The Moral and Intellectual Rehabilitation of the Ruling Class." In *The World of Nations: Reflections on American History, Politics, and Culture*. New York: Alfred A. Knopf, 1973, 80–99.

Lawrence, Karen. *Penelope Voyages: Women and Travel in the British Literary Tradition*. Ithaca, NY: Cornell University Press, 1994.

Lears, T. J. Jackson. "From Salvation to Self-Realization: Advertising and the Therapeutic Roots of the Consumer Culture, 1880–1930." In *The Culture of Consumption: Critical Essays in American History, 1880–1980*, edited by T. J. Jackson Lears and Richard Wightman Fox. New York: Pantheon Books, 1983, 3–38.

———. *No Place of Grace: Antimodernism and the Transformation of American Culture 1880–1920*. New York: Pantheon Books, 1981.

Lewis, Elisha J. *The American Sportsman*. 1855. Philadelphia: J. B. Lippincott, 1906. This is a reprint of Lewis's *Hints for Sportsmen*; see ch. 1 for publishing history.

Lippmann, Walter. *Drift and Mastery: An Attempt to Diagnose the Current Unrest*. 1914. Madison: University of Wisconsin Press, 1985.

Littledale, St. George. "Caucasian Aurochs." In *Big Game Shooting, from the Badminton Library of Sports and Pastimes*, edited by Clive Phillipps-Wolley. Vol. 2. 1894. London: Longmans, Green, 1895, 64–72.

Lohman, Chip. "The North American Model of Wildlife Conservation." *American Hunter*, July 2015.

Loo, Tina. "Of Moose and Men: Hunting for Masculinities in British Columbia 1880–1939." *Western Historical Quarterly* 32 (2001): 296–319.

Lucas, John A. "Caspar Whitney." *Journal of Olympic History* 8 (2) (2000): 30–38.

MacKenzie, John. "Chivalry, Social Darwinism and Ritualised Killing: The Hunting Ethos in Central Africa up to 1914." In *Conservation in Africa: People, Policies and Practice*, edited by David Anderson and Richard Grove. Cambridge: Cambridge University Press, 1987, 41–61.

———. *The Empire of Nature: Hunting, Conservation and British Imperialism*. Manchester: Manchester University Press, 1988.

———. "The Imperial Pioneer and Hunter and the British Masculine Stereotype in Late Victorian and Edwardian Times." In *Manliness and Morality: Middle-Class Masculinity in Britain and America 1800–1940*, edited by J. A. Mangan and James Walvyn. New York: St. Martin's, 1987, 176–198.

———. Introduction to *Imperialism and the Natural World*, edited by John MacKenzie. Manchester: Manchester University Press, 1990, 1–14.

Madeira, Percy C. *Hunting in British East Africa*. Philadelphia & London: J. B. Lippincott, 1909.

Mangan, J. A. *The Games Ethic and Imperialism: Aspects of the Diffusion of an Ideal*. New York: Viking, 1986.

Manore, Jean, and Dale Miner, eds. *The Culture of Hunting in Canada.* Vancouver: University of British Columbia Press, 2007.

Marsh, Margaret. "Suburban Men and Masculine Domesticity, 1870–1915." In *Meanings for Manhood: Constructions of Masculinity in Victorian America*, edited by Mark Carnes and Clyde Griffen. Chicago: University of Chicago Press, 1990, 165–185.

McCutcheon, John T. *In Africa: Hunting Adventures in the Big Game Country.* Indianapolis: Bobbs-Merrill, 1910.

McDannell, Colleen. "'True Men as We Need Them': Catholicism and the Irish-American Male." *American Studies* 27 (4) (Fall 1986): 19–36.

McDowell Group. *Economic Impacts of Guided Hunting.* Juneau, AK. Accessed November 11, 2016. http://www.alaskaprohunter.org/Economic_Impacts_of_Guided _Hunting_Final.pdf.

Melliss, C. J. *Lion-Hunting in Somali-Land, Also, an Account of "Pigsticking" the African Wart-Hog.* London: Chapman & Hall, 1895.

Millais, John. *Life of Frederick Courtenay Selous, D.S.O.* New York: Longmans, Green, 1919.

———. *Newfoundland and Its Untrodden Ways.* London and New York: Longmans, Green, 1907.

Miller, Char. *Gifford Pinchot and the Making of Modern Environmentalism.* Washington, DC: Island/Shearwater Books, 2001.

Mills, Sara. *Discourses of Difference: An Analysis of Women's Travel Writing and Colonialism.* London: Routledge, 1991.

Morison, Elting E., ed., *Letters of Theodore Roosevelt.* Vol. 1. Cambridge, MA: Harvard University Press, 1951.

Morris, Edmund. *The Rise of Theodore Roosevelt.* New York: Coward, McCann, & Geoghegan, 1979.

Mott, Frank Luther. *A History of American Magazines 1885–1905.* Cambridge, MA: Belknap Press of Harvard University Press, 1957.

Murray, William H. H. *Adventures in the Wilderness; or, Camp-Life in the Adirondacks.* 1869. Syracuse, NY: Syracuse University Press, 1970.

*National Cyclopedia of American Biography.* New York: J. T. White, 1940. Vol. 25.

Neihardt, John. *The River and I.* New York: G. P. Putnam's Sons, 1910.

New York Zoological Society. "Report of the Executive Committee." *Eighteenth Annual Report of the New York Zoological Society.* New York: Office of the Society, 1913, 35–43.

Norris, Frank. *Crown Jewel of the North: An Administrative History of Denali National Park and Preserve.* Vol. 1. Anchorage, AK: US Department of the Interior, 2006. Accessed May 7, 2016. http://www.nps.gov/dena/learn/historyculture/park -history.htm.

Ofcansky, Thomas P. "A History of Game Preservation in British East Africa, 1895–1963." PhD diss., West Virginia University, 1981.

Ohmann, Richard. *Making and Selling Culture.* Middletown, CT: Wesleyan University Press, 1996.

———. *Selling Culture: Magazines, Markets, and Class at the Turn of the Century.* New York: Verso, 1996.

Oriard, Michael. *Reading Football: How the Popular Press Created an American Spectacle.* Chapel Hill: University of North Carolina Press, 1993.

Orvell, Miles. *The Real Thing: Imitation and Authenticity in American Culture, 1880–1940.* Chapel Hill: University of North Carolina Press, 1989.

Osborn, Henry Fairfield. "Preservation of the Wild Animals of North America." In *American Big Game in Its Haunts*, edited by George Bird Grinnell. New York: Forest & Stream Publishing, 1904, 349–373.

Oswell, William Cotton. "South Africa Fifty Years Ago." In *Big Game Shooting, from the Badminton Library of Sports and Pastimes*, edited by Clive Phillipps-Wolley. Vol. 1. 1894. London: Longmans, Green, 1895, 26–87.

Painter, Nell Irwin. *Standing at Armageddon: The United States, 1877–1919.* New York: W. W. Norton, 1987.

Pakenham, Valerie. *Out in the Noonday Sun: Edwardians in the Tropics.* New York: Random House, 1985.

Palliser, John. *The Solitary Hunter; or, Sporting Adventures in the Prairies.* New York: Routledge, 1856.

Palmer, T. S., and H. W. Olds. *Game Laws for 1902: A Summary of the Provisions Relating to Seasons, Shipment, Sale, and Licenses.* Washington, DC: UNT Digital Library. Accessed November 6, 2016. http://digital.library.unt.edu/ark:/67531/metadc85555/.

Patterson, Lt. Col. John H. *In the Grip of the Nyika: Further Adventures in British East Africa.* New York: Macmillan, 1909.

———. *The Man-Eaters of Tsavo.* 1908. New York: St. Martin's, 1986.

Peary, Josephine. *My Arctic Journal.* 1893. New York: Cooper Square, 2002.

Peary, Robert. *Nearest the Pole: A Narrative of the Polar Expedition of the Peary Arctic Club in the S.S. Roosevelt, 1905–1906.* New York: Doubleday, Page, 1907.

———. Preface to *My Arctic Journal*, by Josephine Peary. 1893. New York: Cooper Square, 2002, 3–5.

Pettigrew, John. *Brutes in Suits: Male Sensibility in America, 1890–1920.* Baltimore: Johns Hopkins University Press, 2007.

Phillipps-Wolley, Clive. "Big Game of North America." In *Big Game Shooting, from the Badminton Library of Sports and Pastimes*, edited by Clive Phillipps-Wolley. Vol. 1. 1894. London: Longmans, Green, 1895, 346–427.

———. "The Caucasus." In *Big Game Shooting, from the Badminton Library of Sports and Pastimes*, edited by Clive Phillipps-Wolley. Vol. 2. 1894. London: Longmans, Green, 1895, 22–47.

———. "Hints on Taxidermy, Etc." In *Big Game Shooting, from the Badminton Library of Sports and Pastimes*, edited by Clive Phillipps-Wolley. Vol. 2. 1894. London: Longmans, Green, 1895, 413–420.

———. "On Big Game Shooting Generally." In *Big Game Shooting, from the Badminton Library of Sports and Pastimes*, edited by Clive Phillipps-Wolley. Vol. 1. 1894. London: Longmans, Green, 1895, 1–51.

Phillips, John C., ed. *American Game Mammals and Birds: A Catalogue of Books 1582 to 1925; Sport, Natural History, and Conservation.* Boston: Houghton Mifflin, 1930. This title is often referred to in the book as Sheldon, *Catalogue.*

Pope, S. W. *Patriotic Games: Sporting Traditions in the American Imagination, 1876–1926.* New York: Oxford University Press, 1997.

Posewitz, Jim. *Beyond Fair Chase: The Ethic and Tradition of Hunting.* Helena, MT: Falcon, 2002.

Prichard, H. Hesketh. *Hunting Camps in Wood and Wilderness.* New York: Sturgis & Walton, 1910.

———. *Through Trackless Labrador.* New York: Sturgis & Walton, 1911.

Procida, Mary A. *Married to the Empire: Gender, Politics and Imperialism in India, 1883–1947.* Manchester: Manchester University Press, 2002.

Proctor, Nicholas. *Bathed in Blood: Hunting and Mastery in the Old South.* Charlottesville: University Press of Virginia, 2002.

Przeworski, Adam. *Capitalism and Social Democracy.* Cambridge: Cambridge University Press, 1985.

Punke, Michael. *Last Stand: George Bird Grinnell, the Battle to Save the Bison, and the Birth of the New West.* Washington, DC: Smithsonian Books, 2007.

Rainsford, W. S. "Camping and Hunting in the Shoshone." In *Hunting*, edited by Archibald Rogers. New York: Charles Scribner's Sons, 1897, 49–110.

———. *The Land of the Lion.* London: Heinemann, 1909.

Reid, Jane E. *The Joys of the Long Trail: Three Women Adventure-Travellers in Canada at the Turn of the Century.* Ann Arbor, MI: UMI Dissertation Services, 1999.

Reiger, John F. *American Sportsmen and the Origins of Conservation.* New York: Winchester, 1975.

Rico, Monica. *Nature's Noblemen: Transatlantic Masculinities and the Nineteenth-Century American West.* New Haven, CT: Yale University Press, 2013.

Rodgers, Daniel. *The Work Ethic in Industrial America 1850–1920.* Chicago: University of Chicago Press, 1978.

Rogers, Archibald, ed. *Hunting.* New York: Charles Scribner's Sons, 1897.

Roosevelt, Elliott. *Hunting Big Game in the Eighties: The Letters of Elliott Roosevelt, Sportsman, Edited by His Daughter Anna Eleanor Roosevelt.* New York: Scribner, 1933.

———. "A Hunting Trip in India." In *Hunting in Many Lands*, edited by Theodore Roosevelt and George Bird Grinnell. New York: Forest & Stream Publishing, 1895, 107–122.

Roosevelt, Kermit. *The Happy Hunting-Grounds.* 1919. Farmingham, AL: Palladium, 2000.

Roosevelt, Theodore. *African Game Trails: An Account of the African Wanderings of an American Hunter-Naturalist.* New York: Scribner, 1910.

———. *An Autobiography.* 1913. New York: Da Capo, 1985.

———. "At a Meeting of the Society of American Foresters Held at the Residence of Mr. Gifford Pinchot, Washington, D.C. March 26, 1903." In *A Compilation of the Messages and Speeches of Theodore Roosevelt, 1901–1905*, edited by Alfred Lewis. Washington, DC: Bureau of National Literature and Art, 1906, 208–212.

———. *A Book-Lover's Holidays in the Open.* 1916. New York: Charles Scribner's Sons, 1926.

———. "Books on Big Game." *Fortnightly Review* 69 (April 1898): 604–611.

———. "The Deer and Antelope of North America." In *The Deer Family*, edited by Caspar Whitney. New York: Macmillan, 1903, 1–166.

———. "List of Books." In *Trail and Camp-fire: The Book of the Boone and Crockett Club*, edited by George Bird Grinnell and Theodore Roosevelt. New York: Forest & Stream Publishing, 1897, 336–342.

———. *Ranch Life and the Hunting-Trail.* 1888. New York: Readex Microprint, 1966.

———. "The Strenuous Life." In *The Strenuous Life: Essays and Addresses*, by Theodore Roosevelt. New York: Century, 1901. http://www.bartleby.com/58/index.html.

———. *Through the Brazilian Wilderness and Papers on Natural History.* New York: Charles Scribner's Sons, 1926.

———. *The Wilderness Hunter.* New York: G. P. Putnam's Sons, 1893.

Roosevelt, Theodore, and George Bird Grinnell, eds. *American Big-Game Hunting.* 1893. New York: Forest & Stream Publishing, 1901.

———. "The Boone and Crockett Club." In *American Big-Game Hunting*, edited by Theodore Roosevelt and George Bird Grinnell. 1893. New York: Forest & Stream Publishing, 1901, 9–18.

———, eds. *Hunting in Many Lands.* New York: Forest & Stream Publishing, 1895.

Roth, Richard Patrick. "The Adirondack Guide (1820–1919): Hewing Out an American Occupation." PhD diss., Syracuse University, 1990.

Rotundo, E. Anthony. *American Manhood: Transformations in Masculinity from the Revolution to the Modern Era.* New York: BasicBooks, 1993.

———. "Body and Soul: Changing Ideals of American Middle Class Manhood, 1770–1920." *Journal of Social History* 16 (4) (Summer 1983): 23–38.

Russell, Frank. *Explorations in the Far North: Being the Report of an Expedition under the Auspices of the University of Iowa during the Years 1892, '93, and '94.* Iowa City: State University of Iowa, 1898.

———. "Hunting Musk-Ox with the Dog Ribs." In *Hunting*, edited by Archibald Rogers. New York: Charles Scribner's Sons, 1897, 301–327.

Ryan, Mary. *Cradle of the Middle Class: The Family in Oneida County, New York, 1790–1865.* New York: Cambridge University Press, 1981.

Sabin, Edward L. "The Boy Scouts Movement." *Lippincott Magazine* 88 (1911).

Sampson, Alden. "A Bear Hunt in the Sierras." In *Hunting in Many Lands*, edited by Theodore Roosevelt and George Bird Grinnell. New York: Forest & Stream Publishing, 1895, 187–219.

Sanger, William Cary. "The Adirondack Deer Law." In *Trail and Camp-fire: The Book of the Boone and Crockett Club*, edited by George Bird Grinnell and Theodore Roosevelt. New York: Forest & Stream Publishing, 1897, 264–278.

Schaffer, Mary. *Old Indian Trails: Incidents of Camp and Trail Life, Covering Two Years' Exploration through the Rocky Mountains of Canada.* New York: Knickerbocker, 1911.

Schlereth, Thomas. *Victorian America: Transformations in Everyday Life, 1876–1915.* New York: HarperCollins, 1991.

Schwatka, Frederick. *Nimrod in the North; or, Hunting and Fishing Adventures in the Arctic Regions.* New York: Cassell, 1885.

———. *A Summer in Alaska in the 1880s: A Popular Account of the Travels of an Alaska Exploring Expedition along the Great Yukon River, from Its Source to Its Mouth, in the British North-West Territory, and in the Territory of Alaska.* 1893. Secaucus, NY: Castle Books, 1988.

"Secretary Lane's Letter on National Park Management, 1918." America's National Park System: The Critical Documents, 1994. Accessed January 18, 2017. http://www.nps.gov/parkhistory/online_books/anps/anps_1f.htm.

Selous, Frederick Courteney. *A Hunter's Wanderings in Africa: Being a Narrative of Nine Years Spent among the Game of the Far Interior of South Africa.* 1882. London: Macmillan, 1925.

———. *Recent Hunting Trips in British North America.* New York: Charles Scribner's Sons, 1907.

Seton, Ernest Thompson. *The Arctic Prairies.* New York: Charles Scribner's Sons, 1917.

———. *The Book of Woodcraft and Indian Lore.* Garden City, NJ: Doubleday, Page, 1912.

Seton, Grace Gallatin. *Nimrod's Wife.* New York: Doubleday, Page, 1907.

———. *A Woman Tenderfoot.* New York: Doubleday, Page, 1900.

Seton-Karr, Henry. *My Sporting Holidays.* London: Edward Arnold, 1904.

Shaffer, Marguerite. *See America First: Tourism and National Identity, 1880–1940.* Washington, DC: Smithsonian Institution Press, 2001.

Sheldon, Charles. "The Big Game of Chihuahua, Mexico." In *Hunting and Conservation*, edited by George Bird Grinnell and Charles Sheldon. New Haven, CT: Yale University Press, 1925, 138–181.

———. *Catalogue.* See Phillips, John C., ed.

———. *The Wilderness of Denali: Explorations of a Hunter-Naturalist in Northern Alaska.* New York: Charles Scribner's Sons, 1930.

———. *The Wilderness of the North Pacific Coast Islands: A Hunter's Experiences while Searching for Wapiti, Bears and Caribou on the Larger Coast Islands of British Columbia and Alaska.* New York: Charles Scribner's Sons, 1912.

———. *The Wilderness of the Upper Yukon: A Hunter's Explorations for Wild Sheep in Sub-Arctic Mountains.* New York: Charles Scribner's Sons, 1911.

Sherman, Mary. "Our Work for National Parks." *Better Homes & Gardens*, May 1925.

Shields, George Oliver. *Cruisings in the Cascades: A Narrative of Travel, Exploration, Amateur Photography, Hunting, and Fishing, Etc.* London: Sampson Low, Marston, Searle, & Rivington, 1889.

Simpson, Donald. *Dark Companions: The African Contributions to the European Exploration of Africa.* New York: Barnes & Noble Books, 1976.

Slotkin, Richard. *The Fatal Environment: The Myth of the Frontier in the Age of Industrialization 1800–1890.* New York: Atheneum, 1985.

———. *Gunfighter Nation: The Myth of the Frontier in Twentieth Century America.* New York: HarperPerennial, 1993.

Smalley, Andrea. "'Our Lady Sportsmen': Gender, Class, and Conservation in Sport Hunting Magazines, 1873–1920." *Journal of the Gilded Age and Progressive Era* 4 (4) (October 2005): 355–380.

Smith, A. Donaldson. *Through Unknown African Countries: The First Expedition from Somaliland to Lake Rudolf.* London: Edward Arnold, 1897.

Smith, William Lord. "An African Shooting Trip." In *Trail and Camp-fire: The Book of the Boone and Crockett Club*, edited by George Bird Grinnell and Theodore Roosevelt. New York: Forest & Stream Publishing, 1897, 78–123.

———. "The Kadiak Bear and His Home." In *American Big Game in Its Haunts*, edited by George Bird Grinnell. New York: Forest & Stream Publishing, 1904, 225–269.

Spence, Mark David. *Dispossessing the Wilderness: Indian Removal and the Making of the National Parks.* New York: Oxford University Press, 1999.

Spiro, Jonathan. *Defending the Master Race: Conservation, Eugenics, and the Legacy of Madison Grant.* Burlington: University of Vermont Press, 2008.

Sproat, John G. *"The Best Men": Liberal Reformers in the Gilded Age.* New York: Oxford University Press, 1968.

Stange, Mary Zeiss. Foreword to *Two Dianas in Alaska*, by Agnes Herbert and a Shikári. Mechanicsberg, PA: Stackpole Books, 2004, v–xxix.

———. *Woman the Hunter.* Boston: Beacon, 1997.

Stigand, Chauncey. *Hunting the Elephant in Africa and Other Recollections of Thirteen Years' Wanderings.* New York: Macmillan, 1913.

Stone, Andrew J. "The Moose: Where It Lives and How It Lives." In *The Deer Family*, edited by Caspar Whitney. New York: Macmillan, 1903, 289–325.

Stowe, William W. *Going Abroad: European Travel in Nineteenth-Century American Culture.* Princeton, NJ: Princeton University Press, 1994.

Swayne, H. G. C. *Seventeen Trips through Somaliland and a Visit to Abyssinia: A Record of Exploration and Big Game Shooting with Descriptive Notes on the Fauna of the Country.* London: Rowland Ward, 1900.

Thompsell, Angela. "The Expert Knowledge of Frederick Courteney Selous." Presentation at the Britain and the World Conference, Austin, TX, March 29, 2013.

———. *Hunting Africa: British Sport, African Knowledge and the Nature of Empire.* London: Palgrave Macmillan UK, 2015.

Tober, James. *Who Owns the Wildlife? The Political Economy of Conservation in Nineteenth-Century America.* Westport, CT: Greenwood, 1981.

Townsend, Charles. "Elephant Seals of Guadalupe Island." In *Hunting at High Altitudes*, edited by George Bird Grinnell. New York: Harper & Brothers, 1913, 406–420.

Townsend, Whelan. "The Sportsman and His Guide." *Outdoor Life* 19 (2) (February 1907).

Trachtenberg, Alan. *The Incorporation of America: Culture and Society in the Gilded Age.* New York: Hill & Wang, 1982.

Trefethen, James. *An American Crusade for Wildlife.* New York: Winchester, 1975.

Tyrrell, James W. *Across the Sub-Arctics of Canada: A Journey of 3,200 Miles by Canoe and Snowshoe through the Hudson Bay Region.* Toronto: William Briggs, 1908.

"United States Census, 1900," database with images, *FamilySearch* (https://familysearch.org/ark:/61903/1:1:MSKF-KM1: accessed April 20, 2017), Caspar Whitney, Borough of Manhattan, Election District 16 New York City Ward 27, New York County, New York, United States; citing enumeration district (ED) 736, sheet 2A, family 34, NARA microfilm publication T623 (Washington, DC: National Archives and Records Administration, 1972.); FHL microfilm 1,241,113.

Vachell, Horace Annesley. *Life and Sport on the Pacific Slope.* London: Hodder & Stoughton, 1900.

Van Dyke, Theodore S. "The Deer and the Elk of the Pacific Coast." In *The Deer Family*, edited by Caspar Whitney. New York: Macmillan, 1903, 167–256.

———. *Flirtation Camp; or, The Rifle, Rod, and Gun in California: A Sporting Romance.* New York: Fords, Howard, & Hulbert, 1881.

———. *The Still-Hunter.* 1882. New York: Macmillan, 1923.

———. *The Still-Hunter.* 1882. Mechanicsburg, PA: Stackpole Books, 2004.

Veblen, Thorstein. *The Theory of the Leisure Class.* 1902. New York: Random House, 2001.

Vorpahl, Ben Merchant. *My Dear Wister: The Frederic Remington–Owen Wister Letters.* Palo Alto, CA: American West, 1972.

Wallace, Dillon. *The Long Labrador Trail.* New York: Outing Publishing, 1906.

———. *The Lure of the Labrador Wild.* New York: Fleming H. Revell, 1905.

———. *The Lure of the Labrador Wild.* 1905. Halifax, NS: Nimbus, 1990.

———. Papers, Centre for Newfoundland Studies Archives, Memorial University of Newfoundland.

Wardrop, Lieutenant-General Sir A. E. *Modern Pig-Sticking.* 1914. London: Macmillan, 1930.

Warren, Louis S. *The Hunter's Game: Poachers and Conservationists in Twentieth-Century America.* New Haven, CT: Yale University Press, 1997.

Watts, Sarah. *Rough Rider in the White House: Theodore Roosevelt and the Politics of Desire.* Chicago: University of Chicago Press, 2003.

Wegner, Robert. Foreword to *The Still-Hunter*, by T. S. Van Dyke. Mechanicsburg, PA: Stackpole Books, 2004, v–xi.

White, Edward. *The Eastern Establishment and the Western Experience: The West of Frederic Remington, Theodore Roosevelt, and Owen Wister.* New Haven, CT: Yale University Press, 1968.

Whitehead, Charles E. "Game Laws." In *Hunting in Many Lands,* edited by Theodore Roosevelt and George Bird Grinnell. New York: Forest & Stream Publishing, 1895, 358–376.

Whitehouse, W. F. "To Lake Rudolph and Beyond." In *Hunting and Conservation*, edited by George Bird Grinnell and Charles Sheldon. New Haven, CT: Yale University Press, 1925, 258–339.

Whitney, Caspar. "The Cougar." In *Hunting in Many Lands,* edited by Theodore Roosevelt and George Bird Grinnell. New York: Forest & Stream Publishing, 1895, 238–254.

———, ed. *The Deer Family*. New York: Macmillan, 1903.
———. *The Flowing Road*. Philadelphia: J. B. Lippincott, 1913.
———. *Jungle Trails and Jungle People: Travel, Adventure and Observation in the Far East*. New York: Charles Scribner's Sons, 1905.
———. "The Musk-Ox and Its Hunting." In *Musk-Ox, Bison, Sheep and Goat*, edited by Caspar Whitney. New York: Macmillan, 1904, 17–106.
———, ed. *Musk-Ox, Bison, Sheep and Goat*. New York: Macmillan, 1904.
———. *On Snow-shoes to the Barren Grounds: Twenty-Eight Hundred Miles after Musk-Oxen and Wood-Bison*. New York: Harper & Brothers, 1896.
———. "Outdoor Sports—What They Are Doing for Us." *Independent* 52 (June 7, 1900).
———. *A Sporting Pilgrimage*. New York: Harper & Brothers, 1894.
———. "What We Stand For." *Collier's Outdoor America* 42 (March 13, 1909).
Whitney, Harry. *Hunting with the Eskimos: The Unique Record of a Sportsman's Year among the Northernmost Tribe—the Big Game Hunting, the Native Life, and the Battle for Existence through the Long Arctic Night*. New York: Century, 1910.
Wiebe, Robert H. *The Search for Order, 1877–1920*. Westport, CT: Greenwood, 1980.
"William T. Hornaday Awards." *Boy Scouts of America*. Accessed June 8, 2015. http://www.scouting.org/scoutsource/Awards/HornadayAwards.aspx.
Wilson, Christopher P. *The Labor of Words: Literary Professionalism in the Progressive Era*. Athens: University of Georgia Press, 1985.
———. "The Rhetoric of Consumption: Mass-Market Magazines and the Demise of the Gentle Reader, 1880–1920." In *The Culture of Consumption: Critical Essays in American History, 1880–1980*, edited by Richard Wightman Fox and T. J. Jackson Lears. New York: Pantheon Books, 1983, 39–64.
Wister, Owen. "The Mountain Sheep: His Ways." In *Musk-Ox, Bison, Sheep and Goat*, edited by Caspar Whitney. New York: Macmillan, 1904, 167–226.
———. "The White Goat and His Country." In *American Big-Game Hunting*, edited by Theodore Roosevelt and George Bird Grinnell. 1893. New York: Forest & Stream Publishing, 1901, 26–60.
———. "The White Goat and His Ways." In *Musk-Ox, Bison, Sheep and Goat*, edited by Caspar Whitney. New York: Macmillan, 1904, 227–276.
Wright, Sidney. *Adventures among Wild Beasts: Romantic Incidents and Perils of Travel, Sport, and Exploration throughout the World*. Philadelphia: J. B. Lippincott; London: Seeley, 1909.
"Yellowstone Game Protection Act 1894." In *America's National Park System: The Critical Documents*. 1994. Accessed June 15, 2015. http://www.nps.gov/parkhistory/online_books/anps/anps_1f.htm.
Young, David. *The Olympic Myth of Greek Amateur Athletics*. Chicago: Ares, 1984.

# Index

Adirondacks, 18–20, 30–32, 60–61, 150–151, 232, 238–240, 294n63
Alaska, 21, 51, 57–58, 140–141, 147–148, 171–172, 181
   and conservation, 222–223, 232–233, 243–244
   and guides, 61, 190–196, 208, 265
amateur sport, 102–106, 117–118, 123–124.
   *See also* Whitney, Caspar
American Bison Society, 63, 233–234
American exceptionalism, 9–10, 46–48, 65–70, 182, 257–258
Anglo-Saxonism, 66–70, 77, 127, 157, 174–178, 184, 228, 255, 258

Baden-Powell, Robert, 163, 165–166, 180, 301n12, 301n22
Berg, Andrew, 140–141, 191–196, 203, 205, 223
Boone, Daniel, 27, 65–66, 68, 127
Boone and Crockett Club, 48, 65, 71, 74, 98, 172, 259–264, 283n41, 316n45
   and conservation, 228, 231–234, 236, 244, 247–248, 253–264
   and publishing, 1, 26, 65, 73, 98–99, 259–264
   *See also* Grinnell, George Bird; Roosevelt, Theodore; Sheldon, Charles; Whitney, Caspar
Boy Scouts of America, 8, 89, 234
British and American hunting, 157–158
   contrast between, 9–10, 46, 170, 172–174, 177–183
   friendships, 170–172, 174–177

   and publishing, 9–10, 86, 170, 172–174, 182–184
   *See also* Anglo-Saxonism; transnationalism; violence; warfare; wilderness
British East Africa/Somaliland, 71, 147–151, 160–163, 167–173, 180–182, 196–202, 209–210
British Empire, 159–163, 167
   Americans hunting in, 158, 171–173, 175, 178, 180–184
British hunters, 20–21, 159–164, 166–170, 177–180
Buxton, Lord North, 21, 161, 174, 176, 178

Canada
   Barren Grounds, 66, 109–115, 129, 194, 293n31
   Canadian Rockies, 21, 62–64, 139, 191–192, 222, 237
   New Brunswick, 21, 41
   Quebec, 124
Chanler, Winthrop, 108, 180, 198, 200, 212
character
   and conservation, 227–230
   and hunting, 2–4, 17–18, 40, 52–54, 56–64, 271
   judgments of, 34–41, 53–54, 75–81, 117–118, 130
   and pioneers, 45–46
   *See also* manliness; sportsmanship: purpose of; women hunters

337

Churchill, Winston, 168, 170, 173, 183, 302n34
Coleman, Annie Gilbert, 305n8
Colpitts, George, 64, 283n33
conservation
    elite hunters' arguments for, 6, 224, 226–230, 232–236, 239, 241–249, 254–264
    hunters' contributions to, 6, 10–11, 231–237, 245–264, 267–268
    origins of, 221–226, 239–241, 249, 258–264
    popular attitudes toward, 11, 177–178, 240–241, 245–247, 250–252
    and Progressive movement, 229–236, 244–247, 253–258
    race, class, and nativism, 6–7, 229–230, 238–258, 260–261
    and recreational media, 225–226, 228–229, 231–236, 239, 244–247, 249–253, 257
    *See also* Alaska; character; *Forest and Stream*; guides; manliness; sportsmanship; wilderness; women
conservation legislation
    Alaska Game Law, 222–224
    and federal government, 224, 231–233, 238, 243–245, 252–256
    Game Protection Act, 1898 (British Columbia), 222
    and hunting restriction, 6–7, 222–223, 231–239, 246–259, 265
    Lacey Act, 232
    Weeks-McLean Act, 232–233, 247–248, 262, 315n22
    Yellowstone Game Protection Act, 227, 231–232, 249, 254, 260
    *See also* readers
Custer, George Armstrong, 22, 69, 181

Davies, Henry, 22

Elson, George, 192, 213
exploration, 55–56, 67, 70–75, 109, 112, 119, 129, 200, 287n63. *See also* Whitney, Caspar

*Field and Stream* (1874), 25
*Field and Stream* (1895), 137, 191
fishing, 63, 84–86, 122, 137, 196, 254
*Forest and Stream*, 25, 90, 95–96, 125, 137, 170, 269
    conservation in, 125, 225–226, 231–232, 241, 248–249
Forest and Stream Publishing Company, 86, 96
Forester, Frank, 23–25, 33, 52, 84, 271, 277–278n5
frontier, 10–11, 26–27, 45–48, 55–56, 65–70, 127, 255
    race and class, 45–48, 65–70
    *See also* Anglo-Saxonism; violence; West, American

Gilded Age, 12, 25–28, 34–43, 60–61, 104. *See also* publishing
Grant, Madison, 82, 228, 233–235, 244, 248, 254, 260–261, 264
Gray, Prentiss, 139, 171, 191, 226, 317n2
Great Plains. *See* West, American
Greenland, 143, 151–153, 155, 216–218
Grinnell, George Bird
    and Boone and Crockett Club, 48, 259–264
    and conservation, 25, 125, 221, 225, 227, 241, 248–249, 254, 259–264
    and *Forest and Stream*, 125, 170
    and manliness, 56
    and market hunting, 25, 59, 229–232
    as writer, 98
guides, 20, 30, 57, 152, 187–220
    and conservation, 248–249
    fame, 192–193, 200
    hiring of, 190–192, 196–198, 209
    as hunters, 60–61, 190

hunters' dependence on, 24–25, 57, 189–190, 198–203, 210, 212–215
problems with, 189–190, 194, 206–208, 210–211, 214–215, 293n31
race and class, 192, 194–202, 208–209, 218–220
as teachers, 112, 189
*See also individual places*; safari, African; trophies and taxidermy
guides in narratives, 110–114, 208–216
as literary devices, 208–217
race and class, 213–216
guiding, economics of, 194–198, 200–202, 209, 216–220, 265

*Harper's*, 41–43, 85, 96–99, 103–107, 113, 118–120, 131, 150–151
Herbert, Agnes, 143–152, 201–202, 208, 210–212, 308n
Herbert, Henry William. *See* Forester, Frank
Herman, Daniel, 27, 282n21, 283n33, 285n26
Hornaday, William, 73, 210, 226, 258, 266, 269, 271, 286n34
and conservation, 25, 88, 228, 233–234, 237, 248
race, class, and nativism, 62, 82, 157, 174–175, 177, 243
sportsmanship, 53–54, 62–64
*See also* American Bison Society
Hubbard, Leonidas, 66–67, 71, 87, 127, 191–192
hunting, American South, 61, 276n8
hunting, indigenous, 112, 223–224, 241–244. *See also* guides: as hunters
hunting, market, 19, 24–25, 41, 59–62, 223–225, 241–244. *See also* Grinnell, George Bird; trophies and taxidermy
hunting, subsistence, 7, 19, 24–25, 60–61, 74, 112, 167, 223–225, 241–245, 252

hunting techniques
race and class, 19, 23–25, 41, 60–62
stalking, 3–4, 20, 24, 28–34, 40–41, 50–54, 271
variety of, 19–20, 23–25, 60–62, 178–180
*See also* sportsmanship
hypermasculinity, 5, 7–10, 275n3

India, 20, 62, 140, 159–161, 163–167, 171–172, 203–204, 260
Irish, 62, 175–177

Jacoby, Karl, 11, 238, 245–246
Johnson, Martin and Osa, 199, 266
Jones, Karen, 275n4, 278n13

Lacey, John, 232
leisure, 4, 21–28, 32, 40–42, 49, 56–60, 64, 69, 80, 206, 266–267
Lewis, Elisha, 19, 61, 63, 84, 275n4, 286n33
Lewis and Clark, 66–67, 69, 227–228, 255
London, Jack, 7, 96, 130–131
Loo, Tina, 306–307n25

MacKenzie, John, 160, 167, 201, 302n28, 302n33
manliness, 18, 27–28, 34–40, 56–60, 75–81
anxiety about, 2, 4, 7–9, 38–39, 105, 117–118, 126
and character, 34–41, 56–64
and conservation, 227–230, 234
hunting as display of, 11, 17, 28–34, 42–43, 52–56, 258–264
race and class, 8, 19, 35–36, 76–81
and women, 8, 76–80, 143–145, 153–155
*See also* amateur sport; writing
Mexico, 1, 102, 108, 251, 264
Millais, John, 74, 170, 187–188, 193, 235–236, 238
modernization, challenges of, 6, 218–220, 222–226, 229–230, 255–258
Murray, William, 18, 20, 26, 58–59, 240

Index   339

*National Geographic*, 231–233
national parks, 10–11, 227, 231–233, 238, 242, 253–258, 264, 270
National Park Service, 233, 254, 270
Native Americans, 45, 67–70, 255–258. *See also* guides: race and class; hunting: indigenous; women: indigenous
nativism, 35–37, 70, 82, 243. *See also* Anglo-Saxonism; conservation; Hornaday, William; sportsmanship
natural history, 42, 51–54, 70–75, 83, 88, 169, 288n63
Newfoundland, 21, 41–43, 74, 131–132, 203–205, 221–222, 235–238, 249
and guides, 63, 187–188, 193

Ohmann, Richard, 40, 87, 289n4, 291n40
Osborn, Henry Fairfield, 73–74, 233, 248, 261
*Outing*, 68, 80, 83, 89–90, 95–98, 120–133, 137–138, 144–145, 269–270
and conservation, 227–229, 245–248, 252
*See also* Whitney, Caspar
Outing Publishing Company, 44, 130–131

Parkman, Francis, 22, 26, 65, 68
Patterson, Lieutenant Colonel John, 162–163, 166, 170
Peary, Josephine, 8, 140, 143, 151–153
Peary, Robert, 72, 132, 140, 153, 213–218
pig-sticking, 20, 140, 163–166, 197
Prichard, Hesketh, 178, 193–194, 203–205, 220, 230, 238
primitivism, 4, 7–8, 74–82, 268, 275n4
Progressive Era, 12, 28, 36–37, 51–52, 64, 88–89, 95, 138, 256, 270. *See also* conservation: Progressive movement
publishing, 83–100
changing role of editor, 102, 124–125, 132, 269

economics of, 90–91, 94–97, 117, 120, 128, 130–131, 249, 252
and hunting, 1–2, 18, 21, 25–26, 41–44, 99, 107, 113, 258–267
narratives as commodities, 9, 11–12, 84–86, 90–91, 94, 96–97, 117, 257, 268–270
revolution in, 5–6, 9, 28, 87, 94–97, 100–102, 124–125, 174
social world of, 85–86, 97–100, 107–108, 113, 119, 121, 131–132
*See also* British and American hunting; conservation; Second Industrial Revolution; women hunters; writing

readers, 5, 41, 77, 85–87, 89–92, 98–100, 124–127
and conservation legislation, 235–236, 240, 249–252
female, 137–138, 146–149
interactions with editors, 78, 106, 124–126, 130, 232, 249–252
*Recreation*, 78–79, 86, 95, 133, 249–252
redwoods, 253–254, 264
Reiger, John, 11, 222, 231
Remington, Frederic, 42–43, 46–47, 50, 97–98
Roosevelt, Elliott, 22, 28, 36, 171
Roosevelt, Kermit, 58–59, 91, 171, 280n34
Roosevelt, Theodore, 17, 33, 44–48, 71, 73, 176
anomalous position of, 7–8, 45, 53, 180–191, 224, 270
and Boone and Crockett Club, 1–2, 48, 259–263
and conservation, 227, 231–232, 241–243, 254, 259–263
critique of British hunting, 178–180
and flossing, 128
and guides, 192, 199, 214–215
and pioneer West, 44–48, 65, 68–69
social connections of, 107–108, 140, 169–170

and strenuous life, 56–57, 59–60, 285n16
as writer, 83, 88, 92, 98, 105

safari, African, 141–143, 161, 188–190, 196–202, 208–212, 218–220
Second Industrial Revolution, 34, 36–42, 49, 69, 181, 267, 273
   impact on publishing, 87, 94, 100, 103
Selous, Frederick, 92, 131, 168–172, 178–180, 198–200, 227, 235
Seton, Ernest Thompson, 66–68, 82, 88, 110–111, 214–218, 225, 231
Seton, Grace Gallatin, 8, 137, 142–143, 145–155
Sheldon, Charles, 1–2, 57, 128, 140–141, 170–172, 189, 265, 271, 284n4
   and Boone and Crockett Club, 99–100, 261–264
   and conservation, 227, 231–233, 257–264, 271
   hunting narratives, 51–54, 73, 88, 91–93
   library of, 33, 83–87, 99–100
Shields, George Oliver, 78–79, 95, 250–252
Somaliland. *See* British East Africa/Somaliland
Spanish-American War, 118–120
sportsmanship, 55–56, 60–62, 78, 81, 88–89, 93, 122–127
   and conservation, 63–64, 88, 224, 226–227, 241–243, 245, 250–251, 258–264
   contrast with British hunting, 177–181
   early forms of, 23–25, 61, 286n33
   purpose of, 29–32, 60–64, 75–82, 285n26, 286n34
   race, class, and nativism, 23–25, 60–61, 243–246, 266
   *See also* women hunters
Stigand, Chauncey, 166–167, 305n4
Swayne, H. G. C., 161–162, 166–167, 171, 197–200, 208–210, 218–219

Thompsell, Angela, 167, 302n28, 302n36
transnationalism, 6, 9–10, 158, 170, 174–176, 182–183, 270. *See also* Anglo-Saxonism; British and American hunting
trophies and taxidermy
   guides and, 112, 202–206, 293n31
   market in, 203–205, 220, 244, 293n31
   meaning of, 30, 42, 53–54, 62, 73, 114–116, 203–206, 220, 244, 271
Turner, Frederick Jackson, 68–69

Van Dyke, T. S., 28–34, 48, 52–53, 60, 76–78, 84, 180–181, 215, 269–271
Veblen, Thorstein, 289n14
violence
   and frontier, 68–70, 255
   as motive for hunting, 2, 7–10, 29, 53–54, 275n4, 276n8, 284n8
   rejection by sportsmen, 2–4, 8, 29–30, 52–54, 57, 74, 77, 82, 268
   *See also* Roosevelt, Theodore: anomalous position of; warfare

Wallace, Dillon, 66–68, 83, 87, 89–91, 98, 127, 192, 217
Ward, Rowland, 73, 140, 169, 201
warfare
   American hunting and, 45, 67–69, 118–119, 174, 180–182, 304–305n71
   British hunting and, 166, 174, 180–182
wealth, 20–22, 24–25, 27, 37–38, 219–220
West, American, 21–25, 28, 65–70, 176, 189, 253–255, 259–264, 278n13. *See also* frontier; guides: as teachers
Westerns, 40, 276n6
Whitney, Caspar, 56, 61–62, 66, 80–82, 100–133, 244, 269–270, 291nn1–2
   and Boone and Crockett Club, 48, 102, 107–109
   on British hunting, 171, 178–179
   and conservation, 221, 228–230, 235, 244–245, 248–250, 252

Whitney, Caspar, *continued*
    and exploration, 113–119, 128–130
    and publishing, 44, 90, 95–98, 120–127, 130–132, 269
    See also *Outing*
wilderness, 3, 10–11, 18, 45–46, 68–70, 89, 126, 172–173, 206, 214–215, 219–220, 228, 246, 236, 270
    and conservation, 2, 8, 222, 224–225, 227–229, 234, 236, 255–258, 260–264
    contrast with British, 158–159, 160, 172–174, 181, 183
    and women, 138–142, 149
    See also frontier; national parks
Wister, Owen, 67–68, 77–79, 81, 90, 97–98, 108, 113, 177, 227–228
women, 35, 123, 137–138
    and conservation, 229, 234, 243, 248–249
    indigenous, 141, 298n17
    travelers, 138–139
    and writing, 87, 89–90, 142–143
    See also readers: female; wilderness; women hunters

women hunters, 6, 270
    and character, 143–148, 150
    interactions with men, 8, 139–141, 147–148, 153–155
    and publishing, 137–138, 143
    race and class, 141, 147–153
    and sportsmanship, 8, 149–150
    and work, 148–149, 152, 155
work
    changes to, 3–4, 36–40, 80, 281n9
    hunting framed as, 55–60, 64, 69, 109, 213–214
    and writing, 88–94
    See also exploration; manliness; sportsmanship: purpose of; women hunters: and work
writing, 1–3, 5, 11–12, 86–100, 113–116, 258–264, 268–270
    changes to hunting narratives, 26, 40–49, 52, 87
    and manliness, 49, 87–91, 289n8
    motivation for, 26, 48, 53, 86–94, 107, 258, 265–266, 268
    See also publishing: economics of; readers; work